TRADITIONS,
VOICES,
AND DREAMS

TRADITIONS, VOICES, AND DREAMS

The American Novel since the 1960s

Edited by

Melvin J. Friedman
and Ben Siegel

DELAWARE

Newark: University of Delaware Press
London: Associated University Presses

Associated University Presses
440 Forsgate Drive
Cranbury, NJ 08512

Associated University Presses
25 Sicilian Avenue
London WC1A 2QH, England

Associated University Presses
P.O. Box 338, Port Credit
Mississauga, Ontario
Canada L5G 4L8

The paper used in this publication meets the requirements
of the American National Standard for Permanence of Paper
for Printed Library Materials Z39.48-1984.

Library of Congress Cataloging-in-Publication Data

Traditions, voices, and dreams : the American novel since the 1960s / edited by Melvin J. Friedman and Ben Siegel.
    p.   cm.
Includes index.
ISBN 0-87413-556-7 (alk. paper)
1. American fiction—20th century—History and criticism.
I. Friedman, Melvin J.   II. Siegel, Ben, 1925–
PS379.T7   1995
813'.5409—dc20   94-44373
                                                              CIP

Contents

Preface

BEN SIEGEL

Between us, Melvin Friedman and I have many years in the university classroom. But for some time we both have felt the need of a new "text" for our Contemporary American Novel classes. Teachers and students, we thought, would find useful a book in which most of the major American writers of the past three decades were discussed. We wished first to put into clear perspective the work of contemporary masters like Barth, Bellow, Mailer, Oates, O'Connor, Ozick, Percy, Pynchon, Roth, Styron, Updike, and Vonnegut. We also wanted to include discussions of many of the more recent and important ethnic and women writers—and to have represented most of the significant critical approaches. To that end, we invited a baker's dozen of the most perceptive and articulate critic/scholars of contemporary American fiction to deal with the novelist(s) of their choice. As our table of contents makes clear, we have tried collectively to be as inclusive and varied as possible. Still, to claim "completeness," as Mel Friedman makes clear in his Introduction, would be both arrogant and foolhardy. No single volume should rightfully make that claim. Where, for example, are essays devoted to Hawkes and Malamud, McCullers and Gaddis? Or more recent figures like Erdrich, Morrison, and Tan, among others? Several of these writers are dealt with briefly—all too briefly—in our essays. But many readers will feel their absence and begin to formulate mentally an even longer catalog of novelists who merit inclusion in a collection of this type. Simply put, we are keenly, even painfully, aware that more writers could be discussed here. Still, given the contingencies of time, space, and publishing limitations, we have done what we could. Needless to say, we are proud of the results. We feel we have fashioned an informative and useful book which serves a purpose not served by any other current volume. Its one true predecessor, at least to my mind, would be Joseph J. Waldmeir's *Recent American Fiction: Some Critical Views* (Boston: Houghton Mifflin, 1963), in which both

Mel Friedman and I had essays. But even that notable compilation failed to cover the range of ethnic and women writers—or the age span and critical methods to be found here.

As is inevitable in an undertaking of this type, we have accrued a number of debts. Numerous colleagues and students have responded freely to our requests for their counsel and reactions. To them we will make known our appreciation. We do wish to express here our thanks to a few key individuals on both our campuses who helped bring this book into being. At Milwaukee, our sincere thanks for the funds, leave time, and encouragement extended to Professor Friedman go to Dean William F. Halloran and Associate Dean Jessica Wirth, both of the College of Letters & Science, and to Dean George Keulks of the Graduate School. At Cal Poly Pomona, I should like to thank Dean Jim Williams of the College of Arts and Professor Andrew Moss, Chair of the Department of English and Foreign Languages, for their help with needed travel funds, leave time, and general encouragement and Ms. Sherry Allen and Ms. Carol Follett, secretaries without peer, for their tireless retyping of the essays and their smiling assistance with the countless related tasks. Mel Friedman and I also wish to express our appreciation to our respective family members for their untiring personal encouragement, even when they could not figure out what it was we were doing. At the University of Delaware Press, Professor Jay Halio and his Editorial Committee and the indefatigable Elizabeth Reynolds, as they have in the past, helped beyond measure. Also helping to bring this ambitious venture to a successful conclusion have been Julien Yoseloff and his excellent production staff at the Associated University Presses office. Finally, we should like to thank Lisa Rivero for preparing the index. Knowingly and unknowingly, these individuals, among others, have contributed much to this entire venture. Mel and I are grateful to them all.

Introduction: A Brief Overview of the Recent American Novel

MELVIN J. FRIEDMAN

In 1923, T. S. Eliot was trying to decide about the structure of James Joyce's *Ulysses*. He ultimately declared that "novel" was not the proper way to describe Joyce's book, "simply because the novel is a form which will no longer serve." Several sentences later he made his now-famous—if not infamous—assertion that "The novel ended with Flaubert and with James." Yet Eliot subsequently reversed himself on several occasions. In his 1937 introduction to Djuna Barnes's *Nightwood*, for example, he insisted that "this book is a novel." He even underscored this point: "To say that *Nightwood* will appeal primarily to readers of poetry does not mean that it is not a novel, but that it is so good a novel that only sensibilities trained on poetry can wholly appreciate it." Despite eloquent reversals such as this one about *Nightwood* and another about *The Great Gatsby*, Eliot, in sounding the twilight of the novel in his essay "*Ulysses*, Order and Myth," was to have a lasting impact.

The impact was so lasting, in fact, that in 1957 literary critic and novelist Granville Hicks invited ten American fiction writers (Saul Bellow, Flannery O'Connor, and Ralph Ellison, among others) to contribute to a collection of essays entitled *The Living Novel* (New York: Macmillan). The collective intent was to reaffirm the continuing vitality and importance of their craft. In his Foreword, Hicks spoke with defiance: "But there is no substitute now available for the novel, and those who talk about the death of the novel are talking about the death of the imagination." In his "Afterword: The Enemies of the Novel," Hicks concluded with these words of encouragement: "[W]hatever else may be expendable in contemporary American life, the serious novel isn't."

Raymond Federman is an experimental novelist as well as a critic. In a 1977 article entitled "Death of the Novel or Another

Alternative," he reflects the preoccupations of Hicks, if on somewhat different grounds. "The novel is not dead," he states; "it is being assassinated by the big publishers who have turned their businesses into supermarket activities." Federman's complaint is more relevant than ever in the 1990s, as what Hicks called "the serious novel" is often forced to go searching among smaller publishers. Federman has learned this sad truth at first-hand. To reinforce his position he had but to gaze at the best-seller lists and see *The Bridges of Madison County*, the first novel by an unknown writer. That Robert James Waller's book held the selling ladder's top rung for so many months was a clear sign of commercial rather than literary factors. (The many spinoffs from this media event included an album of songs, "The Ballads of Madison County," and Garry Trudeau's sardonic "Doonesbury" acknowledgment of it as "The Washed-Out Bridges of Madison County.")

On a more serious level, Norman Mailer and Saul Bellow have enjoyed both commercial and literary success for nearly five decades. It is astonishing how often they have been paired in critical studies, especially when one considers how little they have in common. Ihab Hassan allows them to share in solitary splendor a section called "Major Novelists" in his *Contemporary American Literature 1945–1972* (New York: Ungar, 1973). Nathan Scott places them with Lionel Trilling "at the absolute center of what is most deeply animating in American literature of the present and the recent past" in his *Three American Moralists: Mailer, Bellow, Trilling* (Notre Dame: Univ. of Notre Dame Press, 1973). Frank D. McConnell groups them with Thomas Pynchon and John Barth in his *Four Postwar American Novelists* (Chicago: Univ. of Chicago Press, 1977) and sees them as being at the cutting edge of the "post-Apocalyptic" experience.

These two "dinosaurs," as some critics see them, are still formidable presences on the American literary scene. (Interestingly enough, Mailer was part of a session titled "The Death of the Novel, the Life of the Novel," held at Town Hall in midtown Manhattan in September 1992. See *New York Times*, 26 September 1992, 13.) Mailer's 1991 novel about the CIA, *Harlot's Ghost*, runs a formidable if uneven thirteen hundred pages, with a sequel apparently in the offing. Bellow, however, seems to have slowed a bit in the past few years—if novel length is a criterion. Mailer's career has been as jagged and irregular as Bellow's has been smooth and straightforward. The *enfant terrible* Mailer changes his stances to accommodate disruptions and fragmentations in the national psyche. He moves with ease from antiwar novelist, to spokesman for American existentialism, to nonfiction novelist, to popular culturist. In short, he remains the most exacting literary and cultural barometer we have. For his part, Saul Bellow continues to honor tradition and remains the darling of the Establishment, as befits a Nobel laureate. Mailer, like the phoenix, keeps rising rejuvenated from his own ashes to assume an unending series of masks and postures; Bellow has created an oeuvre that places him squarely in this country's literary center. Even their Jewish backgrounds have yielded radically different results: Mailer's Jewishness seems an accident of birth whereas Bellow's ethnicity is a staple of his art.

John Hawkes and William Styron also offer an intriguing pairing of alternatives. Hawkes stated his position forthrightly in an interview in the summer 1965 *Wisconsin Studies in Contemporary Literature.* "I began to write fiction on the assumption that the true enemies of the novel," he explained, "were plot, character, setting, and theme." Later, in *Esquire* [See Daniel Halpern, "Checking in with William Styron," *Esquire* 78 (August 1972): 142–43], Styron would plead for a fiction with a "narrative flow. It's when there is no narrative flow that I think fiction is copping out. I don't mean to say it has to be a 'cracking good yarn,' but there has to be a story." Interestingly enough, these differing positions have resulted in two distinguished bodies of novel writing with more in common than the novels of Mailer and Bellow. For example, the first novels of Hawkes and Styron share a fascination with words and with violence. Yet the Styron of *Lie Down in Darkness* (1951) is something of an old-fashioned rhetorician given to Faulknerian indulgences, one who secures his violence in comfortably mythical terms. The Hawkes of *The Cannibal* (1949) seems to have ignored the traditional distinctions between poetry and prose and blended his violence with the surreal and hallucinatory. At present, their careers continue to diverge. Hawkes gropes for different forms and narrative possibilities while seeking new "lunar landscapes." (This is a title he gave to a collection of his shorter fiction.) Styron, however, holds fast to tradition and its comfortable storytelling conventions. Yet one clear point of convergence emerges: both have strived to develop an articulate first-person discourse. The result is that the mature work of each—Styron's *The Confessions of Nat Turner* and *Sophie's Choice* and Hawkes's novels from *Second Skin* and *The Blood Oranges* through the recent *Adventures in the Alaskan Skin Trade, Whistlejacket,* and *Sweet William*—is shaped unfailingly by a controlling narrative voice.

Hawkes and Styron also share a French "birthmark." Styron has a strong literary kinship with the French New Novelists and the Existentialists; Hawkes's principal aesthetic forebears include the Symbolist poets, with their poetics of the blank page and their addiction to the hallucinatory and alchemical property of words. Hawkes also can be said to be in the tradition of the French *roman pur,* wherein language is more important than event or characterization. It can be added, too, that Mailer and Bellow, Hawkes and Styron are strongly representative of that period in American fiction when modernism's techniques and concerns gradually, if reluctantly, gave way to those of postmodernism and metafiction. These four writers had all done important work by the early 1950s, and they continue, if occasionally in an avuncular fashion, to oversee and contribute to the resuscitation of the novel form. This is the very form, it should be recalled, that has been pronounced dead on numerous occasions since T. S. Eliot declared its demise with James and Flaubert. (Three of the above four are discussed in essays in the present collection. The fourth, John Hawkes, is sorely missed.)

II

In his *Sophie's Choice,* William Styron offers an interesting exchange between his narrator, Stingo, and a character of Jewish background, Nathan Landau. Stingo, a Virginian and Styron's literary alter ego, is writing a novel about the South. Nathan suggests that the young man is "at the end of a tradition" and that Jewish writing will soon become "the *important* force" in American literature. In this scene, which occurs in the summer of 1947, Nathan goes on to say: "It's just that historically and ethnically Jews will be coming into their own in a cultural way in this postwar wave." He then offers a nod to Bellow's 1944 novel *Dangling Man* as proof of his contention. Stingo ends the exchange with an ironical sigh of relief: "Well, at least you didn't tell me that the novel's dead."

This exchange pinpoints two of the more active groups among American novelists of the past half-century—one regional, the other ethnic. Nathan's position that Stingo is "at the end of a tradition" cannot be taken too seriously. His remarks about Jewish writing, however, are valid. Southern novelists somehow offer a more unified front than do Jewish ones because they have William Faulkner's commanding presence to inspire them. Many Southerners are Faulkner's heirs in that they look to Yoknapatawpha for literary sustenance. Even a partial list will include Styron, Flannery O'Connor, Truman Capote, Carson McCullers, Eudora Welty, Madison Jones, Elizabeth Spencer, Reynolds Price, Gail Godwin, and Joan Williams. Faulkner's disciples are almost all rather sober storytellers who consider plot, character, setting, and theme (Hawkes's four declared "enemies" of the novel) the essential ingredients of novel writing. They have in large part avoided the experimental temptations to which their mentor succumbed early in his career with *The Sound and the Fury*, *As I Lay Dying*, and *Absalom, Absalom!*.

Southern writing is predominantly rural in setting. From Faulkner through the latest novels of Reynolds Price and Gail Godwin, there is a very precise feeling for landscape and terrain. It is a legacy, perhaps, from the Vanderbilt Agrarians. Carson McCullers and Eudora Welty appeared almost simultaneously on the literary scene in the early 1940s. Their earliest works made it clear the female sensibility was to be a major force in Southern letters. This was strongly affirmed by the abbreviated life and career of Flannery O'Connor, who published two novels and two short story collections between 1952 and 1965. She died at thirty-nine, but her posthumous reputation assures her a position among Southern fiction writers second only to Faulkner's. Yet she falls short of being a major figure because of the sameness of her themes and techniques and the limitations of her vision. Her Catholic background also causes her to stand apart from most of her regional contemporaries. Her characters may be Bible Belt fundamentalists, but they are imbued with a Catholic sense of sin and redemption. (As Michael Patrick Gillespie points out in his persuasive essay in this collection, she joins Walker Percy and John Kennedy Toole in asserting a "Baroque Catholicism.") At present, women writers like Doris Betts, Gail Godwin, Bobbie Ann Mason, Alice Walker, and Sylvia Wilkinson dominate the Southern literary scene. Should one add here Anne Tyler, Baltimore's novelist laureate, who occasionally sets her fiction in Virginia and North Carolina, the resulting list grows quite imposing. Since Faulkner the Southern female sensibility has indeed proved dominant.

A sharp contrast to what I have been saying about recent Southern writers is offered by Jewish novelists. The latter have situated their work primarily in urban or suburban settings, and their central figures have been male. Some years ago, Saul Bellow, Bernard Malamud, and Philip Roth were humorously labeled the Hart, Schaffner and Marx of the Jewish novel. Malamud died in 1986, four years after publishing his last novel, the disappointing *God's Grace*. Of course, Bellow and Roth are still writing. Bellow's recent work has taken no decisive new turn—other than that he has chosen to publish several short novels. Roth has opted to fall back on certain metafictional devices in his novels since *The Counterlife* (1987). Even *The Facts* (1988), which is subtitled "A Novelist's Autobiography," begins and ends with letters exchanged between Roth and his literary alter ego, Nathan Zuckerman. The character confronting his creator has a long history in fiction and drama, and it has become a staple in Roth's recent work. In his *Deception* (1990), Roth himself enters the frame of his novel and makes a number of revealing statements. He declares, for example: "I have been imagining myself, outside of my novel, having a love affair with a character inside my novel." If anything, he intensifies this reflexive process in his more recent *Operation Shylock*. (Two essays in our collection place Roth in intriguing new contexts.)

Raymond Federman and Ronald Sukenick are two Jewish contemporaries of Roth. Both started their careers with some of the same self-reflexive devices. Federman coined the word "surfiction" to describe their early literary maneuverings. Federman's first novel, *Double or Nothing* (Chicago: Swallow Press, 1971), seems to profit from verbal, visual, and narrative experiments he has observed on both the French and American fiction scenes. (Samuel Beckett has always been his master.) Each page tends to go its own visual and verbal way as all traditional distinctions between image and word appear to be rendered obsolete. Readers witness the growing pains of writing a novel while also seeing the grudging, halting fleshing-out of a story. Everything is tentative, with every detail of the story subject to the caprices of the narrator.

Federman's next novel, the unpaginated *Take It or Leave It* (New York: Fiction Collective, 1976), is less eccentric typographically but much denser verbally and narratively than its predecessor. His *The Voice in the Closet* (Madison: Coda Press, 1979) offers unpunctuated and unparagraphed texts in both English and French. Federman describes it as "a complex double book—system of mirrors, echoes, boxes within boxes to accommodate my plural voice." More sharply focused here, perhaps, than anywhere else in his fiction are the matter of Jewishness and the experience of the Holocaust. His *The Twofold Vibration* (Bloomington: Indiana Univ. Press, 1982), like his previous fiction, offers a constant witness to the frustrations and difficulties of writing a novel. Despite some eccentricities of narration and composition, and even of typography and punctuation (commas everywhere but no periods), there is for the reader the sense that Federman is beginning to acknowledge traditional novelistic devices. By the time he publishes *Smiles on Washington Square* (New York: Thunder's Mouth Press, 1985), it is clear he has tired somewhat of his experiments with disrupting the appearance of his text. In his most recent novel, *To Whom It May Concern* (Boulder: Fiction Collective Two, 1990), he turns to the epistolary form. Here the preoccupations of the earlier fiction resurface: the problematical nature of the compositional act, the centrality of the Holocaust, the blurring of the line separating myth from reality. Still, all these elements seem more traditional and finely tuned.

Federman's work is dwelt on here because his fiction is not discussed in the essays that follow. His writing merits extended attention also because it is symptomatic of a kind of experimentation and "literary disruption" marking a movement that, according to Jerome Klinkowitz, dated from the late 1960s. Its practitioners included Ronald Sukenick, Jerzy Kosinski, Kurt Vonnegut, Jr., Donald Barthelme, Gilbert Sorrentino, and William H. Gass. (See Klinkowitz's *Literary Disruptions: The Making of a Post-Contemporary American Fiction*, Urbana: Univ. of Illinois Press, 1975, 1980.) Federman is an exemplary figure also in the literature of the Holocaust. Hence he belongs in the select company of writers like Edward Lewis Wallant, Elie Wiesel, Susan Fromberg Schaeffer, Cynthia Ozick, Norma Rosen, and Isaac Bashevis Singer.

Were Federman's career compared with that of his more celebrated contemporary Philip Roth, for example, sharp differences would quickly become apparent. Roth's traditional, modernist narratives took on metafictional aspects only in later works from *The Counterlife* through *Operation Shylock* (1993). In contrast, Federman began with extreme visual, verbal, and narrative experiments, only to soften some of his Shandyean effects in his most recent fiction. Of course, he is still far from being the conventional fictionist that Roth was for so many years. In his *To Whom It May Concern*, Federman expressed himself rather tellingly. "I would gladly sacrifice all the tricks and gimmicks that have sustained me so far," he stated, "if I could rid myself of the

imposture of realism, that ugly beast that stands at bay ready to
leap in the moment you begin scribbling your fiction." Roth and
Federman do come together occasionally in their subject matter—both confront the Holocaust, the Jewish diaspora, and Israel.
Indeed, Roth has confronted these subjects increasingly in his
more recent novels.

   E. L. Doctorow is another notable novelist who is Jewish. His
place in contemporary American fiction probably has more to
do with his techniques than with his ethnicity, despite the numerous Jewish characters and situations in his work. (Susan
Brienza effectively surveys here a substantial part of his career.)
Doctorow's ability to negotiate the thin line separating fact from
fiction dictates the texture of his novels. Moving between history
and myth or reality and folklore, he blurs with ease the distinctions between categories. In *Ragtime* (1975), for example, he wove
such historical figures as Sigmund Freud and Harry Houdini,
J. P. Morgan and Henry Ford, Stanford White and Harry K. Thaw,
Evelyn Nesbit and Emma Goldman into his fictional narrative.
In *Billy Bathgate* (1989), he made imaginative use of Dutch
Schultz, Bo Weinberg, Lucky Luciano, and Thomas E. Dewey,
among other individuals actually involved in American crime
and punishment in the turbulent 1930s. Here the Jewish gangster
Dutch Schultz (né Arthur Flegenheimer) is fleshed out by an
unlikely fictional narrator who is the sole recorder of the story's
events; he is the fifteen-year-old Billy Bathgate. Certain aspects
of *Billy Bathgate* recall an earlier American novel that mixed
fact with fiction: Scott Fitzgerald's *The Great Gatsby.* Billy has
the same responsibility of making sense of the world of Dutch
Schultz that Nick Carraway had in sorting out the affairs of Jay
Gatsby. Fitzgerald even cast a famous Jewish gangster in a cameo
role, Arnold Rothstein, who appears under the fictional name
Meyer Wolfsheim.

   Doctorow then is not the first to cross fact with fiction. But he
is certainly the most adept at managing it consistently. Admittedly, what he is doing differs somewhat from Truman Capote's
notion of the nonfiction novel. Still the difference is not as great
as might be expected. Imagination and invention control the novels of both writers. Capote starts with historical fact in both *In
Cold Blood* (New York: Random House, 1966) and *Handcarved
Coffins* (included in *Music for Chameleons*, 1980). Both narratives focus on actual murders that so intrigued the author that
he became part of the investigative process. In each instance
Capote enters the frame of the narrative to participate in the

unraveling of events, but in doing so he allows fiction and literary echoes to play substantial roles, especially in *In Cold Blood*.

Three years after Capote serialized *In Cold Blood* in four issues of *The New Yorker* (25 Sept., 2 Oct., 9 Oct., 16 Oct. 1965), Norman Mailer followed suit in *The Armies of the Night* (1968). Capote addresses this matter, with his usual wit and levity, in the preface to his *Music for Chameleons* (New York: Random House, 1980). There he confronts the "Norman Mailer, who has made a lot of money and won a lot of prizes writing nonfiction novels (*The Armies of the Night, Of a Fire on the Moon, The Executioner's Song*), although he has always been careful never to describe them as 'nonfiction novels.' No matter; he is a good writer and a fine fellow and I'm grateful to have been of some small service to him." (Not known for his generosity to other writers, Capote here may have recalled Mailer's calling him "a ballsy little guy" in his *Advertisements for Myself* [1959].)

The nonfiction novel can be said to have gained respectability with Capote and Mailer. This hybrid form was then to prove seductive to any number of American novelists eager to cross fiction with fact. These have included, among many others, Robert Coover in *The Public Burning* (New York: Viking Press, 1977), Don DeLillo in *Libra* (New York: Viking Press, 1988), and Norma Rosen in *John and Anzia: An American Romance* (New York: Dutton, 1989). Readers find this melding troublesome, however, when used by biographers and other nonfiction writers. Indeed, some recent biographers have been roundly criticized for the liberties they have taken with the details of people's lives. Traditionally, they have been expected to be custodians of "facts" about their subjects. So when they begin inventing thoughts and conversations, as did Joe McGinniss in *The Last Brother* (New York: Simon and Schuster, 1993), his biography of Edward M. Kennedy, reviewers question the credibility of their work. The heavy cloud of deconstructionism hovers over a genre which silently permits blurring the line separating truth from fiction. (See, for example, Michiko Kakutani, "Fiction? Nonfiction? And Why Doesn't Anybody Care?" *New York Times*, 27 July 1993, B1, B8.) Still, whatever its faults and dangers, the nonfiction novel and its spinoffs have proved a dominant force on the American literary scene during the past quarter-century. Ironically, this blending of fact and fiction, or "faction" as some have termed it, offers a relatively mild variety of experimentation. Certainly the stylistic extensions of its practitioners pale when measured against the radical "disruptions" of novelists like Raymond Federman, Ronald Sukenick, Thomas Pynchon, Donald Barthelme, and Gilbert Sorrentino.

III

This rightful concern with the nonfiction novel has led our attention away from the Jewish-American literary scene. Yet since midcentury Jewish writers have shared a central position with the South's imposing novelists. Jewish characters and subjects continue to intrigue even non-Jewish writers. Thus John Updike entered the arena with his *Bech: A Book* (1970) and *Bech Is Back* (1982). In his foreword to the first volume, Henry Bech himself traced his American-Jewish genealogy: "I sound like some gentlemanly Norman Mailer; then that London glimpse of silver hair glints more of gallant, glamorous Bellow, the King of the Leprechauns, than of stolid old homely yours truly. My childhood seems out of Alex Portnoy and my ancestral past out of I. B. Singer. I get a whiff of Malamud in your city breezes, and am I paranoid to feel my 'block' an ignoble version of the more or less noble renunciations of H. Roth, D. Fuchs, and J. Salinger?" William Styron, another non-Jew, has flirted with what the narrator of his *Sophie's Choice* calls "the Kingdom of the Jews." In this novel Styron confronts not only the special ambience of Jewish New York but also the human legacy of the Holocaust.

Of course Jews are not the only minority group to assert their presence on the American literary scene. African-American writers have been publishing first-rate novels since the turn of this century. Their honor roll would include, among others, Charles W. Chesnutt, Arna Bontemps, Jean Toomer, Chester Himes, Richard Wright, Langston Hughes, William Melvin Kelley, James Baldwin, and Ralph Ellison. At the center of all this talent is one work that has been declared repeatedly one of the most important American novels since World War II, Ellison's *Invisible Man* (New York: Random House, 1952). The narrative traces a young black man's responses to Southern education, New York radicalism, and the inability of whites to see or know blacks except on their own terms. This novel has brought to African-American fiction the major elements of continental literature and thought from Dostoevsky and Kierkegaard down to the French existentialists. Interestingly enough, in the last decade or so, women writers like Toni Morrison, Alice Walker, Maya

Angelou, and Jamaica Kincaid have come to dominate the black literary agenda. Two essays here address the talents and contributions of these women.

Indeed, the literature of minority groups has become a vital component of the contemporary American scene. The cultural mix these varied ethnic writers offer, most critics suggest, bodes well. On the final page of his *The Politics of Narration* (New Brunswick: Rutgers Univ. Press, 1991), Richard Pearce asks rather rhetorically: "And what are the prospects for the future?" He answers in the affirmative: "Pretty good I would say, considering that the modern (and postmodern) canon in the United States alone is coming to include writers like Toni Morrison, Maxine Hong Kingston, and the remarkable collaboration of Louise Erdrich and Michael Dorris—who create vast decentered and intersubjective fictions of African-American communities, Chinese-American families, and Native-American generations." In short, this country's multicultural agenda appears to be in good hands as the century draws to a close. So does the supposedly vanishing American novel generally. For as this brief survey has suggested, this country's recent fiction suffers no lack of daring, creative, and experimental practitioners. There is every reason then, most critics today would argue, to feel more confident now about the fate of the American novel than did the contributors to *The Living Novel* in 1957. One critic making this point is Jerome Klinkowitz, who strikes a positive note early in his *Literary Disruptions* by titling his opening section "Prologue: The Death of the Death of the Novel." The essays collected here, singly and collectively, offer similar affirmation that the novel is alive and well and thriving in America.

*   *   *

Some material included here appeared in somewhat different form in two of my earlier essays. The first was "Dislocations of Setting and Word: Notes on American Fiction Since 1950," *American Fiction: Historical and Critical Essays*, ed. James Nagel (Boston: Northeastern University Press and Twayne Publishers, 1977): 79–98. The second was "To 'Make It New': The American Novel Since 1945," *The Wilson Quarterly* 2 (Winter 1978): 133–42.

TRADITIONS,
VOICES,
AND DREAMS

Part 1
Using Tradition—Southern, Jewish, European

Baroque Catholicism in Southern Fiction: Flannery O'Connor, Walker Percy, and John Kennedy Toole

MICHAEL PATRICK GILLESPIE

The artist, like the God of the creation, remains within or behind or beyond or above his handiwork, invisible, refined out of existence, indifferent, paring his fingernails.

*   *   *

The coming into being of the notion of "author" constitutes the privileged moment of *individualization* in the history of ideas, knowledge, literature, philosophy, and the sciences. Even today, when we reconstruct the history of a concept, literary genre, or school of philosophy, such categories seem relatively weak, secondary, and superimposed scansions in comparison with the solid fundamental unit of the author and the work.

*   *   *

Writing is that neuter, that composite, that obliquity into which our subject flees, that black-and-white where all identity is lost, beginning with the very identity of the body that writes.[1]

I

In a letter to Mlle. Leroyer de Chantepie, Gustave Flaubert challenged the conventional assumptions regarding the creative significance of any author. Since that 1857 letter, other writers and critics have followed Flaubert's lead. For more than a century they have debated the precise ratio that adequately describes the writer's creative contribution to an individual work's aesthetic impact. Most contemporary critics dismiss the traditional image of the artist/creator as being in exclusive control of the work whose intentionality stands as the ultimate authority for any of its interpretations. The alternative is the abrogation of the im-

25

plicit contract between reader and writer by suppressing all traces of the author's presence. It, too, has proved unsatisfactory to all but the most literal-minded epigones of poststructuralist critics.[2] The more effective approach that has emerged from these extremes seeks to redress the imbalance that comes from giving inordinate significance not simply to either reader or writer but to any discrete imaginative element without not taking into account those relevant elements other than reader or writer.

The act of interpretation creates a bond between the imagination of the creator of a piece of art and that of its most recent reader. Thus, the efforts of any reader can lead to an aesthetically satisfying experience only when his or her responses result from a degree of collaboration with the author of the work. Obviously, for such an endeavor to be successful it must foster a dialectical exchange in which the reader remains sensitive to the writer's creative design. He should not succumb to prescriptive interpretive dictates. The most logical way to achieve this exchange would be through fusion of the extratextual features characterizing the consciousnesses of both the reader and the author. I refer to the social repertoires that define the existence of each consciousness.[3]

I here anticipate the charge that such a method imposes a reductivist perspective upon a complicated critical process. In fact, the obverse is true. A genuinely sophisticated interpretive technique recognizes that numerous features influence the reader's imaginative response to a piece of art. Acknowledging the interplay between reader and writer provides an important perspective. It also establishes clear epistemological limits while allowing writers and readers to experience greater interpretive latitude. For it opens to scrutiny a range of elements shaping the texts they perceive.[4] The social repertoires of audience and of artist stand as the pivotal elements contributing to the impressions derived from an art object. No matter what methodology one chooses to pursue, these repertoires remain a consistent, even inescapable, feature of one's readings.[5]

I have elaborated upon this concept of social repertoires for a specific purpose: I wish to explain the motivation for focusing attention on the cultural features and aesthetic contingencies relating to the Catholic nature of the works of three artistically disparate but culturally analogous writers. I refer to Flannery O'Connor, Walker Percy, and John Kennedy Toole. I believe that by delimiting the religious forces that shape their processes of composition one comes to a fuller awareness of the options open to their readers during the process of comprehension. Admittedly, this approach grows out of a fairly obvious and often-abused interpretive technique. It is one that adduces instances of powerful, even violent images in an author's writing. Such images assert strong proximate influences of specific extratextual forces.[6] What distinguishes my point, however, is an inversion of the standard application: I am not striving to confirm the existence of neuroses within the artist. Instead, my aim is to illuminate structures implicit in the narrative discourse that would otherwise be overlooked. The common feature in the fiction of these writers (their faith as Roman Catholics) remains buried by any number of more overt narrative traits. Still, it becomes a central factor in shaping the diverse personal responses that one may make to the creative impulses of each one.[7] Consequently, the heightened awareness of their manipulations of this religious background defines an important hermeneutic point: it invites the reader to revalue the varying degrees of orthodoxy and of heterodoxy and to shape the resulting impressions into a coherent analysis.

One legitimately might question why a reader need be particularly attentive to any elements within the social repertoires of O'Connor, Percy, and Toole. For the milieus of these three writers—the South emerging to new prominence and struggling to define a new sense of values brought on by post–World War II economic and cultural changes—in many ways merely reflect and refract the moods and settings already made familiar by a previous fictional generation. I refer specifically to that (fictional) sense of the South defined by William Faulkner or by his imitators. In my view, of course, that is precisely the point. These authors must form their narratives with an awareness of the need to confront both the ghost of Faulkner and the ethos of their own Southern heritage. The achievements of their artist forebears persistently threaten their works with the danger of redundancy. Hence their narratives, like those of many other contemporary authors, reflect a sensitivity to this condition—labeled "the anxiety of influence" by Harold Bloom. Seeking to bring individuality to their fiction, they all struggle with a referentiality that the works of their predecessors have made familiar. In a very important sense, their writings evolve out of these efforts to define their natures both as readers and as writers. Thus all three must find ways of resisting the impulse, both within themselves and within others, to relegate their writings to regional associations or to diminish their achievements through comparisons to William Faulkner.

These observations do not take me as far from my point about Catholicism as they might seem. The creative affinities of these authors go beyond the shared problem of individualizing familiar themes or settings. For the compositional strategies that they have adopted for alleviating the burden of influence prove to be broadly similar yet still shaped by the individuality of each writer. Specifically, as Roman Catholics they insinuate into their prose theological perspectives not found in the writings of most Southerners (including many Southern Catholics). At the same time, the ethos forming their attitudes remains relatively close to the Christian temperament of the region. This ethos provides a meaningful counterpoint to their narratives rather than proving an alien commentary on their discourses. Thus each author, in a highly idiosyncratic manner, draws elements of Roman Catholic belief and ritual into various aspects of his or her narratives. As a result, each infuses perspectives into his writings that render them distinct from those dominating the fictional world of the South created by Faulkner.

Thanks to the uniqueness of each perspective, a reader finds relatively little stylistic or thematic duplication when moving from the work of one author to the next. The influence of Roman Catholic doctrine may appear in all three authors, but in every instance it has been transmuted by personal interpretation. It asserts its presence in a manifestly different fashion and reinforces the sense of universality inherent in the very term "catholic." Catholicism operates least overtly in O'Connor's writing. It appears ambiguously throughout Percy's work, and it functions in its most straightforward manner in Toole's novel. The works of each writer, however, convey a sense that the metaphysical presence of the church—or at least of the church's worldview—pervades key elements of the narrative. Acting at the level of metadiscourse, Catholic doctrine invites readers to respond to its implicit commentaries on the narrative strategies of these three authors.

At the same time, this essay is not an effort to impose a consistent, homogeneous rendition of Catholicism on their fiction. In a very real sense, in fact, the Catholicism of each writer can be characterized as idiosyncratic and baroque. The belief of each is a hybrid that accentuates, even exaggerates, certain elements of the church while muting or even ignoring others. Their concepts of dogma and ritual unfold as extravagant elaborations that often border on caricature. Indeed, they repeatedly challenge the more traditional concepts of faith by depicting them as delusions or as willful deceptions. Catholicism remains always recognizable but never exactly congruent with received teachings. At the same time, none feels comfortable with an unreflective, undirected atheism or with a mindless, aggressive pietism. Each writer seeks some version of the church of Christ without Christ. Each strives for a repository of belief that produces confidence and reassurance without incorporating the human flaws. At the same time, each also shows a reluctance to abandon the stability and direction derived from the church.

I should note that my aim is not to affirm either the personal faith or the apostasy of any of these writers. Instead, my intention is to outline an aspect of the creative process that is evident in all three writers: this process acts as a principal factor in shaping discourses within their fiction. The applications differ markedly, but the doctrines and the rituals of the church provide a clearly articulated worldview for each writer. It is a view that provides a consistent metadiscursive commentary: a pre–Vatican II conservatism for O'Connor, an anachronistic solipsism for Toole, and a post–Vatican II ecumenism for Percy.

All three writers received formal instruction in the tenets of Catholicism. Whatever subsequent attitudes toward that religion evolved, some version of the intellectual and cultural heritage of the Catholic faith exerted a shaping influence on their consciousness. This condition in turn has no small impact on their writing. Despite (or perhaps because of) tendencies in their fictions to focus on a variety of the forms of Christian fundamentalism, agnosticism, and atheism, Catholicism implicitly becomes the standard alternative for judging any action. It represents a fixed and unchanging set of beliefs, a moral position that remains uncontaminated by the frailties and the betrayals inherent in ordinary human intercourse.

Paradoxically, Catholicism also has a much more direct and disruptive influence within the various novels: It stands, like Stephen Dedalus's God of the creation, "within or behind or beyond or above" the work. The insinuation of Catholicism into each discourse invites a deconstructive response to the narratives that it glosses. It serves as a basis for measuring the ethical behavior of everyone within the discourses without itself becoming co-opted by participation in the hurly-burly existence of the fictions that it comments upon. For Catholicism operates apparently as a deconstructive ideal, provoking change without undermining itself. I say "apparently" because the baroque nature of their Catholic views—and Catholicism's collective impact on readers—makes the yardstick as protean as the factors that it measures. Nonetheless, Catholicism remains an important benchmark. Catholic hermeneutics offers a contrasting mixture of a mysticism grounded in nonlinear conceptualizing and of habits of obedience that promote deferral to received ideas. Through careful inferences drawn from such hermeneutics, one can break the hegemony of the cause-and-effect thinking that dominates the White, Anglo-Saxon, Protestant worldview of the works that it oversees. Being outside that system allows Catholicism to define a perspective from which to view and to judge the others. At the same time, the Catholicism that each writer hints at does not conform to any of the standard contemporary representations of the church. Its presence in the margins of the fiction of O'Connor, Percy, and Toole may seem to some to trivialize its epistemological impact, but a careful scrutiny of its impact shows the obverse to be true. This displacement to the margins allows Catholicism, in commentaries upon the ethos within each of their works, to unfold its views in a tone distinct and separate. Yet it is a Catholic tone with no less authority than that of the beliefs dominating the consciousnesses of the characters in their stories.

II

Flannery O'Connor, for example, overtly suppresses any traces of a Catholic perception of events. Instead, she focuses with a graphic bitterness on the claustrophobic environment that both nurtures and corrupts Southern Protestant fundamentalist beliefs. She does not restrict her characterizations to practicing Christians, yet most of her characters come out of a common ethos shaped by Protestant fundamentalism. In fact, she traces world views equally crippled by belief or disbelief. For, though putatively antithetical, the same claustrophobic fatalism circumscribes the creeds of both her agnostics and Christians. In implicit contrast, O'Connor uses significant silences to reserve for her own religious faith a privileged position "within or behind or beyond or above" the action. By exempting it from the castigations that both fundamentalist Protestantism and regional agnosticism receive, she allows Catholicism to present a coherent alternative: It offers a moral system with credibility for judging the events of her stories, because it has remained above the scorn that she heaps on sectarian Protestantism. In other words, O'Connor forces us to confront the unsatisfactory manifestations of faith and of agnosticism that one finds in her Protestant world. She does so by implicitly encouraging us to turn to an alternative perspective for an assessment of events unencumbered by the blind spots that she satirizes.[8]

While reading O'Connor's work, one quickly becomes aware of the importance of such a point of reference. Her narratives unfold a complex and confusing social vision that repeatedly calls for clear benchmarks to assist in its comprehension. The fiction of O'Connor seems to delight in positing a fearsome succession of grotesques articulating a nightmarish vision of the South. Her discourses tease us—like the German Expressionist filmmakers of the 1920s—with styles shifting back and forth between realism and surrealism. The narratives edge away from the comfortable confines of naturalism, but they never completely sever the connection with quotidian existence. By integrating a pattern of apparent normalcy into the behavior of outrageous characters, O'Connor imbues their actions with a discernible legitimacy. In turn, this legitimacy impels a reader to confront and to judge their behavior rather than simply to dismiss as aberrations the scenes that the narrative depicts.

Admittedly, one must turn to a separate and independent moral code to accomplish this "acceptance." For even as her discourses foreground images of individuals overcome by malevolence, ignorance, selfishness, and tawdriness, O'Connor's narratives give them all a legitimacy. They do so by establishing these characters in the context of a believable moral system that accepts and even encourages such behavior. Figures who rival Faulkner's Popeye, Abner Snopes, or Anse Bundren in their penchant for evil dominate her fictional worlds, and whatever humor exists manifests itself as *Schadenfreude*. Nonetheless, a systemic consistency sustains their actions. Certainly the harsh misanthropy that governs each individual seems to render all human intercourse equally poisonous. Yet, at the same time, we can see her figures as deviant only when they are measured against values that obtain outside the societies that they inhabit.

A story like "A Good Man Is Hard to Find," for example, builds to macabre conclusion through a steady stream of low-level meanness. The bickering that takes place before the family vacation begins, the acerbic scene in a roadside diner, the querulous exchanges in the car, all contribute to the nastiness permeating the world of the story. When The Misfit finally appears, we easily assimilate him into the ethos of viciousness that already dominates the story. In effect, he stands as simply a more intense manifestation of the social hostility evident in nearly everyone whom we have already encountered. His behavior runs remarkably close in its tenor, if not in its magnitude, to the quotidian cruelty of John Wesley, June Star, and their grandmother. He earns his distinguishing epithet simply because of the energy with which he pursues his goals rather than because his actions deviate significantly from the general ethics of the family.

So convincing is the commonplace cruelty of these characters that the reader never dismisses the violence on any level as gratuitous or unmotivated. Indeed, an aura of unmitigated and undifferentiated barbarity seems inculcated into every level of human endeavor. Even after The Misfit's gang has methodically executed the son, the daughter-in-law, and the grandchildren, and with the moment of the grandmother's own death inexorably approaching, the parallels between the personalities of The Misfit and of the grandmother remain disturbingly pronounced. Their behavior enforces the idea that their shared heritage of Protestant fundamentalism produces striking similarities in their natures. In short, the narrative emphasizes the essential mean-spiritedness of both characters while simultaneously underscoring the perverse religious belief sustaining them. Each maintains a surly resentment of the limitations imposed by conventional values and beliefs. Each offers an interpretation of Christian faith that emphasizes his or her own embittered alienation over any other feeling.

As the moment when the grandmother will be murdered approaches, the thoughts of both characters turn to the death of Christ, and both offer their own interpretation of His redemptive gesture.

> "Jesus was the only One that ever raised the dead," The Misfit continued, "and He shouldn't have done it. He thown everything off balance. . . .
> "Maybe He didn't raise the dead," the old lady mumbled, not knowing what she was saying and feeling so dizzy that she sank down in the ditch with her legs twisted under her.[9]

Although the iconography evokes an immediate reader response, the context in which it appears blurs its significance. At this point neither figure embraces apostasy, yet each reveals an occluded view of Protestant theology. In fact, it seems as if each reflects a basic dissatisfaction not with the guiding principles of Christian behavior—which neither The Misfit nor the grandmother values—but rather with the more spectacular manifestations of divinity. In essence, each wishes to view religion on an ontological plane. Each wishes his (or her) visions of a remote and uncaring God to remain untroubled by the ethical and moral strictures on behavior that are an inherent part of religious belief. Neither wants these limitations intruding into daily life. Neither desires to confront the epistemological choices that inevitably emerge for anyone who accepts the conditions for human relations laid down by the Sermon on the Mount.

Perceiving this ontological preference helps the reader to grasp the paradox in the grandmother's final words. Up to this point she has relegated God to the role of abstract observer: He rather tamely presides over our actions without making specific demands on our daily life. Certainly nothing that precedes it prepares the reader for the grandmother's effort to embrace a Christlike role for herself. Ironically, this gesture of Christian compassion only brings about her downfall.

> [The Misfit's] voice seemed about to crack and the grandmother's head cleared for an instant. She saw the man's face twisted close to her own as if he were going to cry and she murmured, "Why you're one of my babies. You're one of my own children!" She reached out and touched him on the shoulder. The Misfit sprang back as if a snake had bitten him and shot her three times through the chest. (p. 143)

As with the grandmother, ontological rather than epistemological assumptions govern the actions of The Misfit. While adhering to a vague notion of the existence of God, he has resisted accepting the obligations imposed by the fundamentalist concept of Jesus as a personal savior. At the same time, he cannot escape Christianity's domination. Having rejected the intrusion of God in his own life (as well as the displaced divinity figure, the psychiatrist), The Misfit refuses also to tolerate even the slightest effort to meliorate the death of the grandmother. Nonetheless, this nihilistic world view proves no more satisfying than that held by the grandmother.

> "She was a talker, wasn't she?" Bobby Lee said, sliding down the ditch with a yodel.

"She would of been a good woman," The Misfit said, "if it had been somebody there to shoot her every minute of her life."

"Some fun!" Bobby Lee said.

"Shut up, Bobby Lee," The Misfit said. "It's no real pleasure in life." (p. 143)

If we try to come to comprehend these attitudes within their narrative context, we are frustrated by an inner consistency that fails to produce a lucid explanation of the characters' motivations.

On the surface, the narrative invites us to infer radical behavioral differences between The Misfit and the grandmother. Initially, at least, we see The Misfit as an unregenerate criminal and the grandmother as a flawed but basically decent Christian woman. Both designations, however, prove not completely adequate to convey the complexity of the characters' natures. Ultimately, the role that each accepts—that of one who maintains an allegiance (though admittedly tenuous at times) to Christian dogma while torn by ambivalence about its applicability—parallels closely the other's choice. Consequently, to gain a clear sense of how to evaluate the natures of both characters, we must turn to a system of values similar to but independent from that which blurs the distinctions between these individuals: a more catholic/Catholic perception. In essence, we must realize that the deviance between these individual interpretations should not be seen as a measure of morality. Instead, we should view this difference as an index of the environment these figures inhabit. Catholicism proves an alternative to the religion governing the ethos of the story. It brings a fresh perspective to bear on this environment: it recontextualizes the O'Connor characters for the reader.

Catholicism does not, however, prescribe a specific interpretation for the story. For the term itself and the belief it embodies perpetually deconstruct themselves. In speaking of Catholicism as a religion, I refer to a system of theological beliefs that have evolved over nearly two thousand years and that are currently accepted by over 850 million people. To see Catholicism then as a monolithic system would be profoundly reductive. Further, to presume to state definitively the range of O'Connor's personal beliefs would be naive and arrogant. I am convinced, however, that a reading seeking to engage fully the aesthetic potential of O'Connor's fiction (and by extension the fiction of Toole and Percy) must be attentive to the signs of interplay among general notions of Catholicism, O'Connor's personal views, and the beliefs of the fundamentalist Protestant world that she depicts.

Thus Catholicism/catholicism stands as a point of departure for a range of possible meanings that encompass and reconcile the social repertoires of O'Connor and of the reader. Part of the initial dissatisfaction that a reader may experience at the end of "A Good Man Is Hard to Find" results, I suspect, not simply from the actions of the characters but rather from the ethos of the story that apparently condones and legitimizes those actions. In this sense, O'Connor's Catholic perspective (whether overtly or implicitly perceived) insinuates itself into any reading. As we create an interpretation, we attempt to break free of the story's environment. We do so to reconstitute the central figures by measuring them against a set of values outside the Protestant ethics annunciated in the story. Whatever reading we finally derive comes to us through our rejection of the values of the main characters. This rejection is possible only because of the distancing effect of O'Connor's own beliefs.

(One might reply that an atheistic value system would work as well in an effort to constitute such a response. But I contend that any form of secular humanism would implicitly suppress features of the discourse inspired by O'Connor's own social repertoire. This is not to say that one must be a practicing Catholic, or a member of any religious sect for that matter, to read O'Connor intelligently. I would assert, however, that one must be attentive to the religious elements acting upon the creative imagination of an author to derive a full sense of the aesthetic possibilities of his or her work.)

In a sense, one might see O'Connor's writing as a form of proselytizing. She very deftly undermines the efficacy of the dominant religious and nonreligious beliefs in favor of alternatives closer to her own views. O'Connor's brand of Catholicism may in fact seem to reflect a creed roughly similar to its Protestant counterparts, but her "religion" is kept aloof and so retains an appealing logic and consistency. Traditional Protestantism, at the mercy of a panoply of troglodytes in O'Connor's fiction, cannot maintain itself with the same integrity. Her novel *Wise Blood*, for example, plays out the emptiness of Southern fundamentalism with a grim sense of the dire need for faith. At the same time, it offers an equally clearheaded view of the disappointments inherent in most efforts to gain assurance of the efficacy of one's personal beliefs. Like The Misfit, Hazel Motes has refined his attitude toward Christianity into a highly distilled rage; yet, again like The

Misfit, he cannot simply slough off its influence on his consciousness. In proclaiming his Church without Christ, Motes affirms that he cannot remain within the either/or world of Southern Protestant belief. Instead, he is caught in the need simultaneously to testify and to denounce.

Hazel Motes, in fact, seems one of the few characters in the novel imbued with genuine belief. But the anger fueling his faith so blinds him metaphysically that it renders him impotent. (Ultimately, of course, this same rage will lead him to murder, to blind himself literally, and eventually to give himself over to a lethargic despair, to a form of suicide.) Motes presents the paradox of a principled man whose moral system operates according to values unacknowledged by most readers. As with the characters in "A Good Man Is Hard to Find," judging Motes entails a comparison of his behavior to the tenets of more stable and established religious beliefs. Again, Catholicism comes to mind. O'Connor's Catholicism neither vindicates nor absolves the actions of Motes and the others in the novel. It does suggest, however, a system of values both analogous to yet independent of the ones that have inspired so much cynicism and fanaticism in the characters in the novel.

The Violent Bear It Away focuses on ritual, both Christian and secular, in tracing the evolution of belief over three generations. The central figures are the boy Tarwater, his uncle Rayber, and his great uncle Old Tarwater. Their lives embody the decline of sincere faith into mindless ritual in a manner that parallels the movement from Romanticism, through modernism, and finally to postmodernism.[10] As in the previous examples, a degree of cynicism impels the actions of the central figures. Each turns from ritual as an expression of religious faith. Each downplays its communal significance and makes it instead a means of validating personal obsessions. With this transformation as its central concern, the novel unfolds an unflinching analysis of the potential for megalomania, and, by extension, it suggests the potential for oppression inherent in any system of purely personal belief. (This, some would argue, is a characterizing feature of Protestant fundamentalism.)

In the end O'Connor presents a highly complex commentary on the place of religion in the life of an individual. Tarwater, like both The Misfit and Hazel Motes, retains little faith in the Christian tenets that formed a moral code for him early in his life. Still, he cannot simply break free of the obligations of his religion. Like the other characters, he seems disadvantaged not

so much by the stamp of Christianity as by the isolation in which
he pursues his beliefs, whatever these beliefs may come to include. His uncle and his great uncle occupy positions that are
no less contradictory. They stand antithetically opposed in terms
of the faiths that they espouse. But despite the differences, they
display uncanny parallels in their applications of their beliefs.
Ultimately, because each of these three characters is haunted by
an idiosyncratic version of belief, the reader falls back on a stable
and detailed creed—O'Connor's Catholicism—to put their views
into perspective.

Taken together the three works referred to here remind one of
the dictum from St. Paul that faith without good works is nothing. In fact, a reader needs the benefits of Pauline vision, or some
reasonable substitute, to make sense of O'Connor's characters.
They develop as grotesques (a term inextricably associated with
O'Connor's writing), but the full measure of their natures becomes apparent only when set against the backdrop of O'Connor's stable Catholicism. Her belief cannot redeem the characters
in her stories, but it can encourage the reader to pursue complex
responses to the images she creates. I would not go so far as to
join critics who wish to see her as a theologian rather than as a
novelist. However, I do believe that the religious element offers
an important perspective on a singular aspect of her writing.[11]

III

The setting of John Kennedy Toole's *A Confederacy of Dunces*
echoes many of the same broad regional, physical, and metaphysical imperatives to be found in O'Connor's fiction. Toole's
figures, however, respond to life in a manner radically different
from that of O'Connor's characters. Indeed, despite the range of
voices shaping Toole's discourse, all consistently remind us of
the ludicrous aspects of his characters. At the same time, these
characters downplay or at least inhibit their own viciousness.
A number of features other than characterization also help to
transmute commonly accepted values into openly comedic attitudes. These include the carnival atmosphere of New Orleans
and the penchant for costuming and multiple role-playing
among a rich range of individuals. Each character also operates
according to a code of ethics independent of the beliefs of all
the other characters. Like O'Connor's figures, Toole's people occasionally exude a palpable malevolence. Ultimately, however, a

paralyzing lethargy renders them ineffectual and harmless. Hence, readers tend to see them all as comic rather than tragic individuals.[12]

A carnivalesque anarchy then dominates much of the narrative. Here Catholicism becomes both the most overt manifestation of the eccentricities of a majority of the characters and one of the few stabilizing features within the work. The idiosyncratic interpretations of religious faith by a number of the central figures offer significant insights into their natures. Irene Reilly continually turns to the church for moral support in her struggles with her son, yet her efforts repeatedly degenerate into low farce. Her unsuccessful attempt to force her son Ignatius to accompany her to mass, for example, leads to slapstick buffoonery. "[H]e had collapsed twice on the way to the church and had collapsed once again during the sermon about sloth, reeling out of the pew and creating an embarrassing disturbance."[13] Her attempt to invoke the authority of the parish priest only provokes Ignatius's scorn (p. 72). Patrolman Angelo Mancuso still seems traumatized by the treatment he received from the nuns of his grammar school. "You shoulda seen how them sisters beat up on him when he was a kid. One sister threw him right into a blackboard. That's how come Angelo's such a sweet, considerate man today" (p. 185). Santa Battaglia treats the picture of her dead mother like the relic of a saint and ensures that vigil lights still burn for her at St. Odo's Church (pp. 203–4). Here, incidentally, Claude Robichaux dutifully takes his grandchildren to Mass (p. 104). In essence, the characters' attitudes toward Catholicism, while relatively close to conventional practices, provide glosses for the psychological tics distinguishing each church member.

On the other hand, the religious beliefs of the novel's central character, Ignatius Reilly, place him well outside the limits of orthodox Catholicism. His basic beliefs rest on a naive and self-centered interpretation of the philosophy of the Schoolmen mixed with the superstition of the Middle Ages.

> As a medievalist Ignatius believed in the *rota Fortunae*, or wheel of fortune, a central concept in *De Consolatione Philosophiae*, the philosophical work which had laid the foundation for medieval thought. (p. 42)

*   *   *

> I do not support the current Pope. He does not at all fit my concept of a good, authoritarian Pope. Actually, I am opposed to the relativism of modern Catholicism quite violently. (p. 64)

In one sense, of course, Ignatius's reactionary Catholicism serves as a foil for his more outrageous eccentricities and intensifies the satirical aspects of the narrative. However, this highly restrictive view functions rhetorically in much the same way as does Protestant fundamentalism in Flannery O'Connor. So distorted a version of the Catholic religion implicitly draws attention to its obverse. I refer to the more orthodox Catholicism familiar to most people, rather than to an entirely different creed.

Viewing Ignatius's philosophy from the perspective of conventional Catholic beliefs gives the reader a fuller sense of the dimensions of his nature. This conventional perspective suggests that his religious upbringing has shaped and conditioned his behavior. Ignatius gives a perverse twist to every religious impulse that manifests itself in his actions. Still one may find echoes of more conventional Catholic beliefs and traditions in most of the features of his life. It is his personalization of traditional Catholicism that gives readers the deepest insights into his character. In fact, the whole rhythm of Ignatius's adult life becomes clearer when viewed in traditional Catholic terms. His initial encounter with Officer Mancuso and the ensuing automobile accident end the tranquility of his monastic existence, and, at the insistence of his mother, he begins his public life.

Preaching his crusade for Moorish Dignity to the downtrodden workers at Levy Pants and keeping *The Journal of a Working Boy* seem at first glance out of character for Ignatius. They seem so until one recalls how frequently stories of evangelical missionary zeal served as examples in pre–Vatican II Catholic religious education. His stint as a hot dog vendor may seem temporarily to take on a more secular tone. But his eagerness (despite his homophobia) to form a political movement with Dorian Greene to Save the World through Degeneracy combines his own satiric inclinations with a blinding messianic complex. The collapse of these efforts and the pursuit of Ignatius through the French Quarter by a trio of brutish lesbians trace his own Via Dolorosa and lead to his temporary eclipse. Later the appearance in the novel's final pages of Myrna Minkoff suggests that Ignatius may indeed rise again. Of course, none of this is meant to be taken with complete seriousness. At the same time, when one puts all of this against a backdrop of Catholic tradition, the behavior of Ignatius as scapegoat/messiah seems much less haphazard.

Like O'Connor, Toole enforces a strong sense of religious involvement while undercutting the very positions assumed by the adherents. As befits a work set in New Orleans, its Catholicism stands out as an overt aspect of its every discourse. Still, Catholicism's function as a gauge of the central character's deviant behavior remains quite similar to its function in O'Connor's works. Indeed, the narrative even encourages the reader to laugh contemptuously at the superstitious Catholicism of Ignatius Reilly's mother, while also feeding our skepticism of the slightly pompous, medieval mysticism of Ignatius. Nonetheless, Toole's creative strategy keeps conventional Catholicism at the center of the reader's consciousness. Neither the beliefs of Ignatius, of his mother, or of their co-religionists conform to the attitudes of contemporary Catholicism. But it is only with an awareness of traditional Catholic dogmas and doctrines that the reader is able to grasp the significance of their actions.

IV

The renditions of the modern South by O'Connor and by Toole then represent contrasting depictions of human tragedy and comedy. The narratives of Walker Percy, however, offer a hybrid of the two genres: the family romance. Percy's central figures reveal both an ingenuous attitude toward humanity in general and a surprising antipathy toward the discrete excesses of specific individuals. Often Percy's figures combine the traits of Molière's misanthrope Alceste and of Voltaire's optimist Candide. They are trapped in personal dialectics that reach a degree of resolution only in the melodramatic events that conclude his narratives. At times this dialectical impulse is played out through Percy's use of an interlocutor (one might say a confessor). Examples are to be found in the framing scenes with the unnamed priest in *Lancelot* or in the exchanges between Will Barrett and Sutter Vaught in *The Last Gentleman*. More often than not, however, efforts at confession and at absolution remain self-contained. They develop almost exclusively within the consciousnesses of individual characters. It is my contention, therefore, that to grasp the range of interpretive alternatives offered by these exchanges, the reader must examine them from the perspective of the belief conditioning their development.

The biographical details of Percy's entrance into the Catholic Church have been related so often that it would be redundant to repeat them. Nonetheless, I find it of at least parenthetical interest to note the absence in his prose of the proselytizing fervor characteristic of many converts. (The writings of G. K. Chesterton immediately come to mind.) In fact, he appears reticent to dwell in his fiction upon his Catholic affiliation. Rather than affirm his own beliefs through his novels, Percy often displaces the connection into analogous constructions. Such displacement is to be seen in the Episcopalianism of *The Second Coming* or in the renegade Catholic groups of *Love in the Ruins*. As with Flannery O'Connor, this impulse for displacement ultimately has the opposite effect, for in the final analysis it emphasizes the Catholic consciousness as the most effective arbiter of his characters' ethical behavior.

From a purely critical perspective such a religious guide appears eminently useful. For, with much greater frequency than either O'Connor or Toole, Percy repeatedly introduces perspectives in his fiction that contradict one another and often even undermine themselves. It follows only logically then that in this context of shifting viewpoints and displaced associations, the predominant narrative impulse is one of detachment, even voyeurism. The concept itself is by no means alien to Percy's discourses. Two of his novels, *The Moviegoer* and *Lancelot*, center the reader's attention specifically on this impulse to observe without direct engagement. In addition, numerous characters in his other works feel the same need to examine in minute detail the behavior of others while maintaining their own isolation. Paradoxically, only rarely do such withdrawn observations produce a sense of clarity or understanding. More often the resulting feelings are of frustration. In effect, their practices of detached observation cause the characters to experience more deeply their emotional ambivalence and isolation.

Time and again, characters in Percy's fiction seek to establish themselves in positions analogous to artists/gods. Intellectually engaged with their environment, they remain aloof from direct involvement with the world to which they give meaning. Inevitably, however, conflicting contingencies within their own natures frustrate their plans. Their very efforts to impose meaning often undermine their cherished positions of detachment. Will Barrett, for example, buys a powerful telescope as an alternative to continuing the sessions with his psychiatrist that so dominate his consciousness in the opening chapter of *The Last Gentleman*. He reasserts thereby an authority over his life that he had ceded years earlier. Nonetheless, within a relatively short time his observations move from a generally intensified sense of the world around him to a deep concern for the two women whom he observes on a bench in Central Park. At that point his control over his elaborately structured world begins to crumble.

> It was the day after he broke off his analysis that the engineer received a sign: he set up his telescope in the park to photograph the peregrine and had instead and by the purest chance witnessed the peculiar behavior of the Handsome Woman and her beautiful young friend. Every morning thereafter the engineer returned to the park and took his position beside the same outcropping of rock.[14]

Will's obsession with the beautiful young friend of the Handsome Woman takes up the rest of the novel. But the events of their relationship follow a predictable cycle based on his apparently mutually exclusive desires for engagement and separation.

Similarly, the detachment of Tom More in *Love in the Ruins: The Adventures of a Bad Catholic at a Time Near the End of the World* proves to be equally disingenuous. The novel begins with More speaking in an eschatological tone. Indeed, his tone is reminiscent of that used by Old Testament prophets who have rejected the corruption of society and decided to head for the wilderness: "Now in these dread latter days of the old violent beloved U.S.A. and of the Christ-forgetting Christ-haunted death-dealing Western world I came to myself in a grove of young pines and the question came to me: has it happened at last?"[15]

The narrative that follows, however, belies such a position of disengagement. In fact, it details, among other things, his invention of the lapsometer, a clinical device to "measure the depths of the human soul." At the same time, the discourse underscores for its readers the ambivalence inherent in More's attitude. Supposedly, he is withdrawing from a chaotic Louisianan society on the edge of Armageddon. In fact, he retains a deep interest not only in the fate of his immediate community but also in the larger events conditioning the world around him. His concern rivals that of any other middle-class home owner in Paradise Estates, but he is less willing to share responsibility for them.[16] In short, Tom More is a man torn by conflicting doubts with no inclination to resolve the ambiguity:

> I, for example, am a Roman Catholic, albeit a bad one. I believe in the Holy Catholic Apostolic and Roman Church, in God the Father, in the election of the Jews, in Jesus Christ His Son our Lord, who founded the Church on Peter his first vicar, which will last until the end of the world. Some years ago, however, I stopped eating Christ

in Communion, stopped going to mass, and have since fallen into a disorderly life. I believe in God and the whole business but I love women best, music and science next, whiskey next, God fourth, and my fellowman hardly at all. Generally I do as I please. A man, wrote John, who says he believes in God and does not keep his commandments is a liar. If John is right, then I am a liar. Nevertheless, I still believe. (p. 6)

The Will Barrett of *The Second Coming* seems only remotely and imperfectly connected to the character of the same name in *The Last Gentleman*. Indeed, in numerous instances events from the former novel seem retrospectively contradicted by details in the latter. Nonetheless, the later Will does retain the same voyeuristic impulse and the same inability to remain detached as the Will in *The Last Gentleman*. Like other Percy characters, the Will Barrett of *The Second Coming* melds the desire for religious belief with a proud independence that wishes to assert a personal ability to formulate that faith. Perhaps the most striking expression of these inclinations comes as Will determines to set up a confrontation with God by descending into the depths of a local cave in an ironic parallel to Jesus in the Holy Sepulcher. Will, of course, eschews the meekness praised in the beatitudes:

Speak, God, and let me know if the Jews are a sign and the Last Days are at hand. . . . Unfortunately for the poor man awaiting the Last Days and raving away at God and man in the bowels of Sourwood Mountain directly below thousands of normal folk playing golf and antiquing and barbecuing and simply enjoying the fall colors—for on the following day at the height of his lunacy the cloud blew away and the beautiful days of Indian summer began, the mountains glowed like rubies and amethysts, and leafers were out in force— unfortunately things can go wrong with an experiment most carefully designed by a sane scientist. A clear yes or no answer may not be forthcoming, after all. The answer may be a muddy maybe. In the case of Will Barrett, what went wrong could hardly be traced to God or man, Jews or whomever, but rather to a cause at once humiliating and comical: a toothache.[17]

This convergence of the eschatological and the banal typifies the consciousness of a Percy character. It illustrates the need for a stable religious vision to counterbalance these conflicting attitudes and thereby provide the reader with interpretive guidance.

The passages quoted above underscore images of fragmentation and disassociation of sensibilities. Indeed, despite the evoca-

tion of God in several images, one might see all as only
tangentially linked to religious concepts. At the same time, when
one traces references in Percy's fiction to the concept of transcendence and to images of belief, he finds that these ideas function
as central issues. Disjunction still occurs, of course. Ultimately,
however, all of Percy's works incorporate into their discourses
this combined sense of religious allegiance and of an agnostic-
like disassociation. To a degree, his writings may also echo
strong autobiographical impulses. Certainly they reflect the am-
bivalences one might feel after experiencing the struggle for belief familiar to any convert. Then, too, his narratives suggest the
effort at refamiliarization that marked the faith of those Catholics
trying to accept the radical doctrinal and ritual changes of the
reformed, post–Vatican II Church.

The basic question, however, persists: Is it necessary to apply
strictly Catholic views for a valid interpretation of Percy's canon?
Admittedly, none of these observations touches directly upon the
philosophers or upon the philosophical schools often associated
with Percy. I refer to St. Thomas and the Schoolmen, Romano
Guardini, Søren Kierkegaard, Albert Camus, Jean-Paul Sartre,
and the Existentialists. But, of course, that is my point: One can
quite legitimately read Percy from the perspective of these thinkers. Still, the broader/narrower concepts of Catholicism allow
one a much freer range of interpretation. These ideas not only
underscore prominent elements in Percy's work, but they also
establish a context for viewing him outside the conventions assigned to Southern writers. An awareness of the tenets of orthodox Catholicism gives readers the same sense of reference that
it provides in the works of O'Connor and of Toole. Placing Percy's
own idiosyncratic religiosity into a large context, this awareness
highlights specific behavior in key situations and glosses the motivations of central characters in others.

All of this moves an aware reader to conclude that in any
system of reading, whatever the primary emphasis, he can neither exclude the writer nor allow him or her the hegemony once
extended in traditional habits of reading. In approaching the
works of Flannery O'Connor, John Kennedy Toole, or Walker
Percy, the reader needs to focus on Catholicism to grasp at least
one of the systems for generating standards or perspectives that
these authors have adopted. Admittedly, linking the three remains problematic. But by emphasizing the way each writer
draws on Catholicism to escape the influence of Faulkner and

the predictable label of regional writer, I feel I have established
the legitimacy of a new range of possible readings.

Notes

1. James Joyce, *A Portrait of the Artist as a Young Man: Text, Criticism, and Notes*, ed. Chester G. Anderson (New York: Viking Press, 1968), p. 215; Michel Foucault, "What Is an Author?" *Textual Strategies: Perspectives in Post-Structuralist Criticism*, ed. Josué V. Harari (Ithaca: Cornell University Press, 1979), p. 141; Roland Barthes, "The Death of the Author," *The Rustle of Language*, trans. Richard Howard (New York: Hill and Wang, 1986), p. 49.

2. Roland Barthes is the most articulate proponent of this position; in his examination of "Sarrasine," for example, he never attempts to ignore or to suppress the presence of Balzac. See his *S/Z*, trans. Richard Miller (New York: Hill and Wang, 1974).

3. I have drawn my sense of the term "social repertoire," modified to accommodate the argument of this essay, from the work of reader-response critics like Wolfgang Iser and Hans Robert Jauss.

4. I am giving a very precise meaning to the term "text": the imaginative response of reader to an author's images on a printed page. In this sense a text has a subjective, metaphysical existence rather than an objective, physical one. My views parallel, but do not coincide completely with, those of Roland Barthes in his "From Work to Text," *The Rustle of Language*, pp. 56–64.

5. I am using the term "social repertoire" in the manner that Wolfgang Iser defined it in his *The Act of Reading: A Theory of Aesthetic Response* (Baltimore and London: The Johns Hopkins University Press, 1978).

6. One finds examples of this in the closing stanza of Sylvia Plath's anthem of arrested adolescent nastiness, "Daddy." There the narrative voice seeks to purge itself of its anger with the articulation of a series of ferocious images depicting first the destruction and then the humiliation of the hated, parasitic, paternal oppressor.

> There's a stake in your fat black heart
> And the villagers never liked you.
> They are dancing and stamping on you.
> They always knew it was you.
> Daddy, daddy, you bastard, I'm through.

Few contemporary readers will be able to see these lines without recalling countless film versions of the Dracula story (especially those of the now camp performances of Bela Lugosi) or responding to the clear implications of Oedipal/Electral frustration. Individuals will vary in the significance that they assign to these elements, just as Plath's own responses must have varied greatly throughout the process of creation. The point, of course, is not how we respond to these cultural markers embedded in the poem but rather that we cannot avoid responding to them in one way or another.

Much of Plath's thematic and stylistic methodology stands in sharp contrast to the techniques of the writers considered here. Yet in one sense at least, the lines quoted above can serve as an objective correlative for the central issues of this study. Plath's poetry exemplifies some of the most extravagant features of the responses made in America since the Civil War to a persistent and ambivalent sense of the intellectual domination of previous generations. This attitude, of course, has dogged artists of all nationalities for centuries. But one can argue that the trauma that any author must face has become much more intense since Freud's formulating of neuroses for mass consumption. As Plath's poem illustrates, this mixture of obsession and revulsion has often brought about elaborate, bizarre responses that test the creative sensitivities of writers and readers alike. At the same time, one need not feel restricted to images of violence as the only way of expressing artistic frustration. In fact, the works under consideration in this essay, while filled with violent individuals and violent incidents, employ much more sophisticated rhetorical tactics to express their authors' determination to separate themselves from the legacy of their artistic predecessors.

7. I do not accept the logic of German phenomenology that sees subjectivity in a noetic sense, simultaneously privileging its position while burdening it with connotations of anarchy. While subjectivity is synonymous with personalized perceptions, it does not follow that the subject is cut off from the common codes of his or her society that allow the individual to convey to others a sense of these personal responses. Subjectivity is always discursive. The alienated, unresponsive attitude perjoratively referred to as subjectivity is really what many term the objective approach: singular, detached, unchanging, inflexible. Genuine subjectivity must reflect the multiplicity that Bakhtin celebrates, and the truly subjective consciousness remains open to incorporating into its perceptions the variety of experiences and attitudes that it continually encounters.

8. Catholicism is not, of course, free of myopia, nor is O'Connor necessarily unaware of its shortcomings. Its shortsightedness, however, does not figure as a significant drawback when it acts simply as a standard for measuring Protestantism.

9. Flannery O'Connor, Three: Wise Blood, A Good Man Is Hard to Find, The Violent Bear It Away (New York: New American Library, 1964), p. 142. All subsequent references are from this edition.

10. An analogous point about the emptiness of the very name tarwater—used in the eighteenth century as a popular if ineffective folk remedy—has been made in D. G. Kehl, "Flannery O'Connor's Catholicon: The Source and Significance of the Name 'Tarwater,'" Notes on Contemporary Literature 15 (1985): 2–3. Unfortunately, in the final paragraph of the essay, Kehl subverts his own logic by succumbing to a reductive argument and a literalist reading of O'Connor's correspondence.

11. See, for example, Sumner J. Ferris, "The Outside and the Inside: Flannery O'Connor's The Violent Bear It Away," Critical Essays on Flannery O'Connor, eds. Melvin J. Friedman and Beverly Lyon Clark (Boston: G. K. Hall & Co., 1985), pp. 85–91.

12. Lloyd M. Daigrepont has outlined the satiric elements of the novel in his essay "Ignatius Reilly and the Confederacy of Dunces," New Orleans Review 9 (1982): 74–80.

13. John Kennedy Toole, A Confederacy of Dunces (New York: Grove Press, Inc., 1982), p. 20. All subsequent references are from this edition.

14. Walker Percy, The Last Gentleman (New York: Avon Books, 1966), p. 41.

15. Walker Percy, Love in the Ruins: The Adventures of a Bad Catholic at a Time Near the End of the World (New York: Avon Books, 1978), p. 3. All subsequent references are from this edition.

16. At the same time I must note that in his critical writing Percy quite directly assigns to himself and to other novelists the role of modern-day prophet. See especially "A Novel about the End of the World" in his *The Message in the Bottle: How Queer Man Is, How Queer Language Is, and What One Has to Do with the Other* (New York: Farrar, Straus, Giroux, 1975), pp. 101–18.

17. Walker Percy, *The Second Coming* (New York: Washington Square Press, 1981), p. 246.

Voices Interior and Exterior:
William Styron's Narrative Personae

JAMES L. W. WEST III

Oɴᴇ way to approach the novels of William Styron is through
the concept of voice. "Voice" is an elusive feature in narrative fiction, especially in Styron's novels, where many voices
alternate, mingle, and compete with one another for attention.
Some of Styron's voices are meant to be authorial or quasi-
autobiographical; others belong solely to the characters in his
narratives. As we shall see, voice has sometimes given Styron
difficulty during the composition of his novels, but in the fiction
he has chosen to publish one recognizes a genuine mastery of
voice, effective and unobtrusive. And one can see a progression
over time, a developing sophistication from novel to novel, in
Styron's manipulation of voice. From the transparently objective
voice of *Lie Down in Darkness* to the slanted omniscience of *The
Long March* to the double-voicing of *Set This House on Fire* to
the mixed voice of *The Confessions of Nat Turner* to the quasi-
autobiographical voice of *Sophie's Choice*, one can observe
Styron working through a range of voices and learning to exploit
their full narrative potential. One finds this flexibility, this willingness to experiment with voice, in few other writers of Styron's
generation.[1]

Lie Down in Darkness is a profoundly disturbing novel, partly
because of the voices in which it is narrated. There is a central
narrative persona, an apparently objective authorial voice that
speaks from the first lines of the book. The opening of the novel,
with its address to the reader as "you," draws one into the narrative, down from the North into the sullen atmosphere of Port
Warwick on a hot day in August 1945:

> Riding down to Port Warwick from Richmond, the train begins to
> pick up speed on the outskirts of the city, past the tobacco factories
> with their ever-present haze of acrid, sweetish dust and past the rows
> of uniformly brown clapboard houses which stretch down the hilly

48

streets for miles, it seems, the hundreds of rooftops all reflecting the pale light of dawn. . . .

Suddenly the train is burrowing through the pinewoods, and the conductor, who looks middle-aged and respectable like someone's favorite uncle, lurches through the car asking for tickets. If you are particularly alert at that unconscionable hour you notice his voice, which is somewhat guttural and negroid—oddly fatuous-sounding after the accents of Columbus or Detroit or wherever you came from—and when you ask him how far it is to Port Warwick and he says, "Aboot eighty miles," you know for sure that you're in the Tidewater.[2]

The novel proper, it might be said, commences only when this prologue is complete and the second-person form of address has been dropped. The authorial voice can now begin to recount the story of Peyton Loftis and her family. Very little of the story, however, is told neutrally through the consciousness of this authorial narrative persona. The bulk of the tale is recounted instead through the minds and from the viewpoints of the major characters—Milton Loftis, Helen Loftis, Dolly Bonner, and Carey Carr. The viewpoint alternates among these characters and a few others, and the reader's sympathies shift as the perspective changes. The narrative takes on color and bias from each consciousness through which it is filtered, and because most of these characters are obsessive and unforgiving, the coloration is strong. One finds oneself on an old domestic battleground, listening to combatants who have had many years to work up their arguments and self-justifications. Styron's uncanny ability in *Lie Down in Darkness* to listen to the voices of these characters and to reproduce their moralizing and defensiveness makes the experience of reading the novel quite unsettling. One's sympathies change section by section and even page by page as one hears first Milton's side of the story, then Helen's, then Dolly's—and then the voice of the Episcopal priest Carey Carr is heard from its peculiar perspective.

In fiction the omniscient narrative voice usually offers the reader some guidance. Hawthorne's omniscient voice prompts the reader, for example, as do some of the omniscient voices used by Melville, Dreiser, Wharton, and Fitzgerald. But Styron's narrative voice in *Lie Down in Darkness* is for the most part transparent: only in a few places does the voice become didactic, and it never lectures the characters (as is sometimes the case with Hawthorne and Wharton, for example), nor does it point out obvious moral lessons. This voice, in all but one or two places, is transparent and chameleon-like, taking its coloration from the character who has the floor. The approach is entirely appropriate for a novel about guilt and the failure to forgive: On a day such as this one, while the hearse bearing Peyton's body makes its slow progress from the railroad station to the graveyard, it is natural for the minds of the stunned survivors to range back and forth across the past in search of motives, explanations, and excuses.

Still, there is a center of morality in this novel, a perspective that is never truly identified but is present beneath the narrative. That perspective is not exactly Peyton's; it is more nearly that of an advocate who speaks on her behalf, someone of her age and upbringing who laments her passing. Throughout most of the narrative Peyton is a shadowy character, beautiful but, for all the reader can tell, vacuous and materialistic. It is only after we have read her interior monologue near the end, have seen how intelligent and sensitive she is, and have recognized the effect on her of Helen's hatred and Milton's fawning that we can identify her presence and the presence of her advocate in the novel. They have both been there all along, silently listening and judging, holding up Milton, Helen, and the society in which they live for examination and criticism. The implied narrative perspective is that of a talented youth in need of love and discipline but lost to the self-centeredness of adults and the meretriciousness of their social world. This omniscient voice, it might be said, is the voice of Styron's generation.

The voicing of *Lie Down in Darkness* results in part from the manner in which the novel was composed. Styron began the manuscript in 1947 under the working title "Inheritance of Night." He produced a fifty-three-page beginning for his story in late 1947 and early 1948, revised and compressed this opening during the summer and early fall of 1948, and added an additional twenty pages in the early months of 1949. Styron was dissatisfied with this writing, however, and he reworked it extensively for *Lie Down in Darkness*. Fortunately copies of his unrevised drafts have survived, and they are illuminating, especially with regard to the matter of voice.[3]

Styron was much under Faulkner's spell when he began writing *Lie Down in Darkness*; the surviving material from "Inheritance of Night" documents that influence. Styron was particularly taken by *The Sound and the Fury* and *As I Lay Dying*, and he seems at first to have considered using a blend of the narrative techniques in those two books for his own novel.

In a note to his literary agent, affixed to the surviving first draft of "Inheritance," he writes:

> I intend for this novel to be divided into three books of from ten to fifteen sections apiece. Each book is to be preceded by a monologue, direct or interior, which is intended to throw light upon Peyton and her story.

Then, in the first section of Book One of "Inheritance of Night," Styron presents an eight-page passage of direct monologue, spoken by Maudie, the feebleminded daughter of Milton and Helen Loftis. The Maudie character in "Inheritance" is quite different from the severely retarded Maudie of the published novel. In this early version Maudie is only slightly afflicted. Her monologue, though ungrammatical and sometimes repetitive, is told in straightforward English—unlike, for example, Benjy Compson's stream-of-consciousness narrative in the first section of *The Sound and the Fury.* Maudie's monologue is followed by sections, now in limited omniscient narration, which are filtered through the consciousnesses of individual characters—Milton Loftis, Marcus Bonner (a quasi-autobiographical character not present in *Lie Down in Darkness*), Mr. Casper (the undertaker), Marcus Bonner again, and finally Helen Loftis.

Several features are apparent in these early drafts: Styron already conceives of his novel as multivoiced, and the voices are already plaintive, argumentative, and by turns defensive and accusatory. Here, for example, is a section from Maudie's opening monologue. She is thinking of Milton's attitude toward Peyton:

> Oh I reckon she was his favorite, all right. He'd call her his little glamour girl and then Mama would holler out from the sunporch in the back. I could hear her say, "Milton, Milton, please try to be quiet, my migraine is so bad today," and they'd hush up, Papa and Peyton, and then they'd come out of the house real quiet, whispering together like he wasn't any older than her, and go up to Powhatan Road and get some ice cream and bring me back some. Lord, it was hot that summer. . . . Peyton was only nine years old but she was smart, Lord, she was smart, like she is now I reckon, and Papa and her would be talking together like she wasn't any younger than him at all. . . . I am as smart as Peyton, or anybody. Even if Peyton did go to St. Mary's. Even if she can paint pictures and all. Sometimes I want to hate Peyton because she's so smart and beautiful.

Other than Peyton's stream-of-consciousness narration near the end of *Lie Down in Darkness*, there are no long sections of direct

monologue, like Maudie's above, in the published book. The
"feel" of interior monologue permeates the novel, however, and
snippets of the characters' thoughts appear in italics throughout.
It is important to realize that this "feel" is already present in the
very earliest drafts of "Inheritance of Night."

The other noteworthy feature of "Inheritance of Night" is the
presence of the narrative of Marcus Bonner, the quasi-authorial
character mentioned above. A former schoolmate of Peyton's who
has been infatuated with her for years, Marcus works now as a
manuscript reader for a New York publisher and lives in a
wretched room in a "residence club." (Stingo in Sophie's Choice
comes immediately to mind, of course, as does William Styron
himself, who held a similar editorial position and lived in a
similar rooming house in New York City during the spring and
summer of 1947.) Marcus has kept in touch with Peyton, and it
is he who learns of her suicide, has her body exhumed, and
accompanies it down to Port Warwick on the train. Marcus is
not a successful character—he is too ineffectual and Prufrockian
to be attractive—and Styron wisely dropped him from subsequent drafts. But in a curious way Marcus's voice survives in Lie
Down in Darkness. One might almost say that we see the story
from his omniscient perspective. His is the voice of the generation to which Peyton belongs; he is her mourner and chief advocate, and he provides the moral center for the novel.

Styron's next novel, The Long March, is told from the viewpoint of Lieutenant Thomas Culver, who is literally an advocate—that is to say, an attorney—in civilian life. The central
narrative voice in this work is again omniscient, but the Jamesian
vessel of consciousness is Culver alone. His perspective is maintained throughout, and it is moral and judgmental. Indeed, from
now on Styron will always employ a narrative voice that is moral
and didactic, even in The Confessions of Nat Turner. Culver is
appalled by the idiocies of military life—by the posturing, the
game playing, the abuses of language, the waste, and the mind-
lessness of the training exercises. His running reactions, spoken
to others in dialogue or reported by the omniscient narrative
persona, are present in an ironic minor key throughout the story.
But the chief object of Culver's interest is Captain Al Mannix,
the rebellious reservist who is outspokenly critical of the Marine
Corps and who is finally court-martialed for insubordination.
Culver is the first of Styron's "square" observers: he is fascinated
by a rebellious nonconformist but does not have the courage to
rebel. He is friendly with Mannix and functions rather like a

Watson-figure: he is an interpreter, an admirer, an intermediary between Mannix and the reader. Mannix talks to Culver, or *at* him, and we learn something from these encounters, but Mannix never carries the narratives himself, nor do we have access to his thoughts.

Among Styron's papers at the Library of Congress there survives the aborted beginning of a novel which, had it been completed, would have fallen between *The Long March* and *Set This House on Fire* in order of composition. This fragment, recently published under the title "Blankenship," is written in almost precisely the same voice as that used in *The Long March*.[4] The central consciousness in this fragment is a career soldier, Marine Gunner Charles R. Blankenship, who has until the time of this narrative felt entirely at home in the military. The story is set in 1944. Blankenship has been wounded at Guadalcanal and is now stationed as a Warrant Officer at the Naval Prison on Hart's Island in Long Island Sound. Blankenship, an intelligent and capable soldier, encounters a rebellious inmate named McFee and is simultaneously threatened and fascinated by the man. Blankenship allows himself to be goaded into striking McFee with a nightstick—and there the fragment ends.

Why Styron aborted this novel-in-progress is not altogether clear today, but one reason might be that, for all its voltage, the surviving false start represents no real technical advance over what he had already accomplished in *The Long March*. Styron has always pursued technical innovation in his fiction—not radical innovation such as one finds in the fiction of Thomas Pynchon and Gilbert Sorrentino, for example, but innovation nonetheless. He has found it useful to conceive difficult tasks for himself, to tackle challenging technical feats involving structure or voice in his narratives. This is one of the recurrent themes in his published interviews:

> I have a feeling that writers set up barriers for themselves. If they don't, they should. And I know I do. I think that one of the central mystiques of the writer of novels is that you don't take the easy way, you take the hardest way in order to see if you can surmount the problems. And I know that imposing upon myself this kind of tension has, to my mind, produced whatever good stuff I've ever produced. It has always involved taking the most difficult path from point A to point Z.[5]

Styron erected such a hurdle when he began to write *Set This House on Fire*, and the task he set himself involved the concept of voice. In April 1960, only a few weeks before formal publication of the book, Styron described in a letter to *Publishers Weekly* the technical obstacle he had set up for himself before beginning to compose *Set This House on Fire:*

> In writing *Set This House on Fire*, from the very outset I was determined to . . . write a long complex book which would allow me to say all I wanted to about American life, but which at the same time would be written in the first person *and* the third person—two apparently irreconcilable points of view. . . . If *Set This House on Fire* succeeds as a novel it will, of course, succeed for a few other reasons than that I felt determined to weld these two apparently conflicting points of view. At this writing, three weeks before publication, I honestly cannot say whether it will be considered that the book succeeds at all. But I had never seen this welding of two points of view attempted in a work of fiction before: I had never seen a narrator who, beginning in the first person, could convincingly, end up in the third person, the story so merging and mingling that one might accept without hesitation the fact that the narrator himself knew the uttermost nuances of another man's thought; and it was the fight to achieve this new dimension—involving over three-and-a-half years more tearing apart and putting back together than I care to think about—which gives to the book whatever power and tension it has.[6]

Peter Leverett's voice in *Set This House on Fire* is the familiar, conservative voice of the objective narrator-figure, but here for the first time Styron is working in the first-person mode. Peter narrates the story. His voice is reminiscent of the voice of Nick Carraway, another American of high moral character who is intrigued by the aberrant behavior of a neighbor. *Set This House on Fire*, however, fairly quickly takes on a different form—not a monologue by Peter, but a dialogue between him and Cass Kinsolving. Most of the conversation is carried on in Charleston while they are fishing. Peter, the square character, moves in on Cass, the tormented artist—probing and prodding, searching for the truth about what happened in Sambuco. In Part I of the novel, Peter's voice carries the narrative along in the conventional first-person mode, but in Part II, Cass's voice begins to take over. Initially Styron allows Cass to tell long sections of the story in his own voice, in quoted monologue. We hear his voice, become accustomed to it, and learn to allow for Cass's tendencies toward bombast, exaggeration, and self-interrogation. But before we become weary of listening to Cass (who is too garrulous to be an ideal first-person narrator), Styron shifts back to Peter's voice and retains Cass's perspective. Without our really noticing it, Styron has granted Peter access to Cass's mind, thus keeping the advantages of first-person narration but casting the story into something resembling limited omniscience. So smoothly is this transition made that the reader never questions it. The result, in *Set This House on Fire*, is a peculiar double-voicing, ideal for a novel in which the two major characters merge finally into one consciousness in order to examine the moral and philosophical implications of their past behavior.

One finds a forecast of this particular narrative technique in another false start, a twenty-four-hundred-word aborted opening for *Set This House on Fire*, which Styron wrote in 1954 as he was casting about for a suitable voice in which to tell his story. In this discarded opening, Peter Leverett describes two ocean cruises—the first a pleasant journey from America to Europe taken shortly after the conclusion of World War II, and the second a nightmarish trip back to America from Europe taken three years later. Peter has lived through the horrendous experiences at Sambuco (he is not specific yet about what has happened) and now finds himself "a neurotic first-class . . . paralyzed, evil-tempered, humorless, and abominably self-centered." Peter's voice, in this false start, is nervous, talky, and focused relentlessly inward. This is hardly the friendly, self-effacing Peter Leverett of the published version of *Set This House on Fire*. It is instead a single figure who, at this early stage in the composition of the novel, embodies characteristics of both Peter and Cass and speaks in a blend of both voices. (Cass is present, but he is named Ben Kinsolving in this false start and is only mentioned, not developed.) Styron seems to have recognized that this narrative approach would not work, and when he began *Set This House on Fire* a second time, he made a strong initial differentiation between these two characters. Only later did he allow their voices to merge and blend.[7]

A different kind of blending occurs in *The Confessions of Nat Turner*. Indeed, one of the most controversial aspects of the novel is the extent to which Nat's voice is colored by, permeated by, Styron's own. In an interview conducted while he was still composing *Nat Turner*, Styron recalled his initial difficulties in settling on a proper voice in which to have his major character speak.

For years, when I was considering writing this novel, I had no idea how I was going to tackle the thing. I had the idea of telling it from

an omniscient point of view, from many reactive standpoints, such
as that of one of the white victims, one of the farmer types. It just
didn't seem right to me, and I don't know how these things evolve,
but when I began finally to tackle the book itself, I realized that the
only way to do it was to do it from Nat's point of view. . . . I realized
that inevitably one of the profoundly difficult things I would have to
set up for myself would be the telling of this story from the point of
view of Nat himself—a first-person narrative which would somehow
allow you to enter the consciousness of a Negro of the early decades
of the 19th century. It seemed to be the only way out, so I did it.[8]

But Styron chose to narrate the novel in his own literary style.
He placed certain limitations on himself: he avoided anachro-
nisms and the modern vernacular, and he cast all dialogue in a
relatively formal nineteenth-century mode. The vocabulary and
the perceptions that are granted to Nat, however, are Styron's
own. Nat's voice is not limited by place or time or upbringing;
his world collides with Styron's in Styron's consciousness.

When reading *Nat Turner*, one should not forget that the novel
is an artificial construction. The wealth of historical detail in
the novel can easily mislead one into thinking that it is meant
to be a realistic narrative. *The Confessions of Nat Turner* is no
more realistic than *The Scarlet Letter*, for example, or *The Red
Badge of Courage*. Styron's share of the central, first-person narrative voice is historically informed and is modern, even engagé,
in its viewpoint. The narrative voice, for instance, does not *say*
that Virginia's economy, based on slavery, underwent a crippling
depression from 1820 to 1830, but Styron's consciousness *knows*
it. That knowledge is reflected in the narrative and in what happens to Nat when his master must sell him as a valuable item of
chattel. Likewise, Styron's share of the voice knows much about
the history of popular revolution during the twentieth century
and has learned a great deal about the personality of the prototypical revolutionary leader—Lenin, for example, or Castro. That
knowledge is apparent in Nat's self-depiction, in the obsessions
and visions that he reveals in his narration, and in his mingled
love and contempt for the slaves he seeks to free. Styron's voice
is really never far from the surface of *The Confessions of Nat
Turner*. Much criticism has been leveled at Styron for his statement, in the "Author's Note" to *Nat Turner*, that the novel is "a
meditation on history." The phrase can indeed be misleading if
taken literally. Styron's statement to an interviewer in 1965,
about the mode of narration he chose to adopt for the novel,

is perhaps more nearly accurate: "In reality," Styron told the interviewer, "it is a form of translation."[9]

Styron's friend Carlos Fuentes sees *The Confessions of Nat Turner* as something else again—as a novel about language itself:

> By choosing the first person singular, Styron is by no means trying to supplant or reproduce Nat Turner, but creates a completely new figure within a completely new construction, and is doing so, not through traditional techniques (Styron is neither Somerset Maugham nor Irving Stone) but, quite simply, through a creation of language. A novel, a real novel, today, is not a comfortable and comforting psycho-socio-realistic *ancilla*: it is language, and it is as a creation of language that this novel demands to be understood. Unlike the realists (bourgeois or socialist brands), Styron, being a true artist, has not put the cart—significance—before the horse—the sign itself. The real meaning of *The Confessions of Nat Turner* must be sought, I believe, in its approach to language as the first of all master-slave relationships. . . . Nat Turner has been in rebellion against the language on which that system is based. Ironically, his first rebellion is his worst and most radical failure: he rebels against the masters by imitating the language of the masters. He is imprisoned in the language of the elite: by the language of William Styron.[10]

It is important to realize that one is *meant* to hear Styron's language, to listen to his voice, in *The Confessions of Nat Turner*. While he was writing the novel, Styron made no real effort to conceal his presence in the narrative, and he was quite open with interviewers, both before and after publication, about the peculiar nature of his narrative persona. Indeed, it might be said that with *Nat Turner* Styron learned to use his public visibility to instruct his readers about the proper way in which to read a forthcoming book. I make this statement with some hesitation: I do not mean to suggest that Styron consciously planned to use particular interviews as adjuncts to his novel, or that one cannot approach *Nat Turner* without having read these interviews. But it is indisputable that the interviews are a great aid. Styron understood precisely what he was doing with voice in *Nat Turner* and feared (correctly, as it turned out) that his methods would be misunderstood. In his prepublication interviews, he attempted to explain ahead of time what he had done.[11]

The experience of publishing *The Confessions of Nat Turner* and living through the high and low points of its reception seems to have been valuable to Styron. The visibility that he achieved apparently taught him a great deal about the place and status of the author in America and opened for him certain avenues of communication with his public that his predecessors did not have. Certainly the cult of personality in America of the 1970s and 1980s has not had an altogether good effect on the native literature, but the availability of media exposure has not been entirely a bad thing either. At least two other authors of Styron's generation, Norman Mailer and Philip Roth, have learned consciously to use printed and televised interviews and news stories to help create public *personae* for themselves and have appropriated material for their writings from their contacts with the media. Mailer, in particular, has drawn energy from the friction generated by his highly publicized encounters with various groups—liberal activists, for example, or feminists, or advocates of the death penalty. Roth has worked in a somewhat different fashion, taking the notoriety generated by his earlier writings—*Goodbye, Columbus* and *Portnoy's Complaint* especially—and making it a crucial element in the career of Nathan Zuckerman, his fictional alter-ego.

Styron has done something similar in *Sophie's Choice*. In Stingo, the narrator of that novel, he has created a fictional second self who resembles him in several respects and whose life, in many of its details, closely approximates his own. To bring off this bit of legerdemain, Styron has relied in part on his own visibility in the culture, his own fame, his general sense of what the American reading public already knows about his life and literary career. Stingo is the author, for example, of a first novel entitled *Inheritance of Night*, the plot of which is quite similar to that of *Lie Down in Darkness*. Stingo's third novel, *These Blazing Leaves*, closely resembles *The Confessions of Nat Turner* and has been similarly treated by New York reviewers and black militants. Some details of Stingo's personal life are drawn from Styron's own, although here Styron has taken many imaginative liberties. Styron made all of this plain in the printed and televised interviews that took place before the publication of *Sophie's Choice* and that continued for some time thereafter. Again I do not believe that Styron's employment of the media was conscious or manipulative. I would suggest, however, that his relationship with his public is quite different from the relationship that, say, Poe or James or even Cather or Steinbeck could count on with their readers.

What we hear in *Sophie's Choice* is a different kind of fictional voice. It is not the self-reflexive voice of the recent John Barth novels, nor is it the brilliantly self-conscious voice used by John

Fowles in *Mantissa*. It is instead a blending of two voices in a single narrator who is meant to be seen as, simultaneously, Styron and not-Styron. The arrangement might have been imagined by a science-fiction writer: Stingo seems to exist in a parallel but independent universe, perhaps in another dimension—a universe that mirrors our own very closely but not identically. The voice of this character is reflective, relaxed, digressive, self-possessed, humorous, meditative, informed, concerned, and engaged. The voice is more transparently didactic than any other that Styron has employed. Quite frequently it instructs the reader in matters of history and comments on what has been written about the Holocaust by those who participated in it.

The voice that Styron employs in *Sophie's Choice* can be seen as a culmination and blending of most of the narrative techniques used in the earlier novels. Stingo is a later and much more successful reimagining of Marcus Bonner from "Inheritance of Night." Like Marcus, Stingo reads manuscripts at a New York publishing house and inhabits a dreary cell in a rooming house; like Marcus he is also, in his mature embodiment, a kind of moral conscience for his generation. Like Lieutenant Culver, Stingo is hesitant to take action; like Peter Leverett, he is fascinated by someone who has faced a moral dilemma and made a choice; like Nat Turner, he reviews the past and ruminates on its moral implications.

Of all these relationships, the one between Stingo and Peter Leverett, and between *Sophie's Choice* and *Set This House on Fire*, seems the strongest. In fact, the method of narration and the employment of voice in these two novels are almost identical. Stingo, like Peter, begins his narrative in the conventional first-person mode, but he quickly becomes fascinated with the mysterious Sophie Zawistowska and attempts to learn the truth about her past. In the second part of *Sophie's Choice*, Sophie, like Cass Kinsolving, begins to tell her own story in her own voice and accent. But Styron cannot permit her to carry the narrative for very many pages: for all its charm, her broken English is a distraction, and Styron cannot give her the vocabulary that he made available to Nat Turner. So Stingo resumes the narrative in the first person, and again, like Peter Leverett, he is granted powers of omniscience. Styron explained the technique in a recent interview:

> I was determined to make this narrative approach work in *Sophie's Choice*. I knew it couldn't fail if I did it right. If each voice is convinc-

ing in its own mode, then you can start fluidly interchanging them. You have to imprint upon the reader a sense of intimacy. Here's Sophie, who spins out a story about Kraków and her father and her life as a child—a non-stop fifteen-minute monologue. The reader knows that anyone who receives this monologue in its entirety, as Stingo does, and who then in his older reincarnation remembers it all, is perfectly able to set down what really went on in her mind because he heard her telling her story. There's no strain on the reader's imagination. And because you're still using the first-person narrator, the Stingo voice, you get an added dimension—authenticity. You believe the things Stingo tells you. I have always thought that the reader feels convinced by a first-person narrator because of the intimacy of the "I." You lose that in the omniscient mode.[12]

Styron has found this first-person quasi-autobiographical voice a comfortable one. In two long stories published since *Sophie's Choice*—"Love Day" and "A Tidewater Morning"—he has used this voice, and he is currently using it in a novella-in-progress.[13] The names of the narrators change from story to story, but the voice remains that of an older author looking back on his youth and observing the period of history through which he has lived and in which he has participated. This voice is flexible and supple: it allows Styron to move freely over a long span of years, and it combines the verisimilitude of the first-person narrator with the range of the omniscient storyteller. Sometimes by incorporating documentary evidence—letters, diaries, reader reports, journals—Styron is even able to let us hear the narrator's youthful voice. The approach also permits Styron a greater didacticism than one finds in the previous novels, a didacticism appropriate for a public artist who wishes to speak on the moral and political issues of his day.

This most recent voice, the Stingo voice, has developed naturally from Styron's earlier experiments with narrative point of view. In the first four novels, one can see Styron's own voice moving ever closer to the surface. His voice is almost buried in *Lie Down in Darkness*, but it makes intermittent appearances in *The Long March*, is apparent in numerous passages of *Set This House on Fire*, is present throughout *The Confessions of Nat Turner*, and dominates *Sophie's Choice*. There are other "progressions" observable in Styron's novels—thematic, stylistic, ethical, philosophical—but this progression in the use of voice is among the most readily apparent. Styron has experimented with voice in more ways than has any other public writer of his generation;

when we read his novels in future years and look at his career as a whole, we will see this plainly.

Notes

1. Much has been written in the field of narratology on the concept of voice. Three especially useful sources are Seymour Chatman, *Story and Discourse: Narrative Structure in Fiction and Film* (Ithaca: Cornell University Press, 1978), esp. chaps. 4 and 5; Tzvetan Todorov, *Mikhail Bakhtin: The Dialogical Principle*, trans. Wlad Godzich (Minneapolis: University of Minnesota Press, 1984), esp. chap. 5, "Intertextuality"; and Hugh Kenner, "The Uncle Charles Principle," chap. 2 of *Joyce's Voices* (Berkeley: University of California Press, 1978).

2. *Lie Down in Darkness* (Indianapolis: Bobbs-Merrill, 1951), p. 9.

3. The surviving drafts of "Inheritance of Night" are among Styron's papers at Duke University. See James L. W. West III, "William Styron's *Inheritance of Night*: Predecessor of *Lie Down in Darkness*," *Delta* (Montpellier), special Styron issue, no. 23 (octobre 1986), 1–17. The quotation from "Inheritance" in the following discussion is to be found in William Styron, *Inheritance of Night: Early Drafts of "Lie Down in Darkness"*, intro. James L. W. West III (Durham, N.C.: Duke University Press, 1993), pp. 2, 4, 6.

4. "Blankenship," *Papers on Language and Literature*, special Styron issue, 23 (1987): 430–48.

5. Robert Canzoneri and Page Stegner, "An Interview with William Styron," *Per/Se* 1 (Summer 1966): 37–44; repr. in *Conversations with William Styron*, ed. James L. W. West III (Jackson: University Press of Mississippi, 1985), pp. 69–70. The interview was conducted in September 1965 in Roxbury, Connecticut.

6. "William Styron Writes PW about His New Novel," *Publishers Weekly* 177 (30 May 1960): 55.

7. See Arthur D. Casciato, "Styron's False Start: The Discarded Opening for *Set This House on Fire*," *Mississippi Quarterly* 34 (Winter 1980–81): 37–50.

8. Canzoneri and Stegner, "Interview with William Styron," pp. 69–70.

9. Ibid., p. 70.

10. "Unslavish Fidelity," *TLS* (London), 16 May 1968, p. 505.

11. In addition to the interview by Canzoneri and Stegner, one should see Thérèse de Saint Phalle, "William Styron (Héritier Littéraire de Faulkner)," *Le Figaro Littéraire*, 1–7 juillet 1965, p. 16; Frederic Kelly, "William Styron Tells the Story of the Nat Turner Rebellion," *New Haven Register*, 14 August 1966, pp. 7–9; Alden Whitman, "William Styron Examines the Negro Upheaval," *New York Times*, 5 August 1967, p. 13; Maria Clara Moyano, "The Confessions of William Styron," *Book World (Washington Post)*, 1 October 1967, p. 6; Phyllis Meras, "The Author," *Saturday Review*, 7 October 1967, p. 30; George Plimpton, "William Styron: A Shared Ordeal," *New York Times Book Review*, 8 October 1967, pp. 2–3ff; R. W. B. Lewis and C. Vann Woodward, "Slavery in the First Person," *Yale Alumni Magazine* 31 (November 1967): 33–39.

12. Interview by James L. W. West III, 18 September 1988, Vineyard Haven, Massachusetts. This quotation is reproduced with Mr. Styron's permission.

13. "Love Day," *Esquire*, 104 (August 1985); "A Tidewater Morning," *Esquire*, 108 (August 1987). Both stories have been collected in William Styron, *A Tidewater Morning: Three Tales from Youth* (New York: Random House, 1993).

Simply Not a Mandarin: Saul Bellow as Jew and Jewish Writer

BEN SIEGEL

Saul Bellow likes being a Jew and he likes being a writer. He does not like being called a "Jewish writer." Occasionally he even denies such an entity exists, but he repeatedly refers to others as Jewish writers. He is a talented, complicated, often inconsistent individual whose feelings about his Jewishness are frequently difficult to reconcile but which are always challenging enough to merit close scrutiny. He has little difficulty with being a Jew, laying proud claim to his heritage and to strong communal and even "religious" feelings. He acknowledges his Jewishness has been a shaping influence on his mind and imagination and the source of much of his creative energy or power. He makes clear he does not mean this "great power . . . come[s] from the fact that I studied the Talmud, or anything of that sort."[1] Yet his childhood was rigorously orthodox, to the point where, "at the age of six," as he recalls, "I . . . wore a *tallith katan*, or scapular, under my shirt."[2] But as an adult he has "never belonged to an orthodox congregation."[3] The last truly orthodox religious thing he did, he states, "was to have my *bar mitzva[h]*."[4] He feels his creative power "simply comes from the fact that at a most susceptible time of my life I was wholly Jewish. That's a gift, a piece of good fortune with which one doesn't quarrel."[5]

Early Years

Rather than quarrel with his past, Bellow retraces repeatedly the Jewish familial and social elements that shaped his character and thought. So often does he reiterate the importance of this heritage that some critics accuse him of being too preoccupied with his Jewishness. "I have no fight about being a Jew," he responds. "I simply must deal with the facts of my life—a basic set of primitive facts. They're my given."[6] Even his decision to be a writer, he claims, resulted from his Jewish experience. Raised in a bookish environment, he has been always "book-crazy, fiercely concentrated on being a writer."[7] The fourth and last child of Russian Jews, he was born Solomon Bellows in 1915, in Lachine, Quebec, an industrial suburb of Montreal. This was shortly after his parents, Abraham and Liza Bellows, emigrated from St. Petersburg.

Bellow's Lachine impressions blend into those of his years in Montreal, where the Bellows family moved when he was three. But during their six years in that big city they often visited Lachine, a mere fifteen kilometers away. The Montreal move—to a "slum" neighborhood near St. Dominique and Napoleon Streets—was brought on, as usual, by an Abraham Bellows business failure. Not surprisingly, her new locale hardly struck Liza Bellows as a step forward. Her son recalls that she had hated leaving Eastern Europe and crossing the Atlantic. She now found herself and her young family "in a melting pot with French Canadians, Indians, the Scotch-Irish, the Sicilians, and Ukrainians. The mixture of languages and races was confusing to her, fascinating to me." Indeed, languages became for Bellow a natural mode of thought and expression. As a result, he has "never feared to speak foreign languages," he boasts. He always simply assumed "that whatever others spoke I could speak, too. Why not? And I took it for granted—what else was I to do, in childhood?— that this was what life was." He found the nearby "junkyards" to be "just as miraculous as orange groves." But for young Solly the most intriguing element was his neighbors. "On St. Dominique Street, Orthodox Jew mingled with kilted Highlanders and nuns from the parish school. To Henry Adams it would have been a frightful comedown, for me it was all gold."[8]

Bellow does not exaggerate the importance of this rich environment to his fiction. Apparently whatever little Solly Bellows saw he turned into a story. His colorful neighbors and their customs and languages fired his lively imagination and obvious narrative gifts. A then-neighbor, Willie Greenberg, seven years Bellow's senior, still recalls his own mother's accounts of the "tall tales" with which Solly would regale his mother. "After he would leave, she'd put her hand on her left cheek, shake her head and say with a smile 'Oy is dos kind a ligner, a bluffer!' ('This child is certainly a liar, a bluffer!')."[9] These years engraved themselves in Bellow's memory. "My life in Canada," he states, when summing up that early period, "was partly the Middle Ages. My second wife used to say I was medieval pure and simple. I've always been among foreigners and never considered myself a native of anything."[10] In this "medieval ghetto" an orthodox Jewish child like himself, he remembers, "was immersed in the Old Testament as soon as he could understand anything, so that you began life by knowing Genesis in Hebrew by heart at the age of four. You never got to distinguish between that and the outer world."[11] By this time, he says, he "fully accepted the reality of God—but what bothered him was where God was."[12] Bellow has never lacked for guiding texts, sacred or secular. He found, as soon as he could read, that "there were translations: I grew up with four languages, English, Hebrew, Yiddish and French." His was truly "a verbal environment. Writing was really just a continuation of something I had always done."[13] But his first tongue was Yiddish, and he has retained his fluency in the *momme loshen* (the mother tongue) as witnessed by his acclaimed translation of Isaac Bashevis Singer's "Gimpel the Fool" and the easeful pride with which Moses Herzog corrects Valentine Gersbach's faulty Yiddish.[14]

Something else young Solly Bellows did was watch his father fail at various enterprises: a bakery, a chain of shops, and a World War I contract to make sacks for the Canadian government. These failures meant another move. American city life began for the Bellows family when Solly was nine. In 1924, his family moved to Chicago's North West Side, near Division Street. There his father "did all right in coal," Bellows claims, "until one of his uninsured trucks had a fatal accident. For years we all worked to pay it off." On Division Street, he adds, "you could find anything: Yiddish, vegetarianism, Marxism, anarchism, tea, soap boxes. On Friday night you could hear speeches on everything from national tax plans to breathing right."[15] The newspapers in 1924 were filled with the Leopold-Loeb trial, which Bellow recalls following with avid interest.

It is his mother who is always central to Bellow's adult recollections of that period. By then she had been in North America for eleven years, yet, like so many housebound immigrant women, Liza Bellows never got fully used to her new home. She and her husband spoke Russian at home, and "their table talk was still about the Czar, the war, the Revolution."[16] To her this latest move appeared as one more defeat. "She was thinking of her family in Riga all the time." Bellow remembers. "And this was just a sort of exile, purgatory as far as she was concerned. It was very hard to bring up four children in so strange a place."[17]

Bellow's initiation into Chicago street life was not easy. At first the other kids made him "feel like a foreigner, an outsider," says Bellow, by poking fun at his accent and calling him a "Canuck."[18] He recalls vividly his sense of being both a participant and marginal observer of the new life. These feelings persisted "even though I went to grammar school and high school and college in Chicago, lived in the streets and knew it so well. I felt there was a kind of exoticism about the place." He supposes, too, that his mother's sense of displacement contributed strongly to his own feelings of strangeness. As the youngest child he was especially sensitive to her situation.[19] But if he and his family were undergoing dramatic changes, so were most of their neighbors and the country at large. For young Solly even national events often took a personal twist. "On March 4, 1929, when Herbert Hoover was inaugurated," Bellow remembers, "I was out of school with a sore throat and had the new Majestic radio in its absurd large cabinet all to myself. I turned the switch—and there was the new Chief Executive taking the oath of office before a great crowd."[20]

Even at fourteen Bellow appears to have been keenly attuned to his surroundings. Chicago was then, he reports, "a sprawling network of immigrant villages smelling of sauerkraut and home-brewed beer, of meat processing and soap manufacture." Despite its crooked politicians and gangsters, the city appeared to him to be "at peace—a stale and queasy peace, the philistine repose apparently anticipated by the Federalists." Life in the big city then, at least to Solly Bellows and his friends, seemed calm and predictable. "A seven-cent streetcar fare took us to the Loop," he recalls. "On Randolph Street we found free entertainment at Bensinger's billiard salon and at Trafton's gymnasium, where boxers sparred. The street was filled with jazz musicians and city-hall types." Solly's friend "Fish," whose father owned a poolroom, occasionally treated him "to a hot dog and a stein of Hires root beer on Randolph Street. When we overspent we came back from the Loop on foot." Those five miles are scrolled into his memory. He can still summon up the stretch "of freight yards and factories; joints that manufactured garden statuary, like gnomes, trolls, and undines; Klee Brothers where you got a baseball bat with the purchase of a two-pants suit; Polish sausage shops; the Crown theater at Division and Ashland, with its posters of Lon Chaney or Renée Adorée, its popcorn machine crackling; then the United Cigar store; then Brown and Koppel's restaurant, with the nonstop poker game upstairs." It was for him "a good dullness, this Hoover dullness. Higher activities were not prohibited, but you had to find them for yourself. If you subscribed to the *Literary Digest* you might get the complete works of Flaubert as a bonus. Not that anybody read those red buckram-bound books." Yet Solly Bellows was already a voracious reader. His generous friend Fish passed on to him an array of magazines and pamphlets, and through them he "became familiar with Karl Marx and V. I. Lenin; also with Marie Stopes, Havelock Ellis, V. F. Calverton, Max Eastman, and Edmund Wilson" (*IDMR*, p. 535).

But he hardly spent all his time reading. Indeed, Solly was now often outside the house. He enjoyed "a game called Piggie-move-up, which was a baseball game played in the street." His "favorite diversion" was hanging upside down by his knees from porch railings. "Well," he observes, "I was a street kid, although I played the violin and attended a Hebrew school." But he soon "broke with that—the choice was between the Hebrew school and the pool room and the playground, and the pool room and the playground won out. Together with the public library."[21] In fact, before long the library won out over all its competitors. "I began at an early age to read and write," Bellow boasts, "and have never stopped. I used to live in the library and even on the way home, I'd stop in the park to read." For him, he declares, "libraries were liberating as a kid."[22] Clearly, Chicago's streets and libraries helped young Solly adjust to his new country and locale. But despite the neighborhood's insular tone, Division Street and Chicago were in the Protestant Midwest, and he still felt himself a Jew twice-removed from the land of his parents. He needed to find his proper place. He found it easily—in the world of literature and writing. At Tuley High School he and some friends started a group they called the Russian Literary Society. On Friday nights they met in a local hot dog stand (the Mission House), near Humboldt Park, to read their own writings and to argue. Anyone could rise and hold forth on politics, religion, or literature. "We wrote poetry, essays, plays," he says. "All my friends were readers and it was competitive. Someone was ahead of you on Nietzsche, you were up on him on something else."[23]

Solly Bellows was clearly the group's most precocious writer. "Solly was fond of reading his work aloud among friends," reports Chicago attorney Sam Freifeld, a group member. In the back leaf of a volume of Oscar Wilde's poems, Bellow and his friends scribbled titles of books they would someday write, copying their favorite lines from Wilde's verse. "Solly was particularly fond of the phrase, 'Black leaves whirling in the wind,' which he thought would make a terrific book title."[24] Bellow belonged also to his high school debating club. He catches something of that group's emotional intensity in his recollection of his close friend Isaac Rosenfeld, whose much-lamented early death ended a significant literary career. Bellow recalls especially a "late afternoon, a spring day," when the Debating Club convened on the second floor of the old Tuley school building later leveled by fire. "The black street doors are open, the skate wheels are buzzing on the hollow concrete, and the handballs strike the walls with a taut puncturing sound." In the meeting room, Bellow holds the gavel as "Isaac rises and asks for the floor. He has a round face, somewhat pale, glasses, and his light hair is combed back with earnestness and maturity." Despite his short pants, Isaac announces his subject to be "*The World as Will and Idea*, and he speaks with perfect authority. He is very serious. He has read Schopenhauer."[25]

His friends may have shared and encouraged Bellow's literary dreams, but his parents objected to them. "Mama's mind was archaic," recalls Moses Herzog, "filled with old legends, with angels and demons."[26] The description fits Liza Bellows. "My mother lived strictly in the 19th Century," declares Bellow, "and her sole ambition was for me to become a Talmudic scholar like everyone else in her family. She was a figure from the Middle Ages. In her family pictures, her scholarly brothers looked as if they could have lived in the 13th Century. Those bearded portraits were her idea of what a man should be."[27] At fifteen he watched his mother die. "Her hands turned blue, she saw me notice them."[28] Liza Bellows died much before her time, but she likely would be pleased to know critics have found a strong Talmudic or rabbinic imprint on her son's work. Jack Ludwig, in commenting on *Dangling Man* and *The Victim*, observes that Bellow "prefers less to create than discuss. Not the author of Genesis but the Talmudic sages who dissect it are his forebears."[29]

Ludwig considers Bellow to be "possibly America's most intellectual novelist ever." He is a writer who "sets his action and his heroic [values] at a polar extreme from Hemingway's." Let Hemingway and God create legends, he continues. Bellow is less a maker of legend and myth than a Talmudic sage who analyzes, comments, and observes. Bellow's "Talmudic wit," adds Ludwig, lacks the irony that results from an "uncynical acceptance of man's potential absurdity." He rejects the idea man is absurd because he attempts to argue with God. Bellow's idea of man-as-victim provides the key to his fiction.[30] Stanley Kauffmann expresses a similar view. "More and more," he states, Saul Bellow "has become to me the last in the long line of the Wonder Rabbis of eastern European Jewry." Like them, he is given to "ruminating in a world left shaken by Hitler and Hiroshima, Freud and Franz Fanon . . . [and to] presenting his rabbinical tales (yes, even allowing for sex) as flowers of his wisdom. It is an accident of fate, of birthplace and birthyear," concludes Kauffmann, "that made him a novelist instead of a sage."[31]

Abraham Bellows held to a different view. More pragmatic than his wife, he was even more opposed to their son being a writer. Bellow recalls that both parents were raised "in the same tradition," but his father "cast all this off to become a sort of modern type; he was a sharpie circa 1905 in Russia." Having quit the seminary at seventeen or eighteen, he had gone to St. Petersburg, where he took to "importing Egyptian onions, a great delicacy in Czarist Russia." He decided "I should be a professional man or a moneymaker," says Bellow. "Then he thought I was an idiot or worse, a moon-faced ideologist. With that, he about washed his hands of me."[32] Bellow may exaggerate his father's dismissal of him, but the older man's concern is understandable given his own economic failures. In any event, his message was not wasted: money is a significant element in his son's fiction. Bellow has transmuted his father's old and new world disasters into Moses Herzog's family recollections. Herzog remembers his horror when his father—beaten and robbed of his bootleg whiskey by hijackers—returned home to show his wounds. "It was more than I could bear," Herzog laments, "that anyone should lay violent hands on him—a father, a sacred being, a king. Yes, he was a king to us. My heart was suffocated by this horror. I thought I would die of it. Whom did I ever love as I loved them?" (H, p. 147).

The hijacking was but one sad family experience among many. Ten times annually, Herzog's father cataloged his tragic past. Straining to ease the weight of such painful memories, Moses strives for a different perspective. He decides all individual and family experiences "are antiquities—yes, Jewish antiquities originating in the Bible, in a Biblical sense of personal experience and destiny." This century's mass killings had changed standards of human misery, so all that "happened during the war abolished Father Herzog's claim to exceptional suffering. We are on a more brutal standard now, a new terminal standard, indifferent to persons." But try as he may, Moses is not indifferent. He may recognize that "Personalities are good only for comic relief, but that makes little emotional difference." For he remains, he concedes, "a slave to Papa's pain" (H, pp. 148–49). Bellow, too, is hardly indifferent to such family lore. Indeed, his early years and their Jewish ambience were to stamp him indelibly. "The quality of suffering and the verbal form it takes in his work," observes Theodore Gross, "stem from Bellow's poverty-stricken Jewish childhood in Montreal and the Jewishness which he has made a part of his adult vision of the world."[33] Another critic who emphasizes the impact of Bellow's Jewish background on his writing is Alfred Kazin. More than other American novelists of comparable ability, states Kazin, Bellow has absorbed into his fiction "the modern Jewish experience." He literally "connects one novel after another with a representative Jew" in whom he embodies aspects of this experience. Most of his figures are Jews, but even his few non-Jews (like Kirby Allbee or Eugene Henderson) are "wittily agonized definitions of human existence" that resemble strongly his Jewish protagonists.[34]

Bellow treats even the ghetto streets with respect. Rather than quaint backdrops, they are woven into the texture of his plots and characters. In effect, he places the city street at the center of his fiction, so that running through his novels is, as Irving Howe puts it, "a natural, enchanted repetition of the Jewish neighborhood." Montreal's Napoleon Street, Chicago's West Side, and New York's Upper West Side, for example, have been reshaped into Bellow's own special province or locale. His Upper West Side, in particular, states Howe, "is ugly, filthy, dangerous; its streets are crammed with the flotsam of humanity." Among them are the Jewish survivors of pogroms, sweatshops, and concentration camps. "In this menagerie of integration, anomie, and good feeling, people still manage to live. That is Bellow's emphasis—people live."[35] For despite hardships and frustrations, his Jewish elders find along America's streets social and emotional sustenance. Their offspring do even better as they move on and up. Their parents may be locked into the past, but their own first American generation—Bellow's generation—are Jews discovering worlds new to them. They are evolving into college intellectuals, radical dreamers, explorers of high-and-low life. "Look at me, going everywhere!" Augie March cries out, after a long account devoted primarily to the developing of his character and freeing of his senses. "Why, I am a sort of Columbus of those near-at-hand."[36]

Becoming a Writer

Like his characters, Bellow has carried his neighborhood with him. When he moved on to college, his Jewishness influenced even his choice of studies. Entering the University of Chicago in 1933, he transferred two years later to Northwestern University. He now insists he "never had any academic interests"—by which he suggests he did not want to prepare for a writing career by the traditional literature program. Instead, he opted for anthropology and study with the noted anthropologist Melville Jean Herskovit. For anthropology in the 1930s, Bellow explains, seemed the freest and most "radical or liberating of disciplines." Implying radicalism, "especially sexual radicalism," it appealed strongly to young Jews. Anthropology gave them "a greater sense of freedom from the surrounding restrictions" and a means of rejecting snobbery. They were seeking "an immunity from Anglo-Saxon custom" and from "being accepted or rejected by a society of Christian gentlemen."[37]

Receiving his degree from Northwestern in 1937, with honors in anthropology and sociology, Bellow, after a brief graduate stint at the University of Wisconsin at Madison, quit school to marry and to write. Launching his writing career, Solomon Bellows became Saul Bellow. This country's most celebrated novelists then—John Dos Passos, F. Scott Fitzgerald, Ernest Hemingway, William Faulkner, and Thomas Wolfe—were resoundingly non-Jewish. Indeed, American letters in those years revealed a genteel but definite anti-Semitism, especially in Hemingway and Wolfe. Bellow's emergence as a major writer, in the 1940s and 1950s, helped give a new thrust to American fiction. No other novelist portrayed so effectively the confused complexities of wartime and postwar American urban life. His every narrative centered on a sensitive, thinking social adventurer keenly aware of the personal cost of modern existence. Other writers then emerging found in his work a means of confronting contemporary dilemmas. Bellow transformed America's social perplexities into a sort of principle—"a mixture of health and sickness" exemplifying the modern condition. "Would it be excessive to say," asks Irving Howe, "that this principle draws some of its energies from the Jewish tradition, the immigrant past?"[38] Indeed, Bellow's debt to this immigrant tradition is clear, repeatedly acknowledged, but not always understood. With all his gifts and special qualities, he still owes—as do most American-Jewish writers—a considerable debt both to Russian and Yiddish literatures. This dual heritage is a blessing, but it is hardly unmixed. Multiple national or cultural identities are in themselves, as Mark Shechner points out, not necessarily "ennobling or charming." Generally caused by "flight and disruption," such cosmopolitanism can result in "anguish and disorientation." Changing countries and continents may mean "families are broken up, loved ones are lost, and a place in the world is left behind. It is neither a normal nor a happy state of affairs." For those of the Jewish-immigrant generation even the New World's freedoms exacted a heavy cost in "misery and alienation."[39] The writers among them, states Pearl Bell, then had the singular task of bridging their "worlds of the shtetl and of urban modernity." They struggled "to do justice to both the immigrant life they were born to and the assimilationist and cosmopolitan culture in which they had to make their way."[40]

But the goals (social and literary) of the children of those immigrants proved somewhat different. Their collective task—as those of Bellow's generation saw it—was to "reconstruct" their culture to suit their own needs. They were growing up in two worlds: the Old World preserved in the home and the New World confronting them in the street. These first-generation Americans developed a literary sensitivity to their own contradictions and paradoxes and an "ironic awareness"[41] of their own special emotional and intellectual possibilities. Led by Bellow and Bernard Malamud, and then by Norman Mailer and Philip Roth, among others, this generation established the Jewish writer as a significant presence in American culture. Earlier writers like Ludwig Lewisohn, Ben Hecht, Henry Roth, Meyer Levin, Daniel Fuchs, and Howard Fast helped prepare the way. But those of the Bellow-Malamud generation "were the first to make it on their own terms." Having fought a war and earned college degrees, they could relish being "at once alien and American," so that they harbored no doubts about belonging "in the literary mainstream."[42] Despite their confidence and determination, however, they still saw themselves at times as "cultural hybrids." Some proved unable "to achieve wholeness," observes Mark Shechner, whereas others derived from their bicultural situation "strength, an advantage . . . a point of view." One careful observer of Jewish intellectual achievements, especially of Jewish eminence in

Western scientific studies, was Thorstein Veblen. "It is by loss
of allegiance, or at the best by force of a divided allegiance to the
people of his origin." Veblen noted, that the Jew "finds himself
in the vanguard of modern inquiry."[43] Veblen's comments, as
Shechner points out, may be applied validly to this first native
generation of Jewish intellectuals. Its members proved "at their
most creative, masters of discrepancy and accomplished tightrope walkers."[44]

Bellow and Malamud, Mailer and Roth were hardly alone.
Others like Michael Seide, Irvin Faust, Jerome Weidman, and
soon after them, Herbert Gold and Stanley Elkin, were producing
a singular mode of fiction. All could be said, writes Pearl Bell,
to have fused "the racy inflections of Yiddish idiom and diction
with the nervous rhythms of urban life." But Bellow and Malamud and their compeers, as individuals as well as writers,
proved "the archetypal embodiments of a newly complex Jewish
personality." Theirs was a collective personality brimming with
"intellectual ambition, ironic self-confidence, and erotic sophistication." For despite their differences as Jews and writers, adds
Bell, "the novelists of this generation were the first to regard
success as their American birthright."[45] But with their dreams
came responsibilities—as Delmore Schwartz wisely reminded
them. Postwar Jewish writing in America did exhibit moral and
social concerns, but its commitment to communal responsibility
was an old idea. Since earliest times Jews have been characterized by a "craving to be used," to be of service to themselves and
others. This has been true of the Jewish personality, says Judd
Teller, since the first encounter of Jew and Greek. Without denying himself experience or pleasure, the Jew has sought "for some
transcendental meaning . . . for 'a piece of the action' in a greater
universal scheme."[46] Jewish writing (Hebrew, Hellenic, Judaeo-
Arabic, or Yiddish) has been marked by this search for ultimate
meaning and purpose, for order amid chaos, for the rule of law.
Admittedly, this "sense of purpose" has not been restricted to
Jewish writers, and some Jews in every generation have lacked
this concern. For most Jewish writers, however, these purposive
themes have proved central—in particular the desire to be useful
to others. "Who can make use of him?" Moses Herzog says of
himself. "He craves use. Where is he needed? Show him the way
to make his sacrifice to truth, to order, peace" (H, p. 308).

Of course Jewish literature reveals other characteristics as well.
Some elements derive from Russian writings but most come directly from Yiddish fiction. The most obvious borrowings by

modern Jewish novelists from their Yiddish predecessors are the strong use of internal dialogue and a deep concern, says Teller, for "the ineffectual man, the non-achiever in the marketplace." Writers—Jewish and non-Jewish—in other times have treated the nonachiever differently. In the Depression's proletarian fiction, for example, he was lamented as a social and economic victim. Postwar Jewish novelists replaced lamentation with near-celebration. Still, Bellow's Joseph, Asa Leventhal, Tommy Wilhelm, and Moses Herzog share traits with their Yiddish predecessors. Each transmutes much of his thought and energy into internal dialogue. Joseph and Herzog are especially given to this traditional Jewish form. Such inner discourse, Teller explains, "has been the manner of Talmudic study in East Europe, the scholar reciting aloud to himself, in singsong, the arguments of first one, then another disputant, and alternatingly performing in each of these roles." In addition, the postwar emphasis on the material nonachiever has deep roots in Jewish literature. Bellow's intellectual antiheroes resemble strongly their marginal counterparts in both the Russian and Jewish literary traditions. Even without direct interaction between those two literatures, Teller observes, Jewish writers were fated to "produce an identical type" for the spirit of emancipation found in so many Russian shtetlach "was typical of the entire country."[47] He is not suggesting, however, that those American-Jewish novelists familiar with European Jewish writing will always present similar figures. Bernard Malamud, influenced strongly by the Hasidic folktales of Isaac Leib Peretz, turned in his early tales to the unworldly or naive common man as protagonist.

The Postwar Significance of Bellow's Fiction

In focusing in their postwar fiction on the nonachiever, Bellow and Malamud rejected the familiar American hero. They disdained the successful entrepreneur who resembled strongly the rugged frontier individualist of the last century. Most earlier American-Jewish writers had accepted and admired—at his best—the "self-made man." Even Clifford Odets, that redoubtable champion of the "ineffectual man," blamed "the system" for the individual's material failure. Bellow and other postwar Jewish writers, however, found tough entrepreneurs the true failures. Odets saw such aggressive figures as both capitalism's exploiters and moral victims; Bellow sees them as having created

their own moral plight. By deliberately devaluing material accomplishment as a criterion for success, Bellow and his colleagues may be defending, suggests Teller, "their 'unsuccessful'
fathers or grandfathers." They may be repudiating the central
implication of the American success myth that "material failure
is somehow subversive" and likely results from "congenital inferiority" or a "pathological condition."[48] But his emphasis on the
nonachiever was hardly the sole reason Bellow proved so significant to American-Jewish writing. His novels and stories tell—
as the best Jewish stories always do—of this world's confusions
as opposed to God's certainties. Bellow's Jews struggle in a world
run by strangers, with the Jew reduced to the status of "new-
comer, parvenu, displaced person."[49] Thus his "self-ordering"
becomes the individual Jew's basic issue. Maybe the individual's
"business of life, the real business," muses a beleaguered Tommy
Wilhelm, is "to carry his peculiar burden, to feel shame and
impotence, to taste these quelled tears. . . . Maybe the making of
mistakes expressed the very purpose of his life and the essence
of his being here."[50] In the Eisenhower-McCarthy years, many
Americans (Jews and non-Jews) could identify with such emotional confusion. They could do so because Bellow, as well as
some of his contemporaries, did not make his Jewish meanderers
targets or objects of mean-spirited ridicule. In his fiction they
are representative postwar Americans who simply do not embrace the nation's alluring middle-class values. If they indulge
on occasion in foolish acts followed by ironic self-mockery, they
still enjoy Bellow's compassion and sympathy.

In effect, postwar Jewish novelists were less concerned than
their predecessors had been with Gentile opinions of the Jew.
They were involved more with their own "interior world."[51] Earlier Jewish writers—other than those committed to Marxism or
Zionism—had been reluctant to judge Anglo-American culture.
But the new Jewish writers had no such qualms. They had confidence in their validity as Americans and their right to introduce Jewishness into American literature. For example, Bellow
has Moses Herzog voice his impatience with Christian criticism
of Jews. "Do you think that any Christian in the twentieth century has the right to speak to Jewish Pharisees?" he demands
of "calm, Protestant Nordic Anglo-Celtic" Dr. Edvig, his wife's
psychiatrist. "From a Jewish standpoint, you know, this hasn't
been one of your best periods. . . . I don't agree with Nietzsche
that Jesus made the whole world sick, infected it with his slave
morality. But Nietzsche himself had a Christian view of history."

He chose to see "the present moment always as some crisis, some fall from classical greatness, some corruption or evil to be saved from. I call that Christian" (*H*, pp. 53–54).

Bellow did not gain acceptance easily as a major novelist. His struggles to find his proper literary voice reflected in many ways, he feels, the difficulties of two Jewish generations. These are exemplified for him also by the strivings of his own family and their friends to find their proper "place" in American society. "You must appreciate," he explains, "that the American experience is unique; in my opinion it is a tremendous event in world history."[52] It has been also baffling and bruising. "Making it" in this country, he points out, generally has been painful for every immigrant group, and the Jews were no exception. In their quest to be good Yankees, many of his immigrant contemporaries "copied even the unhappiness of the Protestant majority." They embraced "its miseries." Hence he excludes neither his family nor himself from what he terms "that mixture of imagination and stupidity with which people met the American Experience, that murky, heavy, burdensome, chaotic thing."[53]

Bellow tried to cope with the cultural confusion by having "intellectual romances"[54] with varied ideologies like Marxism and Reichian psychology. But he sees now that his major error, a common one, lay in seeking sanctuary in the country's various "corners of culture." He wished to enjoy "high thoughts" and to perfect himself in an art's "symbolic discipline." He overdid it. "One didn't need," he confesses, "as much sanctuary as all that" (*SOC*, p. 77). Yet his concerns were justified. He found he did have reason to fear that he "would be put down as a foreigner, an interloper. It was made clear to me when I studied literature in the university that as a Jew and the son of Russian Jews I would probably never have the right *feeling* for Anglo-Saxon tradition, for English words. I realized even in college that the people who told me this were not necessarily disinterested friends. But they had an effect on me, nevertheless. This was something from which I had to free myself. I fought free because I had to."[55]

More Midwesterner Than Jew

The young would-be novelist reacted to such pressures by trying to think of himself "as a midwesterner and not a Jew." He did not go to the library, Bellow confesses, "to read the Talmud

but the novels and poems of Sherwood Anderson, Theodore
Dreiser, Edgar Lee Masters and Vachel Lindsay" (*SOC*, pp. 72–
73). His specific means of defense was to write like the traditional American or, better yet, English novelist. He wrote his first
two novels, *Dangling Man* and *The Victim*, in that escapist mood.
"I think that when I wrote those early books I was timid," he
states. "I still felt the incredible effrontery of announcing myself
to the world (in part I mean the WASP world) as a writer and an
artist. I had to touch a great many bases, demonstrate my abili-
ties, pay my respects to formal requirements. In short, I was
afraid to let myself go." Self-conscious about being Jewish, he
wanted his first two novels to be "well made." He wrote *Dangling
Man* "quickly," he recalls, but "took great pains with it." He
labored with *The Victim* "to make it letter perfect . . . [having]
accepted a Flaubertian standard." This was "not a bad standard,"
he concedes, but for him it proved "repressive" due to his life
and "upbringing in Chicago as the son of immigrants. I could
not, with such an instrument as I developed in the first two
books, express a variety of things I knew intimately. Those books,
though useful, did not give me a form in which I felt comfortable." Bellow's anger grows palpable: "A writer should be able
to express himself easily, naturally, copiously in a form which
frees his mind, his energies. Why should he hobble himself with
formalities? With a borrowed sensibility? With the desire to be
'correct'? Why should I force myself to write like an Englishman
or a contributor to *The New Yorker*? I soon saw that it was simply
not in me to be a mandarin."[56]

Bellow brought his Jewish sensibilities into more direct play
when he began *The Adventures of Augie March*. He experienced
a significant change in attitude and style as he discarded the
inhibitions of literary Protestantism. He would later feel he overdid it. "I took off many of these restraints. I think I took off too
many, and went too far, but I was feeling the excitement of discovery. I had just increased my freedom, and like any emancipated
plebian I abused it at once."[57] Bellow is keenly aware and proud
of his heritage, but he still considers his—or anyone else's—
being Jewish a quirk of fate, an "accidental exoticism."[58] Hence
he finds all ethnic categorizing "odd" and discomforting,[59] and
he sees no "division" in viewing himself as both American and
Jew. What does bother him—despite his own free use of the
term—is being viewed as a "Jewish writer" rather than a writer
who is Jewish. "I am a Jew, and I have written some books," he
states. "I have tried to fit my soul into the Jewish-writer category,

but it does not feel comfortably accommodated there" (*SOC*, p. 72). He also disdains the Jewish-writer tag for having "a flavor of the ghetto about it"[60] and for being "intellectually vulgar, unnecessarily parochializing and utterly without value."[61] He rejects any attempt to define him in ethnic terms. "Like the exile writers of Paris 50 years go I do not think of myself as representing any national culture. I am simply a modern writer."[62] Thus he bristles at the claim of *Time* magazine that he is "the godfather of a Jewish literary revolution"[63] or at critics who insist he leads a "school" of Eastern Jewish writing. "What point is there in getting into these wrong-headed pygmy battles?" he asks. "I don't live in the East, I reside in Chicago. And I find the whole Jewish writer bit tedious."[64]

He also finds that ethnic tag nothing more than a "sheer invention" created and perpetuated "by the media, by critics and by 'scholars.'"[65] He can conclude only "that when American Jews began to write in English, people were so astonished that they could do so that they quickly gave them a tag. Malamud, Roth and I are all tied together in this way, and it's rather unfortunate."[66] He tries to play down his anger at being squeezed into a literary trio. "Over the years," he states, "I have been faintly amused at the curious linkage of Bellow, Malamud and Roth. Somehow it always reminds me of Hart, Shafner & Marx."[67] Yet the frequency with which he alludes to this "linkage" suggests he is more angry than amused. The three of them, he declares wryly, "have made it in the field of culture as Bernard Baruch made it on a park bench, as Polly Adler made it in prostitution, and Two Gun Cohen, the personal bodyguard of Sun Yat-Sen, made it in China. My joke is not broad enough to cover the contempt I feel for the opportunists, wise guys, and career types who impose such labels and trade upon them" (*SOC*, p. 72).

Still, he does lay himself open to ethnic labeling by writing mostly about Jews. They are the people he knows best, he explains, and "I like to know what I'm talking about. Some readers insist that even his non-Jewish characters—like Eugene Henderson or Albert Corde—are disguised Jews. "Henderson is not a Jew," Bellow protests,

> but he has been accused by some of being a sort of convert. But that's false, that's simply not the case. One has one's character—a given— and that's it. He had better be faithful to the given and if other people don't like it that's unfortunate. I have never consciously written as a Jew. I have just written as Saul Bellow. I have never attempted to

make myself Jewish. I've never tried to appeal to a community, I
never thought of writing for Jews exclusively. I never wanted to. I
think of myself as a person of Jewish origin—American and Jewish—
who has had a certain experience of life, which is in part Jewish.

How much of his experience is Jewish? He rejects the question.
"Proportions are not for me to decide. I don't know what they
are: how much is Jewish, how much is Russian, how much is
male, how much is twentieth century, how much is midwestern.
That's for others to determine with their measuring sticks. I have
no sticks myself."[68]
What he does have is an aversion for those who hold "that any
literature should be so special that it can't be understood by
non-communicants." A literature's "human quality," he counters,
"should appeal to anyone. If it doesn't, it's a mistake. Something
is wrong. It's too parochial. No good literature is parochial." But
then recognizing that he may be pushing this thought too far,
Bellow retracts it in part. "All good literature," he concedes, does
have "some color of this sort because there is no such thing as
a generalized human being. He's an Irishman, or an Italian, or
an Indian, or a Japanese, whatever it is that he is, he is." Bellow's
sensitivity to the Jewish-writer label stems from the occasional
critic's suggestion that readers must be familiar with Judaism to
grasp the "special Jewish slant" of his fiction. "I think that's
nonsense," Bellow flares. "It really is." Yet if he dismisses the
Jewish-writer label as "false and wrong," he does not blame the
Jews for applying it; they have to strengthen their public position
as best they can. "Since the holocaust," he declares, "they have
become exceptionally sensitive to the image the world has of
them and I think that they expect Jewish writers to do good work
for them and propagandize for them. In that respect I was a great
disappointment to them. Since then, Philip Roth has made me
more acceptable by writing *Portnoy's Complaint*. Naturally, they
prefer Malamud and me to the sexual wildmen who have recently appeared in fiction."[69]
Bellow has avoided ethnic "propaganda" in his fiction, but his
nonfiction is another matter. For he, too, has been affected by
the Holocaust. For him, as for most Jews, the Holocaust proved
traumatic. "Of course," he admits. "Until then, like every young
Jew, I had known what is expressed in the phrase 'a feiner Yid.'
But the Holocaust made my generation understand that we might
be annihilated, that everyone else had a right to exist as a member
of a country, but we might be eliminated and nobody would

intervene or care. This is what concerns me at present. I feel that the present attack on Israel is a test of whether Judaism and Jews will survive in the world."[70] His *To Jerusalem and Back* is a booklength expression and analysis of this fear. It is also an emotional defense of Israel and the Jews—and an example of unqualified "Jewish propaganda."

In other words, his fears for Jews everywhere strengthen Saul Bellow's own "parochial" concerns. For that matter, these concerns may be said to move Bellow not only to convert his Jewish heritage into art but also to encourage others to do the same. For he sees in the American Jew elements of the universal human condition—that is, of every man's at least partial apartness. Hence he chides the Jewish writer for his reluctance to exploit fully his cultural situation. In doing so, Bellow does not hesitate to apply to others the Jewish-writer label he so much dislikes for himself. The typical Jewish writer, he charges, "cannot easily accept the historical accident of being a Jew in America that is nonetheless among the first facts of his life. But this accident— the strangeness of discontinuity and of a constant immense change—happens to all and is the general condition."[71] In short, no one can (or should) claim total cultural integration.

Heritage and Prose Style

Nowhere is Bellow's own use of his Jewish heritage more apparent than in his prose style. He is not an experimental writer in the narrow meaning of the term. Even the slight avant-garde elements discernible in *Dangling Man* are missing in the muted, tightly structured style of *The Victim*. Conversely, he avoids also in these early novels that "lifeless lucidity" the postwar realists formulated to counter the experimental styles of the 1920s. Yet in *The Adventures of Augie March*, his "breakthrough" novel, Bellow fashions what Irving Howe has hailed as "the first major new style" in American prose fiction "since Hemingway and Faulkner."[72] Both Howe and Leslie Fiedler detect some stylistic indebtedness to Daniel Fuchs and Nathanael West, but neither critic develops this comparison. They likely are thinking of how those earlier novelists blended American street talk and a submerged Yiddish idiom to produce a sharp, nervous vernacular that echoes the shifting inflections of sidewalk and tenement conversation. Bellow shapes this tough, side-mouthed patois into an original, raucous discourse. Released or muted it is rarely

dull. Indeed, his rhetoric moves always under a tension that echoes somehow both Herman Melville's oral resonance and—to the
practiced ear—an earthy, spoken Yiddish.

What emerges is a rich nonliterary prose mingling formal logic
and street-corner slang, intellectual elegance and immigrant syntax. Its rough verbal texture of rapid images and shifting ideas
breaks traditional verbal patterns by avoiding both the Jamesian
novel's effete sensibility and naturalism's blood and bluster.
Suited to sensory inventories, his language enables Bellow to
catalog easily a delicatessen's smells and sounds, a seedy neighborhood's layered dirt and turmoil, and an array of outer and
inner offbeat human quirks. Then, with the slightest verbal shift,
he can shape his gleanings from Chicago's libraries and muse-
ums into a capsule history of Western culture. No tempo or
rhythm seems beyond his linguistic grasp. The dangling Joseph's
elliptical jottings, Asa Leventhal's sullen uncertainties, Augie
March's larky meanderings, Eugene Henderson's zany outbursts,
or the culturally encrusted ruminations of Moses Herzog and
Artur Sammler, Charlie Citrine and Albert Corde, or Victor
Wulpy and Kenneth Trachtenberg are conveyed with equal ease.
These verbal elements result in a sprawling, episodic style that
embraces a world of cranks and hucksters and thinkers more
varied, vivid, and disorderly than that of any other contemporary novelist.[73]

Bellow's fiction is essentially dramatic. His characters' internal
monologues or external conversations are his novels' most
memorable moments. The spoken word controls his language. A
living voice permeates his most abstract passages. This *voice*,
self-reflexive and mocking, adheres to the ironic, chiding melody
of ghetto speech. What it mocks is the inflated human self: the
speaker and his arguments and analyses, his lamentations and
joys. The lack of power of East Europe's Jews, Bellow observes,
forced them to rely strongly on words. Their "most ordinary"
spoken or argued Yiddish teemed, he declares, with "the grand-
est historical, mythological, and religious allusions." It mixed
philosophical ruminations and the needs of marketplace and
kitchen. Even their discussions of an egg could "involve the Creation, the Fall, the Flood, Egypt, Alexander, Titus, Napoleon, the
Rothschilds, the sages and the Laws."[74] This Yiddish voice might
well have been, as Earl Rovit suggests, the earliest element in
Bellow's development, preceding even his basic concepts or values. Certainly his early absorption of this "kitchen Yiddish" has
energized his style. Bellow has borrowed, however, less from its

diction than its intonations and rhythms. But its affectionate
insults and cosmic curses or occasional blessings are hardly lost
on him. Neither are its needling ironies and "intimate vulgari-
ties" or its easy mix of the "sentimental and sardonic."[75]

His attitude toward American-Jewish life, however, is wryly
quizzical and defensive. "Why did I have to be born among immigrant Jews!" complains Augie March. But Bellow's bonds to
Europe's lost Yiddish culture remain positive and deeply felt.
This Yiddish heritage, Alfred Kazin points out, "is Bellow's tradition. Of the many interesting, talented Jewish novelists in
America, says Kazin, "no other feels so lovingly connected with
the religious and cultural tradition of his Eastern European
grandfathers." Still he remains "the least ghettoized and least
sentimental of 'Jewish Novelists.'"[76] Some critics argue that Bellow's view of women derives from this Jewish religious tradition.
"In part there would seem to be a religious inheritance of female
degradation," states Earl Rovit, "that may be related to the traditional prayer that orthodox Jews recite every morning, offering
thanks to the Almighty that they were born men and not
women."[77] Rovit's idea is intriguing, but Bellow's flawed
women—despite the outraged sensibilities of feminist critics—
ultimately prove no worse than his flawed men. Yet male or female, the Jew remains at the center of Bellow's fiction because
he embodies for the novelist man's basic pains and pressures.
For Bellow the Jew is "man at the end of his tether,"[78] for at
that emotional point traditional demands and individual needs
clash—and there all true drama and literature begin.

Bellow's most curious stance is on Jewish literature. For despite his repeated rejection of "Jewish writer" as a valid literary
description, he uses the term freely. He insists also on the existence of the "Jewish story" as a literary entity. He has even edited
a widely read anthology titled *Great Jewish Short Stories*. In
his introduction he presents his thoughts on Jewish literature,
especially its fiction. The twenty-two stories, ancient and modern, that he has drawn from "Hebrew, German, Yiddish, Russian
and English" sources, Bellow states, are "to a discerning eye,
very clearly Jewish."[79] Including no tale of his own, he does have
stories by Bernard Malamud and Philip Roth. Apparently they
are Jewish writers but he is not. Or, if like him, they are not
"Jewish writers," they are obviously writers of Jewish stories. In
fact, Bellow is adamant on this point: some stories—those of
Isaac Babel offer him example—are, he insists, beyond dispute,
"characteristically Jewish" (*GJSS*, p. 16). Such stories, it follows,

are written by indisputable Jews. That his implied distinction is subtle indeed became evident even to Bellow. Fifteen years after the publication of his anthology, he explained to an Israeli interviewer that the label of "Jewish writer" could be applied validly to an S. Agnon or Isaac Bashevis Singer but not to him.[80] Even for Saul Bellow then "Jewish writers" now do exist. Seemingly, he finds the label bothersome only when it is applied to him.

How valid then, in terms of his own fiction, is his rejection of the description? His central novel, Herzog, suggests that the rejection is not valid, for Moses Elkanah Herzog is a Jew with very Jewish reactions to emotional and intellectual pressures. Admittedly, a non-Jew may be equally concerned with family and children. He may be as opposed as Herzog to popular nihilism or as sensitive to grief. But Herzog responds to his experiences with Jewish sensibility and idiom. For instance, he repeatedly "thinks" Yiddish. Hebrew prayers and curses and Yiddish colloquial phrases—while not always linguistically precise—mingle with Montreal's layered French and English sidewalk locutions. When greatly upset, Herzog is likely to give cry to an English/Hebrew prayer. "Dear God! Mercy! My God!" he exclaims. "Rachaim olenu . . . melekh maimis. . . . Thou King of Death and Life. . . !" (H, p. 304). Wishing to curse those who have injured him, he finds Scriptural phrases leap to his lips. "Yemach sh'mo! Let their names be blotted out!"[81] he cries. Still angry, he adds: "They prepared a net for my steps. They digged a pit before me. Break their teeth, O God, in their mouth!" (H, pp. 202–3).

These reactions are as conscious as they are instinctive. Herzog is keenly aware of his Jewish tendencies. "He could be a patriarch," he says of himself at one point, "as every Herzog was meant to be. The family man, father, transmitter of life, intermediary between past and future, instrument of mysterious creation" (H, p. 202). As a Jew these roles are for him not obsolete but binding. So are certain recognizable feelings. When he attempts to describe his own emotional vulnerability, he notes that he is given to "much heavy love . . . [and, of course] grief did not pass quickly, with him" (H, p. 119). He later pinpoints the cause: "[We Jews] had a great schooling in grief. I still know these cries of the soul. They lie in the breast, and in the throat. The mouth wants to open wide and let them out. But all those are antiquities—yes, Jewish antiquities originating in the Bible, in a Biblical sense of personal experience and destiny" (H, p. 148).

Herzog strains to express these cries, these personal griefs and grievances, antiquities or not. He is given to hastily scribbled, incomplete, and unmailed (and often merely mental) letters to the living and dead: relatives, friends, and enemies, as well as philosophers, scientists, and politicians. Yet despite his agitated emotions, Herzog sees his scribblings in ironic Jewish perspective. They are, he realizes, "fragments—nonsense syllables, exclamations, twisted proverbs and quotations or, in the Yiddish of his long-dead mother, Trepverter—retorts that came too late, when you were already on your way down the stairs" (H, pp. 2–3). Too late they may be, still Herzog keeps up, albeit with a sinking heart, a constant flow of such afterthoughts. Thus his Jewishness literally shapes his perspective and values and even, as noted, his idiom. The same is true of Saul Bellow, who credits Jewish historical experience with providing the positive attitudes and values by which he measures all things. Certainly he employs Jewish history to reject modern fiction's pervasive negativism. "The Jews of the ghetto," Bellow notes, "found themselves involved in an immense joke. They were divinely designated to be great and yet they were like mice. History was something that happened to them; they did not make it. The nations made it, while they, the Jews, suffered it. But when history had happened it belonged to them, inasmuch as it was the coming of the Messiah—their Messiah—that would give it meaning. Every male child was potentially the Messiah" (LG, p. 15). Every new Jewish life held then promise of a better future. This inherited resistance not only to nihilistic views but also to most all-purpose theories helps explain why Bellow heroes resist "being swallowed up by other people's ideas or versions of reality."[82]

Indeed, Bellow declares himself grateful to his Jewish heritage for causing him to reject certain virulently negative ideas espoused by what he terms modern "romantics." He disdains especially the "apocalyptic nihilism" that holds man has reached a "terminal point" in a world so corrupt that it should be destroyed to "rise again." Major non-Jewish writers as different as D. H. Lawrence, Ezra Pound, Ludwig Benn, James Joyce, Louis-Ferdinand Céline, and Thomas Mann, he complains, have accepted this "terminal assumption" as "political fact."[83] Despite its heavy literary endorsement, this fatalistic premise grates on Bellow's Jewish sensibility. Horrendous things have happened, he admits, but civilization persists, and the apocalyptic prophecies have not come to pass. He sees little need, therefore, to call for universal destruction in expectation of a phoenixlike rebirth. In this mental region Bellow has Moses Herzog speak for him. Herzog, in turn, directs much of his mental anger on this point at his child-hood friend Egbert Shapiro, now a respected scholar and author. Shapiro's writings exemplify for Herzog the negative attitude pervading modern thought: they articulate the platitudes of the nihilistic Waste Land mentality. Herzog rejects totally what he terms "the cheap mental stimulants of Alienation, the cant and rant of pipsqueaks about Inauthenticity and Forlornness. I can't accept this foolish dreariness. We are talking about the whole life of mankind. The subject is too great, too deep for such weakness, cowardice—too deep, too great, Shapiro." That Shapiro, a Jew, should engage in such "shivery games" of apocalyptic nightmare and cultural pathology is especially appalling. Tragic experience should have taught any Jew that survival derives from courage, hope, spirit. A learned Jew should be aware how nineteenth-century Romanticism produced a self-anointed elite who con-fused "aesthetic and moral judgments." How could Shapiro then align himself with this clique? "It torments me to insanity," muses Herzog, "that you should be so misled. A merely aesthetic critique of modern history! After the wars and mass killings! You are too intelligent for this. You inherited rich blood. Your father peddled apples." Yet Herzog is also aware that unqualified theories of "progress" are for Jews equally unseemly. Jews are "survivors" in this age, he would remind Shapiro, "so theories of progress ill become us, because we are intimately acquainted with the costs" (H, pp. 74–75).

Saul Bellow sums up Moses Herzog's attitude and his own when he declares that "I may be disappointed in existence, but I feel I have a right to demand something other than the romantic disappointment. I think the Jewish feeling resists romanticism and insists on an older set of facts."[84] Another who insists on this "older set of facts" is Artur Sammler. A seasoned journalist and Holocaust survivor, Sammler finds his life has given him little cause to value man highly. His pessimism has been deep-ened by lifelong reading of Schopenhauer's negative estimates of human nature. But Sammler's intellectual negativism is bal-anced by his Jewish acceptance of man's foibles and worth. Re-calling that Schopenhauer had labeled Jews "vulgar optimists,"[85] Sammler, despite his self-image as an emancipated humanist, accepts the description. Like Saul Bellow and Moses Herzog, he, too, harbors a "Jewish feeling"[86] that resists the modern Waste-lander's cynicism and despair. Despite his death camp traumas, Sammler denounces all who reject any sign of optimism or ideal-ism. He even regains the conviction that every living being has "a splash of God's own spirit" (MSP, p. 189).

If beset then by modernist theories and ideologies, Herzog and
Sammler and Bellow reject most of them for the same reason:
their caution is due in large part to their Jewish heritage. Jews
learned early, Bellow declares, that survival requires a careful
selection of alternatives. Certainly Moses Herzog finds that to
survive he must reject "a great mass of irrelevancy and nonsense." He is learning to say no, and again no, in traditional
Jewish fashion. But this "no" is to be directed not at life's poten-
tials or possibilities, but at all pat formulas and easy answers,
and at daily life's niggling trivia. So Moses Herzog strives might-
ily to resist such daily demands. Indeed, Herzog concludes his
story on that defiant note. In Bellow's eyes, this is not a small
victory. "Any man who has rid himself of superfluous ideas in
order to take that first step" toward survival, he declares, "has
done something significant." In short, both Bellow and his heroes
may suspect all set or formulaic ideas because life has sensitized
them to the gap between theory and practice, promise and fulfillment. But generally their perspective on life is essentially a
Jewish one. So those critics who complain that Bellow's fiction
lacks ideas may simply be seeking the familiar formulas or fash-
ionable ideologies. "Ideas outside the 'canon,'" Bellow argues,
"they don't recognize." If such people mean "ideas à la Sartre or
ideas à la Camus," he adds, "they are correct; *Herzog* has few"
such existential concepts.[87]

Bellow makes clear that what Moses Herzog does embrace is
the Jewish belief in creation's essential goodness and life's ultimate worth. Conversely, Herzog dismisses—it should be recalled—that "Christian view of history" which always finds the
present moment corrupt, in crisis, and falling "from classical
greatness" (*H*, p. 54). Herzog's severest strictures, as already
noted, are directed at Dr. Edvig's Protestant/Freudian downgrading of mankind. It is a pose derived, as Herzog (and Bellow)
see it, from John Calvin and proves "a lousy, cringing, grudging
conception of human nature" (*H*, p. 58). It is a concept neither
Bellow nor his Jewish protagonists—thanks to their Jewishness—can accept. All things considered, a thoughtful reader
today may well decide that theirs does not seem a bad viewpoint
for everyone (Jew and non-Jew alike) to ponder.

Notes

1. Chiranton Kulshrestha, "A Conversation with Saul Bellow," *Chicago Review* 23, no. 4 and 24, no. 1 (Spring/Summer 1972): 15.

2. Saul Bellow, *To Jerusalem and Back: A Personal Account* (1976; reprint, New York: Avon Books, 1977), p. 1. All textual references abbreviated *TJB* are to this later edition.

3. Kulshrestha, "A Conversation," p. 15.

4. Philip Gillon, "Bellow's Credo," *Jerusalem Post Weekly*, 24 December 1974, p. 13. See also the abridged version: "Saul Bellow: Jewish and an Author," *Wisconsin Jewish Chronicle*, 5 June 1975, p. 19.

5. Kulshrestha, "A Conversation," p. 15.

6. Nina A. Steers, "'Successor' to Faulkner?" *Show*, September 1964, p. 38.

7. "Some People Come Back like Hecuba," *Time*, 8 February 1970, p. 82.

8. Matthew C. Roudané, "An Interview with Saul Bellow," *Contemporary Literature* 25, no. 3 (Fall 1984): 267–68.

9. Ann Weinstein, "Bellow's Reflections on His Most Recent Sentimental Journey to His Birthplace," *Saul Bellow Journal* 4, no. 1 (Fall/Winter 1985): 70–71.

10. Jane Howard, "Mr. Bellow Considers His Planet," *Life*, 3 April 1970, p. 59.

11. Steers, "'Successor' to Faulkner?" p. 36.

12. Irving Malin, *Jews and Americans* (1965; reprint, Carbondale: Arcturus Books, 1966), p. 8.

13. Steers, "'Successor' to Faulkner?" pp. 36–37.

14. The late Maurice Samuel, a distinguished Yiddishist and translator, although readily acknowledging Bellow's grasp of Yiddish, playfully pointed out a few slips in Bellow's translation or interpretation of several Yiddish words and phrases in *Herzog*. See Maurice Samuel, "My Friend, the Late Moses Herzog," *Midstream* (April 1966): 11 and n. 9. For a harsher critique of Bellow's linguistic shortcomings in Yiddish and especially Hebrew, see L. H. Goldman, *Saul Bellow's Moral Vision: A Critical Study of the Jewish Experience* (New York: Irvington Publishers, 1983), pp. 74–75, 121–28.

15. "Hecuba," p. 82.

16. Jo Brans, "Common Needs, Common Preoccupations: An Interview with Saul Bellow," in *Critical Essays on Saul Bellow*, ed. Stanley Trachtenberg (Boston: G. K. Hall, 1979), p. 67.

17. Cathleen Medwick, "A Cry of Strength: The Unfashionably Uncynical Saul Bellow," *Vogue*, March 1982, p. 369.

18. Weinstein, "Bellow's Reflections," p. 71.

19. Medwick, "A Cry of Strength," p. 369.

20. Saul Bellow, "In the Days of Mr. Roosevelt," *Esquire*, December 1983, p. 532. All textual references abbreviated *IDMR* are to this article.

21. Medwick, "A Cry of Strength," p. 369.

22. Weinstein, "Bellow's Reflections," p. 63.

23. "Hecuba," p. 82.

24. Walter Clemons and Jack Kroll, "America's Master Novelist," *Newsweek*, 1 September 1975, p. 34.

25. Saul Bellow, "Isaac Rosenfeld," *Partisan Review* 23 (Fall 1956): 565.

26. Saul Bellow, *Herzog* (1964; reprint, New York: Viking Compass Books, 1967), p. 147. All textual references abbreviated *H* are to this later edition.

27. Steers, "'Successor' to Faulkner?" p. 37.

28. Richard Stern, "Bellow's Gift," *New York Times Magazine*, 21 November 1976, p. 42.

29. Jack Ludwig, *Recent American Novelists* (Minneapolis: University of Minnesota Press, 1962), p. 9.

30. Ludwig, *Recent American Novelists*, p. 9.

31. Stanley Kauffmann, "Saul Bellow: A Closing Note," *Salmagundi* 30 (Summer 1975): 91.

32. Steers, "'Successor' to Faulkner?" p. 37.

33. Theodore L. Gross, ed., "Saul Bellow," *The Literature of American Jews* (New York: The Free Press, 1973), p. 226.

34. Alfred Kazin, "The Earthly City of the Jews: Bellow to Singer," *Bright Book of Life: American Novelists and Storytellers from Hemingway to Mailer* (Boston: Atlantic-Little, Brown, 1973), pp. 127–28.

35. Irving Howe, *World of Our Fathers* (New York: Harcourt Brace Jovanovich, 1976), pp. 593–94.

36. Saul Bellow, *The Adventures of Augie March* (New York: Viking Press, 1953), p. 536.

37. Steers, "'Successor' to Faulkner?" p. 36.

38. Howe, *World of Our Fathers*, p. 594.

39. Mark Shecner, "Saul Bellow and Ghetto Cosmopolitanism," *Modern Jewish Studies Annual II* (1978): 37.

40. Pearl K. Bell, "New Jewish Voices," *Commentary*, June 1981, 62.

41. Shecner, "Saul Bellow," p. 37.

42. Bell, "New Jewish Voices," p. 62.

43. Thorstein Veblen, "The Intellectual Pre-Eminence of Jews in Modern Europe," *Political Science Quarterly* 34 (1919): 38.

44. Shecner, "Saul Bellow," p. 37.

45. Bell, "New Jewish Voices," p. 62.

46. Judd L. Teller, "From Yiddish to Neo-Brahmin," *Strangers and Natives: The Evolution of the American Jew from 1921 to the Present* (New York: Delacorte Press, 1968), p. 265.

47. Teller, "From Yiddish to Neo-Brahmin," p. 266.

48. Ibid.

49. Kazin, "Earthly City," p. 133.

50. Saul Bellow, *Seize the Day* (1956; reprint, New York: Viking Compass Books, 1961), p. 56. All textual references abbreviated *SD* are to this later edition.

51. Teller, "From Yiddish to Neo-Brahmin," p. 268.

52. Gillon, "Bellow's Credo," p. 13.

53. Saul Bellow, "Starting Out in Chicago," *The American Scholar* 44 (Winter 1974/75): 77. All textual references abbreviated *SOC* are to this article.

54. Clemons and Kroll, "America's Master Novelist," p. 39.

55. Gordon Lloyd Harper, "Saul Bellow," in *Writers at Work: The Paris Review Interviews, Third Series*, ed. George Plimpton (New York: Viking Press, 1968), p. 183.

56. Harper, "Saul Bellow," pp. 182–83.

57. Ibid., p. 182.

58. Patrick O'Sheel, "Laughter from the Styx," *Humanities*, March 1977, p. 4.

59. Sanford Pinsker, "Saul Bellow in the Classroom," *College English*, April 1973, p. 982.

60. Gillon, "Bellow's Credo," p. 13.

61. "A Laureate for Saul Bellow," *Time*, 1 November 1976, p. 91.

62. O'Sheel, "Laughter from the Styx," p. 4.

63. "Laureate," p. 91.

64. Digby Diehl, "Saul Bellow Waiting for Dreams to Begin," *Los Angeles Times Calendar*, 21 March 1971, p. 45.

65. Pinsker, "Bellow in the Classroom," p. 982.

66. Gillon, "Bellow's Credo," p. 13.

67. "Laureate," p. 91.

68. Kulshrestha, "A Conversation," p. 13.

69. Ibid., p. 14.

70. Gillon, "Bellow's Credo," p. 13.

71. See Earl Rovit, *Saul Bellow* (Minneapolis: University of Minnesota Press, 1967), p. 15.

72. Howe, *World of Our Fathers*, pp. 594–95.

73. See Rovit, *Saul Bellow*, p. 42.

74. Saul Bellow, "Laughter in the Ghetto," *Saturday Review of Literature*, 30 May 1953, p. 15. All textual references abbreviated *LG* are to this review of Sholem Aleichem's *The Adventures of Mottel the Cantor's Son*.

75. Rovit, *Saul Bellow*, pp. 42–43; see also Howe, *World of Our Fathers*, p. 595.

76. Alfred Kazin, "My Friend Saul Bellow," *The Atlantic*, January 1965, p. 53. Kazin incorporates this article in a longer one, "Midtown and the Village," *Harper's*, January 1971, pp. 82–91; see especially pp. 83–85.

77. Rovit, *Saul Bellow*, p. 30.

78. Kazin, "My Friend Saul Bellow," p. 53.

79. Saul Bellow, ed., *Great Jewish Short Stories* (New York: Dell, 1963), p. 9. All textual references abbreviated *GJSS* are to this volume's Introduction.

80. Quoted in Liela H. Goldman, "Saul Bellow and His Israeli Critics over the Past Decade," *Midstream*, May 1988, p. 54.

81. In variant forms, the beleaguered Israelites directed this curse at the hated Amalekites. See, for example, Exod. 17:14 and Deut. 25:17–19. But Herzog would seem to have in mind the general tenor and language of Psalm 109. See also Psalm 3:7 and 9:5 and Jer. 18:22.

82. Harper, "Saul Bellow," p. 196.

83. Ibid., p. 195.

84. Steers, "'Successor' to Faulkner?" pp. 37–38.

85. Saul Bellow, *Mr. Sammler's Planet* (1970; reprint, New York: Viking Compass Books, 1973), p. 209. All textual references abbreviated *MSP* are to this later edition.

86. Steers, "'Successor' to Faulkner?" p. 38.

87. Harper, "Saul Bellow," pp. 193–95.

Jewish Jacobites: Henry James's Presence in the Fiction of Philip Roth and Cynthia Ozick

MARK KRUPNICK

N<small>EAR</small> the beginning of Saul Bellow's novel *Humboldt's Gift* (1975), Charlie Citrine, the narrator, is remembering what his friend, the dead poet Von Humboldt Fleisher, had been like in his heyday, the 1940s:

> He was a wonderful talker, a hectic nonstop monologuist and im-
> provisator. . . . Money always inspired him. He adored talking about
> the rich. Brought up on New York tabloids, he often mentioned the
> golden scandals of yesteryear, Peaches and Daddy Browning, Harry
> Thaw and Evelyn Nesbit, plus the Jazz Age, Scott Fitzgerald, and the
> Super-Rich. The heiresses of Henry James he knew cold.[1]

Bellow's Humboldt is modeled on Delmore Schwartz, who had been the favorite poet of the *Partisan Review* intellectuals around the same time (the 1940s) that Bellow became their favorite novelist. The Jewish writers and intellectuals of New York were bemused, as Henry James was, by the idea of success, and they looked to Bellow and Schwartz to prove that as a group they had finally emerged into the mainstream of American life and letters. We know Bellow redeemed the great hope invested in him. Schwartz, on the other hand, fell apart after his brilliant start and died a miserable death in a seedy hotel off Times Square. His ending found him a long way from the worlds of *The Portrait of a Lady* and *The Golden Bowl*.

Von Humboldt Fleisher was certainly not alone among Jewish writers of the forties in his affection for Henry James and his heiresses. Philip Rahv, a founding editor of *Partisan Review*, had devoted an important essay precisely to these golden girls: "The Heiress of All the Ages" (1943). That essay, together with "Attitudes Toward Henry James,"[2] published in the same year, helped

89

to launch the James boom in academic literary studies. This is not to say that the Jewish intellectuals of New York were the first critics to promote James's work, for they were only following in the wake of pioneers like Edmund Wilson and Yvor Winters and, above all, R. P. Blackmur.[3] But few American critics of old Protestant stock exceeded the literary sons of East-European Jewish immigrants in their enthusiasm for James, and more recent Jewish-American writers have continued to admire James and to use him as a model.

The generation that came of age in the 1930s and established themselves in the 1940s tended to find in James a social legend that satisfied their curiosity about the lives of the American rich and well-born. That curiosity contributed to making Scott Fitzgerald a favorite not only of Delmore Schwartz but also of Lionel Trilling and Alfred Kazin. It had been obvious in the 1920s that no Jewish novelist could write anything like *The Great Gatsby* (1925), simply because no Jewish novelist had Fitzgerald's access to Gentile high society. Two generations later Philip Roth launched his literary career with a novella, *Goodbye, Columbus* (1959), that is a kind of Jewish *Gatsby*; it shows the degree to which by the 1950s Jews had become, for better or worse, like other Americans. It showed, too, how a Jewish writer, and one only twenty-six at that, could command Fitzgerald's perfect pitch and poise.

Those writers who came of age in the 1930s were still alienated from the American mainstream. Thinking of themselves as foreign, they mainly looked to European models. Henry James was a special case. He was an American writer of cosmopolitan taste who had lived his life abroad and studied American society from an ironic distance, all the while continuing to be fascinated, as the Jewish intellectuals were, by the aura of the American super-rich. The depression generation was quite as excluded from Gentile high society as had been that of the 1920s, but the passion of its members to improve themselves socially combined with their depression-born preoccupation with the politics of class to make them avid students of the American patriciate. Philip Rahv, a Communist in the early thirties and an anti-Stalinist Marxist for the remainder of his life, was at the time absorbed by the question of wealth and manners. He even married a Jamesian-type American heiress in his later years.

James attracted lower-class intellectuals like Rahv partly because his novels might be studied as handbooks by which readers could plan their own siege of society. There were other Jewish writers of this generation who were not interested in heiresses but were still drawn to James.[4] Still, those other figures of the forties had in common with Rahv and Delmore Schwartz an interest in James the critic and his chronicles of society. They created James in their own image as members of a generation absorbed in radical politics. At the same time, they were torn between their vaunted "alienation" and a desire to enter into their patrimony as the heirs of Western high culture and beneficiaries of the promise of American life. James was invaluable, for example, to Lionel Trilling in thinking his way free of the simplifying political categories of the Marxist thirties. As much as any writer, James symbolized for Trilling the values (above all "variousness" and "complexity") he opposed to the simplifications of Popular Front leftism. But the novels of James that Trilling wrote about, in well-known essays of 1948 and 1953, were not the master's late-phase major works of complexity and ambiguity, like The Ambassadors. Rather, Trilling wrote about the two novels of James, The Princess Casamassima and The Bostonians,[5] which are the least idiosyncratically Jamesian and the closest in form and intention to the classic European novel of society, as produced by Austen, Dickens, Stendhal, and Zola.

Trilling found in The Princess Casamassima a tension between the opposing ideals of social justice and the glory of high civilization that had been a central theme of his own early intellectual life. He argued that James held these oppositions in balance and that the refusal of Hyacinth Robinson, the novel's main character, to choose between them made him a true hero of the spirit. Irving Howe objected to what he took to be the conservative political implications of Trilling's readings of James. But Howe, too, in his essay on The Bostonians, read James as above all a commentator on great issues of society and the politics of culture.[6]

I

Enthusiasm for James has continued among the Jewish-American writers who came of age in the late 1940s and in the 1950s. The James influence is most marked in Cynthia Ozick (b. 1928) and Philip Roth (b. 1933), who seem to me the preeminent figures of their generation. Ozick and Roth came to James partly because of the essays of earlier Jewish critics like Trilling, Rahv, and Howe. Yet they came to him without the consuming passion for the radical politics of their elders. Because their generational experience was different, their image of James was different as well. Roth was chiefly influenced, at the start, by the author of *The Portrait of a Lady*, whom he read as less a social critic than a moralist, and an abstract moralist at that, concerned with questions of personal identity and responsibility. Ozick was more drawn to the late James, whom she read as a creator of parables and allegories and a magisterial stylist. For both, James was a supreme instance of the religion of art.

Roth is five years younger than Ozick, but I shall discuss him first because he became well known much earlier than she. He found his voice and made his mark in 1959 with a prize-winning collection of stories, whereas Ozick labored in relative obscurity up to the early 1970s. I have already mentioned Roth's early novella *Goodbye, Columbus* and its debt to Fitzgerald. The aura of glamour associated with the vulgar Patimkins may derive from Fitzgerald, but the wit would seem to owe as much to early James. Roth's narrator and main character, Neil Klugman, sounds as much like the arch James of *The Europeans* as like Nick Carraway in *Gatsby*.

But we don't have to guess about James's importance to Roth during the latter's apprentice years. Roth alludes to James three times in his autobiographical memoir *The Facts* (1988). Two references to James occur in contexts of uneasy defensiveness. In the first, Roth is trying to disprove the charge of Jewish self-hatred directed against him by Jews offended by his early story "Defender of the Faith." Contrary to the allegations of his literal-minded Jewish critics, Roth says, he had always been on good terms with his Jewishness. He maintains that his Jewishness had been especially useful to him as a young writer, in making available a certain saving crudeness. Newark-style Jewishness had been "a defense against overrefinement, a counterweight to the intimidating power of Henry James and literary good taste generally." Roth interprets his next decade in similar terms. In a chapter on the making of *Portnoy's Complaint*, he alludes to his psychoanalysis in the 1960s as a model for the confessional style of that novel; that experience proved "a model for reckless narrative disclosure of a kind I hadn't learned from Henry James."[7]

Roth's references to Henry James form part of his carefully nurtured legend of escape. Of course, he would have had no need for escape had he not previously allowed James so powerful an influence over his imagination. In the same chapter of *The Facts*,

Roth says of *Portnoy's Complaint:* "It was a book that had rather less to do with 'freeing' me from an apprentice's literary models, particularly from the awesome graduate-school authority of Henry James, whose *Portrait of a Lady* had been a virtual handbook during the early drafts of *Letting Go.*"[8]

It would be a mistake to think of *The Facts* as the "straight story" of his own life and the preceding fictions merely earlier imaginary versions of the same events. *The Facts* is a version, too, an autobiographical myth, rather than "a novelist's autobiography" as promised by Roth's subtitle. It is a mythic account of the well-behaved Jewish boy from Newark who breaks out of lower–middle-class niceness, and it includes an excessive deference to Jamesian standards of decorum. The fact is that, at least in its final draft, Roth's novel *Letting Go* is not especially decorous. The James influence, detailed below, is complemented by others. There is, for example, the peculiar gloominess and pervasive disenchantment of the novel's male heroes that suggest the tone and subject-matter of Flaubert's *Sentimental Education.*[9] Moreover, the grittiness of detail suggests that Roth was probably also reading Chicago novels in the naturalistic mode, like James T. Farrell's Studs Lonigan trilogy and Theodore Dreiser's *Sister Carrie*. The impact of midwestern realism, notably of Sinclair Lewis, is even more marked in Roth's subsequent novel, *When She Was Good* (1967).

Despite these qualifications, *Letting Go* remains a colossal tribute, all 628 pages of it, to the Jamesian influence. The presence of *The Portrait of a Lady* is felt from the very first pages. There we learn that Gabe Wallach, a college English instructor, had been reading that novel when he received in the mail the letter his mother had written him on her deathbed.[10] Gabe, it seems, is much devoted to James's narratives "of heroes and heroines tempting one another into a complex and often tragic fate." Gabe's involvement in such a story, to which his mother's letter provides a key, begins a few pages later: He meets Libby Herz, who imagines herself to be, like Isabel Archer, the heroine of *The Portrait.*

Roth's narrative has many more explicit references to James's novel. Indeed, *Letting Go* is one of those works of fiction that offer themselves as commentaries on precursor works. For Roth, *The Portrait* is a story of how people interfere in each others' lives, manipulate them, push and pull at them, all in the name of the most high-minded motives. Most of the connections between the two novels by James and Roth are fairly obvious. Libby

Herz, the wife of Gabe's friend Paul, is plainly a version, however pathetic and bedraggled, of Isabel. She dreams of happiness but must settle for a claustrophobic marriage to a man who doesn't love her. Paul, an insufficiently realized character and thus a flaw in Roth's overall conception, plays the Gilbert Osmond role from *The Portrait*, though he is not much like Osmond in temperament. Gabe is a latter-day version of Ralph Touchett, the cousin with independent means who would play fairy godfather to Isabel, hoping to free her to realize the demands of her imagination. Gabe may be the most Jamesian character in Roth's fiction. He is a cool, prudent, self-protective fellow who will always disappoint the women who depend on him. In effect, Gabe proves a variant of the poor but sensitive Jamesian gentleman who is too fastidious or fearful to live any way but vicariously.

Gabe is as innately sour as Roth's subsequent heroes are basically sweet. Nathan Zuckerman may never be quite as sugary as his name suggests, but neither is he so emotionally walled off and constricted as Gabe. Indeed, Gabe seems not only a version of Ralph Touchett but also of Isabel herself. She is torn by her confused desire to enter life aggressively and her fear of emotional commitment. Paul Herz is assigned by Roth the Osmond role, but he appears also to have been intended as a man of feeling and hence an alternative to Gabe. (Names in Roth are always significant, as they are in James.) But Paul is not truly open-hearted (herzlich), and the potential contrast of old-fashioned emotional Jew and cool, smooth Jamesian Jew rather fizzles.

Finally, *Letting Go* is an early 1960s version of *The Portrait* that recaptures the peculiar desolation of the preceding decade. The characters are Jamesian in being detached from large questions of vocation and politics in favor of a near-total preoccupation with the dilemmas of private life. Roth's novel is not violated by any general ideas. Paul and Gabe teach English at the University of Chicago, but they appear as uncommitted to literature as to the women in their lives. Moreover, while both men are Jewish, their Jewishness figures only as a peripheral ethnicity that offers a clue to their difficult relations with their parents. Gabe and Paul may be Jamesian in their concern with their personal identity and fate, but they are completely lacking the generous illusions of James's Americans abroad. Coming of age in the disillusioned 1950s, they start out with certain notions about life, as did Isabel, but they exhibit none of her Emersonian hopefulness.

II

For Cynthia Ozick, as for Roth, Henry James was the great model as she started out. She, too, offers testimony about the nature of her indebtedness. Their relationships to James, however, were very different. Roth has discussed his apprenticeship to James the same way Saul Bellow has *his* early attitude to literary models approved by T. S. Eliot and the conservative-traditionalist critics of the 1940s who had been inspired by Eliot. Bellow and Roth recall having viewed writers like James and Flaubert as icons in a coldly respectable, Gentile-formalist orthodoxy that struck them as hostile to would-be Jewish upstarts like themselves. Ozick's career shows no such pattern of allegiance to academic formalism later replaced by a freer, open-form rebelliousness. No character in her fiction is comparable to Augie March and Alexander Portnoy. She does move from the encrusted, high-modernist style of her first novel, *Trust* (1966), to the looser style and the more casual, homely inflections of "Envy; or, Yiddish in America," published a few years later. The shift is major and, as with Bellow and Roth, involves the question of respectability. But in turning to explicitly Jewish subject-matter, Ozick shows no impulse, as do her male-Jewish counterparts, to present herself as a roughneck.

The surmise of contemporary reviewers that *Trust* was written under the sign of Henry James is confirmed by Ozick's poignant "The Lesson of the Master" (1982).[11] This memoir is presented as a parable, a form that Ozick discussed thirty years earlier in her Ohio State master's thesis, "Parable in the Later Novels of Henry James." Its theme is itself Jamesian: betrayal and the unlived life. The betrayal is self-betrayal, "a stupidity, a misunderstanding, a great Jamesian life-mistake,"[12] that caused a young woman to sacrifice her youth to the dream of Jamesian mastery. For Ozick, at twenty-two, had consecrated herself to James's religion of art and become oblivious to ordinary life; she had obeyed an impulse analogous to that of the protagonists of late-Jamesian stories like "The Beast in the Jungle" and "The Altar of the Dead." Ozick's words convey the spirit of 1950s modernist piety, which differs strongly from the postmodernist mockery of our own moment: "I carried the Jamesian idea, I was of his cult, I was a worshiper of literature, literature was my single altar; I was, like the elderly bald-headed James, a priest at that altar; and that altar was all of my life."[13]

Cultural tastes have changed dramatically. A shift of taste has caused art to become an object of skepticism rather than piety. We also have seen a strong reduction in the cultural status of literature. There is a specifically Jewish aspect to this transition. Ozick's passion for books is recognizably that of the post-immigrant generation. The traditional Jewish avidity for learning, so marked in her work, is less obvious in that of more recent Jewish writers. But Ozick is not given to such sociological speculations. Instead, she likes to point lessons. The moral she draws from her own mistake helps elucidate the Jamesian presence in her early work. Her mistake, she says, was not in becoming an acolyte of James's religion of art but in trying to be Henry James. She should not have tried to write like James at sixty when she was in her twenties and unready for Jamesian presence mastery. At twenty-two she knew, as James's John Marcher in his middle age didn't know, what the beast in the jungle was. It was style, or, as Ozick puts it, "the sinewy grand undulations of some unraveling fiction, meticulously dreamed out in a language of masterly resplendence."[14]

Her first novel, Trust, is the result of her mistaken decision to imitate the style of the master. Its 639 pages make it an even longer work than Roth's first novel four years earlier. Actually, Ozick's novel was completed in 1963, but it languished with an editor at New American Library for a year and a half before being taken over by another editor, David Segal, and published by NAL. With nearly seven years invested in its writing, Trust comes to us as even more ambitious in the high-modernist mode than Letting Go. Still they share the same historical moment: the transition from the somnolence of the Eisenhower decade to the uneasy stirrings of the early 1960s. Indeed, Ozick reports that she finished Trust on the day that John F. Kennedy was assassinated, in November 1963.[15]

These giant novels, both rather neglected, suggest a different view of the early sixties literary situation than the usual one. They have few points of contact with better-known novels of those years, like Joseph Heller's Catch-22 or Thomas Pynchon's V. They convey the ruefulness and distrust—Ozick's title is wholly ironic—of those years without becoming "black comedy" in the manner of early Heller or Kurt Vonnegut or John Barth.

Different as they are from the more innovative fiction of their time, *Trust* and *Letting Go* are similar to each other in their aesthetic high seriousness. This Jamesian attribute contributed to their lack of success in a period increasingly attuned to postmodern parody and playfulness. These early novels of Roth and Ozick are more solemn than playful. More importantly, in terms of their authors' development, they seem now to have been written against the grain of their authors' true talents.

Roth started out as a writer of carefully constructed *New Yorker* short stories. Although he has written mainly novels since *Goodbye, Columbus*, these novels usually take the form of linked novellas. These "sections," of forty to fifty pages each, have tended to be fairly discrete and have often been published separately in magazines prior to book publication. Ozick, on the other hand, dedicated herself from the start to monumentality. She devoted her twenties and thirties to two long narratives, but only *Trust* was published. In the late 1960s, Ozick shifted course and began to attract attention with stories like "Envy" and story collections beginning with *The Pagan Rabbi and Other Stories* (1971). Her reputation today is based mainly on these shorter fictions and on the short nonfiction pieces collected in *Art and Ardor* (1983) and *Metaphor and Memory* (1989). Ozick has been leery of the novel form since her early misadventure. It was not until 1983, seventeen years after the publication of *Trust*, that she published a second novel, *The Cannibal Galaxy*. Significantly, that work is notably shorter and less ambitious than the narratives she was writing in the 1950s. A more recent novel, *The Messiah of Stockholm* (1987), has the feel of Ozick's earlier long stories, like those collected in *Bloodshed* (1976) and *Levitation* (1982).

The chief interest of *Trust* is its language. Ozick has said that this "was conceived in a style both 'mandarin' and 'lapidary,' every page a poem."[16] It is, however, a special kind of poetry, like that of *The Ambassadors* or *The Golden Bowl*. It echoes their exquisite parenthetical hesitations and qualifications and their metaphorical richness: the latter is evident especially in a flood of elaborate quasi-epic similes. The following example from *Trust* appears midway through the novel. It concerns William, the first husband and still the trusted lawyer of the narrator's mother. That trust, however, has come into question:

I had thought William not like Mr. and Mrs. Vand. I had supposed him incapable of betrayal. I had believed him to be—oh, what I had

believed him to be!—it was simple, simple, single and simple, and
the multifold word stuck to my tongue, a stale pearl of honey: it was
only that I had believed William to be trustworthy. Trustworthy!—
that sculptured notion which his son had intervened to sully, like a
boy daubing the blank eye-holes of a stone god with an obscene leer
painted all distastefully in the corners of the proud smooth sockets.
. . . And yet, after all, I had William to lose (William, trampled grotto,
violate shrine), and wondered whether I had already lost him (as
when the spoliation of the lovely thing is still a rumor, though accepted and credited, and one hurries to the place to see the substan-
tiation of one's hideous imaginings, by now as certain and believing
as if the act had been one's own).[17]

Its richly encrusted metaphorical language tends to pull away
from its referents, so that *Trust* calls to mind the later James.
Ozick's novel also makes use of The Master's favorite themes.
One is marriage and its betrayals. Allegra Vand, the mother of
the narrator, has been married twice. Yet her only child, the
unnamed narrator, is the byproduct of yet a third relationship,
with Gustave Nicholas Tilbeck. Ozick uses the marriage, as James
frequently does, to figure a larger crisis of culture involving the
American-European "transatlantic theme" and the fate of the
American upper class. Ozick, again like James, also invokes the
cognate theme of the clash of innocence and experience.

It is not James alone who influences this narrative of an abandoned child's search for her origins. The whole melodramatic
apparatus of wills and trust funds and comic grotesques suggests
Dickens as well. In addition, Ozick's explicitly philosophical
concerns are reminiscent more of George Eliot and, in Ozick's
concern with history, more of Tolstoi, than of James, who was
notoriously indifferent to general ideas. Still, the figure of the
witty girl-child who has been victimized by selfish adventurer-
parents suggests James above all. His *What Maisie Knew* is one
possible model. But the surname of the narrator's stepfather,
Enoch Vand, sounds like a short version of Vanderbank, the
suitor horrified by the "corruption" of eighteen-year-old Nandy
Brookenham in James's *The Awkward Age*.[18] James describes in
his *Notebooks* the germ of *The Awkward Age*. His description
illuminates the central situation also of Ozick's novel: "The idea
of the little London girl who grows up to 'sit with' the free-talking
modern young mother—reaches 17, 18, etc.—comes out—and,
not marrying, has to 'be there'—and, though the conversation is
supposed to be expurgated for her, inevitably hears, overhears,
guesses, follows, takes in, becomes acquainted with, horrors."[19]

By "horrors," James refers to the secrets of adult sexuality, knowledge of which is assumed to be traumatic for innocents, as in the two novels I have mentioned and, most famously, in *The Turn of the Screw*. All three novels were written around the same time, before James wrote his three major works—*The Ambassadors*, *The Wings of the Dove*, and *The Golden Bowl*. The Jamesian horrors seem fairly harmless compared to what Ozick's heroine comes to know. This knowledge includes the evidences of the Holocaust she witnesses when her mother brings her back, as a ten-year-old girl, to a Europe lying in ruins at the end of World War II. The Jamesian preoccupation with sexual knowledge (even the Jamesian preoccupation with voyeurism or the thrill of "seeing") coexists in *Trust* with a post-Jamesian intimation of history as irredeemable evil. Ozick's heroine is recognizably Jamesian in a line that runs from Isabel Archer to Maisie Farrange to Maggie Verver of *The Golden Bowl*. For Maggie, reality is always a phantasmagoria needing to be puzzled out, decoded. For all these heroines, knowledge is a temptation and a fear. Ozick's wide-eyed narrator spies on the lovemaking of her scapegrace father, Nick, and the new wife of William's son, whom she had herself hoped to marry. She reflects: "In me meanwhile knowledge of the private thing: knowledge is the only real event in the world, and something had happened."[20]

III

Henry James's influence, so powerful in the fiction written by Ozick and Roth in the early 1960s, has been muted in their subsequent work. Indeed, their memoirs of the 1980s suggest that their later careers have been dedicated to exorcising that early influence. Although Roth is by no means a literary "redskin" compared with, say, Norman Mailer, he continues the redskin tradition of disavowing "sissy" influences. His fiction, I believe, tells a different tale, but Roth has tried hard to create an autobiographical legend of emancipation from 1950s lower–middle-class Jewish respectability. This effort at liberation has become as much his signature as Sherwood Anderson's comparable legend a half-century earlier of liberation by art from stifling small-town philistinism. Ozick tells a rather different story of her development. As she constructs her autobiographical myth, her decisive move is from the false (Western, Gentile) religion of art to the ancestral (Jewish) affirmation of law and covenant. In her well-known essay "Toward a New Yiddish" (1970), Ozick calls for a specifically Jewish writing that affirms the law and steers clear of what she calls "idolatry," which includes the Jamesian cult of art. Ozick has not confined herself to the narrowly didactic writing that her call for a "liturgical" literature would seem to demand. But since *Trust*, she has substituted a midrashic kind of writing for the lapidary-mandarin gestures of late James and European high modernism. Still, James remains too powerful a presence to be wholly exorcised. An example is *The Cannibal Galaxy*. This work might not have come into being in its present form but for the example of James's "The Beast in the Jungle."[21]

James's shadow continues to haunt Roth's fiction as well. Consider even *The Counterlife* (1987), in which Roth appears to have broken free of traditional modes of mimesis. Here he chooses instead to experiment with narrative methods associated with postmodernists like Borges and Calvino and contemporary Central Europeans like Kundera. Notwithstanding Roth's adventurousness in that novel, however, *The Counterlife* remains traditionally Jamesian in its arrangement of broad oppositions of manners and morals. Basel, New York, Jerusalem, London— Roth's Zuckerman is all over the map, but each new setting makes possible large dialectical oppositions of idea and image. Indeed, it is James's strong opposition of art and life that is his most pervasive legacy to Roth and the preoccupation that links Roth to Ozick. James's late stories of literary acolytes and masters are his central legacy to both.[22] The influence of the stories can be traced in Roth's *The Ghost Writer* (1979) and Ozick's *The Messiah of Stockholm*, the latter dedicated to Roth. In Roth's novel, E. I. Lonoff is the literary idol and spiritual father of young Nathan Zuckerman. He is also a Jamesian artist whose life is consecrated to art. Lonoff's asceticism is the despair of his wife, the ironically named Hope. Of course, Nathan must rebel against this Jamesian self-abnegation, but Roth himself has written a tale that honors James in its method and tone. Nathan's prying and snooping are straight out of "The Aspern Papers," and the theme of the complex, comical relation of acolyte to master derives from any number of Jamesian tales of writers from the 1880s and 1890s. These include "The Lesson of the Master," "The Middle Years," and "The Figure in the Carpet."[23]

In the first full-length study of Cynthia Ozick, Joseph Lowin undertakes to account for Ozick's dedication of *The Messiah of Stockholm* to Roth: "It is not Roth the novelist to whom Ozick is paying homage but rather Roth the editor."[24] Lowin refers to

Roth's editorship of the Penguin Books paperback series "Writers from the Other Europe." That series includes a translation of Bruno Schulz's masterpiece *The Street of Crocodiles*, and Ozick's novel turns on a search for "The Messiah," a manuscript that was lost when Schulz was gunned down by Nazis in 1942. Thus Ozick the novelist shares the intention of Roth the editor of rescuing a murdered Polish-Jewish writer from oblivion. It would seem to make sense, then, to explain Ozick's dedication of *The Messiah of Stockholm* to Roth in relation to his series editorship, especially since Ozick has expressed disdain for the fiction of Jewish ethnicity with which Roth is usually associated. Yet there remain semblances between Roth and Ozick's fictions, notably between *The Ghost Writer* and *The Messiah of Stockholm*. These parallels suggest a firm affinity that links both works to Henry James.

For example, both novels have as their main character a literary man (Zuckerman a novelist, Lars Andemening a newspaper reviewer) who looks to a European-born Jewish literary master as a father-figure. (Zuckerman's Lonoff is asked only to be a literary mentor, whereas Andemening imagines that Bruno Schulz is his biological father.) Moreover, in both novels a writer from a society largely untouched by the Holocaust (the United States, Sweden) fantasizes a relationship with a European-Jewish writer. (Lars focuses on Schulz, Zuckerman on Amy Bellette, imagined by young Nathan to be Anne Frank somehow mysteriously alive after the concentration camp years.) The patterns of discipleship within these fictions reproduce patterns outside—that is, in the authors of these fictions. Each narrative bears witness to its creator's admiration for a great European-Jewish precursor. Schulz is a clear influence on Ozick's conception and style in her *Messiah*, and the Kafka of "The Hunger Artist" is the major influence (apart from Henry James) on Roth's story. Both novels grow out of the complex affinity of a later American-Jewish writer: Schulz was murdered by the Nazis, and Kafka had foreseen in his fiction the imminent destruction of his world.

But what do Schulz and Kafka have to do with Henry James? Certainly James is not the only writer to have made fiction out of the moral ambiguity of the artistic vocation. Joyce, Mann, Gide, and others have made the plight of the artist almost a cliché of modern fiction. Indeed, *The Ghost Writer* might plausibly be read as a *Künstlerroman* indebted chiefly to Joyce's *Portrait of the Artist as a Young Man*. Still, James's stories and novellas of the literary life do seem a more pervasive presence in *The Ghost*

Writer and even in *The Messiah of Stockholm* than does the fiction of his modernist and postmodernist successors. James's presence in *The Ghost Writer* is pointedly explicit: Zuckerman even stands on tiptoe on top of a volume of James's stories (including "The Middle Years") to eavesdrop on an intimate conversation between Lonoff and Amy Bellette. The James connection may be less obvious in Ozick's *Messiah*, but here, too, James's presence is evident in a number of details and emphases. Perhaps the most suggestive examples are Lars's anxious search for some obscure secret and a pervasive haunting of the present by the past.

IV

But the basic question remains: Why has Henry James meant so much to these Jewish writers? Why not Melville or Twain or Faulkner? Irving Howe's famous 1972 attack on Roth points to one answer. Howe argues forcefully that Roth stands outside the main tradition of Jewish-American writing. In his view, Roth's sexual comedies represent the end of the line; they offer evidence of the exhaustion of a once vital kind of writing and mode of feeling.[25] Howe's argument is challenging. Even Roth's admirers must find it hard not to agree that his writing shows few traces of the immigrant sensibility Howe defines as *the* Jewish tradition. It is not simply a question of Roth's subjects but of a structure of feeling to be found everywhere in Malamud and in large parts of Bellow—like the Napoleon Street section of *Herzog* and the story "The Old System."

But is it truly disastrous for a work of art to come at the end of a tradition? Beckett and Borges make that sense of an ending the basis of very significant literary art. Indeed, James, too, was an end-of-the-line writer. He appeared at the end of the New England-Protestant genteel tradition. He then dealt with its exhaustion, as Santayana says, not by working out a new, alternative position (as his brother William did) or by recovering an old attitude (as Santayana himself did in renouncing his Boston Brahmin world in favor of an old Mediterranean Catholicism). Rather, Henry James dealt with the exhaustion of his inherited tradition by applying an unblinking moral realism. He coped with the cultural impasse by looking more deeply into it than did any of his contemporaries. He analyzed modern man's moral problems, but he did not escape them.

Roth and Ozick offer alternative modes of responding to the exhaustion of the tradition as suggested by Howe. Ozick seems the more un-Jamesian in her disposition to go behind the present to recover a lost religious and cultural tradition. That tradition, however, is not Howe's inasmuch as it skips over second-generation literary Jewishness (a mix of Yiddish, late Tolstoi, and memories of working-class immigrant life) to recover Judaism itself. Roth, on the other hand, is the lonely dialectician struggling to define himself (as did James) without any formulated belief system or ideology. Different as they are, however, both Roth and Ozick affirm their Jewishness and see themselves as continuators. Roth is no more an assimilationist or a "swinger" (Howe's misjudgment of him) than is Ozick. Howe has taken it upon himself to decide the vexing question: Who is a Jew? Roth and Ozick both elude his categories, and both seem to offer possibilities for the present that are more pertinent than Howe's piety of the 1930s.

It is important to understand the appeal of Henry James for these novelists of the middle generation. It is not enough to urge the snob appeal of a writer whose favorite characters are moral elitists and material millionaires. Instead, it is necessary to consider the lingering force of the "religion of art" that had replaced radical politics for Jewish writers of the post-war, post-immigrant generation. In Ozick the attraction of this religion of art can be seen in her obsessive struggle against it. Roth's attitude toward art, however, has become increasingly celebratory since the aggressive impiety of *Portnoy's Complaint*. Roth's development in particular reveals how, for writers of the American 1950s, aesthetic invention and freedom may be the only positives to survive the deauthorization of long-held cultural beliefs and institutions. Indeed, that liberating process has been a motif of recent decades.

It is clearly a long way from the Gabe Wallach of *Letting Go* to the Nathan Zuckerman of *The Counterlife* twenty-five years later. But the hypothetical status of Nathan's character and of what happens to him in the later novel are only the most recent forms of the emptiness that is Gabe Wallach's defining trait. In *Letting Go* the "solution" for that emptiness is summed up in a bleak notion of *maturity* Roth had absorbed in the Eisenhower years. The great question (the grand Jamesian theme) is freedom. Is it possible, Roth's characters were asking, to create an actuality that matches the requirements of our imaginations? Roth's own provisional answer in the early 1960s was that people ought to let go of their romantic notions about life and take hold as grown-up, responsible adults. But his characters turned out to lack the energy and competence to change their lives in a positive direction. Hence *Letting Go* proved a dismally pessimistic novel.

In more recent years Roth has appeared to renounce the gloom and pessimism of *Letting Go* and *When She Was Good*. But he has rendered his fiction more playful and inventive only by shifting his hopes and expectations from life itself to the counterlife of art. Freedom may be possible, but only in writing. As for the solution to the vexing problem of identity, it is not marriage or responsibility, says Roth, but invention, performance, art. The self *is* empty; at least that was no illusion. There is no substantial self, no essence; there is only the writing self. Roth the man is lost, as was James, in the steady production of books. His fictions alone offer ever-new constructions of Roth's "life as a man." I have suggested that his "true" account, *The Facts*, is only one version among many. Its artistry is confined by a greater responsibility to history than other Roth books, hence it is also one of his most anemic.

From this point of view it is easier to understand Roth's quarrels with his literal-minded readers, Jewish and non-Jewish, who insist his narcissistic heroes are fragments of Roth's own autobiography. No, he says, they are products of the imagination, which uses but is not bound by the materials of personal history. His quarrel with these readers repeats the famous quarrel between Henry James and H. G. Wells on the art of the novel. Roth's hypothesized counterlives suggest James's own highly intellectual approach to fiction, as revealed in *The Notebooks*. Roth's apologies for his art call to mind James's response to Wells's utilitarian-didactic-mimetic theory of the novel. James wrote to Wells: "It is art that *makes* life, makes interest, makes importance, for our consideration and application of these things, and I know of no substitute whatever for the force and beauty of its process."[26]

The supreme appeal of James will always be to the fineness of his moral sensibility. That sensibility has proved especially congenial to the generation that came of age amid the ruins of Marxism and other great ideological systems. Intellectuals of Irving Howe's generation always found James somewhat suspect. They were put off by his seemingly narrow focus on the private and personal and his lack of general ideas or an overall vision of history. But it was precisely James's reliance on individual consciousness and conscience that recommended him to the

1950s generation. James's individualism and his appeal to the artist's sensibility as final value have had a clear appeal for Roth. Indeed, Philip Roth looks increasingly like James's most distinguished, if most unlikely, continuator.[27] But these qualities appeal also to Ozick, who would, if she could, abjure aesthetic individualism in favor of the communal law. The point is that she cannot, and it is the quarrel between orthodoxy and art that makes up a great part of her interest as a writer.

James is now only one of many figures—others include Jewish writers and intellectuals like Gershom Scholem, Harold Bloom, and Bruno Schulz—with whom Ozick contends in working out her own vision. But so long as the idolatry of art retains its seductive appeal for Ozick, Henry James will remain the lion in her path. Ozick's memoir "The Lesson of the Master" closes on a note of admonition: "Rapture and homage are not the way. Influence is perdition."[28] Certainly the question of influence has been crucial in the fiction of American-Jewish writers. They have struggled toward defining their relationship to their multiple literary and cultural traditions. Their mentors include classic American writers, above all James; major British and Continental figures like Swift, Austen, Dickens, and Forster; American-Jewish precursors such as Bellow and Malamud; and European-Jewish masters, especially Kafka. These ghostly presences have enriched the work of Jewish writers like Ozick and Roth. For them, and writers like them, being subject to literary influences is as unavoidable as having a mother and father. Like biological parents, literary progenitors can be a problem. Both Roth and Ozick have shown that influence is not necessarily perdition.

Notes

1. Saul Bellow, *Humboldt's Gift* (New York: Avon, 1976), p. 3.

2. Philip Rahv's essays are reprinted in his *Literature and the Sixth Sense* (Boston: Houghton Mifflin, 1969).

3. Of course, Ezra Pound and T. S. Eliot were even earlier James advocates.

4. Sanford Pinsker writes: "For Jewish-American critics, a taste for James was at once a credential and a badge, a visible sign that they had left the un-Jamesian streets and kitchen table shouting sessions of Brooklyn forever." See his *The Uncompromising Fictions of Cynthia Ozick* (Columbia: University Press of Missouri, 1987), p. 21.

5. Lionel Trilling's essay on *The Princess Casamassima* is reprinted in his *The Liberal Imagination* (Garden City, NY: Doubleday, 1953), pp. 65–96, and his essay on *The Bostonians* is included in his *The Opposing Self* (New York: Viking Press, 1955), pp. 108–23. For a more detailed discussion of Trilling's

reading of *The Princess*, see Mark Krupnick's *Lionel Trilling and the Fate of Cultural Criticism* (Evanston, Ill.: Northwestern University Press, 1986), pp. 69–74.

6. Irving Howe's discussion of *The Bostonians* was published as the Introduction to the Modern Library edition (New York: Random House, 1956) of that novel. It was reprinted in Irving Howe, *Politics and the Novel* (New York: Horizon Press, 1957), pp. 182–99.

7. Philip Roth, *The Facts: A Novelist's Autobiography* (New York: Farrar, Straus and Giroux, 1988), pp. 115, 137.

8. Ibid., p. 157. James's "graduate-school authority" in the 1950s and early 1960s is manifest in William T. Stafford's collection of critical essays *Perspectives on James's The Portrait of a Lady* (New York: New York University Press, 1967). Included here are influential discussions of the novel by F. O. Matthiessen, Dorothy Van Ghent, Richard Chase, Rahv, and others.

9. Irving Feldman notes the Flaubert connection in his review of *Letting Go*, in *Commentary*, September 1962, pp. 273–74.

10. Bernard F. Rodgers, Jr. offers suggestive comments on connections between James's *Portrait* and Roth's novel in his *Philip Roth* (Boston: Twayne, 1978), pp. 56–58.

11. See reviews by David L. Stevenson and Eugene Goodheart reprinted in Harold Bloom, ed., *Cynthia Ozick: Modern Critical Views* (New York: Chelsea House, 1986).

12. Cynthia Ozick, "The Lesson of the Master," in *Art and Ardor* (New York: Knopf, 1983), p. 293.

13. Ibid., p. 294.

14. Ibid., p. 295.

15. For details on the history of the composition of *Trust*, see Tom Teicholz's 1985 interview with Ozick in *Women Writers at Work: The Paris Review Interviews*, ed. George Plimpton (New York: Penguin Books, 1989).

16. Cynthia Ozick, preface to *Bloodshed and Three Novellas* (New York: Obelisk/Dutton, 1983), p. 5.

17. Cynthia Ozick, *Trust* (New York: Obelisk/Dutton, 1983), pp. 309–10.

18. Joseph Lowin suggests another possible derivation for "Vand." He says the name "may refer to the past participle of the German verb 'winden'—'to turn,' 'to bind.' Is Enoch one who has 'turned' to his tradition and 'bound' himself to it?" See Joseph Lowin, *Cynthia Ozick* (Boston: Twayne, 1988), p. 169.

19. Henry James, *The Notebooks* (New York: Oxford University paperback, 1961), p. 192.

20. Ozick, *Trust*, p. 586.

21. On the presence of James's "Beast" in Ozick's *The Cannibal Galaxy*, see the reviews of that novel by Edmund White and A. Alvarez, in Harold Bloom, ed., *Cynthia Ozick* (New York: Chelsea House, 1986), pp. 127–31 and pp. 133–35.

22. The most useful recent collection of James's tales of writers is *The Figure in the Carpet and Other Stories*, ed. Frank Kermode, in the Penguin Classics series (London, 1986).

23. For a fuller reading of *The Ghost Writer*, see Mark Krupnick, "The Middle Years," *Inquiry*, 15 October 1979, pp. 21–24. Roth summarizes and quotes from James's "The Middle Years" on pages 141–47 of the Fawcett paperback edition of his own novel. But Roth appears also to have been influenced by James's "The Author of Beltraffio." This is another tale in which an eager acolyte visits

his master's home and discovers that perfection of the work does not insure perfection of the life. Mark Ambient's wife despises his writing because it is pagan; Hope Lonoff resents her husband's work because it is not pagan enough. Lonoff never lets go; the basis of his art, as his wife complains, is not-living. In both stories the visiting acolyte becomes a catalyst for violent domestic happenings.

24. Lowin, *Cynthia Ozick*, p. 175. In an interesting article that appeared after I had completed the present essay, Sanford Pinsker also notes Ozick's dedication of *The Messiah of Stockholm* to Roth. Pinsker, too, brings together Ozick's *Messiah* and Roth's *The Ghost Writer*, but in terms of their "reimagining" Kafka and Anne Frank and Bruno Schulz, rather than in terms of their ties to Henry James. See Sanford Pinsker, "Jewish-American Literature's Lost-and-Found Department: How Philip Roth and Cynthia Ozick Reimagine Their Significant Dead," *Modern Fiction Studies* 35 (Summer 1989): 223–35.

25. Irving Howe's essay "Philip Roth Reconsidered" originally appeared in *Commentary*, December 1972, pp. 69–77. It is reprinted in Howe's collection *The Critical Point* (New York: Horizon, 1973), pp. 137–57.

26. *Henry James and H. G. Wells: A Record of Their Friendship and Their Debate on the Art of Fiction*, eds. Leon Edel and Gordon N. Ray (London: Rupert Hart-Davis, 1959), p. 267.

27. I agree with David Denby, who writes: "The Zuckerman books are a brilliant, arduous, and relentlessly ironic investigation of the relations of art and life, perhaps the most brilliant we've had in American literature since the stories of Henry James." See David Denby, "The Gripes of Roth," *The New Republic*, 21 November 1988, p. 40.

28. Ozick, *Art and Ardor*, p. 297.

The Metamorphosis of the Classics:
John Barth, Philip Roth, and the
European Tradition

CLAYTON KOELB

JOHN Barth describes in an essay his literary beginnings as an undergraduate at Johns Hopkins. He mentions that the "freight of literature" he took on as a young man included "Faulkner, Scheherazade, Joyce, Cervantes, and Kafka."[1] We know a great deal about how several of these figures affected him, far less about the others. Scheherazade appears both as a character in his fiction and a subject in his critical writing. Joyce and Cervantes serve as paradigmatic figures in several of his essays, so we know well enough how they affected him—or at least how he thought they affected him. The mention of Kafka, however, is tantalizing and a bit frustrating, because Barth never does tell us exactly wherein lay Kafka's importance for his literary beginnings. Unlike Philip Roth, who has produced a substantial volume of material on and around Kafka, Barth has remarkably little to say outright about this seminal writer. It is not that he says nothing about Kafka but rather that what he does say is uninformative.[2] Furthermore, none of Barth's major fictions is directly comparable to any Kafka story in the way that *The Breast* is comparable to "The Metamorphosis." In addition, Barth's style is nothing like Kafka's. The reader can only conclude that the effect of Kafka on the young Barth must have been powerful, since he cites it so prominently. Yet its traces in Barth's mature fiction are simply not to be found in those places where we normally look for them.

I

Barth never uses Kafka as a source the way he uses Greek mythology, the *Thousand and One Nights*, or even *Tristram Shandy*. From that point of view one should not try to make a

108

case for any significant literary borrowing. A case can be made, however, for another sort of influence; this one did not prompt Barth to borrow Kafka's material but rather taught him how he might profitably borrow material from others. Indeed, it is instructive to compare the ways in which Kafka and Barth transform the classics or pieces of classics into new fictions.

One Kafka story that reveals this method is also one that could well have caught the attention of someone like Barth, who was also so interested in Cervantes. It is called "The Truth about Sancho Panza." In this very short tale the narrator explains that Sancho was afflicted by a "demon, whom he later called Don Quixote," and whom he was able to divert by "feeding him a great number of romances of chivalry and adventure." The demon Quixote

> thereupon set out, uninhibited, on the maddest exploits, which, however, for the lack of a preordained object, which should have been Sancho Panza himself, harmed nobody. A free man, Sancho Panza philosophically followed Don Quixote on his crusades, perhaps out of a sense of responsibility, and had of them a great and edifying entertainment to the end of his days.[3]

Every reader familiar with *Don Quixote* will recognize immediately two things: (1) Kafka knows the story as Cervantes told it and understands what it was about; and (2) Kafka blissfully— and productively—ignores one of the most fundamental features of the novel. Sancho is the hero of Kafka's story, whereas the Don turns out to be a troublesome spiritual force dwelling *inside* Sancho. This reversal more than inverts the relationship described by Cervantes; it completely reimagines it as a matter initially and entirely internal to a single consciousness.

Kafka also reimagines the issue of reading, which is so important to Cervantes's novel. The acts of reading that are the cause of all the hero's difficulties in *Don Quixote* become the solution to the hero's problems in Kafka's story. The powerful influence of chivalric romances is presented as a kind of illness by Cervantes. Here that influence acts as a cure to Kafka's Sancho by exorcising his demon—that is, his reading part.[4] The powerful texts that overwhelm the reader Quixote do not do so to the reader Sancho. The latter stands apart from his reading self and lets it go its own way "uninhibited." We also recognize that Kafka is, in a real sense, doing this very same thing with his own reading of *Don Quixote*. Instead of trying to integrate the text into himself, Kafka lets his reading go off as it were on its own, uninhibited by any obligation to the author's intention.

At times Kafka conceived of reading in a more traditional and less "uninhibited" way, but he very often also did what he depicts Sancho doing. He takes a classic text and empties it of its original meaning so that he can refill it with his own. He does this, for example, when he tells the story of the building of the Tower of Babel in "The City Coat of Arms"; there he notes at the outset that the preparations for the construction included hiring a number of "interpreters." Anyone with the slightest familiarity with the Bible realizes that interpreters ought to be the one thing the Tower builders would not need, because the story is presented as an explanation for the origin of the "confusion of tongues." By introducing interpreters, he makes clear he is ignoring the clear and unmistakable intention of his intertext. He does the same thing when he revises the story of Odysseus and the Sirens, for his Ulysses has wax stuffed in his ears when bound to the mast. The central point of the adventure in Homer's poem is that the hero gets to hear the fatal song without suffering the consequences. Homer's hero has no wax in his ears.

This brief look at one of Kafka's common strategies (the producing of writing by lethetic reading)[5] suggests the technique I think Barth may have learned from his Bohemian precursor. We see Barth using this same strategy in his encounter with world classics of various kinds, including the Bible and Homer. The story collection published in 1968 as Lost in the Funhouse provides a number of excellent examples. The most striking is probably "Glossolalia." This little prose poem obviously calls up the classical tradition by presenting fictional situations derived from mythology and both the Old and New Testaments. Its most important intertext, however, is never mentioned.

"Glossolalia" offers six paragraphs, each of which provides a different example of "speaking in tongues," yet that concept requires broad interpretation to fit the circumstances reported. There are six different speakers, whom the author obligingly identifies in an "Author's Note" added to the second American edition. He lists them as "Cassandra, Philomela, the fellow mentioned by Paul in the fourteenth verse of his first epistle to the Corinthians, the Queen of Sheba's talking bird, an unidentified psalmist employing what happens to be the tongue of a historical glossolalist (Mme Alice LeBaron, who acquired some fame in 1879 for her exotic inspirations in the 'Martian' language), and the author."[6] Barth's special perspective on this material emerges gradually, because he lets Cassandra and Philomela give more or less standard versions of their stories as we know them from classical sources. When he comes to Crispus, however, this "fellow mentioned by Paul" has a different tale to tell from the one we might expect:

> I Crispus, a man of Corinth, yesterday looked on God. Today I rave. What things my eyes have seen can't be scribed or spoken. All think I praise His sacred name, take my horror for hymns, my blasphemies for raptures. The holy writ's wrongly deciphered, as beatitudes and blessings; in truth those are curses, maledictions, and obscenest commandments. So be it. (LF, p. 111)

Crispus is indeed mentioned by Paul in I Cor. 1:14, but the passage most relevant to Barth's text is chapter (not verse) 14. The apostle addresses the issue of glossolalia directly in this chapter. It is clear from the attention he gives the topic that it was of considerable importance to the fledgling community of Christians. Paul is evidently concerned that the practice of speaking in tongues had taken too prominent a position in the life of the Corinthian church, displacing the more community-oriented activity of preaching. The trouble with glossolalia, Paul says, is that it is very hard to interpret:

> So if you in your ecstatic speaking utter words no one can understand, how will people know what you are saying? You will be talking to the empty air! There are probably ever so many different languages in the world, each with its own meaning. So if I do not know the meaning of the language, I shall seem to the man who is speaking to be a foreigner, and he will seem to me to be one too. So since you are ambitious for spiritual endowments, you must try to excel in ways that will do good to the church. Therefore, the man who can speak ecstatically should pray for the power to explain what he says. (14:9–13)

The apostle goes on to recommend that when members of the Christian brotherhood assemble, speaking in tongues "be limited to two or three people at the most" and that someone should be present to "explain what [each speaker] says" (14:27).

Barth presents in his Crispus a glossolalist who does know how to interpret his ecstatic utterance, but one who is unable because of his glossolalia to communicate his interpretation to others. Those who are able to communicate and offer interpretations offer only wrong ones. They assume that human contact with divinity is good for humans. That is the assumption Paul makes: "Anyone who speaks ecstatically does himself good" (14:4). Barth's fiction subverts this traditional and optimistic understanding of contact with divinity. He does so by allowing his reader the privilege of direct access to Crispus's message and presenting it as an assertion of horror. The glossolalist babbles because contact with divinity is an experience of unspeakable ghastliness and unsuited to human speech. Even Holy Scripture, we learn, is the same sort of babble universally misinterpreted in precisely the same way. Crispus resembles Cassandra much more than the Christian community would want to admit. Like her, he has gained from this experience the power to speak the truth. Again, like her, he finds no one believes what he is saying.

The "Crispus" paragraph of "Glossolalia" explicitly directs the reader to find in I Cor. its intertext, but in doing so it swerves radically from that intertext's evident intention. It takes the biblical text "seriously" by accepting as genuine the notion that ecstatic speech results from intimacy with God. Yet it reverses the valorization of that intimacy. The Crispus of I Cor. undergoes a radical metamorphosis—from a bearer of good news into a messenger of the worst possible news. His art, like Philomela's, is no hymn to beauty but the revelation of evil. Just as Kafka has ignored the fundamental narrative concept governing the building of the Tower of Babel in Genesis, so does Barth ignore an essential feature of Paul's presentation of speaking in tongues. In neither case can one properly think of the process at work as simple misreading, because the material at issue is not subject to misinterpretation. Even the most casual reader always gets it right. Kafka and Barth get it "wrong," however, because they have chosen to do so.

Barth goes even further with this game of oblivious reading[7] in "Glossolalia." There is another intertext present in these six paragraphs only as a rhythmic pattern. It is "the only verbal sound-pattern identifiable by anyone who attended American public schools prior to the decision of the U. S. Supreme Court in the case of *Murray v. Baltimore School Board* in 1963" (*LF*, p. xi). Each of the six glossolalists matches exactly the stress pattern of the Lord's Prayer. In so doing, each confirms the opinion offered by the sixth glossolalist, "the author":

Ill fortune, constraint and terror, generate guileful art; despair inspires. The laureled clairvoyants tell our doom in riddles. Sewn in our robes are horrid tales, and the speakers-in-tongues enounce atro-

cious tidings. The prophet-birds seem to speak sagely, but are shriek-
ing their frustration. The senselessest babble, could we ken it, might
disclose a dark message, or prayer. (*LF,* p. 112)

The reference to the "senselessest babble" points the reader to
the "Martian" text of the fifth glossolalist, a passage apparently
lacking any semantic content whatever. (It begins "Ed' pélut',
kondó nenóde, ímba imbá imbá," and continues in that vein.)
When examined closely, however, this babble discloses the
sound-shadow of a text saturated with complex and culturally
powerful meanings.

But of course Crispus, too, is uttering the same shadow-prayer.
That fact adds a significant complication to his explicit contention that the "beatitudes and blessings" of Scripture are in reality
curses and maledictions. Who is really "deciphering wrongly"
here? Now that we examine the case more closely, we might
suspect that Crispus is the guilty party: his denunciation of apparent blessings as actual maledictions is revealed as itself a
form of blessing. At the same moment that Crispus is denying
that he utters hymns, he utters a hymn. His "dark message"
might after all be a prayer.

This is a comforting reading of Crispus's message, but it is
subject to a variety of objections. First of all, one could argue
that Crispus is really quite consistent. He had, after all, declared
that holy writ is marked by curses and maledictions wrongly
interpreted. He also had stated that the Lord's Prayer here invoked is no hymn at all but rather another misinterpreted blasphemy. The spectral presence of the prayer in Crispus's speech
does not so much deny as confirm his contention. Its text no
longer says, "'Our Father, which art in heaven,' [but] I Crispus,
a man of Corinth . . ." Furthermore, the total effect of "Glossolalia" is to empty the Lord's Prayer of its meaning and to transform
it into a series of "atrocious tidings" quite devoid of comfort.
The overwhelming message of Barth's piece is, as he suggested
himself, that "the discovery of an enormous complexity beneath
a simple surface may well be more dismaying than delightful"
(*LF,* p. xi).

There is no easy justification for preferring the reading *in bono*
or that *in malo,* and that may be the most disturbing complexity
to be found beneath the surface of "Glossolalia." The same text
may be read as good news or bad news, as a "dark message" or
as prayer, without altering a single iota of the document. Barth
plays Crispus and the rest against the Lord's Prayer in such a

way as to let "surface" and "depth" come into alarming conflict even as they seem to support each other. Do these six paragraphs accept the authority of the Lord's Prayer? or do they reject it utterly? On the formal level, they pace out the pattern of its stresses with pious regularity, while their semantic content severely undermines the prayer's explicit values. Philomela "warbles for vengeance" according to the same verbal music in which the reverent supplicant proposes to forgive those who trespass against us. Does a "surface" of vengeance hide a "depth" of forgiveness? Or, is that forgiveness merely the exhausted shadow of a set of rejected values?

"Glossolalia" stages a scene of reading in which the discovery of a classical "model" controlling the formal structure of an aggressively modern fiction is at least as disquieting as it is enriching. The materials of tradition have been put to a very untraditional use. One has to wonder whether the tradition is invoked to tap its spiritual power or to divest it of all power and turn it into an empty form. This is the same question that arises when one attempts to evaluate the relation between Kafka's stories and their classical intertexts. For Kafka's careful dismantling of these intertexts is at once both an act of violence and a gesture of reverence. The parable of Sancho Panza suggests just this ambivalence, as Sancho wants both to keep his demon Quixote and to be rid of him. Sancho finds a way to keep him, but with enough distance so that Quixote does no harm. The resulting situation is stable and happy. Barth's "Glossolalia" presents the same ambivalence but puts it in a harsher light. The demon will not stay safely apart but always threatens to overwhelm every attempt to decipher the holy writ of classical texts. This is due to the demon being the driving force behind every act of reading. We may sometimes think the possessing demon that inspires ecstatic utterance is no demon but a god, and we may be right. But we can never be sure.

The notion of ecstatic speech clearly is central and relevant to the relationship between a storyteller and the story being told. Certainly this relationship is one of Barth's favorite topics. The story (especially a traditional or "classical" one) has an existence apart from the narrator, who may be thought of as simply the medium through which the tale propagates itself. The self of the narrator is so taken over by the narrative that the person tends to vanish into the story, to become in effect nothing but story. This occurs with literal precision in the case of another glossolalist in *Lost in the Funhouse*, the narrator of "Menelaiad." This narrator is Menelaus "more or less" (*LF,* p. 127). He is not an actual person but only a voice: "This isn't the voice of Menelaus; this voice *is* Menelaus, all there is of him" (*LF,* p. 127). He is, at the time the tale is told (which is now), a textual remnant of the Homeric poems, a *Menelaiad* that asks to be seen as a minor, fragmentary sibling of the *Iliad* and *Odyssey.* Menelaus actually makes the invitation explicit when he foretells to Telemachus his father's homecoming and recounting of his adventures: "Beside that night's fabrication this will stand as Lesser to Great Ajax" (*LF,* p. 160).

Barth's appropriation of Homer is no less radical or disturbing than his demonic reading of the Bible in "Glossolalia." There the Lord's Prayer undergoes a multiple metamorphosis into the dire tales of Cassandra, Crispus, and the rest. Here the heroic epics change into an antiheroic lament on the price to be paid for the "absurd, unending possibility of love" (*LF,* p. 162). As befits a tale generated out of the transformation of one text into another, "Menelaiad" presents love's possibility as arising out of an unending series of transformations. Indeed, the idea of metamorphosis so dominates this fiction that the reader, and the narrator himself, cannot be sure that the narrator and all his various narratees are not shifted versions of the arche-shapeshifter Proteus. Once Menelaus grasps Proteus on the beach at Pharos, he is prodded toward the realization that "all subsequent history is Proteus, making shift to slip me" (*LF,* p. 160).

"Menelaiad" demonstrates dramatically that (hi)story is a series of metamorphoses, not least by showing itself to be a kind of manic parody of Homeric plot and style. The central formal feature of Barth's fiction is the devotion *ad absurdum* to the structural principle of retrospective narration we are familiar with from the *Odyssey.* Much of Homer's poem, we recall, is taken up with the story of how Odysseus told the story of his adventures to the court of Alcinous, king of the Phaeacians. Barth gives us the story of how the Menelaus-voice tells itself (or us) the story of how Menelaus told to Telemachus and Peisistratus the story of how Menelaus told Helen aboard ship out of Pharos the story of how Menelaus told Proteus the story of how Menelaus told Eidothea the story of how Menelaus told Helen in her bedroom at Troy the story of why Helen chose Menelaus for her husband. The seven embedded stories are kept separate by what soon becomes a bewildering array of quotation marks and *inquits:*

"\'\'\'\"Speak!" Menelaus cried to Helen on the bridal bed,' I reminded Helen in her Trojan bedroom," I confessed to Eidothea on the beach,' I declared to Proteus in the cavemouth," I vouchsafed to Helen on the ship,' I told Peisistratus at least in my Spartan hall," I say to whoever and where- I am. And Helen answered: "\'\'\'\"Love!"/"/"/"

"Love" may be the answer, but who is saying it? We may respond, to put it briefly, that Menelaus says Helen says it. But we must remind ourselves that there are seven Menelauses and at least three Helens implicated in the act. Each of those Helens and Menelauses is a temporally distinct entity, and all are separated from the others by a decisive gap of time. No wonder the Menelaus-voice in the outermost frame exclaims: "I'm not the man I used to be" (*LF*, p. 143). He never was, and none of us ever can be. The device of retrospective narrative, however, brings these temporally distinct selves together in a moment of recursive memory where recollection is embedded within recollection like a set of Chinese boxes. The narrative "I" is always Menelaus, but "Menelaus" is revealed to be a shifting concept. The first-person pronoun is exposed as exactly what linguistics claims it to be, a "Shifter" with a highly context-sensitive meaning.

The hero of "Menelaiad" is this slippery pronoun, an entity quite as shifty as Proteus or the "man of many turns" (*polytropos*), Odysseus. Barth's story thus takes the narrative situation of the *Odyssey*'s central section, in which the hero narrates himself, and makes it into the object of attention. The *Odyssey* eventually returns to a frame in which the hero is no longer his own narrator, but Barth's fiction does not. It constantly shifts narrative frames, to be sure, but in none of them do we find a narrator-separator separable from the self that is narrated. One might suppose that the result would be a text dominated by the presence of that self, but quite the opposite happens. The recursion of Menelaus quoting Menelaus quoting Menelaus, and so on to a depth of seven levels, makes of the narrator an ungraspable, undefinable voice that is remarkable mainly for its lack of *character*. Menelaus would like to be able to pin himself down, but he can't. He cannot even accept that Helen actually sees something in him: "Helen he could hold; how hold Menelaus? To love is easy; to be loved, as if one were real, on the order of others: fearsome mystery! Unbearable responsibility! To her, *Menelaus* signified something recognizable, as *Helen* him. Whatever was it?" (*LF*, p. 151). Menelaus's difficulty is that he wants so much to define himself that he fails to recognize the absolute necessity of others, of an external frame, for the process of definition.

Barth's text, though not his protagonist, recognizes that necessity. It therefore presents itself as a metamorphosis of the Homeric classics. The Menelaus-voice is thoroughly saturated by Homeric rhetoric: however, like the principle of retrospective narration, it is driven *ad absurdum* by the endless reflections of Barth's literary funhouse. Imitation quickly becomes pure parody. The sea is hardly ever simply the sea; it is rather "the pastures of the squid" or "Poseidon's finny fief" (*LF*, p. 142). Even the heavy artillery of epic discourse, the extended simile, makes its obligatory appearance:

> As a sea-logged voyager strives across the storm-shocked country of the sole, loses ship and shipmates, poops to ground on alien shingle, gives over struggling, and is whisked in a dream-dark boat, sleep-skippered, to his shoaly home, there to wake next morning with a wotless groan, wondering where he is and what fresh lie must save him, until he recognizes with a heart-surge whither he's come and hugs the home-coast to sweet oblivion. So Menelaus, my best guess, flayed by love, steeved himself snug in Helen's hold, was by her hatched and transport, found as it were himself in no time Lacedae-moned, where he clings still stunned. (*LF*, p. 160)

The comparison is Homeric in every way. It is not only a travesty of Homer's language, it is a reference to Homer's story of the return of Odysseus to Ithaca, a story Menelaus ought not to know just yet but does know anyway, since he is really a transformed fragment of it: "For all we know, we're but stranded figures in Penelope's web, wove up in light to be uncovered in darkness" (*LF*, p. 145). And then, of course, we are to be wove up again somewhere in another part of the funhouse.

II

Philip Roth's *The Breast* (1972) might also have been titled "Lost in the Funhouse." It is a story wherein the writer takes a trip through a verbal funhouse in which all the mirrors reflect greatly enlarged and distorted images of himself. Most prominent among those distorted self-images is one that is contrived to look like a burlesque version of Gregor Samsa, hero of Kafka's most famous story. Indeed, the more one looks at Roth's story, the more it looks like a zany, yet somehow also serious revision of Kafka's "The Metamorphosis."[8] What is zany about it is perhaps obvious, but the seriousness of it becomes clear only when the reader understands the fundamental nature of Roth's imitation of his European model. For the American writer presents more than an outrageous parody of the European's plot; he offers as well a strikingly perceptive analog of Kafka's characteristic mode of narrative invention.

The narration portrays itself explicitly as a reaction to Kafka's "Metamorphosis." The hero, a professor of comparative literature named David Kepesh,[9] wonders if his transformation into a giant breast is not simply a delusion inspired by the books he has taught for so long: "They put the idea in my head. I don't mean to sound whimsical, but I'm thinking of my European Literature course. Teaching Gogol and Kafka every year—teaching 'The Nose' and 'Metamorphosis.'"[10] Roth himself had taught a course on Kafka at the University of Pennsylvania in the early 1970s, just at the time this story was being composed. He had already displayed his substantial interest in Kafka in others of his narratives. He would shortly offer a fictionalized version of his own near obsession with the Bohemian writer in *The Professor of Desire* (1977). To say that Roth identified with Kafka is to extrapolate only slightly from the substantial evidence in the published work. *The Breast* quite openly demands that the reader see it as an imitation of Kafka's most famous work of fiction.

Roth, far from being embarrassed about engaging in this kind of mimicry, makes the act of imitation into one of the prominent themes of his story. Kepesh-the-breast describes himself as an extraordinarily adept mimic, developing to an extreme a talent he says he had "always had" (*BR*, p. 72). He concentrates on listening to recordings of Laurence Olivier playing Hamlet and Othello and "managed to memorize whole speeches that I could deliver with his intonation, rhythm, and interpretation" (*BR*, p. 71). He feels he is particularly successful with Othello's final speech: "I sounded remarkably like Olivier" (*BR*, p. 72). But he interrupts himself when he is struck by the thought that he might have an audience: "Come now, David, it is all too poignant and heartbreaking, a breast reciting 'And say besides, that in Aleppo once. . . .' You will send the scientists home in tears" (*BR*, p. 72). It is poignant—or funny, depending on your point of view. This is true in part because the locus of Othello's act of self-destruction is his very masculine breast, in part because of the dizzying succession of mimetic acts involved. Kepesh is imitating Olivier's imitation of Othello's imitation of himself (leaving out of account for the moment the mimetic interventions of Shakespeare and Roth as authors).

This lengthy chain puts into question any attempt to fix upon an origin to valorize as primary with respect to a "secondary" (and thus also inferior) imitation. The inclusion of Gogol's "Nose" in the description of Kepesh's European literature course performs the same gesture. We can no more identify "The Metamorphosis" or its author Kafka as an absolute origin for Roth's act of imitation than we can point to Olivier as the ultimate source of Kepesh's version of Othello. The boundary between Roth and the great writers of the past is effaced. The self of the author waxes to include his precursors. Attention is now focused on the chain of literary transformations, indeed on the very concept of "transformation" in both its literal and figurative senses. Kafka, to be sure, had done so as well, in that his title refers both to Gregor's literal metamorphosis and to the transformation that takes place in the life of his family. Roth takes the process one step further, however, by making his story explicitly a part of literary history. Where Kafka had elaborated the concept of the "metamorphosis of the metaphor," in Stanley Corngold's phrase,[11] Roth now presses on to the metamorphosis of "The Metamorphosis." In the process he transforms himself into a comic-opera version of Kafka and Gogol.

Kafka's influence on Roth is, however, more interesting and more fundamental than this borrowing of plot material. Roth, like Barth, appears to have learned from Kafka how to transform the texts of others into texts of one's own. Although it may not be evident, Roth actually follows very closely Kafka's procedure of transforming a commonplace trope into the generative moment of his fiction. Roth, however, follows a slightly more convoluted path. Kafka had taken expressions like "Du bist ein Ungeziefer" and "Kafka" and explored the possibilities, tensions, and energies that arise out of taking such expressions both literally and figuratively at the same time.[12] Roth also begins with a commonplace insult and with his name, but in ways that are perhaps not so easily recognizable. Roth's rhetorical moments are not directly derivable from the principal events of the plot. There is no common trope, for example, that deprecates a man by equating him with a female breast. But it is evident from the way in which Kepesh describes his transformation that this breast is itself a displaced figure for another sexual organ, the penis.

Kepesh's transformation begins with a discoloration of the "flesh at the base of my penis" (BR, p. 5). Although "the bulk of my weight is fatty tissue" (BR, p. 13), Kepesh's entire sensory apparatus is located in tissue that was formerly his penis:

> In that the apertures in the nipple provide me with something re-motely like a mouth and ears—at least I am able to make myself understood through my nipple, and, faintly, to hear what is going on around me—I myself had assumed at first that it was my head that had become my nipple. The doctors, however, hypothesize otherwise ... [and] now maintain that the wrinkled, roughened skin of the nipple—which, admittedly, is exquisitely sensitive to touch like no tissue on the face, including the mucous membrane of the lips—was formed out of the glans penis. So too the puckered pinkish areola that encircles the nipple and contains the muscle system that stiffens the nipple when I am aroused, is said to have metamorphosed from the shaft of the penis under the assault (some say) of a volcanic secretion from the pituitary of "mammogenic" fluid. (BR, p. 14)

And though Kepesh is outwardly transformed into our culture's very image of female sexuality, he inwardly maintains his origi-nal sexual orientation. The "nipple" is still very much a penis: it is "cylindrical in shape, projective five inches from my 'body'; it wants caressing: I just want her to squeeze me and suck me and lick me" (BR, p. 31), but only by a female. Kepesh is uninter-ested in having a male nurse perform these services, and he fantasizes about using it exactly as he would have his normally formed penis: "I want her to sit on me with her cunt!" (BR, p. 36). Kepesh's transformation is a slightly displaced version of a metamorphosis—in Kafka's manner—of the commonplace figural insult "You prick!"

Kepesh himself suggests this possibility in describing his reac-tion to the visit of his acquaintance and colleague, Arthur Schon-brunn. The visit precipitates a crisis because Schonbrunn is unable to contain his hilarity at the sight of Kepesh-turned-breast. In a letter written (but not sent) in response to Schon-brunn's note of apology, Kepesh waxes wroth. He suggests that the two of them might have something in common: "I fail to appreciate the enormous comedy of all this only because I am really more of an Arthur Schonbrunn than you are, you vain, narcissistic, dandified prick!" (BR, pp. 48–49). In other words, if Schonbrunn is a prick, Kepesh is more of a prick. This becomes literally true once we see the interchangeability of breast and penis in the figural economy of the story.

Roth also suggests another kind of rhetorical moment for his story, one that points rather disquietingly to Kepesh's participation in our common humanity. He addresses his audience near the end of his "lecture" as "my fellow mammalians" (BR, p. 77). Used by this character in this context, the term suddenly discloses itself, for all its connotation of scientific precision, as a trope, a metonymy, and a not-quite-tasteful one at that. The biological group to which we belong is designated by that one particular feature of our females. It is the part by which we have come to designate the whole, not just of our bodies but also of our biological class. We are forced to recognize that Kepesh-the-breast is the literal embodiment of that trope: he is the one among us with the strongest claim on the designation "mammalian" that anyone could ever have. He is the most mammalian creature that there ever was. He is *essentially* mammalian, and we cannot escape the possibility that his problems are unique only in their urgency. Kepesh has the right to claim a deep kinship with all the rest of us: *mamilla sum, mammalis nihil a me alienum puto.* It is grotesque, of course, and all the more so when we remember the phallic character of this breast. The term of address "my fellow mammalians" brings about a comic but at the same time earnest confrontation of the literal and the figurative. To the degree that we can "seriously" accept the breast as the token of our biological kinship, so must we "seriously" consider the Breast (Kepesh) as the metonymy of our community. Kepesh's audience (and Roth's) must consider the notion, at once silly and serious, repulsive and convincing, that we are all of us nothing but what he is.

Whether or not we care to see ourselves in these terms, however, we must surely see Kepesh-the-breast as an enormous sexual organ, and indeed a male organ at that. The displacement of penis into breast is more than an indication of a kind of fundamental erotic androgyny—though that element is surely there; it is primarily a device whereby the story can pursue the notion of a person turned into a pure instrument of desire.[13] Roth goes out of his way to set up the equation between Kepesh's affliction and a kind of absolute sexual desire. Kepesh tells us that, in the weeks just before the "incubation period" of his disease, "I began to find our lovemaking boring and pleasureless" (BR, p. 9). His waning erotic interest for his lady friend, Claire, wanes so far that "I just did not care at all about touching her or being touched" (BR, p. 10). It is the first symptom of his approaching transformation (though he knows this only retrospectively) that, all of a sudden, his desire rekindles itself in the most intense imaginable form:

> [It was] immediate sensual delight, purely tactile pleasure. Sex, not in the head, not in the heart, but excruciatingly in the epidermis of the penis, sex skin deep and ecstatic. In bed I found myself writhing with pleasure, clawing at the sheets and twisting my head and shoulders in a way I had previously associated more with women than with men, and women more imaginary than real. (BR, p. 10)

After the transformation takes place, Kepesh still has this capacity for sensual delight, but he can do nothing about it. As a huge, passive object, what is left of the subject in him is reduced almost entirely to *want*, to a great lack that he yearns to fill without knowing quite how. As it turns out, the solution Kepesh works out for his problem entails a further move into the domain of pure objecthood, as object of the admiring (or contemptuous) gaze of large audiences.

But even in this form of pure desire, as a thing that is nothing-but-sex-organ, gigantic and male, Kepesh must still be able to envision the possibility of some form of actual human sexual contact. We note that if he had been transformed into a penis "weighing in at one hundred and fifty-five pounds . . . and measuring, still, six feet in length" (BR, p. 12), this possibility would not exist. It is essential for Roth's story that the fantasies Kepesh harbors about fulfilling the gigantic longings of his gigantic sexual self be realizable by ordinary human females ("twelve- and thirteen-year-old girls . . . three, four, five, and six at a time" [BR, pp. 74–75]). It is essential because the story's principal theme centers on the possibility of fulfilling a huge sexual appetite by means of putting that appetite on display.

In this regard, the story is again very successfully imitative of Kafka. In the first place, we recognize in Kepesh's plan (perhaps actually carried out) to put himself on display an inverted version of the Hunger Artist. The version here no longer involves showing off an ascesis, the limitless suppression of appetite, but now the absolute satisfaction of an unrestrained appetite: "this, my friend, is the Land of Opportunity in the Age of Self-Fulfillment" (BR, p. 75). We might also recognize the slight indication that Kepesh is, in this act of narration, carrying out his plan. The words "Let me conclude the lecture . . ." (BR, p. 75) may be a joking reference to his professorial style of writing. They may also mean that Kepesh is actually giving a public lecture about himself in the manner of the ape Rotpeter in Kafka's "Report for an Academy." More than this is suggested though. We recognize in the entire fictional project the process of turning personal authorial concerns into the stuff of fiction by way of autonomasia—the literal reading of the personal name. Just as "The Metamorphosis" is very much about Franz Kafka, a man with the name of a verminous beast, so is *The Breast* about Philip Roth, a man with the name of the color of sexually aroused flesh.

Here is another connection to the voluble ape of the "Report for an Academy": Roth must have been struck by the similarity of the ape's name to his own. Furthermore, as an English speaker with some knowledge of German, Roth must have seen in the name "Rotpeter" the possibility of a figure of the authorial self, Rot(h) as penis (peter). And if we look at the way in which the transformation of Kepesh into the breast takes place, we find that it is a metamorphosis into "Roth" (red) as much as into anything else. The redness of the stain discoloring the base of Kepesh's penis is stressed: he describes it as "unmistakably red" (Roth's italics). Even the "two fine long reddish hairs . . . on the rim of my areola" that Kepesh identifies as his "antennae" (BR, p. 14) suggest the movement toward "Rot(h)." Significantly, before his transformation Kepesh had been "an emphatic brunette" (BR, p. 13) with "corkscrewed black pubic curls" (BR, p. 4). By becoming a potentially displayable sexual appetite, Kepesh becomes more like his author, and thus more "rot(h)" than he was before.

The Breast follows a very Kafka-like principle of rhetorical construction both in terms of its use of a logomimetic transformation of a commonplace trope and in its play on the name of the author. What makes the novella quite characteristically Roth and very unlike Kafka, though, is its central concern with the problem of a limitless sexual appetite. Certainly Kafka had problems of his own with his sexuality, but they were of a markedly different character from those of a Portnoy or Kepesh. For the Kepesh of *The Breast* the most urgent concern of life is what to do with his boundless desire. The only alternatives seem to him either to find ways to dampen or divert it or to devise a means to satisfy it. Kepesh realizes that the means to limitless satisfaction of his limitless longings lie ready-at-hand: all he has to do is sell himself, put himself on display, and the world will provide out of his audience an unending supply of women ready to minister to his lust:

> And we can find them, pal, you know that. If the Rolling Stones can find them, if Charles Manson can find them, we can find them too.

There will also be women who will want to open their thighs to something as new and thrilling as my nipple. We will be surprised by the number of women, married mothers among them, who will come knocking at the dressing-room door in their chinchillas. Well, we will just have to pick and choose, won't we, select according to beauty, good breeding, and lasciviousness. And I will be deliriously happy. (*BR*, p. 75)

Kepesh is, in his fantasy at any rate, as much figuratively Roth as he is literally *roth*. His display of himself is a dramatization of the process Roth apparently saw himself engaging in with novels like *Portnoy's Complaint* and *The Professor of Desire*. But Roth seems to have attained a distance on the act of artistic self-display that he does not quite allow Kepesh. There is, of course, considerable irony in the assertion, "I will be deliriously happy," particularly in that Kepesh is made to utter the words twice, as if he were trying to convince himself of their truth. There is every reason to believe that Kepesh's proposed career as a celebrity will lead to something other than delirious happiness: "'So you will not be taken on your own terms, ever, you know—this you must realize beforehand.' 'You mean, I'll always be a joke.' 'To many, yes. A joke. A grotesque. A charlatan. Of course'" (*BR*, p. 77). These words must have had a special astringency as they were written by the author of *Portnoy*, who must have at times felt that he had succeeded only in making his fictionalized self a public joke.

The full measure of Roth's irony is disclosed in an unexpected way by his closing his novella—rather abruptly—with Kepesh's quotation of Rilke's famous poem "Archaischer Torso Apollos" ("Archaic Torso of Apollo"). It is a gesture which is at once both stunningly silly and pretentious (given the circumstances) and extraordinarily apt. The silliness and pretension are quite deliberate, to be sure. Kepesh is (to misquote him slightly) "a vain, narcissistic, dandified Breast" who is also a professor of European literature. In addition, he wants to aggrandize himself by association not only with Kafka and Gogol but also with all the great names of modern literature. The aptness of the citation stems from the fact that Rilke's poem is also about a breast, and indeed a breast that has supplanted the rest of a human body. Like Kepesh, this antique Apollo has been transformed into nothing-but-breast, though in this case it is a question of an emphatically male torso and not a female mammary. The torso also resembles Kepesh in that, having no head, it would ostensibly be blind, though the poem asserts that the lack of eyes does not prevent the figure from having a gaze ("Schauen") that, paradoxically, blinds the beholder. Rilke's poem also makes pointed reference to the sexuality of the statue: it asserts the presence of a "smile" that "in the slight turn of the loins (im leisen Drehen der Lenden)" runs "to that middle, which carried procreation (in jener Mitte, die die Zeugung trug)."

Kepesh's recontextualizing of Rilke's poem also points up another similarity between Roth and Rilke's works: an adherence to a logomimesis characteristic of rhetorical constructions. A number of features of the "Archaischer Torso" are the direct result of the same kind of duplicitous reading that generates fantastic stories like "The Metamorphosis" and The Breast. Unfortunately, these features do not survive the process of translation. Where the English text, for example, alludes to the "legendary head" of the statue, the original has "unerhörtes Haupt." The word unerhört means both "unheard" (that is, not perceived by the ear) and "unheard of, amazing, shocking." Obviously, the statue's head is "unheard" in the literal sense, not only because it is absent but also because, being stone, it would not speak even if present. The poet supposed, though, that it would be figuratively "unerhört" and would amaze us with its beauty and nobility—if we had the chance to see it. Perhaps most pertinent of all is another meaning of "unerhört" that lies somewhere between the purely figurative "amazing" and the very literal "unheard"; that is the signification "disallowed, turned down," as a petition that is "not heard" by the authorities. The head of the statue has been "disallowed" to our experience. An even more arresting example of logomimesis occurs in the second line, which describes Apollo's eyeballs as "ripening." The figure makes far more sense in the original German, since the word for eyeball is "Augenapfel," literally "eye-apple." While we do not ordinarily think of eyes as "ripening," we do think that of apples, and Rilke's trope exploits the association. This Apollo's eyes matured in his head, the metaphor implies, as apples ripen on the trees.

Rilke's poem, like Roth's story, is centrally concerned with the question of seeing and being seen. Not only is Kepesh's great fantasy one of putting himself on display before an audience that will "fill Shea Stadium" (BR, p. 74), but he also is convinced that he is constantly being watched—by medical technicians and scientists if not by the general public, either "in an amphitheater" or "on closed-circuit television" (BR, p. 19). In other words, he cannot decide whether he wants to embrace or shun a future in which he is the object of strangers' gazes. He imagines he has found a kind of solution to this dilemma in the ending of Rilke's poem, the poet's single most famous sentence: "You must change your life (*Du mußt dein Leben ändern*)." Kepesh suggests that this "is not necessarily as elevated a sentiment as we all might once have liked to believe." He is proposing then the possibility of a reading of the poem radically different from the conventional one.

The analogy he proposes between his story and Rilke's description of the torso ("Perhaps my story . . . will at the very least illuminate Rilke's great lines for you in a fresh way") requires us to pay more attention to the literal level. When the poem says "there is no place / that does not see you," Kepesh's hopes and fears form the context and insist that the act of being "seen" is not just a figure. Nor is there anything figurative about the alteration in Kepesh's life, which has been as dramatic and physical a change as one could imagine. And if Kepesh does accept (or has accepted?) the supposed invitation of his friend to exploit his altered state by putting himself on exhibit (like a piece of statuary in a museum), he engages in a transformation that is nothing like the noble one usually thought to be intended by Rilke's final line.

Kepesh's narration suggests that changing one's life radically along the lines suggested by works of art may not lead to the happy results we would like to imagine. Rilke's poem seems to exhort the reader to set the classical perfection of the ancient torso as his model (and I use the male pronoun here advisedly). The statue says not only "Change your life" but also, implicitly, "Be like me." Kepesh has done so, though it was not an antique statue but a modern story, Kafka's "Metamorphosis," that he chose for his paradigm. Dr. Klinger says to Kepesh, as he might have said to Rilke, "The world is full of art lovers—so?" And Kepesh replies, as he might have replied to the statue, "So I took the leap. Beyond sublimation. I made the word flesh. I have out-Kafkaed Kafka" (*BR*, p. 73). And out-Rilked Rilke, too, of course. He has made Rilke's poem about the necessity of shaping one's life according to the model of a "breast" into an agenda and has carried it out. Roth has turned Rilke's "*Bug der Brust*" into his own "*Buch der Brust*."

The Breast is a story with the central theme of the metamorphosis of the European classics. Its protagonist is a man so imbued with the power of words, especially the words of modern

European writers like Kafka and Rilke, that he attains the ability to make those words flesh. But this transformation does not bring happiness: it produces anger. Kepesh becomes both "rot(h)" and wroth over what might be understood as the fulfillment of his sexual and literary fantasy. This acting out of the literal signifier, remarkable achievement though it may be, turns out to bring neither illumination nor dignity. *The Breast* serves as a focus for Roth's anger at the "failure of the word."[14] Tropes promise to enrich the world, to help us "change our lives" for the better. But an ignoble and all too worldly literal metamorphosis can undermine and eventually topple lofty figurative sentiments. Kepesh has out-Kafkaed Kafka and out-penised everybody, but the effect has only been to make him into a joke. He is so ridiculous that people like Schonbrunn cannot contain their laughter in his presence.

The transforming power of language, even the language of Roth's own name, has worked to undermine itself by allowing the literal to overwhelm the figurative, the vehicle to efface the tenor. "Roth" should be the name of a man, but the logomimetic languages of *The Breast* has not presented the man to the world, but only a rhetorical reading of the name's significance. Roth, as bearer of a name associated with sexuality (especially because of *Portnoy*) and a certain indignation (*Letting Go, Goodbye, Columbus*) have produced in *The Breast* a document of rhetorical self-fulfillment. As a writer, and an American—that is, a citizen of "the Land of Opportunity in the Age of Self-Fulfillment," he knows about these matters from the inside. *The Breast* is his silly/serious rendering of that knowledge.

Notes

1. "Some Reasons Why I Tell the Stories I Tell the Way I Tell Them Rather than Some Other Sort of Stories Some Other Way" in *The Friday Book* (New York: G. P. Putnam's Sons, 1984), p. 10.

2. Barth mentions Kafka a number of times in his famous essays—"The Literature of Exhaustion," for example—but he says nothing about him that would illuminate this issue. See *The Friday Book*, pp. 62–76.

3. Franz Kafka, *The Complete Stories*, ed. Nahum N. Glatzer (New York: Schocken, 1971), p. 430.

4. See Clayton Koelb, *Kafka's Rhetoric: The Passion of Reading* (Ithaca and London: Cornell University Press, 1989), pp. 91–92, for a discussion of Sancho's demon as his reading faculty.

5. This topic is treated in more depth in Clayton Koelb, "Kafka and the Sirens: Writing as Lethetic Reading" in *The Comparative Perspective on Litera-*

ture: *Approaches to Theory and Practice*, ed. Clayton Koelb and Susan Noakes (Ithaca and London: Cornell University Press, 1988), pp. 300–314. For a definition of "lethetic reading," see Koelb, *The Incredulous Reader: Literature and the Function of Disbelief* (Ithaca and London: Cornell University Press, 1984), pp. 28–40.

6. John Barth, *Lost in the Funhouse* (New York: Bantam Books, 1969), p. xi. Cited henceforth in the text as *LF*.

7. "Oblivious reading" is a concept first proposed in *The Incredulous Reader*, pp. 143–57.

8. There is already a substantial literature that takes note of the Roth-Kafka connection. See, for example, the following: Steven G. Kellman, "Philip Roth's Ghost Writer," *Comparative Literature Studies* 21 (Summer 1984): 175–85; Kellman, "Reading Himself and Kafka: The Apprenticeship of Philip Roth," *NKSA* 6 (June-December 1982): 25–33; George J. Searles, "Philip Roth's 'Kafka': A 'Jeu-ish American' Fiction of the First Order," *Yiddish* 4 (1982): 12–31; and Morton P. Levitt, "Roth and Kafka: Two Jews," in *Critical Essays on Philip Roth*, ed. Sanford Pinsker (Boston: G. K. Hall, 1982), pp. 245–54.

9. That is the same name as that of the hero of *The Professor of Desire*. Indeed, all the characters in *The Breast* reappear in *The Professor*, and one can see the former as a kind of fantastic "alternative future" for the world introduced in the latter. Roth even "sets up" the plot for his earlier story at the end of *The Professor* when Kepesh mentions his "fear of transformations yet to come" (*The Professor of Desire* [New York: Bantam, 1978], p. 248).

10. *The Breast* (New York: Holt, Rinehart and Winston, 1972), p. 55. Citations in the text to *BR* refer to this edition.

11. Stanley Corngold, "Kafka's *Die Verwandlung*: Metamorphosis of the Metaphor," *Mosaic* 3, no. 4 (1970): 91–106.

12. Such "rhetorical constructions" are discussed in detail in Clayton Koelb, *Inventions of Reading: Rhetoric and the Literary Imagination* (Ithaca and London: Cornell University Press, 1988).

13. In this respect, *The Breast* simply carries to the uttermost fantastic extreme the premise explored realistically in *The Professor of Desire*.

14. From the title of Richard Weisberg's *The Failure of the Word* (New Haven: Yale University Press, 1984).

Part 2
Reality's Voices and Languages

Origins, Language, and the Constitution of Reality: Norman Mailer's *Ancient Evenings*

JAMES M. MELLARD

> Yes, it is from Amon that we know our beginning.
> —Norman Mailer, *Ancient Evenings*

Aɴᴄɪᴇɴᴛ Evenings[1] (1983) is likely to puzzle almost any reader who comes to it with even a minimal knowledge of Norman Mailer's career. Beyond the mystifying turns of plot, incestuous sexuality, and repetitions of characternyms, the novel's most puzzling aspect no doubt is why Mailer has chosen to write about Egypt in the time of the great pharaohs, beginning about thirteen hundred years before Christ. The answer is not only surprisingly simple, but it also speaks to something very fundamental in Mailer's work. Curiously, in a novel that seems endless, the end that is so assiduously sought brings readers within view of what may be Mailer's most characteristic theme: origins. Mailer chooses to write about ancient Egypt because he is trying to probe that heart of darkness represented in the origins of the origins of Western culture. He has plunged into the time before the time when Western civilization had its more generally accepted beginnings in ancient Greece.

Mailer's entire career has been devoted to the origins of things. *The Naked and the Dead* (1948) focuses on the origins of human behavior and their relations to a natural determinism. *An American Dream* (1965) concerns what one might regard as a conspiracy theory of history. *The Executioner's Song: A True Life Novel* (1979) seeks the origins of one's fate in the finally mysterious heart of a life. To read much of Mailer is to see that he almost obsessively explores how things come to be, how their vicissitudes are related to their beginnings. The pervasiveness of such questions in Mailer is exemplified in one novel's title—*Why Are We in Vietnam?* (1967). However, this novel is about human ag-

gressivity as the prime component of action and not at all about
Vietnam. The theme of origins, moreover, is securely attached to
Mailer's very identity as a writer. One of his most perceptive
readers has observed that "Questions of origin soon become, for
Mailer, questions also about originality and authorship."[2] Thus
the novelistic details of *Ancient Evenings* eventually seem a mere
cover for the more crucial philosophical theme that has preoccupied Mailer throughout his career.

In contemporary philosophy and literary criticism, the question of origins often is less dealt with than evaded. Jacques Derrida and the deconstructionists, for example, prefer to displace
the problem of origins into the concept of *différance* or displacement. They believe that beginnings invoke metaphysics, and for
them metaphysics is passé.[3] The issue is at the core of epistemol-
ogies, even if we insist that answers are beyond them. One may
grant deconstruction its salutary admonitions and critical uses.
Still, modern phenomenology, given its roots in psychoanalysis,
offers many readers a more functional approach than deconstruction to the problem of origins when confronting those aesthetic structures known as novels. Whereas deconstruction is
critical, phenomenology is descriptive. In its methodology, therefore, phenomenology provides the more effective ways of getting
at a novelist's methods of dealing with beginnings. Whereas
deconstruction splits off ontology from epistemology, phenomenology draws them together, but *within* epistemology.
"Epistemology," says Anthony J. Cascardi, "has come to provide
the foundation for modern philosophy, and, according to [Mar-
tin] Heidegger, it is central to the constitution of all philosophy
since Descartes and Kant." Cascardi continues: "As a consequence of the epistemological revolution, our relationship to the
world is so determined that . . . it becomes a representation to
us. In Heidegger's words, this means that from Descartes onward,
'a theory of knowledge had to be erected before a theory of the
world.'"[4] But in his discussion of art in "The Origin of the Work
of Art," Heidegger outlines a theory of the world as well. That
theory of the world's origins is very perceptively considered in
the essay by David Halliburton that Cascardi introduces. Inspired
by Heidegger, Halliburton formulates three principles that he
terms "endowment," "enablement," and "entitlement." But this
triad is not to be limited to "Heideggerian" thought, says Halliburton. For as principles of "inauguration," "facilitation," and
"adjudication," they may be related also to C. S. Peirce's notions
of "Firstness," "Secondness," and "Thirdness." Beyond Peirce,

moreover, we shall see that the triads are related to important post-Freudian—that is to say, Lacanian—concepts regarding the constitution of human subjectivity. Eventually, we may see that all those other concepts are related to Lacan's notion of a "countable unity." Specifically, he means "Not a unifying unity but a countable unity one, two, three."[5] We shall see that these clusters of Heideggerian, Peircean, and Lacanian notions are relevant here because they are manifested in *Ancient Evenings*. Collectively these concepts finally do much to reveal the tremendous daring, richness, and even *postmodernity* of Mailer's narrative.

I

Let us look first at the concept of endowment. This concept posits a founding or constitutive relation between two objects or elements that does not depend on a pattern of cause and effect, temporal seriality, spatial centrality, or organic teleology. But if endowment does not depend upon our most important *ordinary* notions of constitution or coming into being, it remains nonetheless a principle central to modern phenomenological thought. It comes from Husserl, Halliburton suggests, rather than Heidegger.

> In the course of his investigations into logic, Husserl hit upon a type of relation that does not correspond with familiar conceptual models. It is not causal; neither of its members exists because the other brings it about. It is not serial; neither member antedates the other. It is not spatial, there being no fixed locus that either member must occupy. Nor is it organic, there being no parturition nor any development. Founding occurs when the being of an X is the necessary condition of the being of a Y. In such a relation there can be no Y without X. Therefore Y is said to be founded by X; or, X founds Y.[6]

The principle of endowment is one exemplified in myth. Frequently myths are ways in which cultures address the problem of origins without answering any questions of an ultimate singularity. It is a problem related to Lacan's premise that counting—the countable unity—requires only "a certain number of sets and a one-to-one correspondence" (*OSI*, p. 190).

In *Ancient Evenings*, one sees the inaugurating principle of endowment in Mailer's recourse to a mythic narrative that manifests the Heideggerian fourfold of earth and sky, divinities and mortals. These four constitute the world in a reciprocal relation

that Heidegger captures in a verbal: "worlding." The world, Heidegger tells us, *worlds*.

> This appropriating mirror-play of the simple onefold of earth and
> sky, divinities and mortals, we call the world. The world presences
> by worlding. That means: the world's worlding cannot be explained
> by anything else nor can it be fathomed through anything else. This
> impossibility does not lie in the inability of our human thinking to
> explain and fathom in this way. Rather, the inexplicable and unfath-
> omable character of the world's worlding lies in this, that causes and
> grounds remain unsuitable for this world's worlding . . . . The human
> will to explain just does not reach to the simpleness of the simple
> onefold of worlding. The united four are already strangled in their
> essential nature when we think of them only as separate realities,
> which are to be grounded in and explained by one another.[7]

Mailer shows in *Ancient Evenings* how creation through
"worlding" (endowment) might work. As Heidegger suggests
must happen, Mailer's account of "origins" begins with the element farthest from the human, the one known as "the holy." This
realm in Heidegger represents an opening upon possibility or
potentiality. But Mailer's *novel* opens with a representative of
the mortals for whom the account will be meaningful as inauguration. Thus the myth of origins is offered as a way for an already
posited human—referred to in Mailer's title of Book I, "The Book
of One Man Dead," and eventually identified as Menenhetet
Two—to find his place in the world. The account itself consequently includes, of the fourfold world, the remaining three elements—earth, sky, divinity.

Mailer's myth of origins (found in Book II) begins with the
divinity Amon. Amon's role in *Ancient Evenings* is precisely to
provide endowment. Mailer does not refer to Amon as a god;
rather, he is "the Hidden" whose "hiddenness" represents his
role as endowing founder. In Mailer's account, Amon is not a
creator god, as is the creator in Christian mythology; he is instead
the one who endows life from his position as the invisible. "In
the beginning," says Mailer's Menenhetet One, echoing "Genesis." He is telling the founding story to his great-grandson's Ka
(double or soul) in the Land of the Dead. He states: "Before our
earth was here and the Gods were not born, before there was a
river or a Land of the Dead, and you could see no sky, it is still
true that Amon the Hidden rested within His invisible splendor." But from within his invisible splendor the Hidden does not
create Being so much as he simply "becomes" a being. Continues

Menenhetet One: "Yes, it is from Amon that we know our beginning. He withdrew from the Hidden to come forth as Temu, and it was Temu Who made the first sound. That was a cry for light . . . . The cry of Temu . . . quivered across the body of His Wife, Who was Nu, and She became our Celestial Waters. Temu spoke in so great a voice that the first wave stirred in Her, and these Celestial Waters brought forth the light. So was Ra born out of the first wave of the waters. Out of the great calm of the Celestial Waters was born the fiery wave of Ra, and He lifted Himself into the heaven and became the sun even as Temu disappeared back into the body of His Wife, and was Amon again . . . . That is the beginning" (*AE*, pp. 40–41). In thus ending "The Book of One Man Dead," Menenhetet One's account of origins suggests that out of death or nonbeing comes life. As it is in the myth, so is it in Mailer's novel. Out of a narrative of three elements in the fourfold of earth and sky, divinities and mortals, comes the foundation for the fourth, the mortals. They are "gods" in one sense, but they are really those humans who inhabit the bulk of Mailer's novel's world once it is constituted.

Now endowed with life, Mailer's constituted mythic world proceeds with the work of enablement. If, as Halliburton says, endowment capacitates and enablement facilitates, then we see that what Mailer does in Book II is the latter: facilitation. As Heidegger says, "The divinities are the beckoning messengers of the godhead" (*PLT*, p. 178; *EEE*, p. 251). As such messengers, however, the divinities look in two directions; they look not only toward pure possibility, but also toward nothingness. They mediate between the plenitude of the godhead (Amon the Hidden) and the recognition of negation suffered by the mortals. "They are called mortals because they can die. To die means to be capable of death as death. Only man dies. The animal perishes. It has death neither ahead of itself nor behind it. Death is the shrine of Nothing, that is, of that which in every respect is never something that merely exists, but which nevertheless presences, even as the mystery of being itself" (*PLT*, p. 178; *EEE*, p. 252). When Mailer "peoples" a world, those "people" are called "gods," and they are afflicted by mortality in much the same way as later, ordinary "mortals." Thus, Book II, called "The Book of the Gods," recounts various tales of the Egyptian deities Ra and Nut and their children Osiris, Horus, Set, Isis, and Nephthys. But the implicit purpose of the tales is to show the shift from endowment to enablement, to depict the move from potential action to real-

ized action, as well as the opening up of the constituted world
to change, negation, and death.

II

In Mailer's tale, then, we see several possible ways of arguing
for the constitution of a world. Each way addresses within its
own frame the problems of origins. When the world of the gods
has been endowed with *meaning* in the move that Heidegger
would call "worlding," we see that origins in matter are displaced to a principle of energy; they are displaced to the *process*
by which the world constitutes itself into matter. Once constituted, the gods thereafter enable the entitlements of human beings. The frame here is one of governance, a founding based on
the nature of laws and contracts. Indeed, Halliburton illustrates
the concepts of endowment, enablement, and entitlement
through the specific example of governance. These concepts are
embodied in the executive, legislative, and judicial ones that rest
on the Constitution of the United States. "Through the constitution and the other laws it passes, the legislature confers a worldly
endowment," says Halliburton. "Enablement, for its part, falls to
the executive branch. Through administrative procedures and
enforcement, laws are put into effect and regulations are written
to carry out in greater details the general legislative intent. Finally, the office of entitlement is assigned to the judiciary. The
endowment having been enabled, courts must adjudicate," concludes Halliburton. Because, as Halliburton tells us, "this organization of functions is roughly parallel to the functions of Peirce's
Firsts, Seconds, and Thirds" (*EEE*, p. 260), we are directed to yet
another frame. Beyond these philosophical principles, one
sees—in the move from endowment to enablement to entitlement—an opening onto Lacan's notion not of the constitution of
a world but of the constitution of the human subject *as a subjectivity*. More specifically, one sees it in the move from Firsts to
Seconds to Thirds. For Lacan's "countable unity" depends most
critically on the moves from one to two to three. These numbers
are entwined in Lacan s valorizations of language and the role of
the Oedipus complex. We shall see hereafter how two of these—
language and modes of subject-constitution—are integral to the
theme and structure of *Ancient Evenings*.[8]

Lacan introduces his concept of a countable unity as it relates
to the constitution of the human subject within a consideration

of metalanguages. Lacan is very blunt about metalanguages: "There is no meta-language," he says. "For it is necessary that all so called meta-languages be presented to you with language. You cannot teach a course in mathematics using only letters on the board. It is always necessary to speak an ordinary language that is understood" (*OSI*, p. 188). Lacan draws a parallel between the idea of a metalanguage and the concept of the human subject. He argues that as there is no original founding *meta*language, there likewise is no original founding (meta) subject. Subjectivity is always deferred, retrospective, *Nachträglich*. The subject, therefore, is always elsewhere, in another place. Hence if it is imagined to exist as a thing, it exists as a lost thing, a lost object. "Where is the subject," Lacan asks. "It is necessary to find the subject as a lost object. More precisely this lost object is the support of the subject" (p. 189). He is careful to insist that he does not posit an "intentional unity" of mind or subjectivity such as one finds in phenomenology itself (p. 190). Instead, he proffers the notion of a "countable unity" for the subject precisely because such a unity requires an awareness of retrospection. "Counting," Lacan argues, "is not an empirical fact and it is impossible to deduce the act of counting from empirical data alone. If I take two as a unit," he says, "things are very enjoyable, men and women for instance—love plus unity!" (p. 191). But the number two is not a given. He explains that though this number exists only in a chain, the chain itself does not become visible until at least a second link is adduced.

All theories of number, Lacan points out, depend upon the formula of $n + 1$. "It is this question of the 'one more' that is the key to the genesis of numbers and instead of this unifying unity that constitutes two in the first case I propose that you consider the real numerical genesis of two" (p. 191). One comes into being, Lacan argues, because it is "marked" by two, and two comes into being because it is marked by three. Lacan explains: "It is necessary that this two constitutes the first integer which is not yet born as a number before the two appears. You have made this possible because the *two* is here to grant existence to the first *one*: put *two* in the place of *one* and consequently in the place of the *two* you see *three* appear" (p. 191). The notion of a countable unity is important to Lacan. This is because he posits a subject always *Nachträglich*, one always deferred from any posited original being or entity. The subject is always displaced and always emerges in relation to another. "The question of the two is for us the question of the subject," he states. For "the two does not complete the one to make two, but must repeat the one to permit the one to exist. The first repetition is the only one necessary to explain the genesis of the number, and only one repetition is necessary to constitute it" (p. 191).

Now we may see the significance of Mailer's emphasis on the number two at the beginning of *Ancient Evenings*. In an unnumbered section of Book I that precedes section one, Mailer tells us that his subject—who, we learn, is in the Land of the Dead—questions his identity as human: "Is one human? Or merely alive?" (p. 3). His questions begin to be answered in a number: "A burning number came before me. The Flame showed an edge as unflickering as a knife, and I passed into that fiery sign. In fire I began to stream through the clear and blazing existence of the number 2." Hereafter this subject experiences visions of a filament of two threads wound about each other at one moment, but separating into two at other moments. He takes this filament to be an image of the life of his soul, but the filament disappears from him upon his perceiving it. "I had gained a vision with which to torment myself. For I comprehended the beauty of my soul at just the moment I could not reach its use. I would perish with such ideas even as I gained them!" (p. 4). But Mailer's protagonist comes into his being as body upon the dissolution of that figure 2. "Some totality of me went out of my belly, and I saw the burning figure of the 2 dissolve in flame. I would no longer be what I had been. My soul felt pained, humbled, furious at loss, and still arrogant as beauty itself. For the pain had ceased and I was new. I had a body again" (pp. 4–5).

From this "originating" passage—unnumbered, but constituting the place of zero—we move on to "one," a chapter numbered *one*. Here our protagonist-subject begins to be endowed with subjectivity. Still, it is not yet a subject because it has no memory, no sense of retrospection. It is still merely body. If now a body traversed by thoughts, it remains without mind as such. Instead it acts "like a stranger to my own everyday knowledge," as Mailer puts it (p. 9). Mind-as-such comes with *two*. Chapter two is where "he" begins to be aware of a "friend" whose name is Menenhetet Two. Here, playing on the relations of Menenhetet One to Menenhetet Two and on the ambiguity of the word *Ka*, Mailer's prose imitates something of the dancing of that double filament evoked in chapter "zero." "I think some of us began to regret the nickname, Ka, that we gave [Menenhetet the Second]. It seemed clever at the time, since it not only means *twice* (for Menenhetet Two) but it is also our good Egyptian name for your Double when you are dead" (p. 11). Eventually, by the end of the seventh chapter of Book I, the protagonist-subject begins to realize—with the help of the Ka of his great-grandfather—that as a subject he is in fact that "friend," Menenhetet Two. Finally constituted as a subject (though he lies in the Land of the Dead), Menenhetet Two asks the old man to tell him "the story of Osiris and all the Gods Who lived at the beginning of our land" (p. 40). In other words, he wants to hear that story told in Book II.

Lacan's countable unity may also be seen in the progress of the Egyptian founding myth. Here Peirce's notions of Firstness, Secondness, and Thirdness will enable us to see the gods' functions in Mailer's text. "Firstness," says Halliburton, "is the mode of being that is what it is without regard to any other. Secondness is the mode of being that is what it is with regard to another but not to a third. Thirdness is the mode of being that is what it is by virtue of relating a Second to a First" (p. 245). The sphere of the Second, says Peirce, is that of "brute action" (*EEE*, p. 246). This Secondness is imagined in Mailer's text as largely sexual action and involving the exercise of an "endowment": Ra's phallus. Employed in a manic pursuit of sexual conquests, Ra's phallus is capable of any transformation. "Put a divine lady before Ra," says Mailer's Menenhetet One, "or a slippery old sow—it was all equal to him. He liked them all." But since in the domain of Secondness difference rules in the place of the same, not even that magical phallus can conquer otherness. For despite Ra's great power (essentially the power of materiality itself), he cannot conquer his wife. She is the woman, *the* other to the male. The joke finally is on Ra. Says Menenhetet One: "Ra could change the shape of His prick to [that of] any of the forty-two animals: ram, ox, hippo, lion—just pick the beast!—but He once made the mistake of telling Nut that He did not like to make love to a cow. So She chose to live in the body of one. It is always that way with marriage" (p. 45). For marriage, we may add, is precisely the relation of the same to the different—of "man" to "woman"—in the hope that a Third (Law, Lawfulness) will heal the split.

The progression of Mailer's Book I is thus from Firstness to Secondness, endowment to enablement. In Book II the progression is from Secondness to Thirdness, enablement to entitlement. As brute action or being or pure phenomena, the gods in "The Book of the Gods" fight and fornicate. Yet their actions represent what can be regarded only as matter's manifestations of pure energy without the rule of law, form, formality, or governance itself. Thus a phenomenon achieved in Book II is the ascension to the rule of Thirdness—law or judgment, balance or entitlement. The principle in *Ancient Evenings*, like everything else, is manifested redundantly. Moreover, it is exhibited in ways that suggest Mailer's fundamental "hommosexuality," as Lacan might term it.[9] In Mailer's universe, there is really only one sex, and that one is male. Thus the intervention of the phallic "father" representing law or thirdness may occur in the guise of either biological male or female. Mailer represents it both ways, just so we do not miss the point. For example, we learn on the one hand that law comes into being with the birth of Anubis. He is the son ostensibly of Set and Nephthys, but is claimed as the child of Osiris, who as firstborn of Ra and Nut has endowing priority. "Anubis," says Menenhetet One, "is the jackal who holds the scales of Judgment" (p. 47). Symbolizing this principle of Judgment is the figure of balance, who is exemplified by "the activities of Maat," daughter of Ra (p. 52). "Maat is so devoted to the smallest measure of balance, that She chose a feather for Her face" (p. 53). Identified in that feather, Maat is thus associated with Anubis. "Now that same feather," Menenhetet One tells his auditor, "is used by Anubis to weigh the moral worth of each dead person" (p. 53). The feather thus introduces the notion of a third or mediating, standardizing, and valorizing term. In that respect, therefore, the feather has the symbolic power more generally associated with the phallus and the judgment of the father.

On the other hand, however, Mailer provides a story offering a more conventional symbolization of the phallic function. His tale connects that function to the male and to Thirdness in the countable unity. He identifies the phallic power with the Secret Name of Ra. The tale of Ra now told is mythic in the way we at present think of myths; it is a story of the dying and reborn god, the old king who "dies" in order to be restored in the new king. But in the case of Ra he is simply Ra reborn. The tale is complicated, but the eventuality is that Ra is compelled to reveal his Secret Name to Isis. The latter is charged by the Ka of Osiris to uncover it so that a world slowly sinking back into primal matter—death and negation—may be restored along with Ra. There is first much bluster: "my names are without end. My forms are the form of all things. Every God has His existence in Me" (p. 57). There are also many claims of "I am"—"I am the First and the Son of the First" (p. 57), "I am He-Who-the-Gods-know-not," and the like. Only then does Ra give up his Secret Name to Isis, and Isis receives it as semen into her body. His Name is *Three*. "Temu is One, the Celestial Waters are Two, and Ra, child of Temu and Nu, is Three. So his Secret Name is Three" (p. 58). Thus Ra, as Three or Thirdness, is Law, the rule of Lawfulness. And as Law, Ra thus reveals to Isis—as Menenhetet One reveals it to Menenhetet Two—the fullness of being, a world now fully constituted in its Lawfulness. It is a world made manifest in what Lacan would call the Imaginary duality between light and dark, life and death. But it is also a world now available to the order of the Symbolic because it is ruled by Law. The merely "other" of dualities is subsumed in the "Great Other" of unconscious Knowledge. In Lacan, as in Mailer, the container of that Knowledge is language itself, its function only fully achieved with the introjection of the law of the Father.

III

Thus one sees what Mailer has done in the first two books of *Ancient Evenings*. He has constituted a subject (the containing perspective located in Twoness, Menenhetet Two) and endowed a world with a "constitution." In other words, he has formulated an inaugurating myth that fully constitutes and therein makes fully self-sufficient a fictional world. Thereafter, Mailer is free to attend to the human pursuit of that to which this world's constitution entitles one. In any world, the basic entitlement is perfection: the right to become what one most truly is. However, in the mythos Mailer's novel proposes, this means what one most truly *was*, namely, a god. To that end, a series of homologous relations are there worked out:

One is to Two as Egypt is to Greece;
Osiris is to Ra as the Pharaoh is to Osiris:
Ramses II is to Ramses IX as Menenhetet One is to Menenhetet Two.

The bulk of the novel is then constituted by the relation between the last two sets: the lives of the two Menenhetets as these are entwined with those of the two Pharaohs. We may say that the novel seeks perfection of form in the characters' quest of perfection, as Mailer suggests, by the "self-consuming" form of the novel. Still, that quest is ultimately tragic. The self-consuming form suggests that the second and final death of Menenhetet One (paralleled by the movement of Menenhetet Two into the Land

of the Dead) is further paralleled by the fall of Egypt. For this
land's constituting myths have already been covered over by
those of the Greeks by the end of the novel.

The work of entitlement in *Ancient Evenings* is given over to
the quest of Menenhetet One to achieve perfection through four
lives. In his world, that goal is to become a pharaoh, but he
achieves it only through the unity posited in counting. As One,
he achieves it only *in* Two. Thus the work of entitlement in the
novel is rather complex. There are no simple fulfillments here.
The stages of this quest are bound to Menenhetet One's grasp of
the intricacies of language. These stages are recounted in three
successive books: IV—The Book of the Charioteer, V—The Book
of the Queens, and VI—The Book of the Pharaoh. In the first of
these, he moves from *action* to *speech*. In the second, he moves
from *speech* to *writing*. In the third, through the agency of his
great-grandson, he moves from *language* to *incarnation*: to life
lived "in the voice of the great Pharaoh," in a moment when the
end and the beginning are joined in the middle, a moment when
Menenhetet Two in thought enters his father, Ramses IX, and
Ramses IX (because of Menenhetet One's stories) enters the voice
of Ramses II (p. 538).

Menenhetet One's quest is given him by his mother. She plants
the suggestion that he is the son of Amon and that as Pharaoh
he is destined to rule the world. But he does not simply ascend
to the throne; instead, the steps of the human toward perfection
involve mastery of language. For in language lies mastery of the
power to rule. "Endowment makes possible such enabling as is
necessary to realize the further entitlement of having a language,
or a voice, and participating in a community," says Halliburton
(*EEE*, p. 256). Thus, the measure of Menenhetet One's rise toward
perfection lies in his mastery of various language—or communication—arts. He originates at a level tantamount to the non-
human or even the dead. In fact, Menenhetet's name means
"Foundation-of-speech" (p. 254), and his beginning is so lowly
that he regards himself as being barely above the animals or the
stones or the dead themselves. His original condition, indeed, is
like that of the body at the moment of embalming. We learn
about that seminal condition from the great-grandson: "Like a
stone washed by fog, baked by sun, and given the flavor of the
water on the bank," Menenhetet Two tells us, "I was entering
that universe of the dumb where it was part of our gift to hear
the story told by every wind to every stone" (p. 29). Such also
is the condition in which his great-grandfather, Menenhetet One,

had begun. His mother, he says, "lived with the earth in her hands." Moreover, she and he have a "natural" relation to language: "Our minds were like a stone and each word was scratched upon it" (p. 237). Later, as he tells of preparing to become a charioteer, he admits his identification with the beasts: "Although I did not know it, I was like a horse myself. I did not think, and could barely obey strange commands" (p. 245). But, as he must, he rises toward perfection by his very ability to communicate with those animals. Eventually he becomes First Charioteer to Ramses II because of his ability to direct the chariot team without his hands on the reins. This prompts the pharaoh to tease him about his special skill: "Usually a man has to be dumb as his horse" (p. 256). That identification is not troubling to the charioteer because, "like an animal himself," he was "thereby close to the sound of all languages" (p. 378). He will soon learn, however, that proximity does not give possession.

"The Book of Queens" recounts Menenhetet One's further adventures in the domain of language. He is banished to the desert for fourteen years after the Battle of Kadesh because he was held responsible for the death of Ramses II's pet lion, Hera-Ra. There Menenhetet One ponders the "mystery of many languages" (p. 378). He learns not only the secret art of "being born out of yourself" (p. 379), but also to read for the first time. Upon returning from his banishment, he also learns that the use of language occurs on many levels and that he must become more sophisticated in its usage. In his naïveté, he is often mocked by the noble charioteers. They call him "hero," but they use a word that also could mean "bird" or "coward." He laments that "they mocked me in their noble manner, which was to play with words until the meaning was as hard to catch as a minnow with one's hands" (p. 383). He has a piercing insight: "All I had gained until then had come from the gifts of my body, but, now, if I would thrive in the world, I must learn the arts of speech" (p. 387).

These arts he learns in the Garden of the Secluded. Having served Ramses II as a general, he now serves there as the appointed guardian of Ramses II's queens. One of them, Honey-Ball, represents the highest skills of speech. Among her names is Ma-Khrut, a name derived from Ma-Khru. Hers then is "a title given only to the greatest and wisest of priests, only those who are most True-of-Voice, those who utter the sounds of the most profound prayers in the clearest and firmest tones" (p. 412). As She-who-is-True-of-Voice, Honey-Ball enables Menenhetet One to gain the greatest of all powers of speech: the ability to communicate without or beyond words. She teaches him the art of telepathy. "Honey-Ball knew how to travel alone down those invisible rivers which are formed by the thoughts of us all." Capable of telepathy in his first life, Menenhetet One knows it best in his second, when he is reared as if the child of Honey-Ball: "When I was a priest in my second life, I learned how to draw near to the vast force that rises to the heavens as soon as the servants of Amon, and the worshippers who attend the ceremony, contemplate the Hidden One together" (p. 432). The essence of this power, he learns, is a mode of silence. It is a silence close to thought and underlies the telepathy that Mailer apparently regards as the paramount secret of Egyptian culture. In his four lives, therefore, Menenhetet One comes full circle. He moves from the silence of the stone and the beast to the speech of the human. Then he moves on to the writing of the scribes and priests, and finally to the conflation of speech, thought, and spirit in the mind of the pharaoh and the being of the Ka.

IV

It seems that the main constitutive function of Menenhetet One and Two is to provide a recursive history of a family and its culture. The focus is what one might call, echoing Robert Con Davis, the paternal romance.[10] The paternal, Oedipal, and familial elements become most visible in the final two books, where one can hardly tell the players without a genealogy. The climactic moment of Egypt's history, found in the reign of Ramses II, is recapitulated in Ancient Evenings in the sixth book, "The Book of the Pharaoh." Several sets of narrative and thematic complications come together in this book. In one set, Menenhetet Two—the novel's first point of view—realizes that his biological father is Ramses IX, called Ptah-nem-hotep. He achieves this knowledge by means of the telepathy that his great-grandfather had so struggled to master. Lying between his mother (Hathfertiti) and his "new Father" (Ptah-nem-hotep), the boy (for he is only six years old at this point in the story) "felt again the full force of my Pharaoh's thoughts. They were of me. I was His son. He would accept me as His son" (p. 537). In another set it becomes more clear how the past lives in stories told (p. 446). For Ramses IX, by means of the knowledge gained from the tale told them all by Menenhetet One during the last night of the Festival of Festivals, is prepared to "ascend into the exaltation of His ancestor," the second Ramses, also called Usermare (p. 539). Ramses IX is "enabled" to become one with his ancestor because he is "endowed" with a history and a lineage. Menenhetet One is pivotal in this moment, because he both recounts the history and contains the blood transmitting the lineage.

The Oedipal implications herein are staggering. The moment involves complex paternal and familial recognitions that circle back on Ramses IX. First, Ramses IX realizes that the boy is his son by Hathfertiti. He also realizes that through the boy he is nearer than ever to possessing the knowledge of the first Menenhetet. Second, Ramses IX perceives links to the Great Pharaoh through his mistress Hathfertiti. She is a descendant of Nefertiri, Ramses II's first wife. But this link also forges another connection to Ramses II, for in his second life Menenhetet One is the son of himself and the King's Queen Nefertiri. Third, Menenhetet One is the grandfather of Hathfertiti and through her the great-grandfather of the second Menenhetet. Finally, Menenhetet Two, through descent from Nefertiri, is a half-brother of a son of Ramses II. That son is the murderer of the first life of Menenhetet One, who was murdered while planting his seed in Queen Nefertiri, his murderer's mother. Thus what Mailer offers is family history with a vengeance. For, eventually, all that history comes together in various permutations of the family romance. These are permutations that attempt to transcend the problems of birth, origins, beginnings.

The resolution occurs in a final set of complications in which there is a joining of all threads across time and generations. If Mailer does not give us transcendence, he at least gives us trans-descendants. For example, it is the wish of Ramses IX "to live in the voice of the great Pharaoh" and "to gain the power to become more like the great Pharaoh from Whom His own flesh descended" (p. 538). He gets his wish, but not by himself alone. Its achievement involves two other persons present at the telling: Menenhetet One and the boy, Menenhetet Two. At the climax of the tale of the first Menenhetet's copulation with Nefertiri, the great-grandfather's voice is displaced by—and thus becomes— the voice of Ramses IX. In addition, the boy—Menenhetet Two— becomes incarnated in his father's voice, the voice of Ramses IX, there to join his great-grandfather. Finally, the voice of Ramses IX, as he desires, becomes incarnated in the voice of his ancestor Ramses II.

Forms of incarnation are involved at each transformation. "So

I listened to my *Father's* voice," the boy says. "If my blood was His . . . then my blood came from a God. I came from the Pharaoh, Ramses the Ninth, Who was, with all else, a God. So He was not only my father but of greater eminence, my *Father*, the Good and Great God, a man and a God." But beyond this incarnation is the grander, historically more significant incarnation of Ramses IX into Ramses II. "Now I heard all that was divine in His voice," says Menenhetet Two of his father, the King, "and knew He was seeking to raise Himself to an eminence where He could enter the domain of His ancestor, and live in the power to rule of [Ramses II] the great Usermare" (p. 538). Thus, says the boy, "I was with my Father in the hour He entered into Ramses the Second as the great King awoke on the first morning of His Festival of Festivals." In a sense, all Egyptian history is rolled into this moment. That morning occurred in the thirty-fifth year of Ramses II's sixty-seven-year reign, which ended more than sixty years before the ninth Ramses was even born and some one hundred and thirty years before the time of which Menenhetet Two tells (p. 539). This moment for Mailer's characters, moreover, is the emotional climax of *Ancient Evenings*. But in Mailer's novel it is still an hour in the "middest," with a before and an after. It is a time like that of the gods who "live in the time that has passed and the time that is to come" (p. 542). And the time that is to come brings only disaster for Mailer's human figures.

The tragic dénouement of *Ancient Evenings* is as much entwined with language and discourse as with the novel's climax. Mailer ties the fall of Egyptian culture to just one form of language—writing, even if it is also the highest form of communication. Regarded by Mailer's characters as a form of "telepathy" originating in silence, writing is given power beyond mere speech. Thus Mailer dramatizes the historical truth that a writing culture destroys a speech culture. Menenhetet One describes something of writing's awesome potency that he feels when guardian of the Garden of the Secluded. Speaking of Honey-Ball's skills, he says: "Sometimes I would pick up some of these old temple rolls and open them to their tiny painted birds and the papyrus would tell me much I could not name, so powerful were the thoughts contained" (p. 433). Though Menenhetet One himself joins the writing fraternity of priests in his second life, he still recalls even in his fourth life how it felt to learn to write in his first: "At such times," he says, "a strong man seemed to stir within me and stare with yearning at symbols he could hardly decipher" (p. 671).

But writing for Menenhetet One is not a pure good. It portends, for one thing, the loss of the power of silence. He enunciates the problem it created in his first life. "Watching her write," he says of Honey-Ball, "I would think of all the little scribes I had known who engaged in such tasks, and I would brood on the power of this act, and ask myself why such puny men were able to appeal so greatly to the Gods even though, when they spoke, they were never true-of-voice but frail reeds, scratchy voices most of them. Yet the words they painted onto the papyrus were able to bring forth the power that rests in silence. So they could call on forces the true-of-voice would never reach" (pp. 433–34). But there is another, worse fault attributed to writing. An ironic result, in part, of the power of writing was the downfall of the Egyptian empire itself. Menenhetet One attributes that downfall to two things that metonymically stand for the same force. The first is the papyrus that replaced the cumbersome clay tablet; the second is the uniform alphabet that displaced the polysemous signs of pictography. Thus by his own account Menenhetet One himself contributed in his third life to the fall of Egypt. For as a dealer in papyrus he made widely available the means of written communication of knowledge that undermined the Empire. These included his own methods of chariot warfare. "Too many secrets have been revealed to the Syrians by the gift of papyrus," he complains. "They have begun to copy our sacred letters," he says. "Now, because of the Syrians, everyone can read each other" (p. 676). No knowledge is safe.

Thus writing has for Egypt both a powerfully creative and destructive potential. Its worst effect is that it provides others with the power to penetrate the Egyptians' very soul. Not only does the spreading knowledge endanger a physical world and its culture, but also that civilization's spiritual soul. Because of writing, says Menenhetet One, "we have fewer secrets from other lands. Indeed, we used to have a . . . saying in those years: 'He who has our handwriting, knows our Ka'" (p. 676). It is loss of that cultural soul that is most damaging to the culture. Thus in the novel's final chapter, Menenhetet One tells his great-grandson: "The Pharaohs are gone. Egypt belongs to others." In the thousand years of the second Menenhetet's death, as he searches for his own Ka, the Hittites have risen to supplant the Egyptians. But the Hittites have been replaced by the Greeks, and they in turn are now being displaced by the Romans. The people of Greece and Rome, Menenhetet One tells Two, "were barbarians when you were born. Our Gods . . . are now in their possession.

If you think of the story I told of our Gods at the beginning of our travels, I will now confess that I imparted it to you in the way that these Romans and Greeks tell it to each other. That is why my tale was familiar yet different from what you know. For our Land of the Dead now belongs to them, and the Greeks think no more of it than a picture that is seen on the wall of a cave" (p. 705). But as for Menenhetet, whether he is One or Two is of no consequence in the end: the *end* is to bring the two together. He aims to "enter into the power of the word," there to traverse the fundament of pain. Finally, he will enter the now anachronistic Boat of Ra, whose journey takes him where "past and future come together" (p. 709). Thus, at novel's end, Mailer's final answer to the question of origins appears to be the one with which we are familiar: In the beginning was the word. But, as the novel shows, the word fills the middle as well. So also is the word at the end. The reader may conclude, therefore, that for Norman Mailer the word is all. All indeed is language,[11] for there subject and world are constituted in their evanescent glory.

Notes

1. Norman Mailer, *Ancient Evenings* (Boston: Little, Brown, 1983). All further quotations from *Ancient Evenings* will be cited parenthetically *AE* whenever the context does not make the citation clear.

2. Richard Poirier, "In Pyramid and Palace," in *Critical Essays on Norman Mailer*, ed. J. Michael Lennon (Boston: G. K. Hall, 1986), p. 88. This volume offers a collection of essays and reviews covering Mailer's entire career.

3. See, for example, Jacques Derrida, *Margins of Philosophy*, trans. Alan Bass (Chicago: University of Chicago Press, 1982), and *Displacement: Derrida and After*, ed. Mark Krupnick (Bloomington: Indiana University Press, 1983).

4. Anthony J. Cascardi, Introduction to David Halliburton's "Endowment, Enablement, Entitlement: Toward a Theory of Constitution," in *Literature and the Question of Philosophy*, ed. Anthony J. Cascardi (Baltimore: Johns Hopkins University Press, 1987), p. 242.

5. Jacques Lacan, "Of Structure as an Inmixing of an Otherness Prerequisite to Any Subject Whatever," in *The Structuralist Controversy: The Languages of Criticism and the Sciences of Man*, ed. Richard Macksey and Eugenio Donato (Baltimore: Johns Hopkins University Press, 1972), p. 190. Further citations to this article are abbreviated *OSI*.

6. David Halliburton, "Endowment, Enablement, Entitlement: Toward a Theory of Constitution" in Cascardi, p. 244. Further citations to this article are abbreviated *EEE*.

7. Martin Heidegger, *Poetry, Language, Thought*, trans. Albert Hofstadter (New York: Harper and Row, 1971), pp. 179–80; quoted in Halliburton, p. 253. Further citations will include both text references, the former abbreviated *PLT*.

8. Space here does not permit its elaboration, but the Oedipal theme is

crucial to Lacanian thought in relation to language and to a countable unity. It is also very important in Mailer's works. In particular, it is found in Mailer's often egregious phallicism; noteworthy here is his preoccupation with a *pregenital* phallus that is generally implicated in anality, especially the act of buggery. Poirier's perspective on these two elements supports my claims regarding Mailer's philosophical concerns—"His obsession with buggery," states Poirier, "has in the past carried Mailer into a metaphysics of human biological creativity as a compensation for meaninglessness . . . and from there to a religion of artistic creativity" ("In Pyramid and Palace," p. 87).

9. In his Seminar XX, Lacan discusses fully the complex way in which one may claim that all sexuality is "*hommosexual*"—that is, derived from one sex, which is male. The argument is connected to Lacan's controversial claim that *the* woman does not exist. See *Feminine Sexuality: Jacques Lacan and the Ecole Freudienne*, ed. Juliet Mitchell and Jacqueline Rose; trans. Jacqueline Rose (New York: Norton, 1983), pp. 137–71. It seems clear enough in Mailer's writings that there is only one sex, the male; only one real genital object, the phallus; and only one form of creativity, the phallic.

10. See Robert Con Davis, *The Paternal Romance* (Urbana: University of Illinois Press, 1992). Davis focuses on classical texts such as the *Odyssey* and later Christian texts to reveal the textual construction of the father as the "supreme" authority in Western culture. Mainly deconstructive and oriented by cultural studies and feminism, Davis's book is also indebted to Lacanian theory.

11. For an interesting assault on Mailer's use of language in *Ancient Evenings*, as well as on the faults of solecism and catachresis (mainly) also found in other writings, see Edward Le Comte's "'No One in School Could Read or Write So Well as Me': Our Semiliterate Literati," *Greyfriar* 26 (1985): 31–48. This title is a quote from *Ancient Evenings*. More favorably disposed to Mailer's style in this novel is Christopher Ricks. See his "Mailer's Primal Words," *Grand Street* 3.1 (Autumn 1983): 161–72.

Toward a New American Mainstream: John Updike and Kurt Vonnegut

JEROME KLINKOWITZ

Except for their bibliographic proximity at the alphabet's end, John Updike and Kurt Vonnegut form an unlikely pair. The subjects of their fiction have rarely been similar, and their modes of writing range in quite different directions. Updike has devoted himself primarily to the highly stylized reflection of manners and morals in America's northeast quadrant. It is a region extending from the southeastern corner of Pennsylvania (where he was born and raised), eastward to New York City (where his professional writing career began), and north to the distant suburbs of Boston (where he has lived since 1957). Vonnegut's fictive world has been colloquially familiar but much more expansive. It reaches from his family's roots in Indianapolis to upstate New York (where he worked for General Electric in the late 1940s), out to Cape Cod (where he published family-magazine stories and wrote his first novels in the 1950s and 1960s), and back down to Manhattan (his home since 1970). His fictive characters, however, have made stops on the transgalactic planet Tralfamadore and on a moon of Saturn along the way.

Age offers another difference. Vonnegut is a crucial decade older. He was born in 1922 and Updike in 1932. This difference gives him the dubious privilege of recognizing with painful immediacy what the Great Depression was doing to his parents' lives and fortune. It also accorded him the ambiguous honor of fighting in World War II. As a prisoner of war in Dresden, Germany, Vonnegut was bombed by the American Eighth Air Force and nearly killed by strafing P-51 Mustang fighters flown by pilots from his home town. For Updike, the Depression also existed, but within his parents' stories, not as a reality he could consider rationally firsthand. The war, however, was merely an event to be read about in newspapers and watched on newsreels at the movies.

The operative distinction between them is where—for the first two decades of their careers—they were published. From the start, Updike's short stories appeared in *The New Yorker*. For these same twenty years, Vonnegut's work was directed to and printed in less sophisticated, family-oriented magazines such as *Collier's* and *The Saturday Evening Post*. Their novels followed these same markers. Updike maintained an unbroken succession of publication with the prestigious house of Alfred A. Knopf. Vonnegut drifted from one firm to another, at times resorting to the declassé medium of paperback originals. Here is where the original contrast in their fiction is most apparent. For the first twenty years of his career, John Updike wrote novels and stories about kids from Pennsylvania seeking their fortunes at Harvard University or in New York City (or occasionally at home in the Keystone State). He also liked to focus on young married couples followed by philandering couples, divorcing couples, divorced singles, and eventually remarried couples—working out the fine particulars of their lives in the suburbs north of Boston. All of the above made perfect material for the self-consciously sophisticated readers of *The New Yorker*. During these same two decades of the 1950s and 1960s, Vonnegut's readers formed a decidedly different audience, to the point that they were really no definable audience at all. They can be described generally as barbershop readers of *Collier's* or the *Post* whose eyes might be caught by a story's illustration and who might then read on until their time for a haircut. Some were the browsers of paperback racks who might chance upon *The Sirens of Titan*, packaged as tawdry space opera, or upon *Mother Night*, marketed as a supposedly authentic World War II spy thriller.

Yet, as the years have gone by, John Updike and Kurt Vonnegut have grown closer. From the confluence of their middle-class backgrounds, interests, subjects, and techniques, a new American mainstream for fiction has emerged within the general style of writing they now share. Vonnegut was relatively late in publishing. He began, in 1950 at age twenty-seven, following military service, graduate school, and an abortive career in industry. Updike started early—in 1954, at age twenty-two, almost immediately after graduating from Harvard. Hence their works coincide in time. In his four novels detailing the life of Harry "Rabbit" Angstrom—*Rabbit, Run* (1960), *Rabbit Redux* (1971), *Rabbit Is Rich* (1981), and *Rabbit at Rest* (1990)—Updike has showed himself to be as interested in the lower-middle-class as in the upper-middle-class suburbanites of his *New Yorker* stories. He has also reached afar into African politics for *The Coup* (1978) and has delved into increasingly bizarre permutations of the spiritual and mystical for such novels as *A Month of Sundays* (1975), *The Witches of Eastwick* (1984), *Roger's Version* (1986), and *S.* (1988). For his part, Vonnegut has looked upward from his original common heroes to such increasingly public figures as a future U. S. president (*Slapstick*, 1976); a dishonored official in the Nixon administration (*Jailbird*, 1979); a privileged rich boy (*Deadeye Dick*, 1982); a writer who must chronicle the devolution of humankind in a manner correcting Darwin's thesis (*Galápagos*, 1985); a genius in terms of America's one original contribution to the art of painting (*Bluebeard*, 1987), and a high-ranking army officer reconstructing his life in post-Vietnam America (*Hocus Pocus*, 1990).

Moreover, in the third and fourth decades of their careers as writers (the 1970s and 1980s), both Updike and Vonnegut have become available public spokesmen. Each is ready at a moment's notice to speak on anything from America's classic novelists to the country's international policy. By the start of the 1990s Updike's nonfiction filled four volumes (*Assorted Prose*, 1965; *Picked-Up Pieces*, 1975; *Hugging the Shore*, 1983; and *Odd Jobs*, 1991) and Vonnegut's three (*Wampeters, Foma, and Granfalloons*, 1974; *Palm Sunday*, 1981; and *Fates Worse Than Death*, 1991). There is also the promise from both of more such books. Writing has brought them fame and, once again, proximity. In the late 1960s they would sometimes meet on the Eastern Airlines shuttle from Boston to New York. In fact, since the mid-1970s Vonnegut has lived across the street from Updike's editor and moves in the same social circle. As one of Vonnegut's protagonists might suggest, this style of convergence has been no accident: the path American fiction has taken in the past thirty years conforms to the particulars of their progress as writers.

II

John Updike's first published story, "Friends from Philadelphia," which appeared in *The New Yorker* for 30 October 1954, also serves as the portal to his first collection, *The Same Door*.[1] One of the *Olinger Stories* included in the 1964 Vintage paperback reharvesting,[2] it announces what would become, over the next quarter century, Updike's favorite theme, style, region, and technical approach. He notes in his Foreword to *Olinger Stories* that town and countryside may be similar to his own native region surrounding Shillington, Pennsylvania, yet the two, he cautions, are not the same. "Shillington is a place on the map and belongs to the world; Olinger is a state of mind, of my mind, and belongs entirely to me" (p. v). Turning to *The Same Door*, we see that it introduces a protagonist and a style upon which Updike would draw for many subsequent stories and at least one major novel, *The Centaur* (1963). He here presents a young man who will be "rewarded unexpectedly" as the "muddled and inconsequent surface of things now and then parts to yield us a gift" (*Olinger Stories*, p. vii).

The young man's name is John Nordholm, called "Janny" in the dialect of his girl friend, Thelma Lutz, whose own last name in this Pennsylvania Dutch region of America sounds more like "Lootz." Such specific pronunciation is the story's first signpost in the world of manners, for Thelma has only recently learned that people in New York City pronounce both John's name and hers differently than do folks at home. Thelma wears "quite short shorts" (*The Same Door*, p. 3), John notes in the story's first paragraph. He also reflects that she has been plucking her eyebrows, something he wishes she wouldn't do, for it sends signals of which he disapproves. When Thelma's mother speaks, chiding her daughter for keeping John standing in the doorway, the scene broadens to reveal key features that carry their own clear message: Mrs. Lutz "was settled in the deep red settee watching television and smoking. A coffee cup being used as an ashtray lay in her lap, and her dress was hitched so that her knees showed" (p. 4). By this point, just two dozen lines into the story, Updike's *New Yorker* readers might suspect that "Friends from Philadelphia" is nothing other than a technical reprise of countless John O'Hara stories appearing in that magazine since the 1930s. The social signs are certainly similar: identification of a character's status, his or her pronunciation, if not diction, accompanied by all those details signaling that the Lutz household is thoroughly working class.

It is just here that Updike's storytelling turns away from a simply manneristic approach and anticipates the path it will take over the next four decades as it converges with Vonnegut's. Instead of confirming that these materials are arranged to reward the reader for his or her attention to prejudicial detail, Updike's story moves almost at once to another level of plot—that of an adventure in language. The details of social milieu soon take second rank to the story's competing dialogues. These include

John's with Thelma (a sexual fascination); Thelma's with John (a certain pretentiousness, based on sexual superiority but also on the language she can draw from books and films); Mrs. Lutz's with John (an honest willingness to help solve his problem, whatever it might be), and, finally, John's with Mrs. Lutz (whose help is needed to buy wine for his family's dinner guests).

The O'Hara-like codings of status remain but become less directive as the story proceeds. When Mr. Lutz arrives home from work, new dialogues are factored into Updike's theorem: John with Mr. Lutz, Mr. Lutz with his wife and daughter, Mr. and Mrs. Lutz between themselves, and all four people with the television set (which emits a sign system John can't read because his own home doesn't have a TV). Even when the action moves out of the house and into another world of more obvious social codes—such as the fact that Mr. Lutz lacks a college education yet never wants for an expensive new automobile—Updike's narrative emphasis remains on language. This extends even to the point of Mr. Lutz recalling a nonsense sentence, "Paint No Dimes Light Red" (p. 9), that he has devised to teach Thelma about the car's automatic transmission sequence of Park, Neutral, Drive, Low, Reverse. When Mr. Lutz puts John in the driver's seat for an impromptu lesson, he assumes the position of John's father, whose financial success as a college-educated teacher has just been challenged. During the drive to town John does not understand Mr. Lutz's sly quoting of television comedians, and Mr. Lutz does not comprehend the boy's simple attempt at making metaphors. Pauses in the conversation loom as gaps that Thelma fills to her own sexually sophisticated advantage, although John naively misinterprets most of her innuendoes. When they reach the liquor store, there is more miscommunication: John's errand to buy some California sherry, "inexpensive but nice" (p. 11), is corrupted by Mr. Lutz into the cruelest prank yet. He sends the boy home with a hundred-dollar bottle of prewar French burgundy as if it has been purchased for seventy-four cents.

A John O'Hara story would focus on the wine. But, as a prototypical Updike narrative, "Friends from Philadelphia" slowly but deliberately focuses its action on the language of culture rather than on this culture's static catalog of signs. How semiotics can prove a dynamic system of differences is clarified by Updike's most typical subsequent work—from his first novel, The Poorhouse Fair (1959), through the serious acclaim for The Centaur and popular notoriety of Couples (1968), to his self-apparent use of language systems in his recent work, S. Along the way are his story collections, an impressive shelf of nine volumes comprising a career's work in itself. In them, the manners and morals of a contemporary America are subjected to a lyrical, almost musical, analysis in terms of their propensity for semiotic song. Now, in the 1990s, John Updike presents himself as a thoroughly representative mainstream writer, propounding not just the "what" but also the "why" of current American lives. He does so always within a narrative structure cognizant of (if not entirely in league with) the philosophic developments of our time.

III

That Kurt Vonnegut had arrived at the same stage of development as the 1980s ended is scarcely less remarkable, given the circumstances with which he began. His first published story, "Report on the Barnhouse Effect," appeared in 1950, just four years ahead of Updike's premier effort. But it was published in a magazine light years away from *The New Yorker* in style. *Collier's* was a venerable family weekly then in its 125th volume. Its 11 February issue featured not just Vonnegut's futuristic tale but also human-interest journalism on world traveler Lowell Thomas's latest jaunt, Nanette Fabray's new Broadway musical, lobbying groups in Washington, postal inspectors, and a critique of socialized medicine. Vonnegut's "Report," drafted in the form of a magazine writer's candid if self-consciously confused summary analysis, fit right in with *Collier's* standard fare. It also served as a good introductory aria for his short story collection, *Canary in a Cat House.*[3] By 1961, however, the bulk of Vonnegut's material for *Collier's* and *The Saturday Evening Post* was already written. The first magazine had folded and the second was soon to go under, leaving the author with markets no more dependable than those of paperback originals (the form of *Canary in a Cat House*) and actual feature journalism (to which he would turn in 1964). Yet "Report on the Barnhouse Effect" survived in the author's canon and graced the more comprehensive collection of his short fiction, *Welcome to the Monkey House.*[4] This volume appeared just after his earlier novels had found a new generation of paperback readers among college undergraduates and a year before his first best-seller, *Slaughterhouse-Five*, would establish him as a leading popular author.

"Report" opens with a confession disclaiming any narrative authority. "Let me begin by saying that I don't know any more about where Professor Arthur Barnhouse is hiding than anyone else does," Vonnegut's storyteller insists. "Save for one short, enigmatic message he left in my mailbox on Christmas Eve, I have not heard from him since his disappearance a year and a half ago" (*MH*, p. 156). He also warns his readers that they will be disappointed if they expect to learn how to achieve the Barnhouse Effect itself. Vonnegut employs the intertexts of this popular-magazine market to subvert them, attracting curiosity even as he disavows it.

As will be the pattern in his fiction for the next twenty years, Vonnegut carefully establishes the low-level authority of his narrator. In *Mother Night* (1962) and *Cat's Cradle* (1963), it is the authority of one who participates in the story through no major intention of his own but who is swept up in the text he begins narrating. "Report on the Barnhouse Effect" is drafted by a nameless underling who has worked under Professor Barnhouse's direction but who has never been privileged to know *how* the man's astonishing principle worked. Hence the writer's object in this text is as much to understand as to explain. The Barnhouse Effect itself is a typically Vonnegut subject; it shares properties with military science, organized religion, and popular hysteria, yet it is ultimately explainable in simple axioms. How the most basic device of the human imagination can have consequences at once apocalyptic and utopian is one of Vonnegut's genuine insights. Indeed, it generates most of his narratives, and in this inaugural short story he structures his understanding of that principle from the inside. Nearly half the tale is over before the reader gets a clear idea of what the Barnhouse Effect is, yet in the process all principles of narrative authority have been called into question.

Averring the Effect's fundamentally natural basis, but without telling what it *is*, Vonnegut's narrator digresses to tell stories about its inventor; he delves into "deep background," as a professional journalist would say. These stories-within-stories include a report on the Professor's Army service as an artillery private, where he discovered he would win the barracks' craps game by just concentrating on the roll he needed. Here is Vonnegut's method in a nutshell: by operating a double proof in which the scientific is perfectly complemented by a justification in popular or commonly understood terms, the narrator achieves credibility without sacrificing his ultimately serious intent, even though the contrast in modes can be hilarious. By the end the narrator has become the next practitioner of the Barnhouse Effect. In addition, the cause of world pacifism is advanced by the handing

down of a totally effective antimilitary secret from one generation of scientists to another. That the scientific device happens to
be something called *dynamopsychism* is not intimidating, since
Vonnegut's narrator makes it clear that all he means is *mind over
matter*, a familiar piece of popular wisdom.

Vonnegut's textual joy in such popular materials as the double
proof is evident throughout his work. In *The Sirens of Titan*,[5] he
explains the technicalities of a *chronosynclastic infundibulum*
(space opera terminology for a time warp) by using a children's
science textbook. An *infundibulum*, it turns out, is a funnel, and
if you don't know what a funnel is, "Get Mommy to show you
one" (p. 15). Later in this same novel he describes how earth's
history has been structured as a series of intergalactic messages
to a flying-saucer pilot whose vehicle is stranded on the seventh
moon of Saturn, awaiting shipment of a spare part for repair. The
banality of these messages ("You will be on your way before
you know it," p. 271), contradicts their loftiness of form. In this
instance the spell-out message is formed by the building of the
Moscow Kremlin. It follows such earlier spell-out devices as the
Great Wall of China summary of his struggles to write the book
and chapter 10 as a reminder of his role as author in completing
it. He thereby cues the story's concluding action in Dresden during the spring of 1945 to his own typing of the final pages on
Cape Cod during the first week of June 1968. That was just a few
days after Vonnegut and his eventual readers had heard the news
of Robert Kennedy's assassination. To emphasize that these
opening and concluding chapters are not mere relabelings of an
otherwise conventional preface and afterword, Vonnegut includes himself thrice within the story's central action. His aim
is to relate his own behavior within the narrative to that of his
characters' acts. This technique finds fulfillment in his next
novel, *Breakfast of Champions*. In it he initially steps back to
write a preface, but then two thirds of the way through the book's
action, he enters the ongoing narrative as its creatively active
author. In this role he does everything from making phones ring
to moving characters from one part of the room to another, to
speculating on the debilitating models for life that conventional
short stories and novels have become. Like *Slaughterhouse-Five*,
Vonnegut ends *Breakfast of Champions* shoulder to shoulder
with his characters, but this time the levels of action are not
separated by twenty-three years (corpse mining in Dresden during 1945, as recalled from a typing desk on Cape Cod in 1968).
Instead, the action levels are simultaneous: they release Kilgore

Trout from further service while this particular creation cries to the author, in the voice of Vonnegut's late father, to keep him in the cast of characters so that next time he can be made young instead of old.

IV

From the start of their careers through their first sustained acceptance as major American writers, Updike and Vonnegut exploited complementary but distinct features of literary theory that have come to characterize our age. In the early 1950s critical discussions about fiction were conducted without compelling attention to such matters as semiotic readings of cultural signs and self-conscious textuality. So it is with a generation's hindsight that one can look back to the first two decades of their careers—from "Friends from Philadelphia" through *Couples* and *Rabbit Redux* and from "Report on the Barnhouse Effect" to *Slaughterhouse-Five*—and see how instrumental such social systems have been to Updike and how textually self-conscious Vonnegut's works have been. Isolating such elements now would prove little about their development. Yet comparing the courses their writings have taken in their third and fourth decades of work reveals that they built on these respective techniques of semiotic reading and self-conscious textuality. It also suggests that each writer has moved closer to the other in terms of adopting techniques and embracing subjects each formerly considered his own.

Updike's move toward textuality begins in 1977, with his Introduction to the new Knopf edition of *The Poorhouse Fair*. That 1959 novel, Updike's first, had projected its action into a future now, in 1977, just a few years hence. Thus what was dystopian back in 1959 becomes virtually contemporary in 1977; it also enables Updike to emphasize how his appraisal differs from Orwell's of *1984*: "As in our mundane reality it is others that die, while an attenuated silly sort of life bubbles decadently on" (p. x). It is impossible, given Updike's dedication to manners as a readable but not predictable "blueprint," to foretell the future in any terms other than those presently at hand: "We can extend the graph curve of present trends and be certain that existent vitalities will decline, but we cannot conceive of the new, of the entities born by intricate synthesis from collisions of the broadly known. Models of the future tend therefore to be streamlined models of the present, the present with its corners cut off. But it is these very corners that move into the center and become the future" (pp. xiii–xiv). So the future projected in this novel becomes one "wreathed in mists as of nostalgia" (p. xiv). Thus an authorial awareness of textuality complements the reader's historic location of this novel's sign system, whether it be read in 1959 or 1977.

A similar sense of how his texts control him even as he presumes to control their semiotic order catches Updike's attention in the Foreword he writes in *Too Far to Go*.[6] This paperback original forms a special collection of the seventeen short stories he had written since 1956 that featured a just-married and eventually just-divorcing couple, Richard and Joan Maple. The social signs that make these two people are as readable as those that form the pieces assembled in *Olinger Stories*; only now the lesson is not the authorial reassurance that there may be unexpected rewards among such close observations. Instead, there is suggested his material's own advice, based on inexorable historical progress, that "all blessings are mixed" (p. 10). With poetry, Updike has learned that as mixed as blessings become when they are generated by a textual situation, they are even more fugitive when it comes to light verse. He notes this sad truth in the "Foreword to the 1982 Edition" of his first book of poems, *The Carpentered Hen* (1958). Each of his successive collections contained less of the poetic style that characterized his first, until by the present time he finds that he writes in a totally different way. He links this transition to the time of the Kennedy assassination.

But the deepening self-conscious textuality of Updike's work is more than just a response that happens to coincide with a move toward greater seriousness in American culture. True, a certain political topicality becomes evident in his novels of the 1970s. It ranges from the interrelated thoughts on the American space program and urban racial relations in *Rabbit Redux* to the geopolitical concerns voiced in *The Coup*. These topical events broaden Updike's interests beyond the almost restrictively tribal sign systems employed in his first manneristic fictions. At the same time, *A Month of Sundays*, *Marry Me*, and *The Witches of Eastwick* delve into the theological, irrational, and supernatural. *Marry Me* is itself a somewhat unstable text that suggests three possible alternative endings. In his writing of the later 1980s Updike begins to consider textuality in a classic sense; he looks back to the work of another Massachusetts-based writer, Nathaniel Hawthorne, as a model.

In 1979, on his introduction into the American Academy of Arts and Letters, Updike paused to consider the lessons Hawthorne's major novel, *The Scarlet Letter*, might have for his work. Collected in *Hugging the Shore*,[7] his essay "Hawthorne's Creed" singles out *The Scarlet Letter* as the only one of Hawthorne's four completed romances in which "we do not feel the social surround of the principal characters to be thin, for it is solidly composed of ancient Boston's communal righteousness." Updike then adds: "And Dimmesdale, insofar as he speaks for Puritanism, is not the hero but the villain, so that we rejoice in his fall; thus D. H. Lawrence read the novel as the triumphant story of a husband and wife, Mr. and Mrs. Chillingworth, conspiring to seduce and torment an insufferably flawed agent of iron domination" (p. 76). Updike began his essay by noting also that this most religious of novelists had not been a churchgoer, although matters of theology and spirit suffused his work. Updike casts his own novel, *Roger's Version* (1986), as a restatement of *The Scarlet Letter*'s themes and action from Chillingworth's point of view. Thus it is significant that when his wife concludes her adultery and they resume their family routine, she sets off to church simply to annoy him.

Roger's version of the Hawthorne story is presented in a straightforward manner. It is buttressed by the solid surroundings of social signs that characterize Updike's most typical work. But in its sequel, told from the adulterous wife's point of view, the author makes a bold leap into virtually complete textuality. Indeed, his novel *S.*[8] is named for the style in which its protagonist, Sarah Worth, likes to sign herself. Her signature is placed upon the novel, for Updike does not choose a narrative voice to speak for her or even let her narrate her own story. Instead, the novel comes to us as a bundle of letters, postcards, and audiotapes. It begins with her letter written on airline stationery as she deserts her husband, and it continues through 264 pages of material variously addressed to his and her attorneys, her best friend, her daughter, Pearl (who alone among the characters is named for one of Hawthorne's originals), and others involved in the ongoing progress of events. Most of these individuals are dedicated to a reexamination of the past. Sarah needs them to construct a viable identity she feels has been denied by the circumstances of her married life and the rules by which it had been lived.

Of the two paragraphs from *The Scarlet Letter* that Updike uses as an epigraph, the first reports how suddenly beautiful

Hester Prynne had looked when she emerged from prison. The second indicates the immensity of what she must now do:

> Much of the marble coldness of Hester's impression was to be attributed to the circumstances that her life had turned, in a great measure, from passion and feeling, to thought. Standing alone in the world,—alone, as to any dependence on society, and with little Pearl to be guided and protected,—alone, and hopeless of retrieving her position, even had she not scorned to consider it desirable,—she cast away the fragments of a broken chain. The world's law was no law for her mind. (p. 1)

Independent of society, Sarah Worth, too, must exist as a character in her own text, apart from the social system identifying traditional Updike characters. That system itself now exists only in her letters' references to it. She herself is swept up into an entirely new, artificially (and somewhat questionably) created order of guruistic Hindu thought—for which Updike thoughtfully provides a thirteen-page glossary at novel's end.

The action Updike portrays in S. is like that of his typical novels: the protagonist faultily yet persistently strives to create a space for herself amid the semiotic clutter of the contemporary social world. In *Rabbit, Run*, for example, Updike had Harry Angstrom look about his new family's apartment. It is cluttered with tacky furniture, dirtied by dustballs behind the doors and beneath the radiators, and suffused with the banalities broadcast by daytime TV. He wonders if his own soul could amount to much more than this. In *S.*, Sarah leaves an attractive upper-middle-class suburban homelife that impinges on her independence. The difference in Updike's method in these two novels published over a quarter-century apart is clear. In *Rabbit, Run* the items of semiosis are taken from such cultural artifacts as television programs ("Queen for a Day" and "The Mickey Mouse Club") and from social signposts like year and make of cars and Harry's job (demonstrating kitchen gadgets in a dime store). In *S.* they exist as language expressed in specific textual circumstances. The tape recordings Sarah sends to her friend Midge encapsulate what Updike wishes to portray as the full context of the language of middle-class American women. The tapes convey their attitudes, the postures of their social group, and even the found poetry in collage-like juxtapositions of references to husbands, daughters, mothers, dentists, and lawn care.

Sarah is learning to function within a new social code with its unique terms for everything; hence she is able to report back to Midge about the linguistic process as well as its social product. At one point, she smuggles her cassette tape recorder into a meeting with the guru himself, who propounds the following theory she in turn sends back to Midge:

> English is strange in its little words. In German there is the same thing, the strange little floating words only the natives can dispose properly. I have often considered that language is stranger than it seems. It conveys meaning, we perceive that, yes, but also it makes a tribal code, a way to keep out others. It is that intricacy which in paper currency is meant to defeat counterfeiters. The religion of the Hindus and even more of the Jains has this repellent intricacy, which to be ideal must be endless, which piles upon the mind until the mind goes blank and may receive enlightenment. (pp. 131–32)

These repellent intricacies fascinate the Updike we recall from *Rabbit, Run,* and much of *S.* is devoted to capturing the odd little stylistic habits of the guru, Shri Arhat Mindadali. But the self-consciously textual nature of this new approach to his material allows Updike to show how totally artificial and conventional language structures are. For example, at the book's climax, the exotically colorful Arhat is shown to be not an Indian at all, but rather "a Jewish Armenian from Watertown, Massachusetts" (p. 218) who has constructed his own elaborate identity for personal gain. "I wasn't getting stateside publicity in those days," he tells Sarah when recalling his adventures in India. "I was just one more obscure guru. Coming to the States was [his manager] Durga's idea, and she was right: this is the place to score" (p. 219).

The Arhat's voice is an interesting set-piece for Updike's talents, but Sarah's textuality remains his principal interest. As a character, she has one voice for her letters to her husband, another for her daughter, a third for her mother, and so on down the list of her correspondents. Because her reader is formally identified, and because Sarah controls both her own image and its context by virtue of being the writer, the material of *S.* has an objectivity that Updike can play with on its own terms, such as catching Sarah in moments of intertextuality when she uses realtors' language in bargaining with her husband. "These legal pranks of yours are pathetic," she declares. "Tell Gilman [his attorney] I will settle for half the value of the two houses as appraised for *fair market value in today's skyrocketing New England real-estate market,* half the New Hampshire land ditto, the stocks and bonds and I divided them, my Mercedes (I hope you rev the engine now and then), all the silver and furniture that came from my ancestors with their single insistent initial, and all my legal expenses" (pp. 170–71).

Much of the novel's humor and no small portion of its thematic effect are achieved by this intertextuality. Sarah will show herself to be well meaning but witlessly condescending when writing her hairdresser. She is especially so when dropping cheery little postcards to her hairdresser's imprisoned son. She endeavors to maintain a specific identity for her husband (tough independence and bitterness over his impositions), for her mother (a sense of ancestral superiority from her father's side), for her daughter (a combination of motherly caring and image consciousness, based on her displaced ideals), and for the others to whom she writes. Yet the powers of intertextuality forbid such compartmentalization. The result is that her true personality emerges through such unintended interweavings. Her assigned task in the guru's community is to write his letters. This endeavor allows a subtle blending of his philosophy and the organization's practical politics and her own religious aspirations and physical reality. This intertextuality enables Updike to create his story of manners and morals in full view of the reader. In fact, he draws on the reader's ability to compare texts from letter to letter and to form an image of Sarah from the comparison and contrasts. And like all textual projects, the action deconstructs. For the guru is actually an American in disguise, while Sarah's two principal readers—the sympathetic Midge and the hostile Charles—end the novel by marrying, thereby dismantling the structure Sarah has created as an audience for her texts. Yet in S. the letters exist side by side. This means that Updike and not Sarah has controlled the text and that Updike's readers (not just Charles, Midge, and the other characters) are the real audience.

V

Kurt Vonnegut's parallel move toward a systematic understanding of social manners begins with *Slapstick* (1976). Its plot device derives from the author's studies in anthropology. Specifically, it is grounded in Robert Redfield's theory that the ideal tribal group totals two hundred, with distinctive and useful jobs for each member. In *Slapstick* the protagonist, Dr. Wilbur Daffodil-11 Swain, grows up learning how the nation's wealthy bond together by virtue of their family names. So, when he becomes president of the United States, he institutes a system of randomly assigned but socially binding middle names to create a new system of extended families. The members of each family group are responsible for the moral support of their own. *Jailbird* (1979) features a protagonist whose Slavic name is changed to Walter F. Starbuck, to sound better at Harvard (a technique appreciated and employed by Swain in *Slapstick*). Starbuck then begins a career noteworthy in the world of manners and morals, that of dedicated government service. The Watergate scandal of the Nixon administration dismantles all that, however, as is the world of values shared by Rudy Waltz undone in Vonnegut's next novel, *Deadeye Dick* (1982); it is deconstructed by the nickname fastened on him by an act of adolescent irresponsibility. In *Galápagos* (1985), Vonnegut steps back to view the human race from the greatest distance imaginable: from one million years in the future, when its regeneration from a few South Seas survivors of nuclear war is traced through the social and moral habits that eventually reform the species into something not even recognizable in contemporary terms.

John Updike has not abandoned his manneristic orientation but has rather deepened and extended it by virtue of self-conscious textuality. Similarly, Vonnegut maintains his own customary awareness of the text as he prefaces *Slapstick*, *Jailbird*, and *Deadeye Dick* with the style of autobiographical integrations he used in *Slaughterhouse-Five* and *Breakfast of Champions* (and in the later editions of *Mother Night* and his collected short stories). In *Galápagos*, this textuality is evidenced in the persona of the narrator, a distant relative of his familiar SF writer type, Kilgore Trout, who comments on the making of his story even as it unfolds. But an awareness of the systematic nature of social and even biological behavior, including a reformulation of Darwin's thesis in *Galápagos*, pervades this new approach.

In *Bluebeard*,[9] Vonnegut implements an important part of his ongoing textuality by making his protagonist Rabo Karabekian. He is the abstract-expressionist painter whose color-field rendition of human self-awareness as a band of light was first described in *Breakfast of Champions*. But in this novel the sociology of art interests Vonnegut far more than does its aesthetics, although the former is eventually related to the latter. Karabekian is an Armenian American (an odd coincidence with the guru of Updike's novel S.) whose parents apprentice him to the era's most successful magazine illustrator, Dan Gregory. In Gregory's *ménage* Karabekian learns not only the principles of representative, thematic art, but also the ways and means of power—sexual, financial, and artistic. His own fame as an artist comes in a completely different style. As one of the so-called Irascibles—the group of emergent abstract-expressionist painters active in New York City during the 1940s and 1950s—Karabekian participates in the sociology of an artistic revolution: Painting is transformed from figurative representation to an arena in which its proper subject is its own action on the canvas.

Here Vonnegut's graduate training in the comparative study of cultures once more comes into play. His proposed thesis topic at the University of Chicago involved the comparison of two revolutionary groups—the Ghost Dance of American Indians during the 1890s and the cubist painters in Paris a decade later. The Irascibles were a widely publicized crowd, and Vonnegut combines in the painting style of Karabekian elements of the action painting and rip method of Jackson Pollock, the textural layering of color by Willem de Kooning, the push and pull of compositional elements by Hans Hofmann, the biomorphic figuration evident in William Baziotes, the harsh expressiveness of Franz Kline, and the color field mysticism of Barnett Newman, Ad Reinhardt, and especially Mark Rothko. Interestingly enough, an immediate precedessor of this group was Arshile Gorky, an Armenian immigrant. Because this group's morals and manners make such a well-documented story, Vonnegut is able to employ it as a context for Karabekian's development among the social life of its members. In addition, these artists provide not only the most thoroughly systematic background, but also the most verifiable in the documents of art history and cultural commentary to be found in any of his works.

Karabekian's own life is detailed through his social relationships and aesthetic innovations. At the center of both are questions about the role of money in the arts and the role of the arts in moral philosophy. These concerns square with history. The abstract-expressionist masterpieces of the 1940s, which were often taken in trade to satisfy bar bills, became, within a decade, million-dollar properties. Much of Karabekian's wealth derives not only from sales of his own work but also from having acquired the world's best collection of his colleagues' art simply by accepting their paintings as settlements for small debts. This style of art also raises questions about how abstract painting can make a moral statement. Dan Gregory's broadly illustrative canvases are in fact a parody of the opposite tendency, wherein attitudes are enforced by strict depiction; this latter tendency is

related to the artist's own embrace of Italian fascism. But Karabekian is constantly challenged by those around him for the supposedly empty content of his own mature work. It is an argument
he is forced to undertake with people from all social levels—not
just the artistically erudite but also with his housekeeper and her
semiliterate daughter. Yet when Karabekian's final masterpiece is
revealed, it becomes a combination of a systematic debate and a
textual reference within Vonnegut's canon. For it is a panoramic
depiction of figures acting out the dramatic scene from the final
pages of *Slaughterhouse-Five*—that is, after the bombing of Dresden in World War II's final days. In this earlier novel, Dresden
had been an undepictable emptiness, a thematic void that the
author could structure only by surrounding it with the textual
material of his struggle to write. In *Bluebeard*, a painter whose
genius centers on the artistic rendering of blankness as a silent
presence is able to produce a work that actually structures the
void. It is a void not just in Karabekian's previous vision, but
also one that has been the generative substance of Kurt Vonnegut's fictive work.

The point here is that Vonnegut and Updike started from
widely separated stylistic and thematic poles but yet have spent
the third and fourth decades of their careers working toward
a common center. Their coming together suggests that a new
American literary mainstream may be forming. The systematic
attention of each author to manners and to the self-conscious
use of textuality recalls the two major theoretical principles of
our age. Other, less traditional writers have been more emphatic
in their implementation of these theories. But as the 1980s progressed, these innovators abandoned such obvious experiments
in the hope of finding popular acceptance by writing straight
realism. Ronald Sukenick in *Blown Away*,[10] Clarence Major in
Such Was the Season,[11] and Steve Katz in *Florry of Washington
Heights*[12] offer obvious examples. These novels have prompted
some critics to accuse their authors of selling out, while others
have claimed their new work signals the end of the novelists'
characteristic style of fiction. But when major figures such as
John Updike and Kurt Vonnegut can be seen adopting these innovative devices as a way of deepening and extending the strongest tendencies in their own work, it becomes apparent that a
new mainstream has emerged from what were once avant-garde
techniques. At the same time, the avant-garde has been able to
retire, at least momentarily, from its usual shock-troop duty.

Notes

1. John Updike, *The Same Door* (New York: Alfred Knopf, 1959).

2. John Updike, *The Olinger Stories* (New York: Harvest Books, 1964).

3. Kurt Vonnegut, *Canary in a Cat House* (Greenwich, CT: Fawcett Books, 1961).

4. Kurt Vonnegut, *Welcome to the Monkey House* (New York: Delacorte Press/Seymour Lawrence, 1968). Citation to this volume is abbreviated *MH*.

5. Kurt Vonnegut, *The Sirens of Titan* (New York: Dell, 1959).

6. John Updike, *Too Far to Go* (Greenwich, CT: Fawcett Books, 1979).

7. John Updike, *Hugging the Shore* (New York: Knopf, 1983).

8. John Updike, *S.* (New York: Knopf, 1988).

9. Kurt Vonnegut, *Bluebeard* (New York: Delacorte Press, 1987).

10. Ronald Sukenick, *Blown Away* (Los Angeles: Sun & Moon Press, 1986).

11. Clarence Major, *Such Was the Season* (San Francisco: Mercury House, 1987).

12. Steve Katz, *Florry of Washington Heights* (Los Angeles: Sun & Moon Press, 1988).

Writing as Witnessing: The Many Voices of E. L. Doctorow

SUSAN BRIENZA

> The moment you have nouns and verbs and prepositions, the moment you have subject and objects, you have stories ... nothing is as good at fiction as fiction. It is the most ancient way of knowing but also the most modern, managing when it's done right to burn all the functions of language back together into powerful fused revelation.
>
> —Doctorow, in *Esquire*, August 1986

> Father kept himself under control by writing in his journal. This was a system too, the system of language and conceptualization. It proposed that human beings, by the act of making witness, warranted times and places for their existence other than the time and place they were living through.
>
> —Little Boy, in *Ragtime*

Because of his genius and versatility, E. L. Doctorow is equally and simultaneously comfortable in both the mainstream and the margins of American fiction, the realm of realism and the edges of experimentation. He creates recognizable characters and compelling plots with social import, yet he is boldly innovative with time, structure, point of view, syntax, and prose rhythms.[1] Even his most political comments on history, he says, must be conveyed through distinctly literary language, because factual speech cannot recreate or even depict the past: "My premise is that the language of politics can't accommodate the complexity of fiction, which as a mode of thought is intuitive, metaphysical, mythic."[2] A writer with many voices, many styles, Doctorow can be as minimalist as Joan Didion or as baroque as Nabokov. Often playful with forms, syntax, and punctuation, he is always deadly serious in his social treatises on America. But until recently, critics have focused on his themes of injustice, class, and democ-

racy, his critique of American history and politics, and his blend-
ings of fact and fiction, all to the relative neglect of his style.[3]

In Doctorow's many interviews and articles, the motif of language and voice emerges as often as concerns with truth and
moral character; he implies, while he does not state, the connections between style and ethics. In his appeal to Congress on support for the arts, "For the Artist's Sake," he applauds programs
"that suggest to people that they have their own voices, that they
can sing and write of their own past."[4] History is the supreme
fiction, he argues, one that we must continuously recompose.
Elsewhere Doctorow suggests a direct link between style and
moral vision, especially in that the version of history of those
in authority becomes the privileged rendition, and confines the
individual imagination. "There is a regime language that derives
its strength from what we are supposed to be and a language of
freedom whose power consists in what we threaten to become,"
he states. "And I'm justified in giving a political character to the
nonfictive and fictive uses of language because there is conflict
between them."[5] Specifically, one of the bridges between linguistics and politics, as he sees it, is the metaphors one chooses (as
Orwell has argued and our century has shown). In Doctorow's
view, therefore, "the development of civilizations is essentially
a progression of metaphors."[6] Those metaphors are often determined by the government, but they also may be supplanted or
co-opted by writers, just as Daniel/Doctorow switches the metaphor of electricity and "connections" from negative to positive
meanings in The Book of Daniel.

To begin with beginnings, language is an important impetus
for Doctorow's work. An example was the word "ragtime" that
kept suggesting new complexities of that novel, or the road sign
"Loon Lake" that sparked his next fiction. The germ, he says,
"can be a phrase, an image, a sense of rhythm, the most intangible
thing," any verbal element that makes a book "yield" to the
writer.[7] In the introduction to his one play, Drinks Before Dinner
(a long essay-like preface that Shaw would have liked but judged
too short), Doctorow affirms that language has been essential in
his work. He states that the play started with his noticing the
similar sound of two voices, that of Gertrude Stein and Mao Tse-
tung (significantly, one of them literary and one political). He
then explains his desire to explore their similar voices—that is,
their speech patterns, syntax, and repetitions:

> This play originated not in an idea of a character or a story, but in
> a sense of heightened language, a way of talking. It was not until I

had the sound of it in my ear that I thought about saying something.
The language preceded the intention. . . . Writers live in language,
and their seriousness of purpose is not compromised nor their con-
victions threatened if they acknowledge that the subject of any given
work may be a contingency of the song.[8]

He goes on to argue that the style is the moral man, that in the
play Edgar's opinions derive from and are in turn fostered by a
particular way of speaking: "I must here confess to a disposition
for a theatre of language [as opposed to character], in which the
contemplation of this man's fate or that woman's is illuminated
by poetry or philosophical paradox or rhetoric or wit."[9] This is
a corollary to Wittgenstein's famous generalization that the limits
of one's language mark the limits of one's world. Susan, the
daughter in The Book of Daniel, dies of "a failure of analysis,"
concludes her brother. Susan's political rhetoric is limited, her
voices few. Over and again in Doctorow's characters, language
creates a personal fiction, and that fiction determines a personality. This idea of a self constructed through style, blatantly illus-
trated in Loon Lake, clearly articulated in The Book of Daniel
and Lives of the Poets, and subtly presented in World's Fair, operates in every novel. Moreover, and quite self-referentially, several
of his novels—especially The Book of Daniel and World's Fair—
are, at one of their many levels, about language. I will discuss
each of his fictions in order to reveal Doctorow in his multi-
talented variety. But I will concentrate on these two novels because they are the richest linguistically and because their two
protagonists, Daniel and Edgar, are the most self-conscious
writers.

Doctorow's first novel, Welcome to Hard Times (New York:
Simon and Schuster, 1960), shows in part how either the speech
or the silence of Eastern businessmen is just as lethal as an outlaw's gun in destroying a Western town. It explores the age-old
theme of moral courage through an Old West story about the
outlaw Bad Man from Bodie, who terrorizes towns and challenges men and who is recorded but not conquered by the
"mayor," Blue. Doctorow narrates this familiar tale that plays
with the genre of the Western in a manner reminiscent of Faulkner: Blue chronicles the town's history in three parts, as he
writes in three huge ledger books he inherits from a lawyer. Not
for the last time in Doctorow does writing confer power: "I kept
the books and they called me Mayor." Blue wants to believe that

justice, law, order, and goodness derive from accurate and orderly language:

> ... it pleasured me to feel the legal cap or read the briefs all salted down with Latin. In all my traveling, whenever I came across a Warrant or a Notice of any kind I never failed to read it through. Some people have a weakness for cards, or whittling, my weakness has always been for documents and deed and such like. (p. 100)

The ledgers begin simply as lists of inhabitants and their property, but then they expand to become the very novel we are reading.[10] Blue realizes that his story may be told in different ways, and that his writing has various purposes—legal, psychological, emotional, practical. The reader realizes that what starts as a list of transactions asserts the poverty of language itself:

> No, maybe I'm not telling it right. When I dipped my pen in the ink it was not just for celebration, it was as something that had to be done. . . . What other way was there to fix people's rights? (p. 132)

This word "fix" recurs in several contexts in *Welcome to Hard Times*. Nobody is fixed in place, and thus towns materialize and evaporate overnight: "Nothing fixes in this damned country, people blow around at the whiff of the wind." But marking names down does affix marital, family, and property rights; writing helps Blue to remember, to fix events in time. It allows him to fix the Bad Man in his mind, to fix events in space. But ultimately writing does not fix. It does not mend the town or Molly. Nor does it fix the situation, for the Bad Man "fixes" or "takes care of" or kills or terrorizes everyone. At the end the dead are fixed to the spot ("they're all as they are") because Blue has only one good hand left, so he writes instead of digging graves.[11] "I scorn myself for a fool for all the bookkeeping I've done; as if notations in a ledger can *fix* life, as if some marks in a book can control things" (pp. 184–85, my italics).

Bleeding into a cotton rag, and bleeding onto the page, Blue admits that writing brings suffering and never "fixes" anything accurately in prose, even as—*Tristram Shandy*-like—narrative time chases clock time:

> I'm trying to put down what happened but the closer I've come in time the less clear I am in my mind. I'm losing my blood to this rag [cf. journal or newspaper as "a rag"], but more, I have the cold feeling everything I've written doesn't tell how it was, no matter how careful

I've been to get it all down it still escapes me. . . . [H]ave I showed the sand shifting under our feet, the terrible arrangement of our lives? (p. 199)

Paradoxically, in his final lament about the ineffectiveness of his expression, Blue expresses himself most beautifully, and the earlier pages in his ledger have a lyrical, almost biblical quality.[12] In fact, these passages show that early on Doctorow the novelist was part poet. Later in his work, poetry surfaces to capture the emotional climaxes in The Book of Daniel, and Warren Penfield's verse becomes one of the three main voices in Loon Lake.[13] In Welcome to Hard Times, Blue is especially moving when in down-home Western images he tries to describe the indescribable. He sounds here like Thornton Wilder at his best:

"We've both suffered," she said, but words don't turn as the earth turns, they only have their season. When was the moment, I don't know when, with all my remembrances I can't find it; maybe it was during our dance, or it was some morning as a breeze of air shook the sun's light; maybe it was one of those nights of hugging when we reached our ripeness and the earth turned past it; maybe we were asleep. Really how life gets on is a secret, you only know your memory, and it makes its own time. (p. 138)

Yet, as an unrelenting optimist, Blue still writes for a purpose. He hopes that the ledgers will be recovered and read, as in fact they are—by us. He wants his writing to be an act of making witness, a warning.

At the end the novel circles around to its beginning; it suggests that young Jimmy Fee, earlier orphaned by the Man from Bodie, is transformed into another Bad Man himself. Doctorow implies this with one simple verbal echo: both outlaws vent their rage with the senseless and malicious destruction of the Indian's garden. So the series of disasters continues, not just the double leveling of the town of Hard Times, but evil multiplying evil. The conclusion is so disheartening that when Blue finishes his chronicle, he states that "it scares me more than death scares me that it may show the truth." While false language is inaccurate, true language can be terrifying. Yet even surrounded by death and burning buildings, Blue admits: "I have to allow, with great shame, I keep thinking someone will come by sometime who will want to use the wood." Although Blue is envisioning wood to rebuild a new town, the reader can imagine the pulp required to write a new history.

Another test of moral courage motivates the plot of the next novel, which offers a different twist on popular materials. Although the author himself has disowned his second fiction effort, *Big as Life* (New York: Simon and Schuster, 1966) demonstrates Doctorow's early experiments with modes and forms. He here creates a science-fiction scenario about two giants, a modern Adam and Eve, suddenly appearing in New York harbor next to the Statue of Liberty. Since the events are told cinematically through a splicing of three subplots from three different perspectives, the novel is able to satirize by turns government bureaucracy, scientific research, and media sensationalism. It also probes the mind of the historian, Wallace Creighton (a reincarnation of Blue), who sees the creatures as neither an alien invasion nor a huge welfare case. For all of Doctorow's author/historians (Blue, Wallace, Daniel, and Edgar) reinforce the idea that the writer remakes history. "The principle which interests me," says Doctorow in many different formulations, "is that reality isn't something outside. It's something we compose every moment."[14] That is why he speaks not of history versus fiction, but only of "narrations" of events.

The optimist/survivor side of Blue is here represented by a hippie jazz musician named Red, who uses the syntax of music to describe the giants. Each type of character—Wallace, Red, the scientists, the General and the army, and the agents of NYCRAD—has his own type of language that reveals not only his view of the two "monsters" but also his worldview. The style of the agency, in particular, operates with Orwellian logic—that corrupt policies cause and are caused by corrupt language: "There seemed to be growing numbers of public relations and mass media executives in halls. Their vocabulary depressed him [Wallace]. They spoke of morale control and the manipulation of public attitudes" (p.88).

Kahn the sociologist, who usually speaks the pseudolanguage of statistics, makes Wallace see that the agency NYCRAD (New York Crap?), whose main purpose is its own promotion, has mutated into an inhuman monster itself (p. 89). Government rhetoric becomes even more bureaucratic than in noncrisis times, and individuals are transformed by the disaster: the terms for the creatures constantly change as public attitudes shift. Creighton is sympathetic to "the big fellow's" pain, but the scientist is cool, comic, and irreverent; he calls them "Tarzan and Jane," "these bozos," "these honeys." New Yorkers turn the creatures into something familiar, a game, in the "Name-the-Giants contest."

174   SUSAN BRIENZA

And the tone of letters about the giants becomes more belligerent and sexually violent as the "siege" continues. In a top secret report from NYCRAD, English is reduced to governmental acronyms, PSDs or "practical systems for destroying" the creatures (p. 211). Thus the final solution is to "take care of them," with the officials using that perfect Mafia phrase that transmutes affection to annihilation. It is the same phrase that Daniel employs ironically in *The Book of Daniel* when he laments, after the death of his sister, that "They are still taking care of us, one by one." In modern America the language of love is distorted into the language of murder.

In the repressive, bureaucratic world of *Big as Life* even Creighton's "objective" historical language begins to lie and languish. The only mode, ultimately, that maintains its purity, integrity, and dignity is the language of music. Indeed, inspired by the creatures who have aroused his emotions, Red composes some of his best jazz pieces:

> Red's arrangement called for six variations which progressed in complication and length, and in the third variation the crowd began to understand what was happening and the air began to charge. . . . The emotion was tightly locked in the form and there was nothing random about the instrumentation. At its most intense polyphonic moment the full passionate voices were in perfect tension and almost antagonistic, like four entwined dancers struggling to get out of step with one another. (pp. 130–31)

Stylistically, the jazz descriptions are the best passages in the novel. Here, for example, Doctorow borrows a concrete image from dance to convey an abstract concept of harmony. (Of course in *Ragtime* he would use musical metaphors to structure an entire novel.) In *Big as Life*, however, even the salvation promised by art flounders: the last of Red's concerts, extended beyond the official curfew, deteriorates into a riot, which destroys his bass. Incorporating social satire and political commentary in *Big as Life*, Doctorow aspires to moral fable. Yet here he does not achieve the moral conclusion of a fable. Sadly enough, the novel does not really conclude at all. In fact, its nonending and stilted formulas are probably why Doctorow has dismissed *Big as Life* as his one mistake. It may satirize bureaucratic language, but it fails to create any new narrative voice. Thus, for the only time in Doctorow's career, a poverty of style produces a poor fiction.

Many critics have marveled that just a few years after this semifailed novel Doctorow published *The Book of Daniel* (1971).

It has proved to be his masterpiece and has been honored by inclusion in the Modern Library Classics series. Concentrating his interest in politics and history, Doctorow here fictionalizes the story of the Rosenbergs' execution and its aftermath, as told from the son's perspective. His narrative technique is brilliantly conceived. He uses a self-conscious adult Daniel to relate the present though first-and second-person perspectives. But he also intersperses first-and third-person child Daniels to depict the family's tragic past. Several other distinct American voices (friends, lawyer, foster parents), each with his or her own version of the truth, tell parts of the social saga. In addition, Doctorow infuses the whole with allusions to the biblical Daniel, bits of family myth, and "objective" descriptions of religious and political imprisonment and torture. The skillful choreography of a fragmented, nonlinear chronology allows him to superimpose the political events of the 1940s and 1950s on the upheavals of the 1960s and 1970s. This temporal overlay also means that emotional cause and effect (Daniel and Susan's childhood trauma and adult disorders) become intertwined and thus indirectly explained. A stylistic *tour de force, The Book of Daniel* resembles Joyce's *Ulysses* in its wordplay while it transcends Dos Passos' *U. S. A.* in its brilliant comminglings of fact and fiction.

To appreciate fully the style and narrative techniques of *The Book of Daniel*, the reader must keep remembering that the Rosenbergs/ Isaacsons are Jewish. In fact, one critic sees in the fictional last name the implication that Paul, Rochelle, Susan, and Daniel are all "Isaacs," sons of Abraham who become sacrificial victims of U. S. politics.[15] Indeed, Rochelle declares that their deaths will be their son's bar mitzvah, and Daniel has the old Jewish men sing Kaddish for his family at the end. Hence the sensitive reader is likely to hear echoes from Jewish rituals—in particular the Yom Kippur service—in the novel's texture: "Rachel is weeping for her children, refusing to be comforted for her children, for they are gone."[16] Daniel concludes after his intellectual quest that truth is ambiguous, justice and certainty are elusive, and even God is elusive. He also realizes at the end that he can feel emotion. His reactions are echoed in another prayer from the Yom Kippur service:

> This is the vision of a great and noble life:
> to endure ambiguity and to make light shine through it;
> to stand fast in uncertainty;
> to prove capable of unlimited love and hope.

(p. 446)

The biblical "Book of Daniel" is an even richer source—for dual time frames and for shifts in point of view, as well as for other technical and stylistic devices. Of course Doctorow makes the correspondence clear through the very title of the novel, *The Book of Daniel* rather than *Daniel's Book*. But he also does so by alluding explicitly to Israel's Daniel as an interpreter of dreams, and by drawing a parallel between Daniel's three friends as religious dissenters in the fiery furnace and the American Daniel's parents as political dissenters in the electric chair. (Doctorow tells us that he views electricity as the metaphor for fire.) The associations, however, extend beyond these to the deepest levels of verbal mode and style. First, neither the events nor work are told in chronological order, as they have temporal gaps. In fact, most biblical scholars consider chapters 7–12 as an abrupt departure, reasoning that they are, perhaps, authored by a different person than the writer of Books 1–6. Again, most scholars agree that a dual time frame operates: The "Book of Daniel," though set during the Babylonian exile, actually was written about four hundred years later, in the second century B. C. E.; this would be "shortly after the Maccabean rebellion against the Syrian king Antiochus IV." Thus Daniel's story is told as a moral lesson, as "a call to arms, to defiance, and to faith. What Daniel and his three friends did, the second-century Jews, many of them already Hellenized, are exhorted to do: resist and pray and hold fast."[17]

The king's dreams, then, figure not as prediction but as history: the various elements of the "great beast" dream were designed by the later writer to represent kingdoms that had already risen and perished. Similarly, Doctorow shifts time frames to overlay two different periods and thus to suggest what the New Left can learn from the Old Left. He also appears to argue that the repressions of the seventies replay the McCarthy era, that history repeats itself. To make this point he has the hippie Artie Sternlicht entitle his collage "EVERYTHING THAT CAME BEFORE IS ALL THE SAME." The biblical Belshazzar asks: "What was that? A hand, writing giant words on the stone? . . . What mean these words?" Only Israel's Daniel can read the writing on the wall. Hence Susan Isaacson says to her brother, Get the picture?

Point of view also swerves and shifts in the Bible's "Book of Daniel," as it does in Doctorow's. Mark Mirsky has written that the biblical "book is full of voices, the autobiographical 'I' of Daniel, Nebuchadnezzar, the Aramaic of the Chaldean necromancers, and moves from third to first person and back to first again."[18] It even includes sentences in the second person—"But you, go to the end!" (12:13)—that find their counterpart in the modern Daniel's several taunts or threats to the reader. Repeatedly, in virtually every interview, Doctorow recounts that he originally wrote *Daniel* as a straightforward third-person chronicle and was stymied until he decided to have Daniel tell his own story: "That moment when I threw out those pages and hit bottom as it were I became reckless enough to find the voice of the book which was Daniel's. I sat down and put a piece of paper in the typewriter and started to write with a certain freedom and irresponsibility and it turned out Daniel was talking . . . and then I had my book."[19]

Analogously, in the Bible's chapter 3 Nebuchadnezzar is being discussed as "he," when suddenly in chapter 4 he begins narrating his own story in the first person. Significantly enough, it is a conversion story. His movement to faith and wisdom requires, perhaps shapes, a new "I." Daniel in Doctorow undergoes an emotional conversion—from sadistic to sensitive, from "What is the matter with my heart?" to "I think I am going to be able to cry." Understandably, Daniel swerves abruptly from first person to third at moments of emotional crisis. At such times he needs distance and detachment. One example is when he recalls his mother leaving home, never to return. Another is when he feels remorse as he recounts his past survival mechanism in the orphanage, imitating and therefore becoming the Inertia Kid.

Here and elsewhere Doctorow's Daniel is reminiscent of the biblical writer in that he makes stories out of his suffering.[20] He also specifically resembles his biblical namesake not only because he and his family (like Daniel and his people) undergo tests and trials, but also because he analyzes his family's nightmares just as Daniel interprets the king's most difficult dreams. Doctorow transposes Nebuchadnezzar's dreams into his novel's riddles; these become puzzles that the narrator poses to the reader, riddles of doom comparable to the king's nightmares of destruction:

> om om om omm omm omm om om ommmmmm
> ohm ohmm ohm ohm ohm ohhmm ohm ohmmmmm
> what is it that you can't see but you can feel
> what is it that you can't taste and can't smell and can't
> touch but can feel . . .

> What is it that you can't feel but you look as if you do
>   ohm
> what is it that can't move unless you put something in
>   its way
>
> (p. 242)

In meditating (om) on the unit of electrical resistance (ohm), Daniel would have us guess the answer—that the same General Electric that sponsors Disneyland, with its Nazi-like crowd control, helps to kill his parents, a death where the human body closes the electrical circuit. Daniel's interpretation brings him closer to the truth about the past and closer to his own separate peace: if "Susan dies of a failure of analysis," then Daniel, just as his predecessor did, survives through success in analysis.

But most important, both books of Daniel focus on the artist and the power of the word. Lynne Sharon Schwartz points out that when early in the biblical book Daniel and his three friends are given new names (like black slaves in America) their positions are subordinate ones. The namers are the ones in authority, since naming automatically confers power, starting with Adam naming the animals. In his turn, Israel's Daniel is quick to realize the rhetorical powers of language as he debates and reasons with the eunuchs and as he flatters and fawns over the king. Schwartz's conclusion is that Daniel is the Bible's first real artist; as rhetorician, as interpreter of dreams, as prophet, he says what will happen, and his "words are proved powerful."[21] The idea that naming grants authority (or "fixes" truth) is repeated in Doctorow's courtroom scene. There Rochelle keeps a running tally of all the times she and Paul are referred to as "traitors" and their alleged activities as "treason." She realizes that the logic of the government is guilt by association of nouns. Her wisdom does not save her, and the grandmother's curses (speech acts, words again as power) neither damn the government nor transcend poverty and tragedy, yet the son inherits a similar kinship with words. His research into the past—his actual writing—saves, if not his soul, then his heart. At the end of the biblical book the pages are sealed, and at the end of The Book of Daniel Doctorow echoes these words and allows Daniel to "close the book" on the past: his writing has "liberated" him.

Daniel's authorship entailed self-consciously trying to make "connections," positive and productive connections rather than the deadly electrical ones that killed his parents. This is one reason why Doctorow constructed the novel from fragments, from disparate assaults on the reader's mind, thus echoing the fragmented biblical "Book of Daniel." The original Hebrew and Aramaic, as one critic describes it, "is a language in which every other word is a concealed metaphor. . . . There is no room in it for niceties of relation expressed by subordinate conjunctions. The thoughts are flung at you in succession and you are left to relate them for yourself."[22] Doctorow imitates this style, thus suggesting that "The Book of Daniel" may be the first postmodern work, and that Daniel as prophet is the prototype of the modern artist who exploits dramatic devices to hold his audience.

> At issue is the human mind, which has to be shocked, seduced, or otherwise provoked out of its habitual stupor. Even the Biblical prophets knew they had to make it new. They shouted and pointed their fingers to heaven, but they were poets too, and dramatists. Isaiah walked abroad naked and Jeremiah wore a yoke around his neck to prophesy deportation and slavery, respectively, to their soon to be deported and enslaved countrymen. Moral values are inescapably esthetic.[23]

By turning themselves into walking metaphors, the biblical prophets had hoped to awaken the Israelites from their lethargy. A few thousand years later, a new generation of prophets—the seventies radicals and protesters—created similar dramatic metaphors (Artie Sternlicht argues that the battle is fought in images) to compel their brethren to revolutionary action. The "connection" was not lost on Doctorow.

Experimentation with style in the service of political statement takes a new turn in *Ragtime* (New York: Random House, 1975). Here Doctorow invents narrative analogies to musical structures and artistic and cinematic techniques. These include syncopation from ragtime and cartoon silhouette in fast motion.[24] Initially, Little Boy's secretive fantasy life provides clues to Doctorow's narrative modulations. The Boy "was alert not only to discarded materials but to unexpected events and coincidences" (p. 131). Doctorow, too, is alert to unexpected turns of plot and coincidental meetings of his characters. For this is the way he intertwines the three ordinary (though allegorical) families of his novel and then has them intersect with the extraordinary figures of history. Besides the unexpected, the Boy is enchanted also by Ovid's stories of transformation. These teach him that all life is volatile and cause him to search for sudden change in himself (pp. 132–33). The same principles of volatility and transformation apply to most of the characters in the novel. For example, Tateh deteriorates into an old man with white hair and then is reincarnated as the middle-aged, black-haired Baron. Throughout all the transmutations, Little Boy grows into Boy, scrutinizing the mirror to see the change; instead, what he sees is a mirror image, a magical self-duplication. Doctorow then employs duplication as metaphor and motif. Characters feel a doubleness within themselves, and some characters are doubles of each other—white and black, rich and poor, powerful and helpless. They are the "haves" and "have nots" that have always divided America.

Even in Harry Houdini's sleights of hand and body (dramatizing and repeating his death and resurrection), we can see metaphors for Doctorow's stylistic maneuverings. But most of his techniques derive from the Boy's artistic imagination, from Tateh's artistic creations, and from the musical form of the time. Tateh constructs portraits through complicated paper silhouettes: "With his scissors he suggested not merely outlines but textures, moods, character, despair" (p. 51). With his words, Doctorow creates vignettes that capture the textures and moods of his characters, and of an entire era. Of the turn of the century, he writes: "Women were stouter then. They visited the fleet carrying white parasols. Everyone wore white in summer. Tennis racquets were hefty and the racquet face elliptical. There was a lot of sexual fainting. . . . On Sunday afternoon, after dinner, Father and Mother went upstairs and closed the bedroom door" (p. 4). Each sentence is a silhouette, and then the silhouettes move in sequence. Each vignette, each concept is framed by the surrounding ones. We see this process just as Mother sees the two children on the beach: "The idea of examining through a frame what was ordinarily seen by the eye intrigued her. She composed them by her attention, just as if she had been holding the preposterous frame" (p. 298). The word "compose" here applies to the reader as well as to Mother. We must formulate some of the narrative pictures ourselves, using as background what we already know of the age.

If we then take the silhouetted sentences and link them together, we move associatively from stout women to demure parasols to summer whites to summer sports to repressed sex to half-repressed sex. Similarly, Tateh takes his silhouettes and binds them together in a book to create the "moving pictures" of the girl on ice skates. After technical refinement and big business intervene, the Baron makes his moving pictures, his films, with quickly succeeding frames that show us Life in a new way (as Mother re-sees the children when she frames them). "In the movie films, he said, we only look at what is there already. Life shines on the shadow screen, as from the darkness of one's own mind" (p. 297). With this explanation we shift back to Little Boy looking at his changing image in the mirror. Yet we can also expand the metaphor outward from Tateh's string-bound silhouettes to Doctorow's images in the sentences, scenes, chapters, and sections, all bound into *Ragtime*. By transforming history into a novelistic narrative, Doctorow (like the big screen) is merely showing us what is "already there." In effect, he represents the period through a narrator who seems as distanced, as detached, as a camera eye.

The verb "compose" suggests musical as well as visual composition. Coalhouse Walker, Jr., plays a Scott Joplin piece while Doctorow plays with aural and visual images: "This was a most robust composition, a vigorous music that roused the senses and never stood still a moment. The boy perceived it as light touching various places in space, accumulating in intricate patterns until the entire room was made to glow with its own being" (pp. 183–84). *Ragtime* (which Doctorow says has a furious pace, never standing still) accumulates unexpected events in intricate patterns. It shows the robust changes of post-Victorian America, and it does with characters and plot structure what ragtime does with syncopation and polyrhythm. Syncopation is a shifting of accent so that the normally unaccented beats are stressed. Transposed to the novel form, narrative syncopation means that *Ragtime* will not be concerned with the great historical figures of the time, but rather that the average people will be stressed. Not just the "accented beat" or ordinary families take part, but also the marginal groups. In chapter 1 Doctorow suggests the mood of the era with just a few flat, simple sentences: "There were no Negroes. There were no immigrants" (p. 4). Arthur Saltzman shows that flat language is used in *Ragtime* both for "the sentimental misrepresentations of history"—the "nostalgic catalogues" of the era—and for their refutations. For example, Doctorow writes matter-of-factly: "One hundred Negroes a year were lynched. One hundred miners were buried alive. One hundred children were mutilated." Saltzman sees this interplay between "the charmingly nostalgic and bitterly ironic" as another representation of the complex rhythms of ragtime.[25] Soon the counterpoint rhythm asserts itself, and the upper-class white family of New Rochelle must share its narrative space with two other families, one black and one immigrant. Shifting the normal accent, Doctorow elevates these families to the major roles and puts the geniuses of the age in the chorus. In syncopated motion, Father helps explore the Arctic, while Freud and Jung share a carnival car through the tunnel of love.

Doctorow's transposing of ragtime's polyrhythm (simultaneous and sharply contrasting rhythms) means that the shifts of accent between the rich and the poor, the famous and the mundane, co-occur. This provides another reason for the large number of coincidences and intersections of plot, and the many repetitions of phrases like "at this same time in our history." The little people make themselves bigger, like the children enlarging and exaggerating every limb in their sand figures of each other. Simultaneously, the grand figures become diminished: Coalhouse Walker grows into a tragic hero, while Henry Ford shows up J. P. Morgan as just a two-bit Egyptologist. These syncopations and polyrhythms are played in numerous variations, thereby echoing yet another property of ragtime pieces—seemingly endless repetition. Little Boy perceives repetition all around him, both in the natural and the artificial, and many repeated actions suggest futility. Thus the ice skaters decomposing their tracks as they make new ones is a metaphor for history repeating itself: "The boy's eyes saw only the tracks made by the skaters, traces quickly erased of moments past, journeys taken." By the end the boy has become a mature and imaginative author, our narrator. Since all time is the present, he can yell after Houdini "Warn the Duke"; this is long before Houdini meets Archduke Ferdinand, whose assassination later will spark World War I. The boy's roving imagination again becomes the parallel for Doctorow's skipping in time and juxtaposing asynchronous events, for his ragtime structure and language.

Finally, this tale of ragtime America resolves itself in a parody of the fairy-tale plot, as Doctorow continues his innovative toying with standard genres, forms, and formulas. It becomes a rags-to-riches story when the poor Tateh, like a cinema Cinderella, overnight becomes the wealthy Baron. In addition to the musical references of "ragtime," there is, Doctorow has said, "a sense of satire in the word 'rag.' Also an idea of impoverishment, of something sewn together from bits and pieces of colored cloth."[26] Then we recall Blue bleeding onto his "rag" and Coalhouse pouring his suffering into his ragtime. Resonance from this one word provided ongoing and expanding creative inspiration for

Doctorow as he composed a "true" story of turn-of-the-century America.

He continued to focus on the problem of class in the United States but shifted to the 1930s. In *Loon Lake* (New York: Random House, 1980), he also moves to other voices and an intertwining of three different styles. He interweaves a first-person saga of his hero Joe (poor boy turned CIA wizard), prose poetry by a failed writer, and a computer-printout terminology to imitate and reflect CIA thinking. Throughout the novel Doctorow builds a refracting series of character doubles, visual and verbal echoes, and allusions to Hollywood. His purpose is to depict Joe as he seeks wealth and power in Depression America by imitating and role-playing, and thereby becoming a wealthy, influential figure, F. W. Bennett, the industrialist Joe both hates and loves.[27] Joe's dissatisfaction with his original station in life begins the novel. His first sentence—about his real parents—is "They were hateful presences in me." By the second page we are reading of Joe as a child. "I knew my life and I made it work," he declares, and then "I only wanted to be famous" (p. 4). No huge leap seems necessary from these goals to the self-made WASP and CIA man who appears on the last page. En route he compromises his morals while adopting the appropriate style and language. As a street kid, Joe practiced stealing and running. He also "went after girls like prey," and his quick hand promises animal survival: it was "like a frog's tongue, like a cobra" (p. 5). Instinctively, he later identifies with the loon at Bennett's lake: "Up he popped, shaking and mauling a fat fish. And when the fish was polished off, I heard a weird maniac cry coming off the water, and echoing off the hills" (p. 76). This cry of power echoes and expands so that the boy grown older admires men who reach out quickly and grasp wealth. One who does precisely that is F. W. Bennett who owns the entire lake—land, water, and fish. Even the mansion on the property exudes an "enormous will" (p. 75), and the servants metaphorically, as well as the linens literally, are embossed with, and possessed by, the initials FWB. Thus when Joe scans the Bennett guest book and intuits that it contains "some powerful knowledge I could use," albeit "in code" (p. 70), he reaches out suddenly and deceptively for a pen to add his newly composed persona to the list of royalty and industrial magnates. "Joe, I wrote. 'Of Paterson. Splendid dogs. Swell company.'" Joe learns that power resides in names, the company one keeps, and the language one uses. By imitating the form and format of the wealthy, he begins to join them. Joe-as-cobra strikes again. Ruthlessly, he tricks the maid, erases his immigrant past, and begins his re-creation—all with a few adroitly written sentences.

This forging of a personality and philosophy takes place through shifting points of view and ambiguous personal pronouns within a temporally fragmented story. The resulting non-linearity lends the novel a fantasy quality which makes Joe's description of a dream serve as an analysis of Doctorow's technique: "The account in helpless linear translation of the unending love of our simultaneous but disynchrous lives" (p. 254). Characters replay each other and break into each others' stories (as in *Ragtime*), because their lives are at once parallel, intersecting, and tangential. At three strategic places in the novel, Joe hears the tune "Exactly Like You." This is a hint to the reader that the women characters form two basically identical series and that Joe becomes the moral equivalent of Bennett while trying not to become exactly like the failed poet Warren Penfield. Doubles and mirror images govern not just characters and plot elements, but also the prose of the novel. For example, Penfield's poems and anecdotes, while initially appearing digressionary and whimsical in terms of the novel's structure, actually mirror ethical problems and esthetic issues surrounding the poet's younger alter ego, Joe. They also reinforce the motifs of role-playing and self-made man. Penfield's *Child Bride in a Zen Garden* contains a stanza on the emperor who was "A self-impersonator, a self impersonating a self in splendor" (p. 98).

Role playing (saying the right lines at the right place) fashions a persona and thereby becomes a means to power. Since Joe of Paterson seeks both a new identity and the power of wealth, it is logical that his play-acting gathers momentum as he grows in ambition and cleverness. Joe admires "pictures with high style," and he gleans from the movies that he, too, can play different roles for different audiences and purposes. That most of his later lines derive directly from the movies, Joe concedes with a perceptive analysis: "He fitted himself out in movie stars he discarded them. I was interested in the way I instantly knew who the situation called for and became him" (p. 8). His acting lessons intensify at the carnival, and, as he had learned on the street as a kid, good acting meant survival: "It was as if I had to acclimate myself to the worst there was. . . . I knew it was important not to *act* like a rube" (p. 20, my italics). Once at Loon Lake, in Act I Joe portrays a trespasser/interloper and later cannot decide whether to play rich boy or servant. As a compromise, he works for Bennett by day and dons argyle socks by night. Joe and Libby play millionaires by dressing the parts; they take possession of Loon Lake temporarily by appropriating the Bennett wardrobes. In his early scenes with the intimidating leading lady, Clara, he feels as if he needs a "script" for his lines (p. 83). He reasons astutely that he must feign supreme calmness to win Clara (p. 104). He must *pretend* that he has a right to her in order to claim that right. A quick study, he easily learns to repeat possessive pronouns to appear to possess objects. Like Jay Gatsby's talk of "his" house, "his" car, "his" river, Joe appropriates his own "personal ethyl" for his auto. To complete the drama, he must lie to Penfield and concoct a story about Clara to insure their escape. Again Doctorow links morality and language: Joe attains power by lying and then believing and acting out his own lies, and by performing his part well. As a fugitive his very subsistence depends on the right props, costumes, and lines. On the road, when it comes time to register for a hotel room, Joe finds the right words not from experience but from the movies (p. 143). Then trading in the Mercedes for a common station wagon necessitates a new script. He weaves an elaborate fiction about Bennett as his father, which by now acquires a measure of truth, as he has acted the part of son so well and has inherited Bennett's legacy of amorality.

Ironically, the runaway lands himself in a sticky legal predicament with the Jackson police because he has revamped a typical cinema revenge plot: he chooses a job at Bennett Autobody expressly to taunt and goad the owner. The interrogation scene at police headquarters comes straight out of Bogart movies. "You've got the wrong man," protests Joe. Then he becomes a self-conscious scriptwriter, director, and actor simultaneously, as he fabricates a personal biography and a union history. By manufacturing his story piece by piece, the way F. W. Bennett manufactures cars, he illustrates what many of Doctorow's protagonists show in different ways—that language confers power. By playing innocent he is declared innocent. Joe's routine (part James Cagney and part Red James, his fellow worker and exposed spy) demonstrates the power of words for pure survival. Words represent "survival at its secret source," he explains, working against that which "threatens my extinction," a murder charge. "I had found a voice to give authority to the claim I was making—without knowing what that claim would be, I had found the voice for it, I listened to myself to the performance as it went on" (pp. 226–27).

In similar fashion, Joe talks himself out of confining romantic relationships and into inheriting Loon Lake from Bennett (his spiritual father all along). He probably also talks his way into a job at the CIA. Of course Joe will excel there—though some reviewers found the ending of *Loon Lake* contrived and unrealistic. After all, this government agency is a domain of power where role-playing, pretense, and disguise on a grand scale create a new reality, and where moral issues are routinely bypassed. Greed and lust for power have made Joe as mechanical and unfeeling as one of Bennett's automobiles: "Calculating, heedless, and without gratitude, I accepted every circumstance that had put me there, only gunning my mind [cf. gunning the engine] to the future, wanting more, expecting more, too intent on what was ahead to sit back and give thanks or to laugh or to feel bad" (p. 120). A lust for power has reduced him to an "autobody" indeed, a machine—one of the central metaphors (since T. S. Eliot) for modern, mechanized man.

Yet Doctorow does "feel bad" about ethics and morals in America. It matters little whether the period be the ragtime era, the Depression, the repressive forties or the radical sixties. In *Ragtime* and *Loon Lake* especially, he uses his many voices and styles not for their own sake but to show that both victors and victims are the losers. Desire for wealth may indeed be the root of all evil, concludes Doctorow, and the serious writer must address this truth: "No system, whether it's religious or anti-religious or economic or materialistic, seems to be invulnerable to human venery and greed and insanity. . . . In the largest, most philosophical sense, the writer has to be subversive, of course. If he exists simply to endorse the complacent vision or the lies of the society then there's no reason for him to exist."[28]

Doctorow's most recent works of fiction are less political, more personal explorations. Closer to the writer himself, they still ask a socially important question: What precisely *is* the role of the artist in America? *Lives of the Poets* (1984) demonstrates experimentation with shorter fictional forms. It consists of six short stories, each in a distinct voice, and climaxes in a novella, the title piece. Here the self-conscious, self-reflexive writer talks about his domestic situation (the life of the poet) and his difficult creative process. He deals also with the troubled marriages of his artist-friends (the lives of the poets) and (implicitly) about his stories, the lives that we have just read. The first story, "The Writer in the Family," shows how, quite literally, a voice can construct a world. Here a young boy gets his artistic initiation when he is called upon by his wealthy and therefore powerful aunt to write letters in the name and style of his dead father. The idea is to keep the father alive for the grandmother. From the beginning, then, his art is co-opted: he is used by the aunt just as his father was used by his mother and sister. The boy skillfully mimics his father's voice and succeeds too well in this fiction; he can call a halt to the ruse only by killing off his father verbally. But before this, he perceives his father clearly for the first time.[29] He sees and understands Jack by matching a picture of his father in a sailor outfit with a remembered image of a shelf of books his father had given him, all sea tales. Now he is ready to write his last letter. He does so in a voice blending his father's with his own, in a moment of genuine truth that demonstrates to us, if not to his aunt, his real power as an artist. In an act of imaginative reconstruction, he gives his father's life the conclusion it deserves by placing his remains at sea:

Dear Mama,
    This will be my final letter to you since I have been told by the doctors that I am dying. . . . I know that I am simply dying of the wrong life. I should never have come to the desert. It wasn't the place for me.
    I have asked Ruth and the boys to have my body cremated and the ashes scattered in the ocean. (p. 17)

This is the end of the first story, that of a life of a young poet. It suggests that the artist is controlled by society's powerful forces and questions whether the artist can write freely and in his own voice. But Doctorow also suggests that there may be positive ways of taking on other personas. The final and longest story, "Lives of the Poets," quotes the voices of Delmore Schwartz and Robert Lowell, and it also alludes to the voices of Shakespeare, Mailer, Oates, Vonnegut, and Updike. But the voice it begins with is that of Samuel Beckett, which here sounds like Molloy or Malone:

My left thumb is stiff, not particularly swollen although the veins at the base are prominent and I can't move it backward or pick up something without pain. Have I had this before? It's vaguely familiar to me and it may subside, but it feels, bulging veins and all, as if it won't, it is either gout or arthritis unless, of course, death to the writer, it is that monstrous Lou Gehrig thing, God save us all.
    . . . And then of course this subtle hearing impairment. Every once in a while I hear the voice but not the words. Is the cervical pinch constricting sound, pinching me into silence?[30]

The narrator's descriptions of the scrotum (p. 105) and the sex act (p. 127) borrow from Beckett's Irish humor, but the tone of the rest of the story is humorous in a uniquely American idiom. "Lives of the Poets" contains the lightest and yet some of the most scathing social satire on the absurdities of America in the 1980s. It mocks everything from do-it-yourself bookcases and middle-aged joggers to gourmet health food. In fact, every page of this story demonstrates a quality of Doctorow's language apparent since *Welcome to Hard Times*—he is a very funny writer.[31] Yet the subject of this fiction is a serious issue, that is, "the infinite task of the human heart," to quote Doctorow quoting Schwartz. We are traveling in the Updike country of American marriage, adultery, separation, and divorce. But in this particular Doctorow vehicle the question becomes how should one, how can one, *express* ideas about affairs, love, relationships, for couples who are "no longer entirely together"? This is especially puzzling if one is ambivalent about the desire for confessional writing: "But everyone talks too much. . . . They violate their own privacy and everything gets hung on the line as if we all live in some sort of marital tenement. Whatever happened to discretion? Where is pride? What has caused this decline in tact and duplicity?" (p. 84).

Of course, one way to write about a difficult subject, besides through self-mocking humor, is through metaphor and analogy. In his stories of crumbling marriages, Jonathan intersperses his observations of the wrecking and reconstruction of a nearby building with his analysis of the emotional scaffolding of a relationship and the threads of a union—all the while chronicling the destruction of the United Thread Mills.[32] For example, he muses about "the lapse into dereliction of men who have taken down their establishments" (p. 122). Metaphor, along with euphemism and humor, also becomes the method the narrator/protagonist adopts to describe his feelings to his wife. He argues that writing is actually a form of imprisonment, which is why he considers himself justified in joking about giving Angel "visitation rights." Yet the reader also knows (as Jonathan begins to suspect) that his writing and fantasizing are divorcing him from the real world—or is his imagined world just as real?

Jesus Christ, after a while you know you just don't look up in New York when you hear the sirens. There was just a full-complement arrest right out the window nine stories down on Houston, three cop cars parked askew, couple of blue-and-white motor scooters, a dozen

cops and plainclothesmen milling about at the Mobil gas station and
one slender man, hands cuffed behind his back, being shoved into
an unmarked car with a turning red light on the roof. And sitting
with the last paragraph, I missed the whole thing. (p. 90)

Ironically, he hasn't missed the whole episode but has recreated
it in great detail. Hence he gives Art supremacy over Life.

The lover he awaits, his Dark Lady, materializes only through
words—that is, through the narrator's lyrical descriptions of
their loving and lovemaking and the woman's own scant words
on postcards. When "Lives of the Poets" was interpreted as autobiography, Doctorow stated quite directly in an interview that
the Lady was not a former lover but the Muse. Again, inspiration
means the right language: "To do your job properly, always let
the language do it for you."[33] As Jonathan traces the letters of a
sentence announcing her absence ("I have met some people and
am going on with them"), he recalls one of her observations:
"Language is something that almost isn't there." What is there is
not art but existence, not poetry but lives. His wife and children
are very much present, and also there, newly arrived in New
York, is a family of Spanish immigrants, needing shelter. Now
the narrator gets the opportunity to literalize the metaphor Doctorow has stated repeatedly in interviews: the role of the writer
in America is to tell the truth, to witness. When Jonathan tries
to avoid taking in the poor family ("I want to help out but I have
to confess I had in mind a less fervent participation"), the priest
replies, "This is what it means to bear witness" (p. 143). Yet he
does participate, even though his displacement complicates his
creative work and may force him to experience "reentry" shock
on a return to his old home in Connecticut.[34] By the end of the
self-referential story, Jonathan combines witnessing with bearing
witness, good writing and good deeds, by playing typewriter
with the little boy of the immigrant family: "Little kid here want
to type. OK, I hold his finger, we're typing now, I lightly press
his tiny index finger, the key, striking, delights him, each letter
suddenly struck vvv he likes the v, hey who's writing this?" Thus
The Lives of the Poets ends with joyous, childlike pleasure in
writing combined with a metaphorical scene of the truly engaged, witnessing writer.

We are tempted to read World's Fair (1985) as autobiography,
since the protagonist happens to have the same first name, birthday, and childhood experiences as Edgar Doctorow. Still, it is
more valuable to read it as a contemporary American portrait of

the artist as a young boy, as well as a view of the young artist as "a little criminal of perception" (similar to Daniel, or to Huck Finn). Here again truthful language leads to moral vision. Doctorow says that he "wrote the book on the presumption—which I realized after I started—that a child's life is morally complex, and that a child is a perception machine. A child's job is to perceive."[35] Indeed, one critic argues that perception or artistic understanding is the only hope and "counter-force" Doctorow offers against the injustice and disillusionment that are the norm for his characters.[36] In its form, World's Fair presents what Doctorow calls "the solace of shared perceptions." It offers a series of numbered chapters by the first-person protagonist, the young boy Edgar. These are interrupted at strategic junctures by chapters named either "Rose," "Donald," or "Aunt Frances," in which mother, brother, and aunt expand and correct the vision of the young son.

Doctorow here gives the child the same kind of cloudy understanding he gave to Daniel and Susan, so that Frederick Karl's analysis of The Book of Daniel applies equally to World's Fair: "Doctorow has located the material in a kind of limbo or stillness that recalls Kafka's searching narratives. For the world of the children, while full of personally observed details, never contains the totality of experience; it is always partial, a search for missing elements."[37] Thus style and structure mirror perfectly Edgar's growing awareness and his attempt to learn the past from the vantage point of the present. In this and many other ways, World's Fair abides in James Joyce's world of Dubliners and Portrait. It, too, unfolds in a place of missed or partial epiphanies, visions and revisions of family history, moments of terrible disillusionment, and childish confusions of cause and effect. The most disturbing discovery for Edgar—and the most effectively portrayed by Doctorow—is the child's "insufficient knowledge" of his parents' coupling: "My mother and father, rulers of the universe, were taken by something over which they had no control. . . . The devastating truth was that there were times when my parents were not my parents; and I was not on their minds" (p. 78).

For both young artists, Stephen Dedalus and Edgar, the world is a universe of words, and ultimately through language comes knowledge, control, and power. Edgar's vision focuses on particular words: "This was a place called Kensico, an Indian name" (p. 51). His mind moves from events to names. He shifts, for example, from "They were the ones, I knew, who chalked the strange marks on our garage doors" to "it's bad, Donald told me. . . . It's a swastika" (p. 53). To the young Edgar, the strange yet "American" language of Yiddish connotes persecution and funerals, "mostly Jewish death words. Jewish death was spreading" (p. 101). Here and elsewhere Edgar confuses denotation and connotation, literal and figurative. Even as he tries his first metaphors ("I was a dust mop of emotions"), he is fearful of figurative language when the literal level is too bizarre, as in some song lyrics and in the images in *Alice in Wonderland*. He analyzes his mother's confounding image, "'I'm going to knock the spots out of you,'" by concluding, "maybe it was a dust metaphor." But even when he cannot measure the meanings, his way of uncovering reality is by language, whether written or spoken. Later, from the radio Edgar learns that words can create a new fictional universe as well as peopling the real world: "Listening to programs, you saw them in your mind" (p. 130).

There are famous scenes in *Portrait* where Stephen Dedalus experiences moments of transcendent understanding. These include when he sees the word "fetus" and later when he hears and profoundly recognizes his own name. These scenes are echoed in *World's Fair* when the boy ponders the word "scumbag" and thereby sees the world anew:

> It seems to me now that in this elemental place, these packed public beaches in the brightest rawest light of day, I learned the enlightening fear of the planet. . . . Beyond any name's recognition, under the shouting and teeming life of the world's public on their tribal Sunday of half-nude ceremony, was some quiet revelation in me of unutterable life. I was inspired in this state of clarity to whisper the word *scumbag*. It was as if all the sound had stopped, the voices, the reedy cry of gulls, the sirens and the thunderous surf, for that one word to be articulated to illumination. . . . All of this astonishingly was; and I on my knees in my bodying perception, worldlessly primeval, and home, fearful, joyous. (p. 63)

Significantly, by the end of this passage he sounds much like the Stephen Dedalus of the "Proteus" chapter of *Ulysses* remaking the world in his own images.

Words bring not just fear and elation but also power and honor in the development of both *Portrait* and *World's Fair*. Just as Stephen earns praise and family attention with his prize-winning essays in school, Edgar wins the joy of bringing his parents to the World's Fair (the reversal of his earlier childish wish) by writing on the ironic subject, the all-American boy. A good performance, Edgar had intuited earlier (like Joe before him), can get you what you want. In his mother's linguistic universe, life is a series of warnings and lessons. Edgar incorporates her vocabulary yet individualizes it when he learns the "lesson" of art, of writing, from the circus clown's disguises:

> I took profound instruction from this hoary circus routine. . . . There was art in the thing, the power of illusion, the mightier power of the reality behind it. What was first true was then false, a man was born from himself. . . . [That] there were ways to dramatize this to an unsuspecting world was the keenness of my understanding. You didn't have to broadcast everything you knew all at once, but could reveal it suspensefully, and make them first cry out in fear, and make them laugh, and, above all, make them applaud, when they finally saw what an achievement had been yours by taking on so well and accurately the comic being of a little kid. (p. 116)

The clown's achievement, of course, self-consciously and self-referentially explained, is Doctorow's achievement in this very novel. He reveals Edgar's revelations gradually; he gives us all the moods of childhood, thereby taking on the comic persona of the little-kid version of himself.[38]

The child voice moving toward adult perceptions is one of many "oppositions" in World's Fair. In general, a cluster of cumulative images surrounding and subsuming the World's Fair of 1939–40 illuminates, for Edgar and for Reader, the basic dichotomies of male and female (figured in the pointed needle and round hemisphere of the fair, pictured at the beginning of every chapter), youth and maturity, innocence and experience, grand scale and miniature scale, and especially fictional world and real world. The adult Edgar realizes that his child view was only one of many possible fictions; he knows now that he must merge the language of Donald, Rose, and Frances to construct a truer history.

Doctorow was asked by Bill Moyers in an interview if he had ever considered following Tolstoy's example—that is, to do something about the world rather than merely describe it, to quit fiction writing and become "a prophet for justice." He replied:

> Well, I cannot imagine not writing. . . . I love language. I love to be in it. I love to have my mind, sort of, flowing its way through sentences and making discoveries that I hadn't anticipated. It's really very selfish. You want to make something that's good and true and something that didn't exist before and hope it will last, that's all. That's all, but it's everything.[39]

Indeed, Doctorow has demonstrated that he can simultaneously create fictions that are stylistically sound, socially true, and culturally lasting. Traditional in his enjoyment of storytelling, Doctorow nevertheless is innovative in his fragmentation of form. He often plays against some other genre, convention, or mode in each of his novels, yet matches the technique perfectly to the content. As Red says of his music, Doctorow could say of his fiction, "The emotion was tightly locked in the form and there was nothing random about the instrumentation." Orchestrating self-conscious narrators, metafictional devices, the collage technique, multiple perspectives, or whatever he adapts or invents, E. L. Doctorow displays a linguistic richness and structural versatility that make each succeeding fiction a new departure.[40] Each proves an unexpected, unpredictable—but fully realized— experiment. And with each novel, each fusion of language and moral vision, he bears witness to and recomposes America, for in his writings "moral values are inescapably esthetic."

Notes

1. For more on Doctorow's placement within this dichotomy, see Paul Levine, *E. L. Doctorow* (New York and London: Methuen, 1985), pp. 11–15; and Geoffrey Galt Harpham, "E. L. Doctorow and the Technology of Narrative," *A Writer in His Time: A Week with E. L. Doctorow* (Davenport, IA: Visiting Artist Series, 1985), p. 20.

2. Doctorow quoted in Victor S. Navasky, "E. L. Doctorow: 'I Saw a Sign,'" *New York Times Book Review*, 28 September 1980, p. 44.

3. One exception is Arthur Saltzman, "The Stylistic Energy of E. L. Doctorow," in Richard Trenner, ed. *E. L. Doctorow: Essays and Conversations* (Princeton, N.J.: Ontario Review Press, 1983), pp. 73–108. But Saltzman finds the merger of the "artistically venturesome and socially conscientious" coming only with *Loon Lake*, whereas I locate it from the beginning of Doctorow's work. Also, Saltzman is more interested in structure and theme than in language.

4. Reprinted in Trenner, *Essays and Conversations*, p. 14.

5. In Doctorow, "False Documents," an essay included in Trenner, *Essays and Conversations*, p. 17.

6. Ibid., p. 26.

7. Doctorow quoted in Bruce Weber, "The Myth Maker: The Creative Mind of Novelist E. L. Doctorow," *New York Times Magazine*, 20 October 1985, pp. 25ff.

8. E. L. Doctorow, *Drinks Before Dinner* (New York: Random House, 1979), p. xi.

9. Doctorow, *Drinks Before Dinner*, p. xiii.

10. That Blue uses ledgers tends to literalize life as an inhuman "system of debits and credits," with relationships based on "a series of transactions rather than on emotional ties." See Saltzman, in "Stylistic Energy," p. 77.

11. Ibid., p. 76. Saltzman notes that the bad man who consigns people to their graves has the perfectly morbid name of Clay Turner.

12. However, Saltzman disagrees; he describes the language as "sparse, severe" and "without embroidery."

13. See Daniel L. Guillory, "Doctorow as Poet," *A Writer in His Time: A Week with E. L. Doctorow* (Davenport, IA: Visiting Artist Series, 1985), pp. 13–19.

14. Doctorow, as recorded by Navasky, p. 44. Quoted in Levine, *E. L. Doctorow*, p. 11.

15. Frederick Karl, *American Fictions: 1970/1980* (New York: Harper & Row, 1983), p. 262.

16. *Gates of Repentance: The New Union Prayerbook for the Days of Awe* (New York: Central Conference of American Rabbis, 1978), p. 434. Other references are to this edition.

17. Lynne Sharon Schwartz, "Daniel," in David Rosenberg, ed. *Congregation: Contemporary Writers Read the Jewish Bible* (New York: Harcourt Brace Jovanovich, 1987), pp. 428–29.

18. Mark Mirsky, "Daniel," in *Congregation: Contemporary Writers Read the Jewish Bible*, p. 441.

19. Paul Levine, "The Writer as Independent Witness," in Trenner, *Essays and Conversations*, p. 62.

20. Schwartz, "Daniel," p. 419.

21. Ibid., p. 422.

22. Bernhard W. Anderson, *Understanding the Old Testament* (Englewood Cliffs, N.J.: Prentice-Hall, 1957), p. 12. Quoted in Schwartz, "Daniel," p. 434.

23. Doctorow, "False Documents," p. 25.

24. For a fuller analysis, see my earlier article, "Doctorow's *Ragtime*: Narrative as Silhouettes and Syncopation," *Dutch Quarterly Review of Anglo-American Letters* 11 (1981/2): 97–103.

25. Saltzman, "Stylistic Energy," pp. 90–91.

26. Interview with Charles Ruas, *Conversations with American Writers* (New York: Alfred A. Knopf, 1985), p. 200.

27. For a fuller discussion of the motifs, techniques, and doubles in *Loon Lake*, see my article "The Cry of Power Once Heard: Patterning in Doctorow's *Loon Lake*," in *A Writer in His Time: A Week with E. L. Doctorow* (Davenport, IA: Visiting Artist Series, 1985), pp. 1–12.

28. Paul Levine, "Interview with E. L. Doctorow," *Ideas*, CBS Radio, Spring 1978.

29. Images of vision and perception pervade this book, especially in "The Water Works." Here a detective, as he performs his private-eye work, notices himself being watched.

30. E. L. Doctorow, *Lives of the Poets* (New York: Random House, 1984), p. 81. Other page citations of the book refer to this edition.

31. Someone, not I, should write an entire article on Doctorow's satiric humor. Just one example from "Lives of the Poets" should make this clear: "A call from my mother: I saw your friend Norman's name in the newspaper, I see him all the time on television, why don't I ever see you on television? I don't know, Mom, I value my privacy. Why, she says, what are you hiding?" (p. 136).

32. Trenner points out that throughout his fiction Doctorow exploits "the symbolic force of architecture." He uses the details of buildings "to symbolize—generally to ironic effect—moral conditions" (pp. 7–8).

33. Doctorow in Weber, "The Myth Maker," p. 76.

34. The narrator often uses science and space metaphors to illuminate contemporary problems.

35. Doctorow in Weber, "The Myth Maker," p. 78. The boy admits that, on some subjects, "I could only make do, like a detective with the barest of clues, inaudible words, an indefinable sound of panic, a dim light, going on and off" (pp. 78–79).

36. Richard Trenner, Introduction, *Essays and Conversations*, p. 6.

37. Karl, *American Fictions*, p. 261.

38. In another nonfiction context, Doctorow again terms the artist a clown: "As clowns in the circus imitate the aerialists and tightrope walkers, first for laughs and then so that it can be seen that they do it better, we have it in us to compose false documents more valid, more real, more truthful than the 'true' documents of the politicians or the journalists or the psychologists" ("False Documents," Trenner, *Essays and Conversations*, p. 26). In his interview with Weber, Doctorow again returns to the circus metaphor for the writer. Ideally, he says, "you get rid of the lights, you get rid of the music, you forego the drum roll, and finally you do the high-wire act without the wire" (p. 78).

39. Doctorow was speaking on Bill Moyers's T.V. special "World of Ideas" that aired 11 October 1988.

40. As I complete this article, Doctorow's novel *Billy Bathgate* (1989) has just been published.

Panoramic, Unpredictable, and Human:
Joyce Carol Oates's Recent Novels

LINDA WAGNER-MARTIN

A̲ʟᴛʜᴏᴜɢʜ Joyce Carol Oates must be named among America's most successful contemporary novelists, she remains strangely marginalized. The value of her fiction keeps getting displaced, subsumed under arguments about who she is, what her concerns as a writer really are, what role her fiction plays in the paradigm of current literature. Throughout a sprawling labyrinth of reviews and personal interviews, Oates has long evinced her belief that the novelist's function is moral and at least partly didactic. The writer observes culture, lamenting its travesties and tragedies. He or she uses technical virtuosity to write effectively about any theme, any character, any concern. Oates has frequently been compared with Faulkner because of her command of craft, her technical daring, her general artistic sophistication—and her admittedly dark vision of human possibility.

That she is a woman writer is probably less significant than that she draws from all kinds of belief and "knowledge." Yet her gender has skewed reviews of her books throughout her career, beginning in 1964 with *With Shuddering Fall.* She recently wrote that "the impulse to create, like the impulse to destroy is utterly mysterious." It is "one of the primary mysteries of human existence."[1] Once those mysteries are accepted, and the power of the sub (or supra) conscious acknowledged, the writer's work becomes chameleon. It is then realistic, fantastic; labored, effusive; predictable, oblique; naturalistic, mythic; utopian, dystopian; generic, avant-garde; exaggerated, understated. Each of these terms has been used at some point in Oates's career to describe her fiction. Panoramic in theme, unpredictable in method, her writing reflects the human condition as she acknowledges it to be in the latter third of this century. For the most part, her assessment of that human condition is critical. Hence her recent novels have charted themes that society as a whole would rather ignore. Among these are sexual abuse, incest, and the enslavement of physical passion and its consequent betrayal.

One of Oates's most controversial stands within her fiction is that culture is male-determined. In her fiction, women do what they do because of the men of power in their lives. Women are wives, fearful of what their husbands will think or do. They are unquestioning in their submission, or they are young women or adolescents waiting to trap the man who fathers their child, learning early the tricks of sexual manipulation. Or, they are children, sensing where family power lies and responding to the (usually male) sources of it. There are few families anywhere in Oates's fictions that are not male-dominated. There are few women or female adolescents who have lives of their own; their ambition rather is to keep their man, whether father or lover, happy. Because of this schema of domination, most of Oates's main characters are male. They are the determinants of the culture; their actions and decisions count in the lives of all Oates's characters. Oates is often criticized for writing about powerless women and for focusing her attention on men, yet the American culture she describes is still male-dominated. It is in this context of describing gender power that Oates's fiction of the 1980s begins to differ from her earlier work.

Oates's *Marya, A Life* (1986) ostensibly creates a different milieu for the title character. In Marya's "night of patchy dreams, strangers' voices, rain hammering on the tarpaper roof close overhead,"[2] the reader realizes that Marya's union organizer father has been killed. Marya comes to understand the meaning of his death—and the depletion of her family's economic and human resources—later. This occurs when her mother takes her into the morgue and she sees a body, but the body "hadn't any face that you could recognize" (p. 11). Abandoned by their mother, Marya and her two young brothers live with her father's people. Sexually abused during the years she is eight, nine, and ten by her cousin Lee, "who liked her" (he is twelve, thirteen, and fourteen), Marya learns to exist by going "into stone." From her early life on, Marya typifies Oates's fragile, damaged characters, who are often so numbed by the pain of their existence that they perform at what appear to be subhuman levels.

Oates's fiction of the 1980s increasingly focuses on the subhuman, not as a criticism of these characters but as a criticism of the society that forms them. Many are as dehumanized as Richard Wright's Bigger Thomas in *Native Son* (1940). But

Oates's most brutalized characters are women. Victimized by older male relatives—fathers, uncles, cousins—and unprotected by the obtuse or blandly uncaring women of their families, Marya and Enid, the protagonists of her shattering novel *You Must Remember This* (1987), barely survive their frequent psychic mutilations. *You Must Remember This* begins with Enid's suicide attempt: "She swallowed forty-seven aspirin tablets between 1:10 A.M. and 1:35 A.M. locked in the bathroom of her parents' rented house. . . . She stood five feet three inches tall in her bare feet, she weighed eighty-nine pounds."[3] Victimized by her adored young uncle, Enid acts out the horrifying fear that she—though innocent—will be found out, that her uncle will be discovered, that (most realistic of Oates's plot machinations) she will come to enjoy this evil. Wearing her thin silver chain with the Virgin Mary stamped on the medal, she dresses herself all in white like a bride and goes to find death. She seeks the death she has convinced herself she deserves, the death only she can control. Through her chosen death, she will finally come to some kind of power. Oates's poignant cry for women to have control of their bodies and their lives shapes both *Marya, A Life* and *You Must Remember This*.

In both books, Oates resolves her tormented narratives through reconciliations of daughters with mothers, through resolutions of the matriarchal bond. The books are unlike *A Garden of Earthly Delights* or *them*, two of Oates's earlier novels in which mothers are perpetrators of male coercion. These two more recent books explore the ways women come to know both their "selves" and their potential as women in contemporary culture. Even in these efforts, however, Oates's women are very male-dependent. Marya goes through countless debilitating relationships with men, including a dying priest, as well as teachers and other lovers. Like Enid, she leads her life with a relentless subtext of romance, watching for the man who will make her dreams come true— despite the fact that she never dreams. Marya is too numb to have a normal subconscious life. Oates portrays one of her heroine's early high school romances so that the reader is reminded of the cultural imperative for Marya's behavior: "In the beginning she had pursued him [Emmett Schroeder]. . . . Falling in love— 'romance' of one kind or another—behaving like all the other girls. . . . Her 'feeling' for boys, for men, was largely a matter of daydreaming" (p. 101).

Both Marya and Enid have accepted what Oates, in her preface to *You Must Remember This*, describes as the "green of romance, of nostalgia, of innocence." Oates's working title for *You Must Remember This* was "The Green Island," retained here as a subsection title. It provides an image that pulls together the notion of the fresh innocence of adolescence with the highly romanticized fantasy of being shipwrecked on an island with someone. The metaphor of life as some uncontrollable sea and of a woman's safety dependent on her being rescued by a man (any man, regardless of the source of his power) prompts most of Oates's women characters' behavior.

Growing up through a 1950s girlhood that was itself dominated by this myth, Oates knew too well that conventional wisdom Marya and Enid accepted. She has referred to both these novels as her "most personal" books. She also has compared herself as an adolescent to Enid, "The contours of whose soul so resemble my own," not in the experience of sexual abuse but in the painful development of an independent psyche.[4] Women in the world Oates depicts in *You Must Remember This* (carefully dated 1946–56) followed the injunctions of their culture: "You Must Remember This" is not only the title of a maudlin, mindlessly romantic ballad, but it is also a prescription for living the female life. A woman's role was to serve, to listen, to follow orders, and not to originate anything.

> He instructed her to hold still. Not to move. *Not* to move.
> And not to look at him either. Or say a word. (*Marya*, p. 15)

> She remembered his voice, Don't tell anybody will you. (*Remember*, p. 4)

> "Get in! Close the door!" Felix said. . . . He was nerved up, angry. "Does your father know you hitch rides?" he asked. . . . It's cheap and it's asking for trouble—I don't want any niece of mine doing it. . . . You led me on, acting the way you did fooling around the way you did you knew damn well what you were doing didn't you!—and now I see you out on the street hitching rides! . . .
> He lit another cigarette, he let her cry for a while, then said, "It's stopped raining," though in fact it hadn't quite stopped yet. "You can get out now, Enid. Get out." (*Remember*, pp. 130–32)

Even as adults, Oates's women characters continue these patterns; they are frozen in the psychological states abuse has created for them. In Marya's later relationship with Professor Fein, she again takes orders and lets herself be manipulated. She is used and reused, both sexually and professionally. Yet it is the much older and cynical Fein who tells her that she must find her mother. The novel builds to that predictable ending, but the effect of Marya's finding her mother is left ambiguous. She has written to the woman she has not seen since childhood, and her mother has replied. In the novel's last scene Marya prepares to open her mother's letter:

> As if a dream secret and prized in her soul had blossomed outward, taking its place, asserting its integrity. . . . She placed the envelope carefully on a table and sat in front of it staring, smiling, a pulse beating in her forehead. How odd to see her name—Marya Knauer—her name in a handwriting that belonged to her mother, a handwriting she did not recognize.
>   Marya, this is going to change your life, she thought, half in dread.
>   Marya, this is going to cut your life in two. (p. 275)

The ending of You Must Remember This is much more ambiguous. Oates's layered structure has Enid leaving for college, the appropriate demise of Felix, the reunion of her parents (which culminates in an almost powerless sexual act), and the poignant letter from Enid's brother, Warren. In following his example (leaving "home"), Enid has saved herself—the reader supposes. But Warren's closing letter to Enid expresses the unpredictable—and ungovernable—power of physical passion:

> Strange isn't it—how "love" seems to carry with it no knowledge. The people I have loved most in my lifetime (including you) I haven't known at all. Nor have they known me.
>   The blood ties are so powerful and deep and mute. Something terrifying there. How we feel about one another—even about the house on East Clinton Street—so strange, helpless, paralyzing and exciting both. It's only away where people don't know me or haven't known me for very long that I am myself. (p. 416)

In You Must Remember This, Warren takes a positive maternal role. Although Enid's mother does find a professional life for herself—in her sewing and designing, her physically leaving the house—the ending of the novel shows her once again locked in the sex act, repeating her husband's hesitant profession of love. But she has provided for Enid the beautiful quilt the latter takes with her to school; it is an emblematic gift of women's understanding and power (albeit worked in the wedding ring pattern). The ending of Oates's 1987 novel seems to countermand the comparatively simple ambivalence of Marya, A Life.

Elaine Showalter, in her essay on Oates and this novel, finds
Marya's reaching back "to find the mother who has abandoned
her, and to reclaim a matrilineage that is both painful and em-
powering,"[5] to be mostly positive. Showalter states that for Marya
to deny "the mother's country. . . is to be a permanent exile"
(p. 152). Yet she also acknowledges—in response to the grim
tone of the book—that Marya's gesture of reconciliation is not
itself a panacea.

> The community of women is not idyllic, but torn by rage, competi-
> tion, primal jealousies, ambiguous desire, and emotional violence,
> just like the world in which women seem subordinate to and victim-
> ized by men.

In this comment, and in other reviews of *You Must Remember
This*, critics have again taken up their pastime of making Joyce
Carol Oates into a feminist writer. One of the reasons *Marya, A
Life* and *You Must Remember This* were well received is that in
these books comparatively strong women characters endured,
even succeeded, though undeniably damaged by the gender
struggles of their culture. It seemed to Oates's many readers as
if she had become more interested in the problems of women and
might be moving toward writing about fully achieving women
protagonists. (The thirty-five years of Oates's career as novelist
have engendered a tapestry of criticism about the absence of
feminist themes in her writing.[6])

Oates has repeatedly spoken to the conflicts of being both
writer and woman—not about any inherent conflict in being a
woman who writes, but about critics' reaction to women writers.
In her essay "(Woman) Writer: Theory and Practice," she stated:
"She is likely to experience herself, from within, as a writer
primarily: perhaps even a writer exclusively. . . . When the writer
is alone with language and with the challenging discipline of
creating an art by way of language alone, she is not defined to
herself as 'she.'"[7] Oates then declares—though less militantly
than she might have in either the 1960s or the 1970s (as she has
no desire to discount her female being and psyche): "Is memory
gender-bound? Are impressions filtered through the prism of
gender? Is there a distinctly female voice?—or even a conspicu-
ously feminine voice?" (p. 23).

Most of Oates's essays and prefaces that deal with the gender
issue have been negations of the Gilbert and Gubar position that
now dominates the critical world. This view suggests that women

writers suffer under an "anxiety of authorship" different from, and more intense than, the anxieties of male writers. Oates is confident enough of both her vision and her voice to downplay the effects gender has on the writer's natural state of hesitancy. Hence when Oates herself writes about *Marya, A Life*, she sees the importance of the closing episode: She perceives Marya's attempt to find her mother as less a matriarchal connection (the search for parent become thoroughly gender based) than a humane one. Oates states that Marya's action is positive because she makes the choice "finally"; she chooses "not to accept the terms of their [her] own betrayal."[8] She acts against the betrayer, the parent who happens to be mother rather than father.

Some critics believed they were seeing some pattern of more self-assertive women protagonists in Oates's 1980s fiction. For them, her 1989 novel, *American Appetites*, reversed whatever tendency they might have anticipated. Ian McCullough, highly esteemed research Ph.D., and his wife, Glynnis, author of successful cookbooks, lead a chic upper middle-class social and intellectual life. Disturbed only by the emotional vicissitudes of Bianca, their nineteen-year-old, their life runs to predictable busyness: Ian leads a remote, conventional intellectual life; Glynnis punctuates her suburban days with short-lived affairs— several with Ian's best friends. When Ian becomes fascinated by Sigrid Hunt, one of Glynnis's young protégées who had formerly been a dancer, the outer fabric of their life is shredded by Glynnis's jealousy. After Glynnis's quasi-accidental death, the reader is left to determine motives for Ian, Sigrid, and Bianca—motives for their subsequent behavior, not for their actual or fantasized complicity in Glynnis's death.

Despite the semblance of power each woman in this novel pretends, none is self-actualizing. Glynnis arranges not only her husband's existence but also a great many other people's. (One key anecdote is her memory of having sex with Ian's best friend, Denis, just minutes before the two of them go to lunch with their respective spouses as a foursome.) Bianca's defiance of her mother is a move against that awesome control. Her "present" for her father's fiftieth birthday is the parodic sexual dance, and it provides a useful glimpse into her understanding of the forces that motivate adult culture. Glynnis sits at the center of the web that shapes life in Hazelton-on-Hudson. Hence the shattered glass in the picture window represents Glynnis's webs or lines of power, as well as the actual cracks in the glass as she falls through it to her death.

Rather than equating Glynnis's control with strength, however, Oates shows how frightened Glynnis is once she suspects that Ian might have a lover. His asexuality, which had shown itself in occasions of impotence throughout their twenty-six-year marriage, now becomes more threatening than any overt hostility. In her drunken, violent response to him, Glynnis shows the hidden passions, the hungers, that had prompted so many of her actions in the past. By making Glynnis the proprietor of foods, cooking, and homes, Oates aligns the natural hungers for food and sex with the matriarchy.

Lest the reader miss the horror of Glynnis's complicated life because of the coolly understated prose, Oates underscores the vapidity of suburban women's lives. She does so by creating a macabre affair between Ian and Meika (whose older husband, Vaughn, had been one of Glynnis's lovers) soon after Ian is accused of Glynnis's murder. Meika, like Glynnis, is every bit the predator. By the close of *American Appetites*, Ian is living with Sigrid and planning a marriage, and Meika and Ian's attorney, Ottinger, are living together. Sexual liaisons are reasonless, impermanent, destructive, Oates's novel warns, but they are an expected part of all hearty and elite "American appetites." Her listeners understand full well the pathetic confession Sigrid makes on the witness stand: "I was caught up in this love affair which seemed to be sucking all the life from me. It was just a state I had drifted into . . . a pathological state of the soul."[9]

The closing coda has two of Ian's best friends (one is Denis, the lover Glynnis has taunted him about) come for a lunch that Sigrid has prepared. She has unwittingly contributed to a closed male camaraderie that shuts her out and makes her only a sexual object. The incident shows the mystery and the impenetrability of every human relationship. Supposedly Ian's best friend, Denis, has lied to him about his affair with Glynnis. Both lunch guests, Denis and Malcolm Oliver, have been Meika's lovers. Ian has no idea why he plans to marry Sigrid. He says in a later part of the scene, "I will blow my brains out when the season turns" (p. 337). The rapacity—conscious or unconscious—of these upstanding male professionals lies just under their veneer of accomplishment and wit.

Oates foreshadows our bleak knowledge that Sigrid will be left to bear the loss—and probably the guilt—of Ian's death by having her speak only once during the male-dominated luncheon. In that scene she tells the story of her dancing the role of the doomed Princess Creon in *Medea,* an oblique parallel to her triangle with Ian and Glynnis. Just as Medea in her bitter jealousy sends the princess the beautiful poisoned gifts that melt her flesh from her bones, so Glynnis has given Sigrid the anguishing work of caring for Ian. She is covered by his body in the sex act just as Princess Creon was by the poisoned robes. Sigrid states that "the Princess is so innocently vain, or . . . vainly innocent, she accepts the gifts immediately, and puts them on, and preens in front of a mirror, and dies an agonizing death" (p. 327).

Becoming lovers the night of Ian's acquittal, Sigrid and he as couple are the immediate result of Ian's fear *of* death (his own) and his fear *from* the death (of Glynnis). His fear gives him a sexual power that he had earlier lost. The *Medea* narrative also suggests incest—in that it includes the Princess's father, the Creon who—in trying to remove her flaming garments—also dies. Oates uses many references to Ian's and Sigrid's ages, to Sigrid's estrangement from her father, to Bianca's estrangement from Ian, and to Sigrid's appearance at the luncheon "like a tall somber child in a nightgown"; the allusions suggest that the sexual bond between Ian and Sigrid, as their names suggest, is incestuous. Sigrid has already had one abortion; the next fruit of her passionate involvements will be Ian's death. The reader is reminded of Ian's irrational binary statement to Nick Ottinger as they wait for the jury to bring in its verdict: "I will blow my brains out . . . or I will get married again and begin my life over." "I will blow my brains out or I will marry" (pp. 328, 330).

As if to illustrate her statements about gender-determined imaginations, Oates creates in *American Appetites* a novel in which gender is less important than morality. Men and women alike break codes of marriage and friendship and professional loyalty. Only the "innocently vain, or vainly innocent"—Ian, Bianca, and to a lesser degree Sigrid—can be hurt by disillusion: What does marriage "mean"? What does family "mean"? *American Appetites*, one of the most graphically bitter of Oates's novels, implies that language—like the social and moral codes it represents—"means" nothing. The most chilling scene in the novel is Denis's lying to Ian about his former relationship to the now-dead Glynnis.

As Sigrid's single narrative suggests, the misleading and oversimplified romance script is to blame for much of the novel's and the culture's sorrow. Dissatisfied with professions and roles, women look for fulfillment in sexual relationships. Sigrid's life was such a paradigm, and one can assume Glynnis's was, too. As Sigrid says, "at the time I became involved in this love affair,

I was feeling ill-used and embittered about losing my job at Vassar" (p. 313). The appetites of Oates's characters are explicable, however, not only in terms of the late twentieth-century culture but also as ramifications of primordial gender patterns. In Oates's 1979 novel *Cybele*, she established the same patterns, creating in the unaware Edwin Locke a precursor of the equally unaware Ian McCullough.

Her *Cybele* is the story of a middle-aged man whose quick and destructive love affairs with a half-dozen women lead to the actual death with which the novel opens. At forty-four, Edwin Locke was a prosperous businessman, stable in his love for his wife, Cynthia, and his two sons. The family is part of an established suburban social group. At forty-six, he is depleted from sexual and drug experimentation, living on the fringe of society, ready to become a child molester. The explanation for Locke's perversion is given by the mysterious narrator of the novel, the *I* of Chapter One ("*In Memoriam.* Edwin Locke") and of subsequent brief references, Cybele. With characteristic whimsy, Oates gives the reader no way of identifying the narrator except through the title.

Cybele is the great earth mother, nature goddess, mother of the gods, and wife of Cronus. She is known also as Demeter, Rhea, Op, protectress of the wild things of the earth. But she is probably best known in mythology for her relationship with Attis. Jealous of his turn to other women, Cybele drives him mad so that he castrates himself. He dies under a pine tree, where violets eventually grow. In other versions of the myth, Attis, like Adonis, is killed by a boar. Spring was the season for Attis to be celebrated because he was the god of vegetation. Other objects or images connected with the Cybele-Attis myth are the lions that either accompanied Cybele or drew her chariot, the drum or cymbals she carried, and the dancing and wild music used to celebrate her being. (Without extensive elaboration, it is clear that *American Appetites* makes use of a great many of these characteristics.)

Oates's narrator/author points out in chapter 1 that the story will accelerate greatly as it continues. It assumes the form of dance itself, so that by the end of the narrative "no one will see him [Locke] at all and he certainly will have lost even his incomplete vision of himself."[10] The novel fulfills that promise, so that the last chapters become more and more fragmented and less connected to previous segments. As Locke changes lovers rapidly, we know less and less about them and about his state of mind. Oates's narrative method changes to show the precipitous changes in the man and in his social behavior.

The character of Edwin Locke can be read as an ironic re-creation of seventeenth-century philosopher John Locke, creator of the idea of the pleasure principle. The travesty which the search for pleasure becomes in *Cybele* is far removed from the ideal balance that Locke wrote about in 1690 in *An Essay Concerning Human Understanding*. Oates's Locke exemplifies the horrors of ignorance, of the equation of sexual pleasure with "love," and of a male's complete ego absorption in the sexual act, without thought for his partner. "He knows only that the October night is beautiful, that the future lies all before him, rich with the surprise, the continual shock, of sensual pleasure; it lies in wait for him. The past does not exist. The past is falling away, moment by moment, helpless to impede him. . . . *this is why we are born*, Edwin Locke thinks" (p. 98). No other human being is important to this man; his ego has become the center; what matters is his experience, his sensual pleasure. The rest of *Cybele* chronicles a succession of meaningless relationships—with a hint of homosexual, group, and child partners. These illustrate the indiscriminate search that obsesses Locke.

That search finally becomes faceless. A body is any body, and all sex partners become

> An immense hill into which he wants to burrow. Head-first. Trembling with desire. Sobbing with desire. And the hill becomes flesh, and the flesh seems to flinch from his violence, his need, whimpering as if it were alive; but still he forces himself into it. Like this! Like this! Like this! And as he forces himself into it it does give way, it succumbs, he pounds at it with his head, plunging, burrowing, half-choking with the rage of his desire, until he has penetrated my very core.

Cybele's speech gives her identity away to the reader: "my" very core is the feminine principle, the earth mother, who first entices and then traps irretrievably. The passage above continues,

> And then the flesh, which has parted for him, in fear of him, begins to contract.
> And horribly, he is caught in me. Trapped.
> Swallowed alive!
> He screams for help, for release. But of course no one hears. His screams are not audible, nor is there anyone to hear. For I have him now, I have him fast, and tight, in the hot tight blood-thrumming

depths of me, and he will never withdraw, no matter how frantically he struggles to get free, no matter how valiantly his poor strained heart beats: I have him, I have him forever. (pp. 200–201)

Oates continues, "it's the oldest story in the world, isn't it?" She reinforces the image of Cybele, waiting till Locke plays himself out, winding to the inevitable end of the saga—his own death.

Death comes to Locke not by castration, which has been grad-ual throughout the novel in various episodes of impotence, but by scissor stabs to the heart. The real seat of passion, this change from the Attis legend implies, is the heart and not the genitals. Locke dies from the scissor injuries, but he is immolated as well, burned after his murderer "dribbles" gas over his body "with a certain ceremonial grace." Locke's death occurs, Cybele makes clear, because he hadn't "the insight. He never understood." His burned body, found by the very children he would have liked to use as sex partners, is finally mistaken for that of a dog. It is not only bereft of gender distinctions, but also of humanity.

In *Mysteries of Winterthurn* (1984),[11] Oates creates another of these men for whom sexual passion is all-important. Xavier Kil-garvan, the detective-hero of *Mysteries*, is as passionately fool-hardy as Edwin Locke or Ian McCullough. Xavier, at sixteen, falls irresistibly in love with his distant cousin Perdita. Because of horrible crimes occurring in his cousin's home, Xavier (with the idealism suggested by his named saint, Francis Xavier) becomes a detective. Oates gives the reader scene after scene in which conventional religious accouterments carry sinister meaning. For example, the cherubs surrounding the Virgin Mary in a ceil-ing painting attempt to seduce Xavier as he keeps watch in the murder bower, just as Perdita has earlier enticed him to the attic of her home where Xavier eventually finds wire-choked infant bodies swaddled and laid in bureau drawers. The sensual and depraved grow from, or into, the religious, as Oates follows the familiar Gothic interpretation of humanity's quest for emotional gratification.

Although the novel falls into three seemingly separate tales—horrific accounts of strange and never-solved crimes—*Mysteries* is the story of Xavier and his obsessive passion for Perdita. Ironi-cally—or with the mockery of narrative conventions so obvious throughout Oates's work—the novel has a "happy ending" as Perdita and Xavier finally marry. When Xavier gives up his occu-pation as detective, however, the reader assumes that he becomes a lost man. But this irony is never apparent, and the reader—

lulled by the conventions of the genre—gives a sigh of relief when the marriage occurs. The reader is convinced that Xavier's efforts have finally paid off in this long-anticipated but unexpected reward.

If anything, *Mysteries* is a comic novel—although the relationship of Erasmus Kilgarvan to his oldest daughter, Georgina (the self-styled poet Iphigenia), is difficult to read as comedy. Incest is one way of murdering the child, just as Agamemnon tried to sacrifice his daughter to the gods. In her description of Georgina as Emily Dickinson, Oates carefully underplays the macabre. Instead, she makes an important comment about family power structures, the coercion by the religious community, and the impossibility of women using their talents and finding freedom—unless that freedom is sanctioned by patriarchal power.

Her *Mysteries of Winterthurn*, like its triad genre novels *Bellefleur* and *A Bloodsmoor Romance*, shows Oates's easy versatility. Such a deviation from her usual intense naturalism or fantasy as to be found in this trio proves again that Oates's writing, collectively, merits the same kind of explicative and diverse critical methodology that is generally applied to Thomas Pynchon's fiction. The chief difference between the two writers is that Oates's sense of humor is even more madcap. She directs her humor at the most sacred cultural and literary conventions while offering so few clues that her fiction becomes a great, wry mystery. In *Mysteries of Winterthurn* she gives the reader the most rational of frameworks: "Editor's Notes," "Postscripts," "Epilogues," and the detective-novel tradition itself. It proves an organization that suggests ends and reliable conclusions (the three-part, separate mystery structure) and a sane narrative voice that describes a seemingly sane detective figure. What we are left with, however, is a completely inexplicable novel; it is not one of the mysteries explained in any way. We also are left with an ever-widening rift between the rational and the irrational: in the case of Xavier, it is between the psychic health we associate with sanity and his own brand of passionate madness. Oates's *Mysteries* then is a conundrum of literary conventions, even to the concrete poems created by the entries in her table of contents.

To see these two earlier novels—*Cybele* and *Mysteries of Winterthurn*—in the light of Oates's three later fictions—*Marya, A Life, You Must Remember This*, and *American Appetites*—is to see how differently she has come to approach the same themes. These include sexual passion and enthrallment, the cultural adoption of the panacea of sex, and the underlying destruction of women's freedom as a result of these attitudes about sexuality during the later 1980s. What might have once become a text that could evoke some humor has become fiction of the highest possible seriousness. Oates is convinced that her writing mirrors life and that life exists in some part to teach and to admonish. This conviction has given her many readers these embittered and embittering novels about women's lives, lived in the strangleholds of the men their culture has empowered. It is not a satisfying vision, but it is a true one. And Oates is once again fulfilling her own role as Cassandra in the panorama of contemporary American fiction.

Notes

1. Joyce Carol Oates, (Woman) Writer, Occasions and Opportunities (New York: E. P. Dutton, 1988), p. 3.

2. Joyce Carol Oates, Marya, A Life (New York: Berkeley, 1988), p. 1.

3. Joyce Carol Oates, You Must Remember This (New York: Harper & Row, Perennial Library, 1988), p. 3.

4. Oates, (Woman) Writer, pp. 379–80.

5. Elaine Showalter, "Joyce Carol Oates: A Portrait," Ms (March 1986), reprinted in Modern Critical Views, Joyce Carol Oates, ed. Harold Bloom (New York: Chelsea House, 1987), pp. 137–45. See esp. p. 137.

6. See my collection, Critical Essays on Joyce Carol Oates (Boston: G. K. Hall, 1979), especially the Introduction and essays by Charles Lam Markmann, Sanford Pinsker, Eileen Bender, and Joanne V. Creighton. See also Victor Strandberg, "Sex, Violence, and Philosophy in You Must Remember This," Studies in American Fiction 17 (Spring 1989): 3–17.

7. Oates, (Woman) Writer, pp. 22–23.

8. Ibid., p. 378.

9. Joyce Carol Oates, American Appetites (New York: E. P. Dutton, 1989), p. 314.

10. Joyce Carol Oates, Cybele (Santa Barbara, CA: Black Sparrow Press, 1979), pp. 11–12.

11. Joyce Carol Oates, Mysteries of Winterthurn (New York: E. P. Dutton, 1984).

Women's Life-Writing and the Minority Voice: Maya Angelou, Maxine Hong Kingston, and Alice Walker

SUZETTE A. HENKE

Both autobiography and the autobiographical or confessional novel offer a unique conflation of history and discourse, of verifiable fact and aesthetic fabulation. To a large extent, every biography imposes narrative form on an otherwise formless and fragmented personal history. Every novel, confessional or otherwise, incorporates shards of individual and social history into the baroque texture of its ostensibly mimetic world. The question I shall address in this essay is how the autobiographical novel can provide a new understanding of the lives of women of color who have been marginalized in contemporary American culture. How can African-American and Asian-American women create the personal space necessary to conquer and transcend prevalent stereotypes of gender, race, and class that limit expectations and circumscribe future possibilities? And how, in particular, does sex-role enculturation affect personal and artistic growth in a world that tacitly oppresses both the minority artist and the autonomous female creator?

What I should like to suggest here is that autobiography is, or at least has the potential to be, a revolutionary form of writing. As such, it lends itself particularly well to the evolution of an enabling feminist discourse rooted in a diversity of ethnic backgrounds. As a genre, autobiography has always encouraged the author/narrator to reassess his or her past and to reinterpret a plethora of racial, sexual, and cultural codes inscribed on personal consciousness. It is no wonder, then, that minority women authors have reacted to the impetus of the second wave of feminism in the 1960s: they have appropriated the autobiographical act as a potential tool for liberation. Women's life-writing, cast in the form of memoir or confessional narrative, promises mastery over a fluid, shapeless, episodic history. Whether relating an individual life-history or transforming experience through fictive fabulation, the author can reinscribe an alienated and marginal self into the pliable body of a protean text. An epiphany or "conversion experience" often takes shape as compensatory fantasy. Then a new, revised self, emerging as autobiographical or fictional protagonist, is free to rebel against the values of the dominant culture. Through the autobiographical act, a female persona creates herself anew and calls herself into being as the protagonist of a fabulated history. As both author and mother to her own identity, she gives birth to a heroine mythically resurrected from the ashes of patriarchy. She becomes empowered to define her subjective identity in a narrative that offers her control of a chaotic, alien, and antagonistic environment.

In my own thinking about autobiography, I have defined the genre broadly, and sometimes metaphorically, to include both confessional writing and the autobiographical novel. Women's life-writing can emerge in a variety of experimental texts. These may range from historical diary and memoir to the *Bildungsroman* whose protagonist clearly shares its author's own youthful trajectory. Maya Angelou's *I Know Why the Caged Bird Sings*, for instance, claims to be self-consciously confessional, but Maxine Hong Kingston's *The Woman Warrior* filters autobiographical experience through a glittering net of narrative embellishment. Alice Walker's epically designed *Bildungsroman, The Color Purple*, stretches the integument of the self-imaging genre to its modal limit by offering ostensibly autobiographical accounts of the lives of its female characters. These extraordinary women of color are all struggling to provide themselves and their sisters with a panoply of mythic themes that will valorize both female and racial identity. Women daring to name themselves, to articulate their private histories in diary or fictional form, reinscribe the claims of feminine desire onto the text of a resistant patriarchal culture. In so doing, they begin to celebrate a maternal subculture that has long served as a fertile source for utopian visions of a feminized and egalitarian society.

Maya Angelou: *I Know Why the Caged Bird Sings*

"The Black female," writes Maya Angelou, "is assaulted in her tender years by all those common forces of nature at the same time that she is caught in the tripartite crossfire of masculine

prejudice, white illogical hate and Black lack of power."¹ To be
black and female in the United States is to be doubly marginal,
twice removed from the dominant power group and handicapped
by a burden of racial prejudice and gender stereotypes. It is little
wonder that, in the persona of her younger self, Marguerite Johnson, Angelou felt convinced that she existed as a kind of change-
ling. Fed on celluloid fantasies of Shirley Temple as female
figura, the ingenuous Ritie harbored extravagant dreams of physical transformation and found herself unable to relate to a dark,
ungainly body with sludge-colored skin and nappy hair. Beneath
this outer shell there surely resided a slim, white-skinned, blue-
eyed, blond-haired sylph. Only no one knew it—not even God.

In Angelou's *Caged Bird*, negritude and femininity make contradictory, irreconcilable demands on Ritie's sense of personal
identity. The color of her skin, the kinkiness of her hair, and the
fullness of her lips all contribute to intense feelings of physical
self-hatred. During the 1930s and 1940s, the social ideal of blond
feminine beauty was touted in newspapers and in ladies' magazines and, most powerfully, in romantic cinematic representations. In the American South at midcentury, there was little
consciousness of the kind of black pride that grew out of the
Civil Rights movement of the 1960s. To be young, gifted, and
black in Stamps, Arkansas, was, quite simply, to be lonely. The
dominant tone of Ritie's narrative, modulated by wry humor and
a pervasive vitality, is one of painful isolation.

Ritie's own childhood experiences border on the grotesque. At
the age of eight, she is raped by her mother's frustrated and
demented lover, Mr. Freeman. The narrative voice recounting
this humiliation is taut, laconic, and deliberately restrained. Verbal control offers mental compensation for emotional shock and
physical trauma. "The act of rape on an eight-year-old body,"
Angelou tells us, "is a matter of the needle giving because the
camel can't. The child gives, because the body can, and the mind
of the violator cannot" (p. 65). Through the helpless, vulnerable
body of his lover's daughter, the male exacts sexual satisfaction
and psychological vengeance. Shattered by this betrayal of filial
trust and accusing herself of complicity, the traumatized child
retreats into silence and self-imposed exile. By naming the unspeakable crime, she has, she believes, condemned her assailant
to death. The young girl is bereft of language to articulate the
double pain of rape and emotional betrayal. "I liked him holding
me," she confesses. And because she responded warmly to those
brief moments of physical affection, Marguerite fully expects to

be stoned as a biblical harlot. Her only guide to the mysterious terrain of adult sexuality is the New Testament—a tract that would ostensibly condemn her as an adulterous sinner.[2]

The traumatic assault robs the female child of both dignity and language. She spoke, and a man was killed. Like Shakespeare's Iago, she determines never more to speak words. Sent back to Stamps, Arkansas, she lives in a private cage of self-imposed isolation until she is released by the skilled and patient tutelage of Bertha Flowers. Ritie slowly begins to reclaim a hard-won mastery over speech and writing. Literature opens doors and worlds that stretch far beyond the limits of a small southern town in provincial America. Shakespeare and Dickens win her intellectual commitment, and she finds herself able to identify with a vast human panorama that liberates her mind and fires her curious imagination. It is through literature, moreover, that she begins to discover her black heritage as well. When young blacks attending a grade-school graduation are humiliated by a white-dominated world of limited, circumscribed expectations, the poetry of James Weldon Johnson consolidates their energies and gives them a sense of community that inaugurates the first stirrings of black political rebellion.

Ritie's adolescent rites of passage are, like those of most teen-agers, acted out in relative seclusion. Searching for the freedom of personal expression, she must, as a black woman, prove her competence in meeting a complex set of emotional challenges. Her narrative becomes a picaresque series of adventures, some-times comic and sometimes dangerous and bizarre. In the slums of Los Angeles, she survives in a community of homeless, vaga-bond children who sleep in abandoned cars. On a pleasure trip across the border to Mexico, she rescues her inebriate father and learns spontaneously to drive an automobile. Through sheer per-sistence and stubbornness, she becomes the first black ticket-collector on the San Francisco cable cars, and this socially incon-sequential challenge to the unwritten color bar has, for her, the force of a momentous personal victory. If discrimination can be overcome by the patient self-assertion of a lone, determined teenager, what might racial solidarity and a communal black struggle for empowerment not achieve? Ritie feels that she has, by her own small step toward equality, taken a giant leap toward the cultural liberation of oppressed peoples everywhere.

Angelou's *Caged Bird* is not Joyce's *Portrait of the Artist*, nor does it claim to be. Many of Ritie's battles, like those of Stephen Dedalus, have to do with adolescent sexual crises and the need

of the postpubescent child to establish gender identity. When
sixteen-year-old Stephen visits the red-light district of Dublin,
he can luxuriate in furtive sexual acts, then atone for his transgressions through the auspices of a kindly father-confessor. But
Ritie must face the complex ambiguities of female sexuality—
anatomically interior and hidden from consciousness by a society that defines femininity through Freudian images of genital
castration. Without benefit of sex education, she becomes panic-
stricken at the sight of her developing labia—an effect of maturation that she confuses with freakish hermaphroditism. If society
looks upon feminine sexuality as a nothingness, a hole or vessel
to be filled by the phallus, then the adolescent girl has no
positive icon to explain her blossoming genitals. Baffled and
perplexed, Ritie feels compelled to engineer her own sexual re-
searches: "What I needed was a boyfriend" (p. 238). Taking a
kind of initiative that startles even herself, she boldly invites an
attractive young man to "have sexual intercourse" with her.
When he eagerly complies, she finds herself both reassured and
pregnant. Ritie has proved her womanhood to herself and to the
world, and the results of her carefully choreographed defloration
are palpable and life-transforming. On graduation from high
school, she simultaneously becomes a mother and an adult member of black society. "I had had help in the child's conception,"
she observes, "but no one could deny that I had had an immacu-
late pregnancy" (p. 245).

   Luckily, Marguerite Johnson is not Hester Prynne, and no scarlet letter awaits her. African-Americans have traditionally been
more compassionate in matters of sexual fallibility than their
white puritanical brothers. Women facing single parenthood, by
choice or by necessity, have usually found family and community
support for their so-called "illegitimate" offspring. Ritie's sexual
fall is cause for temporary alarm, but no one in her family interprets it as irreparable tragedy. After all, her lapse has resulted in
the birth of a beautiful, healthy baby. And Ritie finally attains
through her infant son much of the warmth and affection she
desperately craved as an isolated young girl. She has collaborated
in the creation of a child whose presence reinforces something
she has always unconsciously known: black is beautiful, or potentially so, and she is worthy of a dignified place in a society
of caring adults. As her mother assures her, "If you're for the
right thing, then you do it without thinking" (p. 246).

   The end of Caged Bird is comic and triumphant. Unlike Stephen Dedalus, who defines his manhood in proud opposition to

family, church, and state, Marguerite Johnson realizes her womanhood by symbolic reintegration into black society. Her victory suggests an implicit triumph over the white bourgeoisie, whose values have flagrantly been subverted. The final tableau of Ritie and her son offers a revolutionary paradigm of the black anti-Madonna. At the conclusion of the first volume of her autobiography, Maya Angelou/Marguerite Johnson has stopped serving white masters, and she has become mistress of herself. A proud Maya emerges from the cocoon enveloping a younger, trembling Ritie. Killing the celluloid spectre of Shirley Temple, she gives birth not only to a child, but also to a new, revitalized sense of her own competence. She is now a self-empowered black woman triumphing over the vicissitudes imposed by an antagonistic patriarchy.[3]

Maxine Hong Kingston: *The Woman Warrior*

Maxine Hong Kingston grew up in the Chinese-American community of Stockton, California. It was an ethnocentric microcosm that struggled to preserve Asiatic roots despite violent transplantation into the world of Western ghosts. Like blacks in the American South, Chinese immigrants saw Caucasians as "spooks." Whites were impalpable presences that remained curiously unreal, even while they controlled the factories, mines, and businesses that employed immigrant labor. It was not the teacher-ghosts or the merchant-ghosts that haunted Maxine's Chinese-American childhood. Instead it was the pervasive spectre of an ethnic heritage that manifested itself in arbitrary rules and incomprehensible traditions. Throughout adolescence Kingston was torn between allegiance to a close-knit emigrant community and the foreign American culture that surrounded her. She had two languages and two identities and, from early childhood, was forced to reconcile their contradictory demands. Would she remain Chinese and agree, in fantasy, to be sold into a marriage arranged by her tyrannical parents? Or would she rebelliously claim personal freedom as an "American feminine" autonomous individual?[4]

Like Joyce's Stephen Dedalus, Kingston sets out to analyze and discard the shackles that bind her imagination, just as linen cloth once bound the feet of her female ancestors. Ironically, she cannot abdicate Chinese tradition without losing the myths and legends that constitute her identity. Hence she must propitiate the ghosts that haunt her by articulating all those fabulous legends that once fired her childhood fantasies. Self-consciously, she moves "away from an ethnic tradition the distance required to memorialize and cherish it."[5] In telling the story of her ancestors and herself, Kingston simultaneously creates a second *fabula* that rewrites the self in its ethnic and racial context. Weaving Chinese legends into her autobiographical story, she begins to reclaim the heritage of the warrior woman, Fa Mu Lan, who offered a model of female heroism. For by narrating the tale of Chinese women abused, rejected, or punished, she comes to terms with those scapegoat images that nudged her toward revolutionary ardor.

The first tale she recounts is that of No Name Woman, the aunt who brought shame upon her family and death to herself through an adulterous love affair with an unknown suitor. The Chinese community refuses to forgive such a flagrant violation of its ethical sanctions. Wearing white masks and screaming for blood, the villagers descend on the outcast's cottage, throw stones and rocks, sacrifice livestock, splatter blood, steal possessions, and hurl epithets of infamy on the humiliated household. The book begins with a *Walpurgisnacht* of violence, a witch's sabbath that destroys two lives. "Your aunt gave birth in the pigsty that night. The next morning . . . I found her and the baby plugging up the family well" (p. 5). The scapegoat is resurrected by Brave Orchid as a haunting paradigm of female vulnerability: "Now that you have started to menstruate, what happened to her could happen to you. Don't humiliate us" (p. 5). The message is clear: female sexuality, unless contained in socially acknowledged patriarchal forms, is a curse and a threat. An illegitimate child, begotten by love or by violence, de-legitimizes the female in the eyes of an implacable, unforgiving community. The prodigal daughter may have self-consciously chosen to defy society through the sexual extravagance of adultery. Or her act might simply have been a frightened capitulation to male power. Women "at sex hazarded birth and hence lifetimes" (p. 8). Did she do so in a moment of weakness, yielding to charm, affection, or promises of love? Or was her act of love meant as an act of iconoclastic self-assertion? In either case, the villagers punished her for claiming the right to "a private life, secret and apart from them" (p. 14). Infuriated that they could not control her uterus and her offspring, they sacrificed her as a scapegoat to the "firm roundness" of inbred, tribal solidarity.

The defiled renegade, cast out by the tribe, gave birth in a pigsty and carried her precious newborn to the well in a vengeful suicide that would inevitably contaminate her family's water supply. The ghost of this female scapegoat must wait generations to be forgiven. In effect, she must wait until her brother's daughter can make reparation to her restless spirit wandering the earth in search of vindication. The aunt is a martyr to her gender, a ghost of feminine vulnerability. Filled with adulterous seed, she gives birth to a child that brings shame and despair.

She then continues to perpetuate the spectre of feminine deviance in the minds of those who have escaped to the new world. Maxine Hong Kingston tries desperately to make peace with the ghost of this long-lost aunt, whom she offers the paper gift of verbal immortality—hieroglyphs scratched on parchment in honor of her memory. The narrative rewrites the woman's private, subjective story and gives voice to a grief that remains unspoken. Kingston's family biography is intended as an offering and a propitiation; it is an artistic tribute to the aunt's maligned memory. Through her own mastery of language, Maxine rebelliously names the woman who has no name and resuscitates her wandering spirit. She calls into existence the spectre of a woman wronged by her lover, by society, and by irrational physiological processes. The dramatic tale that the author devises re-creates childbirth as pain and metaphysical delight: "The black well of sky and stars went out and out and out forever; her body and her complexity seemed to disappear. She was one of the stars, a bright dot in blackness, without home, without a companion, in eternal cold and silence" (p. 16).

These women, too, must be remembered as the females whose subversive behavior distinguished them as rebels. Refusing to be identified as wives or slaves, they became sinners, renegades, witches, and outcasts. Paradoxically, No Name Woman would be remembered only for her crimes and celebrated in her anonymity. Her ghost stalks the earth and must be mollified by a substitute victim—a talk-story that can elevate her life history to the status of art. "The real punishment was not the raid swiftly inflicted by the villagers, but the family's deliberately forgetting her" (p. 18). By consciously remembering the aunt so cruelly forgotten, Kingston resurrects her from the grave as a hero rather than a criminal, a martyr to the mob violence that ended in self-destruction.

Kingston's Chinese heritage is paradoxical indeed. For within the Chinese patriarchal tradition there resides a slippage or a split between the universal contempt expressed toward females

and an underground legend of feminine heroism. Kingston lives
in a society that once practiced infanticide and that traditionally
sold girl children into slavery. Brave Orchid, the shaman-doctor,
tells of the snuffing-out of female life still practiced in rural
China at the beginning of this century: "The midwife or a relative
would take the back of a girl baby's head in her hand and turn
her face into the ashes" (p. 101). "There's no profit in raising
girls," Chinese relatives insist. "Better to raise geese than girls"
(p. 54). No better than geese, or maggots feeding on the carcass
of a dying tradition, girl children are at best marginal; many are
murdered, battered, or sold into bondage. "There is a Chinese
word for the female I—which is 'slave'" (p. 56). Chinese women,
Kingston implies, collude in their own victimization when they
bind the feet of their daughters or sing songs celebrating a lunatic
fidelity that doggedly worships the beating stick:

> Married to a cudgel, married to a pestle,
> Be faithful to it. Follow it.
>
> (p. 225)

Wife-battering is so acceptable that it can be treated as a cultural
joke in Chinese opera. As the daughter-in-law shrieks "Beat me"
to an applauding crowd, spectators laugh until tears wet their
cheeks. Female masochism is little more than an ethnic joke, a
familiar refrain in the patriarchal configuration of Chinese society. "A husband may kill a wife who disobeys him. Confucius
said that" (p. 225).[6]

Fortunately, Chinese legend offers another female model, that
of Fa Mu Lan, the woman warrior. Trained in swordplay and
self-control, she is celebrated as a Chinese Joan of Arc, leading
armies into battle, conquering a wicked, tyrannical emperor,
birthing a son on the battlefield, and saving her people from
political despotism. Kingston's mother (Brave Orchid), despite
her prolific warnings of feminine vulnerability, gives her daughter an invaluable role model: "She said I would grow up a wife
and a slave, but she taught me the song of the warrior woman,
Fa Mu Lan. I would have to grow up a warrior woman" (p. 24).
Fa Mu Lan has the wrongs of her people tattooed on her back,
but they are inscribed, it seems, in a patriarchal register. For she
bears the weight of ancestral agony cut by her father with a phallic knifeblade that tears the flesh of her female body/text. Disguised as a man, she raises an army and leads a revolution that
redeems her people from misery and oppression. But despite

unprecedented valor, she eventually returns to her community to assume the traditional duties of a submissive wife and a conscientious mother. As Sidonie Smith observes, the truly subversive story embedded in the narrative of Fa Mu Lan is the emergence of legendary "witch amazons" who embody "all that is unrepressed and violent in ways both sexual and textual."[7] "Later, it would be said, they turned into a band of swordswomen who were a mercenary army. They did not wear men's clothes . . . but rode as women in black and red dresses. . . . When slave girls and daughters-in-law ran away, people would say they joined these witch amazons" (p. 53).

Like the Amazonian women, young Maxine seems obstreperous, willful, strong-minded, and petulant. She clings to deviance as a sign of "manly" stature, a mark of individuation that will endow her with uniqueness and dignity. But even now, she feels, "China wraps double binds around my feet." Kingston's own revenge will imitate that of the woman warrior insofar as she uses art to exorcise cultural bondage. It was, finally, the story of her fight for justice that made the swordswoman great—even more so than her military victories. Kingston herself has discovered that the autobiographical act is itself a valorous achievement. Rewriting the self and rewriting the tale of her Chinese heritage are ways of perpetuating the glory of the mythic swordswoman and her band of Amazonian avengers. "The ideographs for revenge are 'report of a crime. . . .' The reporting is the vengeance—not the beheading, not the gutting, but the words" (p. 63). Through language she will avenge the sufferings of her people, and, in particular, she will vindicate and exorcise the sufferings of Chinese women. Humiliated and demeaned by historical misogyny in China, Kingston metaphorically emblazons on her own body/text grotesque tales of foot-binding and infanticide, of female torture and self-destruction. She seeks "atonement" with all the women of the past who infiltrate the memories of her girlhood and even haunt her adult Chinese-American consciousness.

Ironically, Brave Orchid (Kingston's mother) once followed the path of the woman warrior, who was a slayer of dragons and a seeker of autonomy.[8] In quiet rebellion, she went to medical school and became a doctor—a female shaman with magical healing powers. Characteristically, she considered herself a kind of bisexual exemption from the universal law of female inferiority. Yet she had no compunctions about purchasing a bright young girl as a personal slave and medical trainee. Nor did she

allow her American-born "biggest daughter" to forget the igno-
miny of being traded for that maidservant. When compared with
the Chinese bondslave purchased for fifty dollars, a daughter
seemed a bad bargain: "And here I was in the United States
paying two hundred dollars for you" (p. 98), she complains. Once
in America, however, the exalted shaman falls into economic
servitude. She is enslaved to drudgery in a Chinese laundry, to
poverty, maternity, and racial inferiority. Secretly, Maxine fosters
the conviction that both she and her mother bear the proud tradition of Fa Mu Lan. "I am really a Dragon, as she is a Dragon,
both of us born in Dragon years" (p. 127).

Legend, of course, can deceive an individual into heroically
minded behavior that runs amok in the modern world. The ancient Chinese parable of the good Empress of the East inspires
Brave Orchid to goad her sister into a bizarre quest for an absent
Chinese husband. "You are the Empress of the East, and the Empress of the West has imprisoned the Earth's Emperor in the
Western Palace," Brave Orchid tells her sister. "You must break
the strong spell she has cast on him that has lost him the East"
(p. 166).[9] Moon Orchid has neither the desire nor the fortitude
to carry out such a pilgrimage. But Brave Orchid nonetheless
choreographs for her sister a ludicrous drama of female vengeance, modeling her scenario on a Chinese fairy tale. Her inter-
ference erupts into an absurd "soap opera" script. Brave Orchid's
husband, confronted with his marital breach, explodes in fury
and refuses to act the part of a character from a Chinese comic
book. To the faithless spouse in Los Angeles, Moon Orchid and
her sister are spectral grandmothers, ghosts of an ancient land
and a forgotten past. "It's as if I had turned into a different person," he explains to Moon Orchid. "You became people in a book
I had read a long time ago" (p. 179). Although technically a
bigamist, this wealthy and prestigious brain surgeon refuses to
acknowledge the moral and ethical ties that bind him to his
Chinese roots. "No Name Woman" had paid the price of martyr-
dom for betraying a husband who had abandoned her. In contrast, Moon Orchid remained faithful to an emigrant spouse only
to be callously destroyed by this nameless husband who rejects her.

This humiliating confrontation robs Moon Orchid of the one
thing that gave her life meaning—the dream of an adolescent
marriage vow that might one day culminate in joyous, self-
affirming reunion. Deprived of her homeland, her marriage, her
identity, and her illusions, the pathetic old woman falls into ver-

tigo, then paranoia. She has fantasies of apprehension by the U.S. government and fears erasure by the partriarchy in a holocaust of ashes. Once uprooted, Moon Orchid withers like a fading flower. Haunted by ghosts of her Chinese past, she is metamorphosed into a spectral stick figure, skeletal and unreal. Her "skin hung loose, like a hollowed frog's, as if she had shrunken inside it" (p. 180). Brave Orchid tries desperately to resurrect her sister's flagging spirit. However, her sororal vigil at her sibling's bedside, filled with magical chants and loving ministrations, fails. Because she cannot name herself, Moon Orchid falls into dementia. "Mad people," Kingston observes, "have only one story that they talk over and over" (p. 184). Without the ability to rewrite the self, to manipulate talk-story in new, imaginative configurations, one becomes the victim of hostile obsessions. Moon Orchid can find sanctuary from her paranoid fantasies only by fleeing to a state mental asylum. There she feels safe and happy in a community of like-minded women. Brave Orchid and her daughters have, in turn, learned a painful lesson about marital infidelity and the patriarchal erasure of female identity.

Brave Orchid functions as the matriarchal center of the Hong family, and she displays a good bit of imagination and folk wisdom in rearing her daughters. She tells Maxine, for instance, that the child's tongue was bifurcated at birth. In a fairy-tale fantasy, Kingston imagines that her mother "pushed my tongue up and sliced the frenum" (p. 190) in a liminal rite of female initiation. "I cut it so that you would not be tongue-tied," Brave Orchid explains. "Your tongue would be able to move in many languages" (p. 190). The myth evokes an image of female castration—a bizarre *brith*, a circumcision of frenum rather than frenulum, intended to endow the girl-child with the gift of tongues. A "split tongue," metaphorically, ought to be capable of mastering several dialects. The legendary rite reassures the child of her power to articulate a new self in an unfamiliar world, and the story serves as a maternal precaution against the confused dumbness of bilingualism.[10]

Maxine, however, is morbidly shy and, like the legendary Philomela, must cast the tale of her suffering in lyrical, poetic language. Like the Greek heroine, she is forced, tongueless, to weave her story on the looms of written language. Art is the one vehicle that can unbind the cleft tongue of this dragon daughter. Her creative powers are released through the ancient tradition of Chinese "talk-story," the art of manipulating language until it soars like a bird with every flight of the imagination. As a child,

Maxine feels that her ethnic heritage condemns her to mute alienation. In a society of ghosts, she must control the baroque, ideographic figures that dance in her head. Wrapped in protective silence, she stares confusedly at the white ghost-teachers and releases her tongue only in the chanted notes of Chinese instruction. Ethnic security restores the gift of voice, though it also imperils the individual tongue: "You can't entrust your voice to the Chinese, either," Maxine observes. "They want to capture your voice for their own use" (p. 196). Just as the parents of Fa Mu Lan insisted on etching their ancestral grievances on the back of their virtuous daughter, so the parents of Chinese-American children inscribe their own racial histories on the resistant backs of helpless offspring. They bind the tongues and imaginations of their children as mothers once bound their daughters' feet in China. The tongue, unbound, sings its own song of unselfconscious lyricism. But how can it do so in a society that rejects high-pitched sounds inherited over centuries? The American-Chinese cultural gap seems to be primarily auditory, as Chinese utterances fall "chingchong ugly" onto xenophobic American ears. "Most of us eventually found some voice, however faltering," Kingston tells us. "We invented an American-feminine speaking personality" (p. 200).

The one exception to this gesture of linguistic conformity is the doll-like Chinese child who remains imprisoned in autistic silence even when bullied by an outraged Maxine in the private recesses of a basement lavatory. This ubiquitous alter-ego haunts Kingston's childhood like the ghost of a repressed ancestral self, speechless and unresistant. A symbol of the historical weakness of Chinese women, the girl arouses in Maxine a sadistic need for mastery over a Jungian shadow self. "I hated fragility," Maxine confesses. Locked in psychological battle with this silent antagonist, she is desperate to make her dumb self speak, to force the voiceless females of Chinese history to articulate their misery and protest their crippling pain. With unbound feet and clanking shoes, she fantasizes stomping on the figuratively bound feet of her adversary. But the victim stands mute and helpless, first screaming like a trapped animal, then reduced to vegetable passivity. Maxine learns the bitter humiliation of authoritarian power: a self-defined torturer, she bursts into tears, pleading with her victim for an excuse to be merciful. The confrontation leads to mutual anguish and to a mysterious, regressive, no-name illness that immobilizes the penitent Maxine for the next eighteen months. "It was the best year and a half of my life," observes Kingston. "Nothing happened" (p. 212).

Because her own speech sounds, she believes, like the quacking of a pressed duck, Maxine attempts to compensate for her handicap through the beautiful sounds of written language. The alternative is madness: "I thought talking and not talking made the difference between sanity and insanity. Insane people were the ones who couldn't explain themselves" (p. 216). Maxine's "buried self" is a deviant witch-lady with red hair, a "frivolous and violent" spectre riding a white horse and screeching like a vampire. Or perhaps she *is* a vampire—wild, uncontrollable, sadistic, and raving. "I had vampire nightmares; every night . . . blood dripped from my fangs, blood of the people I was supposed to love" (p. 221). Madness, of course, is one escape from the sentence of female bondage. Deviant and crazy, with arms flailing and disheveled hair flying (like those Amazonian avengers liberated by Fa Mu Lan), this vampire self will refuse the shackles of race and gender. She will be revolutionary in her madness, reclaiming the ghostly freedom of an androgynous warrior. In a manic burst of logorrhea, Maxine claims to have mastered the "ghost powers" that will set her free—intelligence, language, and art. "I am not going to be a slave or a wife" (p. 234), she triumphantly announces. She is determined to defy Chinese cultural expectations and, at the same time, to refuse assimilation into the dominant American culture. As a liberated artist, the adult woman can finally begin to confront childhood ghosts. She can appropriate their stories of misery, oppression, heroism, and endurance. The patriarchal culture of China, transplanted to the new world, may be transformed into a strongly matrifocal and woman-centered society.

The woman warrior may be the legendary hero of Kingston's childhood. Yet it is, finally, not Fa Mu Lan but Brave Orchid who proves to be the heroine of this autobiographical tale. Proud shaman of her people, she brings from the old world a sense of wisdom and magisterial dignity, even when laboring in a torrid Chinese laundry. It is to the remote figure of Brave Orchid that the romantic adolescent longs to confess her "207 transgressions." Clearly, Brave Orchid has replaced the "chief magician" of Maxine's pietistic devotions. But precisely because her mother looms so powerful in Maxine's adolescent imagination, she becomes a threatening and domineering matriarchal figure.[11]

In writing her autobiography, Kingston discovers that she is telling the story not only of herself, but also of her mother, her aunts, her grandmother, and of all those Chinese women who appear before the mind's eye and demand voice for their grievances. Like the woman warrior, the author will display the tableau of her maternal ancestry annealed in etchings on her artistic imagination. In telling the story of Chinese women, she writes herself into the narrative and "atones" for her ostensible rejection of ethnic bonds. She becomes reconciled with the ghosts of her past. She is "at one" with those brave, silent women who once threatened to bind her feet and her psyche, to sell her as bondslave to husband or master. These spirits are a part of what she is and what she has become. Propitiated by the gift of talk-story, these are transformed into beneficent presences, muses that fire her dreams and inspire her confessional art.

In the end, language liberates the author from all the ghosts that have haunted her Chinese-American childhood. Stripped of power to judge and to punish, they prove interesting, friendly, and ultimately harmless. Articulating the poignant story of her own maternal heritage, Kingston confronts the silent spectres of her past and masters their presence by relegating them to the play frame of artistic fabulation. Like Ts'ai Yen, Maxine Hong Kingston composes a lyrical tribute to her Chinese heritage on the "Barbarian Reed Pipe" of English autobiography. No matter. Her paean is universal and may some day be translated into "a song that Chinese sing to their own instruments" (p. 243). We suspect that it will translate well. Fictionalized autobiography proves, for Kingston, a way of reinscribing the self into the complex intertextual codes that define a feminine/feminist Chinese-American identity.[12] In *The Woman Warrior*, the author/narrator gives voice to a set of enabling narratives appropriated from Oriental legend. Myth, Kingston insists, is a form of "non-fiction." When individuals, particularly women, "make up these fictions about themselves ... it's not just for fun. It's a terrible necessity."[13]

Alice Walker: *The Color Purple*

In her prize-winning novel *The Color Purple*, Alice Walker is revolutionary in the frankness and lucidity with which she depicts the fragmented lives of black women in twentieth-century Southern society. Walker has reiterated the story of Job through the life experiences of Celie. The latter is a protagonist who, like Samuel Richardson's Pamela, writes and rewrites the story of her life in a series of letters addressed first to God, then to her long-lost sister, Nettie. The one structural flaw in the novel is, perhaps, its epistolary style. It is difficult to believe that Celie, with crushing responsibilities to father, mother, siblings, husband and stepchildren, would be able to summon the time and energy to articulate her misery. But if one accepts Walker's format, then the novel unfolds in vivid black dialect as a powerful autobiography of a young woman victimized by intolerable handicaps of race and gender. Rape and emotional incest are climactic in Maya Angelou's *I Know Why the Caged Bird Sings*, but they are simply the point of departure in Walker's bold depiction of female reality in the deep South at the beginning of this century. "He never had a kine word to say to me. Just say You gonna do what your mammy wouldn't. First he put his thing up gainst my hip and sort of wiggle it around. Then he grab hold my titties. Then he push his thing inside my pussy. When that hurt, I cry. He start to choke me, saying you better shut up and git used to it."[14]

Both rape and incest are brutal facts of Celie's childhood. Patriarchal authority is absolute and unquestioned: the demonic Alphonso can attack his stepdaughter, blame her for immorality, and freely dispose of her "bastard" children. Celie is battered, humiliated, and finally gotten rid of—sold as "spoiled property" to an anonymous suitor, Mr. _____, only later identified by the name Albert. Celie, meek and humiliated, becomes a battered wife, and the cycle of relentless male domination continues. "I don't know how to fight," she confesses. "All I know how to do is stay alive" (p. 26). Only those who endure will live to prevail. And Celie is a survivor. In the depths of her misery, she writes letters to God. And God is, for Walker's characters, that which is loved best—whether it be Jesus, or Nettie, or the African roofleaf, or trees and animals, or simply the color purple blossoming, unexpectedly, in a meadow of grass. Walker is intent that all her principal characters—the "good ones" worthy of salvation— discover God through communion with the Spirit. Celie and Shug Avery have long colloquies on metaphysics that wean them from psychological dependence on a white male deity. What does that bearded, irascible figure in the white man's Bible have to do with *them*? With the help of Shug, Celie finally rejects her mental image of an all-white God—"looking like some stout white man work at the bank" (p. 91) and surrounded by albino angels.

Such anthropomorphic fantasies are infantile and demeaning.

The Olinka are closer to the divine presence when they worship the roofleaf as that which is most necessary to their existence. "We know that a roofleaf is not Jesus Christ, but in its own humble way, is it not God?" (p. 142). Shug, like the Africans, insists that God is neither male nor female, but an androgynous "it." This "it" is to be found nowhere but in the great spirit of nature and life that unites the isolated individual with the surrounding cosmos. The spirit manifests itself in playful acts of desire and satisfaction—in trees, flowers, birds, laughter, and sexual delight. It allies itself with all that is beneficent in the universe, and it rarely, if ever, is to be found in a church. For Celie, Shug Avery becomes both mother and God, a matriarchal spirit of loving devotion. And Celie, ministering to her husband's ailing and debilitated lover, becomes a redemptive figure in the life of this brash, rambunctious singer who longs for maternal solicitude. Shug's mama "never love to do nothing had anything to do with touching nobody. . . . I try to kiss her, she turn her mouth away" (p. 115).

The white missionaries who preach Jesus and Christian marriage to the natives feel dumbfounded by an African social structure built on polygamy. How, they wonder, can wives work together in the fields, laugh together, help one another, and nurse each other's children? Female solidarity is just as much a mystery in the American South. "Not many women let they husband whore lay up in they house" (p. 59), exclaims Celie's intrusive father-in-law. Shug is not only welcomed by the adoring Celie, but she also is the first person to offer Celie the gift of unqualified affection. The interaction between Celie and Shug is fraught with tactility. The two women comb each other's hair, laugh, kiss, preen one another, and gradually begin to share female secrets. Celie climbs out of her nacreous shell of isolation and diminished self-esteem as she begins to understand that identity is largely contingent on loving and being loved. When Shug dares to name a song after Celie and dedicates it to her, Celie is virtually overwhelmed by feelings of affection that remain rapturous and inarticulate. By her warmth and healing affection, Shug miraculously resurrects this ugly duckling of a child from a life of loneliness and physical self-hatred.

Layers of social distance and female hostility are slowly peeled away. The two women weave a tender cocoon of candor and solicitude that forms an emotional shelter for both. They talk together like two wives discussing the same husband, though each seems to know an entirely different Albert. Shug experiences his devotion, sexual tenderness, passion, and masculine worship. Obsessed with Shug, Albert has treated Celie contemptuously. She knows him as an irascible patriarch—father, owner, judge, jailer, and domestic tyrant. Committed to a life of service and devotion, she can never enjoy the connubial relation that has degenerated into a kind of ritual humiliation. Copulation is joyless and perfunctory. Like a dog "doing his business," Albert climbs on top of her and ejaculates, treating Celie like a wastebin for his excess sperm. She feels desecrated, exploited, violated, and diminished. She remains, in fact, a virgin in terms of sexual pleasure. It is Shug who introduces Celie to the delights of female sexuality—first by word, then by mouth. She tells Celie about the clitoral "button" and shows her the beautiful, budding flower of her own genitalia, looking "like a wet rose" (p. 79). Shug becomes mother confessor to the distraught Celie, who cries because "Nobody ever love me" (p. 109). Albert just "clam on top of me and fuck and fuck" (p. 109).

In a poignant scene of mutual affection, Shug offers Celie the tenderness denied her by father, mother, husband, and children: "She say, I love you, Miss Celie. . . . Then I feels something real soft and wet on my breast, feel like one of my little lost babies mouth. Way after a while, I act like a little lost baby too" (p. 109). Shug becomes surrogate parent and child simultaneously. She is the mother who rejected and abandoned Celie, as well as the lost baby, and the children taken from her. In a moment of passionate commitment, Shug fulfills all the roles of those who have failed to love the innocent girl/child/woman. Her lovemaking is a little like "sleeping with mama." To Celie, "It feel like heaven" (p. 110). An androgynous figure, Shug serves as the bisexual lover who finally resuscitates the dogged, downtrodden Celie. She literally brings her back to life. By pilfering Albert's pockets and trunk, she *also* unearths the letters from Africa that resurrect Nettie. Walker uses Dickensian strategies of missing characters, coincidental meetings, and improbable journeys to reveal the startling fate of Nettie and the long-lost children, Adam and Olivia. For the first time in her life, Celie is stirred to revolutionary anger. She is furious that Albert could have kept from her the thing she most loved, her sister Nettie. With Shug as lover and surrogate sister, Celie finally rebels. Seething with rage, she wants to *murder* Albert. Instead, she makes pants. She sews. She fumes. Finally, she leaves and starts a new life in Memphis.

By introducing Nettie's African experiences halfway through the novel, Walker adds an unexpected dimension of historical and cultural breadth. What started out as a personal biography becomes nothing less than an epic of the race: It is an oft-told story seen from the fresh perspective of black missionaries determined to save their pagan brothers and sisters on the "dark continent." They find in Africa a strong tribal culture gradually destroyed by imperialistic incursions—a road, rubber plantations, resettlements, and the annihilation of the sacred Olinka roofleaf. The Africans have a proud heritage, but they are not romanticized in a Rousseauesque posture as "noble savages." The Olinka scorn women, mutilate female bodies, and scar their children's faces. The men take numerous wives and are pampered by them. Males enjoy the bliss of perpetual childhood, while their wives labor to make the crops grow and to bring forth children. African patriarchy evokes both admiration and distress in the missionaries, who try to mitigate tribal contempt for women and educate the Olinka children in the practices of "civilized" life.

The novel spans a broad chronology from the early twentieth century to the present day. Hence the reader can witness gradual social and historical changes that occur over several generations. Celie learns that her real father was lynched and that her mother went mad. The widow married a ruthless opportunist who drove her to the grave after raping her daughter. Celie takes it for granted that Albert has a right to beat her at will. But Albert's son Harpo knows better than to strike his fiery wife, Sophia. When he does, she blackens his eyes. After Sophia assaults an impudent white mayor, she lands in prison and is forced into a kind of indentured servitude as "mammy" to the mayor's children. There exists no place or space for uppity black females in Southern white society. Racial integrity, Walker implies, must first be found in the heads and hearts of a people long bowed down by slavery and subservience. The master/slave pattern of the nineteenth century is psychologically mirrored in more recent paradigms of conjugal ownership. As Friedrich Engels would remind us, in traditional marriage the patriarchal husband resembles the socially empowered bourgeoisie, and wife and children play the role of oppressed proletariat. In Southern black society at the beginning of this century, the master/slave Hegelian dialectic was frequently replicated in an aggression/frustration syndrome characteristic of domestic violence.

In Walker's The Color Purple, Shug Avery emerges as a feisty revolutionary spirit who teaches Celie lessons of black pride. She makes the younger woman capable of raising both head and fist in rebellion against her "nameless" husband/father/master. Naked men, Celie observes, remind her of frogs, and none of the croaking lot will ever turn into princes. Shug, on the other hand, proves to be a princely consort, and together she and Celie effect a quiet revolution by asserting the strength of female solidarity. In search of creativity, they turn back to the traditional female arts of song, sewing, cooking, and affectionate nurturance. At the end of the novel, even the ruthless Albert is sufficiently mollified to appear as an androgynous figure. He sits sewing with Celie, as both enjoy the shared pleasure of iconic devotion to Shug. Celie is patient, resigned, altruistic, and nonpossessive. She has learned, finally, the most important lesson of all: "I try to teach my heart not to want nothing it can't have" (p. 235). Her spirit has been tempered by the fires of love and loss. She waits, contentedly, for Shug, for Nettie, and for the restoration of her long-lost children who have blossomed on the shores of an African homeland.

Walker ends *The Color Purple* with glimmers of a utopian vision. There is some hope that the new generation will be gentler, less violent, and more civilized in their conjugal relationships. They will be so even as the outside world continues to threaten black communities, in both Africa and the United States. The native Africans consider the white man "naked." They view him stripped of dignity and nobility, and determined to compensate for physical exposure to the elements by resorting to threatening gestures of technological mastery and cultural oppression. (Walker is giving us, perhaps, a parodic version of Freud's theory that female modesty is responsible for the weaving of cloth.) Traditional African society cannot survive the onslaughts of capitalistic greed. Therefore, the best features of tribal-familial allegiance must be replicated and cherished, then disseminated throughout the world by means of a modern black diaspora.

In a radical gesture of compassion and self-sacrifice, Celie's son, Adam, scarifies his face not to prove his manhood, but as a testimony of love for his disfigured bride, Tashi. Symbolically participating in the consequences of her barbaric mutilation, he makes a covenant with the woman who will share his life in America. In this *new* world of hope and promise, both men and women will be freed from traditionally sanctioned hostilities and liberated from atavistic rites. Violent and aggressive sex-role stereotypes will give way to ethical values of compassion, respect, fidelity, and cooperation. After the revolution, men will not be scarified, and women will be neither beaten nor sexually abused. Such a revolution, Walker implies, is already in progress. But the complex problems of race, class, and gender, springing as they do from identical sources of patriarchal hegemony, have yet to be fully resolved, even in the supposedly enlightened society of contemporary America.

Conclusion

Some of the most interesting developments in the genre of self-imaging have occurred in recent experiments in life-writing by women of color in the United States. African-American, Asian-American, and Native-American women tend, even more than their white sisters, to "think back through their mothers" in clear matrifocal patterns. Their writing is often woman-centered and female-identified as part of a larger mythic heritage passed from mothers to daughters in a long line of orally transmitted "talk-stories." Always threatened by multiple marginalities, these authors take refuge in powerful and enabling psychological attachments to mothers, grandmothers, sisters, aunts, daughters, and female friends. Angelou, Kingston, and Walker have learned to envisage themselves as poets of their race. They see themselves as shamen whose magical and mysterious powers of language will be used to name and to legendize exemplary female heroes. As the authorial self is converted and reincorporated into a supportive society of women, the image of the lonely romantic artist gives way to a shared vision of collective struggle, joy, celebration, and communal triumph.

Notes

1. Maya Angelou, *I Know Why the Caged Bird Sings* (1970; reprint, New York: Bantam, 1971). Hereafter cited in the text by page number only.

2. Sondra O'Neale observes that at this point in the novel "the tenuous psyche of a gangly, sensitive, withdrawn child is traumatically jarred by rape, a treacherous act from which neither the reader nor the protagonist has recovered by the book's end. All else is cathartic . . . even her absurdly unlucky pregnancy at the end does not assuage the reader's anticipatory wonder: isn't the act of rape by a trusted adult so assaultive upon an eight-year-old's life that it leaves a wound which can never be healed?" ("Reconstruction of the Composite Self: New Images of Black Women in Maya Angelou's Continuing Autobiography," in *Black Women Writers*, ed. Mari Evans [London and Sydney: Pluto Press, 1985], p. 32.)

3. As O'Neale remarks, the "process of her autobiography is not a singular statement of individual egotism but an exultant explorative revelation that she *is* because her life is an inextricable part of the misunderstood reality of who Black people and Black women truly are" (p. 26). Selwyn Cudjoe goes on to explain that the "Afro-American autobiographical statement emerges as a *public* rather than a *private* gesture," as *me-ism* gives way to *our-ism* and superficial concerns about *individual subject* usually give way to the *collective subjection* of the group" ("Maya Angelou and the Autobiographical Statement," in *Black Women Writers*, ed. Evans, p. 10). For reasons of space and compression, I have limited my discussion to the inaugural volume of Angelou's multi-volume autobiography, which continues to elaborate a similar chorus: "Black people and Black women do not just endure, they triumph with a will of collective consciousness that Western experience cannot extinguish" (O'Neale, p. 28).

4. Maxine Hong Kingston, *The Woman Warrior: Memoirs of a Girlhood Among Ghosts* (New York: Random House, 1977), p. 6. Hereafter cited in the text by page number only. For the sake of convention and clarity, I have chosen to treat *The Woman Warrior* as fictionalized autobiography and to refer to its narrator as Maxine Hong Kingston, a persona contiguous with the author of the text. Kingston, however, might demur. In an interview with Phyllis Hoge Thompson, she describes "that narrator girl" as a prankster and declares: "It's hard for me to call her me, because this is an illusion of writing. She is so coherent and intense always, throughout.... And I'm not like that." ("This Is the Story I Heard: A Conversation with Maxine Hong Kingston and Earll Kingston," *Biography* 6, no. 1 [Winter 1983]: 6–8). In her essay "Threads of Identity in Maxine Hong Kingston's *Woman Warrior*," Margaret Miller reminds us that in China "individualism was not an operative cultural concept until the May 4 Movement." Kingston "is caught between Chinese and American models of development. As an American her growing is marked by tantrums and resistance to the group's definition of her function and value.... As a Chinese, these acts of rebellion mark her as 'unfilial'" (*Biography* 6, no. 1 [Winter 1983]: 14–15).

5. Diane Johnson, *Terrorists and Novelists* (New York: Knopf, 1982), p. 6. In "Narrative Technique and Female Identity," Suzanne Juhasz observes that Kingston's "search for self necessarily involves a definition of home. Is it America, China, or some place in between? For Kingston the question of national identity complicates the search for self. Yet it is possible to understand how gender identity and national identity can be versions of one another, how home is embodied in the mother and father who together stand for the primary source of the self" (*Contemporary American Women Writers*, ed. Catherine Rainwater and William J. Scheick [Lexington: University Press of Kentucky, 1985], p. 174)

6. In her book *About Chinese Women*, Julia Kristeva notes that Confucius "put women in the same class as 'slaves,' '*xiao ren*,' 'inferior men.' This treatment, which goes along with the oppression of women under the hierarchy of authorities in the feudal family, earned Confucius the name of 'eater of women....' Cloistered in their houses, *nei ren* ('humans for the inside'), they [women] are, according to Confucianism, destined only for housework and reproduction. Consequently, there is no need for them to learn to read and write. The arts—poetry, drawing, singing—don't have to be learned except by the 'ladies of the night,' the various categories of courtesans who are employed

less for the pleasures of the body than for the joys of aesthetic conversation" (*About Chinese Women*, trans. Anita Barrows [New York: Urizen Books, 1974], p. 75).

7. Sidonie Smith, *A Poetics of Women's Autobiography* (Bloomington: Indiana University Press, 1987), p. 159. Smith believes that Fa Mu Lan's story serves as symbolic paradigm of "perfect filiality" in the phallic order, since the warrior woman is ultimately tamed, "recuperated as publicly silenced wife and slave" (p. 158).

8. As Miller explains, Kingston has structured her narrative in terms of a traditional Chinese dialectic: "The first two chapters set up the dialectical terms of the 'symbolic, archetypal situation' which will help Kingston understand her present identity: first slave (the no-name aunt), then warrior (the fantasy based on the story of Fa Mu Lan). The third section gives us the warrior in her modern realistic guise: this is Brave Orchid at medical school and as a doctor. The fourth transports Brave Orchid to America and contrasts her to another slave figure, her sister. . . . The final chapter is Kingston's attempt to come to a synthesis of these archetypes and her final effort to relate them to her present" ("Threads of Identity," p. 18).

9. In *About Chinese Women*, Julia Kristeva speculates that Chinese legend and Chinese writing have proved to be particularly enigmatic to the Western mind because of the highly stylized, pictorial, symbolic, and ideographic qualities that characterize a semiotic system closely allied with unconscious, prelogocentric modes of experience. "The logic of Chinese writing," she tells us, "presupposes, at its base, a speaking, writing individual for whom what seems to us today a preoedipal phase—dependency on the maternal, socio-natural continuum, absence of clear-cut divisions between the order of things and the order of symbols, predominance of the unconscious impulses—must have been extremely important" (p. 56). In its description of narrative crisis, Chinese writing proves disconcerting because of its insistence on presenting a schematized, archetypalized version of events: "Rather than proceeding to an explanation which, for us, is the only logical one . . . the Chinese give us a 'structuralist' or 'warring' (contradictory) portrait. Behind the event itself there appears a combinatorium or an association that bears the seed of an overthrow of the previous order; a battle between good and evil; two-faced people: persecutions, conspiracies, sensational turns of event" (pp. 57–58). Hence the curious passion with which Brave Orchid recounts a traditional Chinese tale of "good and evil" empresses warring for the favor of an "entranced" or enchanted patriarch. The legend motivates a powerful psychodrama that proves disastrous when enacted on the stage of twentieth-century America society.

10. Smith observes that Kingston's "mother passes on a tale of female castration, a rite of passage analogous to a clitoridectomy, that wounding of the female body in service to the community, performed and thereby perpetuated by the mother" (p. 168). The event may have been real and not fantasized: I am told by medical people that such practices used to be standard in U.S. hospitals.

11. The thrust of Kingston's narrative is toward the resolution of an inscrutable and contradictory maternal *imago*: "The mother is the significant other in many female autobiographies. She is both an agent of the patriarchy, socializing her daughter to her role with an intention as protective as the emperor's . . . and at the same time a potentially subversive model" (Miller, p. 23). As Suzanne Juhasz points out, the "factual and fantastic tales of Brave Orchid combine to make of her a complete person in her daughter's eyes, a person with a

separate identity both to be proud of and of necessity to reject, to move beyond" (p. 181).

12. Asked in an interview with Arturo Islas whether or not she would consider herself a feminist, Maxine Kingston replied: "I have always been a feminist but feminism is just one modern political stance, like being an ethnic writer. One has to have an even larger vision. I don't think my writing would limit itself to whatever is politically useful" ("Maxine Hong Kingston," in *Women Writers of the West Coast: Speaking of Their Lives and Careers* [Santa Barbara, Calif.: Capra Press, 1983], p. 16). In describing the role of Chinese myth in her narratives, Kingston explains: "I know all of these great heroes from the high tradition and they're not helping me in my American life. Such myths need to be changed and integrated into the peasant's life as well as into the Chinese American's life" (p. 14).

13. "This Is the Story I Heard," p. 12.

14. Alice Walker, *The Color Purple* (New York: Washington Square Press, 1982), p. 11. Hereafter cited in the text by page number only. In describing her inspiration for "Writing *The Color Purple*," Walker tells us that she first began to conceptualize the narrative when her sister Ruth, in talking about a lovers' triangle, expressed astonishment at the fact that "one day The Wife asked The Other Woman for a pair of her drawers." Thus Walker's fictional history "starts not with the taking of lands, or the births, battles, and deaths of Great Men, but with one woman asking another for her underwear" (*In Search of Our Mothers' Gardens* [London: The Women's Press Ltd., 1984], pp. 355–56). Much of Celie's autobiographical narrative incorporates, disguises, and transmutes some of the emotional experiences of Alice Walker's own autobiography—in particular, an early sense of isolation and marginality, culminating in an unplanned pregnancy and traumatic abortion. In an interview published in the collection *In Search of Our Mothers' Gardens*, Walker explains: "I have always been a solitary person, and since I was eight years old (and victim of a traumatic accident that blinded and scarred one eye), I have daydreamed—not of fairy tales—but of falling on swords, of putting guns to my heart or head, and of slashing my wrists with a razor" (p. 244). She describes spending a summer in Africa and returning "to school healthy and brown, and loaded down with sculptures and orange fabric—and pregnant" (p. 245).

I felt at the mercy of everything, including my own body, which I had learned to accept as a kind of casing over what I considered my real self . . . but now it refused to function properly. . . . I vomited incessantly, even when nothing came up but yellow, bitter bile. . . .

For three days I lay on the bed with a razor blade under my pillow. My secret was known to three friends only. . . .

On the last day for miracles, one of my friends telephoned to say someone had given her a telephone number. . . . I went to see the doctor and he put me to sleep. When I woke up, my friend was standing over me holding a red rose. . . .

Then I wrote the suicide poems. . . . I also began to understand how alone woman is, because of her body. (pp. 245–48)

Part 3
Hopes, Dreams, and Desperation

Desperate Hopes, Desperate Lives: Depression and Self-Realization in Jamaica Kincaid's *Annie John* and *Lucy*

I

ON the surface, everything about *Annie John* suggests the traditional *Bildungsroman*: it traces the central episodes in the life of a young girl from prepubescent familial bliss to her ambivalent turmoil about her mother and a permanent departure from home at seventeen. Along the way she struggles through alternate moods of embracing and rejecting her parents, the satisfying and troubling subterfuge of social expectations, the awakening of an uneasy sexuality, and the gradual formulation of an internal life that seeks release from the strictures of home and the culture of Antigua. In the background are a host of secondary values. These include a legacy of slavery and deprivation and the rich texture of Annie's family life (with its exotic foods and rituals), as well as the English cultural overlay on the social patterns of Antigua. Exemplified by the eminence of the Anglican Church, there is also the interplay of European Christianity with the folk rituals of potions and curses and evil demons. Everything in this society has a dual foundation, even the local dialect (an amalgam of English and patois). In addition, it manifests in a double psychological and social identity a people who live in a world not of their own creation.

Against this complex background, Annie John grows up to tell her story, one greatly enriched by the fact that it is told in retrospect. As a result, there is, inevitably, a dual time scheme: the time of the action related from the time of the telling. The action progresses through seven years of Annie's young life. It moves through her increasing maturation to a fierce declaration of sovereignty when she leaves home. The time of the telling seems

237

constant. It occurs at an indeterminant point anterior to her departure from home, and allows for a wiser and less strident perspective that enables her to reveal her struggle in its full complexity. Although in one dimension her story constitutes a traditional *apologia pro vita sua*, it is less a polemical treatise than a confessional. For much of what Annie reveals about herself and her family does not, ultimately, redound to her credit.

There are two other implications to this narrative strategy: The first is that Annie as narrator renders the childhood scenes in progressively more sophisticated language so that the narrative matures linguistically at the same rate as Annie's development. The second is that there is a continual narrative irony, as the older teller depicts reality from the perspective of the child, as when she suggests that dead people would occasionally "show up standing under a tree just as you were passing by."[1] The underlying assumption of this technique is that what is told, the principle of selection of scenes from a multitude of possibilities, is determined not by the child but by the adult narrator. The latter seems motivated by a desire to depict the most salient crises of her voyage toward self-realization.

It is an exciting but painful journey. Essentially, it proves a tragic "coming of age in Antigua," despite the overlay of humor and charm throughout the narrative.[2] The central issue from start to finish is Annie's relationship with her mother. The central image is that of the trunk, one that contained mementos of the mother's youth in Dominica and then comes to hold the treasured reminiscences of every stage of Annie's childhood. It is appropriate that Annie brings a similar trunk with her when she leaves Antigua at seventeen. In the matter of the trunk, as in so much else, Annie's life recalls that of her mother and brings them as close together in their separation as they were on their island. This is an awareness the adult narrator would have that the child would not. It is buttressed by the special irony that although the child Annie sees the mother as a heartless despot, the Annie who narrates portrays "no tyrant but a beautiful, loving woman who adores her only child and is wise enough to wish her daughter independent."[3] The act of telling a story of rebellion with such a loving portrait of a mother is, in effect, an act of psychological reconciliation that never achieves material fulfillment. For there is no indication that Annie ever returns home. On one level, she need not, for what her story reveals is the process by which, in striving for independence, she recapitulates the life of her mother. It is no small point that both the child and the mother share the same name, "Annie John."

The book begins with ten-year-old Annie's childhood fascination with death, a subject with somber values set off against the sunny and carefree world of her everyday life. Her conflicts are with the world of the supernatural, with the imponderable causal forces that live in shadow and sign and that wrest a comforting meaning from random events. Her preoccupation with death is a normative fixation and an attempt to understand the most profound developments around her. Beyond the charm of innocent grotesquerie, her fixation offers the revelation of Annie's character and of a lively and creative mind. It reveals also a love for storytelling, an unsentimental confrontation with the most unpleasant realities, and a child's faulty logic that accepts folklore as transcendent reality.

In a sense Annie must reach outward for conflict. The world she lives in, at least on her level of engagement, is prelapsarian, an antediluvian feast of family love and lore. Her mother is not so much long suffering as long rejoicing. She is so in love with her daughter and life as to celebrate even its most minute details, from routine household tasks to the bark she uses to scent Annie's bath water. Indeed, the artifacts of the young girl's existence speak of adoration: Her father built the house she lives in with his own hands. He even lovingly crafts the furniture in her room, the spoon she eats with, the entire household. It is a brilliant context in which to begin the story: For this caring household is the world that Annie will come to resent and rebel against in her final departure.

Although as narrator she stresses these details, at the time of the action Annie is oblivious to them. She is obsessed instead with her immediate concern for a progression of expirations—from Nalda to Sonia's mother to Miss Charlotte and the humpback girl, whose passing inspires in Annie not compassion but a desire to rap on the hump to see if it is hollow (p. 10). Even these episodes bring her back under the sway of her mother, however. For it is the latter who tells the stories of death in the family, and it is she who is holding Nalda in her arms when she dies. This tragedy is given cruel interpretation by Annie:

> I then began to look at my mother's hands differently. They had stroked the dead girl's forehead; they had bathed and dressed her and laid her in the coffin my father had made. . . . For a while, though not for very long, I could not bear to have my mother caress me or

touch my food or help me with my bath. I especially couldn't bear
the sight of her hands lying still in her lap. (p. 6)

It is the first negative transformation in Annie's attitude toward
her mother. Annie begins to visit funeral parlors, an obsession
that brings her home late one evening without the fish she was
supposed to deliver. She lies about the incident: "That night, as
a punishment, I ate my supper outside, alone, under the breadfruit tree, and my mother said that she would not be kissing me
good night later, but when I climbed into bed she came and
kissed me anyway" (p. 12). It is a warm and forgiving world
Annie lives in but it is a childhood paradise, one she will have
to leave to become an adult.[4]

When Annie turns twelve everything changes. She enters the
first stages of the love-hate relationship with her mother that
informs the central plot of the narrative.[5] Ironically, it is not the
terrors of death that lead to the schism but the act that brought
her life: she discovers her parents making love and is revolted.
To provide a context for this event, the narrator sketches a background of familial closeness, how mother and daughter would
bathe together in water scented with flowers and oils. Annie tells
of her mother's departure from Dominica with the trunk and of
the many times the mother later removed Annie's things from it,
caressing each item as an emblem of her daughter's previous
growth: "As she held each thing in her hand she would tell me
a story about myself" (p. 21). In contrast, the father's background
is rich in love of a more perverse and complex variety. He has
loved and abandoned a series of women, leaving several with
children he does not now acknowledge. This is a fact that hangs
over their lives, seeking expiation. Abandoned as a small child,
he grew up with his grandmother, sleeping with her until he was
eighteen, when she died. The father weeps when he relates this
story, and Annie experiences a sudden growth of sensibility in
her compassion for him (p. 24).

The turning point for Annie comes when her mother informs
her that it is time for her to have her own clothes, not simply
imitations of her mother's dresses. Annie is shocked at this demand for her discrete identity: "To say that I felt the earth swept
away from under me would not be going too far" (p. 26). Here
Annie would seem to be confronting the classic confusion of a
girl in her relationship with her mother: She desires the closest
possible identification and shows distress when the mother suggests any degree of separation. Nancy Chodorow suggests that

"the child's reaction to its mother in such a situation is not true hate but confusion that is part of the failure to recognize the mother's separateness."[6] Her mother exhibits disgust at Annie's many lies, but the event from which their relationship never recovers is the parental sex scene, particularly the image of her mother's hand, making a circular motion, on her husband's back. It proves an imagistic referent that lends the title "The Circling Hand," indicating that it is the preeminent event. This image is invested with Annie's confrontation with adult sexuality, a development that will prove more difficult for her than the discovery of death. In the absence of siblings, Annie must share love with the "other" parent, a fact that inspires not rivalry toward her father but a bitter resentment of her mother: "I was sure I could never let those hands touch me again; I was sure I could never let her kiss me again. All that was finished" (pp. 31–32). In her place Annie proclaims her love for a schoolmate, Gwen, and this and other surrogate loves sustain her through the break with her mother.

Annie's ambivalence toward her mother intensifies in the second chapter devoted to Annie at twelve; the implication is that the year was pivotal in her development. Annie is in a new school, and much of the chapter is a description of a typical school day. Yet the salient dimensions of the episode deal with Annie's growing maturity. There is here a nostalgic look back at the unconditional love she has received throughout her childhood from her mother, as well as her compelling need to move beyond the family to the larger social world around her. The key document is an autobiographical essay she writes in school. In it she describes swimming with her mother and the profound sense of isolation and abandonment she feels when her mother momentarily slips from view.[7] Annie is not simply puzzled or startled; she experiences a momentary crisis of being: "A huge black space then opened up in front of me and I fell inside it. . . . I couldn't think of anything except that my mother was no longer near me" (p. 43). When her mother sees her crying, she hugs her closely and promises never to leave her again, but Annie is left with the sensation of abandonment.

The depth of Annie's dependence and antipathy here adumbrates the more exaggerated passage she will make through her dark night of the soul in the penultimate chapter. Yet even now there are pathological implications to the depth of her emotion. That these events are juxtaposed with an account of her first menstruation is also important in that Annie's struggle toward

emotional maturity is linked to her biological coming of age
(p. 51). Similarly, the intensification of Annie's love for Gwen[8] is
set against the diminution of her love for her mother, a diminution that continues until Annie reflects that "I could not understand how she could be so beautiful even though I no longer
loved her" (p. 53).

From this point on every episode contains another expression
of Annie's continuing rebellion and of her substitution of other
emotional alliances for the close bond she formerly shared with
her mother. Soon these ideas take the form of Annie's stealing
and lying and playing marbles, all forbidden activities. There is
also her infatuation with the Red Girl, who is the personification
of familial anarchy in that she refuses to bathe more than once
a week. Gwen, the socially correct young lady who has Annie's
mother's full approval, is replaced by the Red Girl, who is free
from convention and discipline: "Oh, what an angel she was,
and what a heaven she lived in!" (p. 58). That this expression of
betrayal contains portions of both pain and pleasure is expressed
in Annie's relationship with the Red Girl. The latter pinches
Annie and then kisses the injured spots: "Oh, the sensation was
delicious—the combination of pinches and kisses" (p. 63). That
all of this activity takes place at a time commensurate with the
previous chapter becomes clear when Annie starts to menstruate,
the second rendering of that event in the book. Once again it is
a transitional event in that it coincides with the departure of the
Red Girl and the cessation of playing marbles. But through this
episode Annie has expanded the terrain of her rebellion. Embracing forbidden friends, and violating the most sacred shibboleths
of social behavior, she masks her true nature behind a conventional facade. This double life will come to exact its bounty.

The theme of rebellion is taken then into another dimension.
Annie begins to confront the social history of her world: the
legacy of slavery and exploitation under British colonialism and
the meaning for people of color of the expeditions of Christopher
Columbus. She does not perceive society in explicitly racial
terms, but the figures of authority around her seem to be white:
her doctor, the Methodist minister, her teachers. The history Annie knows is British, as is her religion, currency, holidays, flag,
and middle name.[9] Peer relations seem to be conducted without
racial restriction, as in Annie's friendship with the daughter of
the minister: "Ruth I liked, because she was such a dunce and
came from England and had yellow hair" (p. 73). But even here
there is a powerful sense of the differences between them: "Her

ancestors had been the masters, while ours had been the slaves. She had such a lot to be ashamed of."[10] As she did in *A Small Place* in 1988, Jamaica Kincaid here attributes the moral high ground to the exploited rather than the powerful.

These kinds of concepts, contemporaneous with the time of the action rather than the time of the telling, lead Annie to relish the portrait of Columbus in chains. She writes beneath his picture the very words that her mother had used to respond to the news that Pa Chess was incapacitated: "So the great man can no longer just get up and go. How I would love to see his face now!" (p. 78). This comment, even to the exact words, is yet another element in Annie's recapitulation of her mother. Yet the chapter ends with an additional step in their estrangement with the mother tricking her daughter into the eating of breadfruit and with Annie portraying her mother as a crocodile.

In "Somewhere, Belgium," a title derived from an escape fantasy, Annie has turned fifteen and has entered into a deep depression, the etiology of which would seem to be an emotional schism. Many aspects of her life are warm and protective. These include the stories of her father's youth and the many objects around her crafted by his own hands, as well as the familiar story of Annie's mother leaving home at her age. But on another level Annie's already tenuous circumstances have grown worse. Promoted two grades, she is no longer in the same class with Gwen. Their relationship falters while at the same time the younger Annie suffers in the company of older girls well into adolescence. Her own hesitant steps toward courtship all end badly, even the games she plays with neighborhood boys; in each instance her mother expresses not so much outrage as disgust. When she stops on the way home to flirt with one of the boys from her youth, her mother observes the event and later accuses her of behaving like a slut. Her words move Annie to say "like mother like daughter" and the mother to respond that "until this moment, in my whole life I knew without a doubt that, without any exception, I loved you best" (p. 102).

Annie becomes deeply torn: she is filled with a sense of her mother's love for her, which moves her to tears; at the same time she wishes the older woman were dead. Their duplicitous relationship—outward harmony concealing a deep inner antipathy—is now an obstacle to any integration of self for Annie: "I could not be sure whether for the rest of my life I would be able to tell when it was really my mother and when it was really her shadow standing between me and the rest of the world" (p. 107).

Annie needs desperately to be part of the rest of the world, hence the fantasy about escaping to Belgium.

These unresolved conflicts lead to Annie's dark night of the soul at fifteen, a sleep that continues throughout a long rain of more than three months. Caused by no discoverable physical illness, Annie's sleep is a mechanism to escape emotional irresolution.[11] It is also an episode that allows for one last family summation, even the mysterious appearance of the maternal grandmother, who comes, still dressed in black since the death of her son decades before, with ritual cures and potions. It is clear, however, that the causative factor does not lend itself to these cures nor to those of Western medicine: "I looked inside my head. A black thing was lying down there, and it shut out all my memory of the things that had happened to me" (pp. 111–12). This illness resembles in many respects the archetypal pathology in the female *Bildungsroman*: "Sleep and quiescence in female narratives represent a progressive withdrawal into the symbolic landscapes of the innermost self. . . . Excluded from active participation in culture, the fictional heroine is thrown back on herself."[12] In this case, however, Annie's conflict results less from the problems of acculturation than from the more fundamental issue of growing up in her family.

Annie's illness takes her back through the progression of her life, with her parents' tender solicitations; they treat her like an infant, seeing to her every need. The complexity of her feelings toward her parents is omnipresent, as when Ma Jolie suggests that the cause of the illness may be the curses of the women Annie's father abandoned (p. 117). Other familial objects also possess a negative resonance for her, as does the photograph of her in her communion dress, wearing shoes her mother had forbidden. It was another confrontation that had led Annie to wish her mother dead. Annie's need to break free of the constraints of this heritage is exemplified by her washing the images off the family photographs, except for her own portrait and that of the forbidden shoes. All of this is consistent with the theories of Nancy Chodorow, who postulates that

> mothers feel ambivalent toward their daughters, and react to their daughters' ambivalence toward them. They desire both to keep daughters close and push them into adulthood. This ambivalence in turn creates more anxiety in their daughters and provokes attempts by these daughters to break away.[13]

The illness does not abate, however, until Annie begins to realize that she never wants to see her mother again, that her world has become an "unbearable burden." As soon as she is able to articulate this awareness, she quickly recovers. It has been a transforming respite, one that leads to the resolution of the book in the last chapter.

Even the temporal structure of the final chapter suggests its seminal role in Annie's life. For it covers but a single day, and it does so not in the broad sweep of the previous sections but hour by hour, moving ever closer to Annie's departure from Antigua. There is never any doubt about the psychological need for Annie to leave. (She is revolted by nearly everything associated with her mother.) However, at the time of the telling, the summation of this day constitutes a revisiting of the scenes of her youth. The objects and places of Antigua are described in great detail in the book's most sophisticated language, for Annie is now seventeen. Awakened by the bell in the Anglican Church, she walks down the road she has trod all her life. She walks past the familiar library and offices and stores she has always known to the jetty and the ship that will carry her to England. Beneath the bitterness that demands her departure at the time of the action, the anterior act of narrating allows for another farewell: to the lush environment of Antigua, to the smell of the sea, the white sand of the beaches, the rich sounds of the voices. The narrator knows what the young girl cannot—that she will never return.

On the level of action, Annie's story is thus one of progressive antagonism and disenchantment that winds inevitably toward her escape. As a narrative act, however, her story constitutes an imaginative return to the world of her youth in its full complexity, the pains as well as the pleasures. The submerged implication in the story being told at all is that the spatial departure from Antigua did not resolve all of the emotional issues of Annie's childhood. They still seek resolution though their cathartic reiteration.[14] It may well be the reflective narrator as well as the liberated adolescent who, on the final page, is preoccupied with "an unexpected sound, as if a vessel filled with liquid had been placed on its side and now was slowly emptying out" (p. 148).

II

Nearly all of the themes and devices of *Annie John* are continued, or deepened, in *Lucy*, published in 1990.[15] The two volumes must be considered as independent fictional constructs, and Lucy Josephine Potter as distinct from Annie Victoria John. But the parallels between the two are extremely close. Both Annie and Lucy grow up on Caribbean islands, and both long to escape the restrictions of a solicitous mother by leaving home and becoming a nurse. In each volume the love-hate relationship between mother and daughter is a dominant issue, although manifested in rather different terms. Also, the young girl in each knows she must escape to have any chance of personal growth. In each work the mother's name is "Annie" and the child is referred to as "Little Miss." Both have a father who was raised sleeping in the same bed as his grandmother. In addition, the father's promiscuity and lack of responsibility toward illegitimate children are a subtheme in each case. The differences in the two stories are minimal but interesting. Both girls leave home to become nurses; Annie walks to the jetty at seventeen on her way to London, and Lucy flies to New York at nineteen. Annie feels a painful separation at age twelve when her mother urges her toward independence. Lucy has the same feeling at ten when her mother gives birth to the first of three sons, and a decade later she is still mourning the loss of maternal affection in New York. The details are different, but the psychic history and emotional struggle are the same.

In both works the young girl becomes aware of the legacy of slavery and British colonization. Both Annie and Lucy chafe against this legacy and its domination of their church, social life, and, especially, education. *Annie John* traces the development of the protagonist from age ten to seventeen and *Lucy* from nineteen to twenty; essentially, however, the same internal conflict is at issue: the extent to which the prerogatives of "self" are limited by familial and social circumstances. The young girl's quest in each book is to transcend nonvolitional factors and to aspire to self-realization, and to become the person she is interested in becoming, and none other. Each work is a moving and surprising feminine *Bildungsroman*. Each concludes in a nostalgic reminiscence of Caribbean life and lore, maternal love, cultural resentment, and the final exhilaration of starting a new and independent life.

For Lucy that process takes her through an emptiness and depression not unlike the dark night of the soul Annie endures. As in Annie's case, the foundation of Lucy's despair rests in an unresolved conflict with her mother. Lucy experiences a desperate and consuming need for maternal affection at odds with an

incipient desire for separation and independence. These antithetical emotions are expressed in a series of contradictory reali-
zations. Homesickness is an example, juxtaposed as it is to Lucy's
anger when she realizes that she misses the people and things
of her island:

> What a surprise this was to me, that I longed to be back in the place
> that I came from, that I longed to sleep in a bed I had outgrown, that
> I longed to be with people whose smallest, most natural gesture
> would call up in me such a rage that I longed to see them all dead
> at my feet. (p. 6)

Lucy's thoughts of leaving home inspire a sense of emptiness, a
bleak and cold depression she has never known before: "Something settled inside me, something heavy and hard" (p. 24). This
feeling seems to result from many of the same causes that torment Annie: a resentment of her mother, a sense of restriction in
the culture of Antigua, bitterness at the pervasiveness of British
colonial rule, and a desire to explore what she is capable of
becoming. Because she is no longer home, however, and perhaps
because she is several years older, these matters are easier for
Lucy to resolve than for Annie.

Analogous to the many important dreams in *Annie John* is the
one Lucy has in the very center of the book:

> There was a present for me wrapped up in one of my mother's beauti-
> ful madras head-kerchiefs. I did not know what the present itself
> was, but it was something that would make me exceedingly happy;
> the only trouble was that it lay at the bottom of a deep, murky pool,
> and no matter how much water I bailed out[,] I always woke up
> before I got to the bottom. (p. 87)

This dream of unattainable happiness first seeks expression in
the replacement of her mother with a surrogate, Mariah, whose
children are in Lucy's care. Another form of the quest for fulfillment is in sexual gratification: Lucy rejects all social constraints about sexuality and takes a series of lovers. Finally, she
is brave enough to risk independence, and it is on this rising
action that the book ends.

Early in her narrative Lucy clarifies the basis of her discomfort
with the kindness of Mariah, who assumes a maternal role in
her life:

> Mariah was like a mother to me, a good mother. If she went to a store
> to buy herself new things, she thought of me and would bring me

something also. Sometimes she paid me more money than it had been agreed I would earn. . . . Always she expressed concern for my well-being. (p. 110)

As Lucy rebelled against her true mother, it is inevitable that she will eventually need to free herself of Mariah's influence as well, however well intentioned and supportive. Mariah, of course, has no way of knowing the depth of Lucy's need to be independent. Lucy remembers not only her awareness that "I was not like my mother—I was my mother" but also her mother's response to any attempt at independence: "'You can run away, but you cannot escape the fact that I am your mother, my blood runs in you, I carried you for nine months inside me'" (p. 90). Given the enormity of the parental control she seeks to escape, Lucy's resentment of any authority is understandable.

The sad irony of the situation is that the more kindness Mariah demonstrates, the more she is seen as "mother" by Lucy:

> But I already had a mother who loved me, and I had come to see her love as a burden and had come to view with horror the sense of self-satisfaction it gave my mother to hear other people comment on her great love for me. I had come to feel that my mother's love for me was designed solely to make me into an echo of her; and I didn't know why, but I felt that I would rather be dead than become just an echo of someone. (p. 36)

Lucy is not insensitive to Mariah's warm feelings toward her. When Mariah exhibits confusion and foreboding at turning forty, Lucy comments: "I did not understand why she felt that way about her age, old and unloved; a sadness for her overcame me, and I almost started to cry—I had grown to love her so" (p. 36). The problem is that the more Mariah plays the role of mother in Lucy's emotional life, the greater the need for Lucy to reject her.

As Lucy transfers her affection, this affective duality becomes increasingly clear: "The times that I loved Mariah it was because she reminded me of my mother. The times that I did not love Mariah it was because she reminded me of my mother" (p. 58). Mariah has become identified with the mother's control of her daughter, hence she can do nothing to sustain her relationship with Lucy.[16] Lucy's dreams of becoming independent rest in part on her need for a sense of autonomy and individual sovereignty, and these feelings underlie the resentment she ultimately feels toward her employer. The inevitable fruition of this emotional development comes when Lucy leaves Mariah for a new position.

Lucy is filled with exhilaration at the prospects of her new life. Mariah clearly feels hurt and betrayed: "Mariah helped me put my things in a taxi. It was a cold goodbye on her part. Her voice and her face were stony. She did not hug me" (p. 144).[17]

One expression of Lucy's need for independence is her rejection of a mother figure; another is her exuberant interest in sexual exploration. Although this obsession links her more closely with her father's profligacy than with her mother, it is essentially another mode of self-realization. Frank discussions about sexuality between mother and daughter were apparently as difficult for Lucy as they were for Annie. It is only with Mariah that Lucy can openly discuss her burgeoning desires. When Mariah displays a bouquet of peonies for Lucy, the young girl responds to their smell with a surprising comment: "I told her that this smell made you want to lie down naked and cover your body with these petals so you could smell this way forever" (p. 60). Rather than being shocked, Mariah is greatly amused and mocks a prudish response, to Lucy's enjoyment. Her reflection as narrator is sensitive: "This was the sort of time I wished I could have had with my mother, but, for a reason not clear to me, it was not allowed" (p. 60). Despite their racial differences, Mariah is in many ways a better parent to Lucy than her biological mother had been.

Lucy's sexual explorations seem composed of rebellion (at the time of the action) and the necessity to shock (at the time of the telling). Her adventures are formulated to be startling, from her reminiscence of adolescent flirtations with a young boy named Tanner to her sexual fulfillment with Hugh. Although she certainly does not love Hugh, or any of the other men with whom she becomes involved, she does seem to enjoy the pleasures of sexual activity, a close relationship with another person, and immersion in immediate experience. Perhaps more than anything, erotic activity is associated in Lucy's mind with her longing for an eventful life, with a need for a dramatic experience, as was clear even in her youth. When as a child her friend Myrna told her about how Mr. Thomas used to meet her in the dark for brief sexual interludes, performed with his middle finger, Lucy's response is not shock or surprise but jealousy: "Why had such an extraordinary thing happened to her and not to me?" (p. 105). This memory also explains why Lucy is later so receptive to Peggy's suggestion that they watch the hands of men in the park, associating the size of the hands with the size of a phallus.

Exploring sexuality is one way Lucy has of searching her own being. She shares the experiences with Mariah, telling her about trysts with Paul: "I told her what everything felt like, how surprised I was to be thrilled by the violence of it . . . what an adventure this part of my life had become, and how much I looked forward to it" (p. 113). Mariah responds not with moral judgment but with a reflection on the state of her own marriage: "We have such bad sex." The comment further associates her with Lucy's mother (p. 114). Lucy then becomes involved with Roland, a camera salesman, and they too have an intense, brief relationship. In all of these escapades, however, there is no sense of commitment, no mention of love or marriage or desire for family. Jane Mendelsohn rightly has observed: "Lucy's 'only true love' is her mother, back in Antigua, and the death she has been mourning is the death of childhood."[18] Lucy's erotic frolics are more internal examinations than emotional conquests, and they relate to another dominant motif in the book—her progressive formulation of a new identity for herself.

The heart of the story Lucy narrates is of her struggle toward self-realization in the two years immediately before the telling. Lucy reflects on her love for her mother and the restrictions she felt in her presence. She explores how Mariah replaced her mother in America and how she came to break with her to begin a new life. She reveals the details of her sexual experimentation, focused not on romantic interests or even sensual gratification so much as on personal exploration. In the last section of her story she recounts in some detail the process by which she invented herself. It is clear that she did so in the context of a profound sense of longing for home, of isolation and emotional loss, of the death of her father and the destitution of her mother, to whom she sends virtually all of her savings.

It is significant that the final section of the book is entitled "Lucy," in that the conclusion is about the formation of a new self. The section begins with her musings about how she is no longer the girl who grew up in Antigua. Indeed, she has rejected all that was expected of her there, not only a career as a nurse but also "a sense of duty to my parents; obedience to the law and worship of convention" (p. 133). On the other hand, she is still in the process of character formation; she is still "becoming": "I understood that I was inventing myself, and that I was doing this more in the way of a painter than in the way of a scientist" (p. 134). Part of this process of invention is a kind of summing up of her life. It is here that she discusses the "colonial" theme so pronounced in *Annie John*—her bitterness focused on Christopher Columbus, her refusal to sing "Rule, Britannia," and her observation that "I was not a Briton and that until not too long ago I would have been a slave" (p. 135). Her resentments have their humorous aspects:

> I disliked the descendants of the Britons for being unbeautiful, for not cooking food well, for wearing ugly clothes, for not liking to really dance, and for not liking real music. If only we had been ruled by the French. (pp. 136–37)

She reviews the stages of her personal growth, through puberty and menstruation, her employment by Lewis and Mariah, her love affairs, and the death of her father.

It is indicative of Mariah's sensitivity to this formative process that she gives Lucy a necklace from Africa, for part of Lucy's new life involves a definition of herself ethnically as well as personally. She leaves Mariah's home with new clothes, books, a new camera, and a new sense that she is unwilling to be the servant to Mariah's master (p. 143). Even though she will share an apartment with Peggy, it is clear that Lucy feels liberated when she awakens her first morning in her new home: "The next day I woke up in a new bed, and it was my own" (p. 144). The most graphic emblem of her new identity is that, for the first time in the book, she is able to articulate her full name, "Lucy Josephine Potter," and to reveal why the title of the volume uses her first name only: "The Lucy was the only part of my name that I would have cared to hold on to" (p. 149). This concept of "naming" reveals other matters as well, for she had earlier experimented with calling herself "Emily," "Charlotte," and "Jane" after writers she admired. For a time, as a child, she tried "Enid," only to learn that it was the name of a rejected lover of her father who attempted to murder Lucy's mother. She does not accept "Lucy" until her mother tells her that it is short for "Lucifer," which inspires Lucy's ironic response: "I went from feeling burdened and old and tired to feeling light, new, clean. I was transformed from failure to triumph. It was the moment I knew who I was" (p. 152).

But Lucy does not become that independent self until the end of the experience she is relating, until she has not only fled her island but also left Mariah and established a life of her own. Her new position in an office provides employment and further assurance that she can create her own identity. That is the significance of her enrolling in a photography course at a university.

In this new sense of identity she can make friends with Mariah once again, and she discovers that her former employer is going to live in a commune: "Everyone who lived in this place, she said, was filled with love and trust and greeted each other with the word 'Peace'" (p. 162). Lucy has the better of it, for her approach to a new life acknowledges pain and harsh realities. Mariah, in contrast, speaks of her utopian dreams amid the desolation of her life, the artifacts of a failed marriage. As a final act in the story she tells—a gesture of profound self-affirmation—Lucy picks up the notebook Mariah had given her and writes in it her full name, Lucy Josephine Potter. Under her name she inscribes "I wish I could love someone so much that I would die from it" (p. 164). Having become someone, Lucy is now ready to embrace someone else, not just with lust but also with love, and it is this sensation that constitutes the conclusion of the book.

Annie John and *Lucy* have the emotional power and artistic integrity to be read as independent of one another, essentially two books by the same author. But they are also very much of a set, a two-volume *Bildungsroman* with a traditional form and an innovative pattern of details. On this level, the first volume explores the life of a young girl on a Caribbean island who comes to realize that she must leave home to find herself. The second book continues the story in New York, tracing the life of a similar young girl who ultimately finds her identity and establishes an independent life for herself. Both stories are filled with hope and expectation. Both also portray the process of self-realization as involving the pain of separation, a sense of desperation and loneliness, and an unsettling affirmation of individuality against the constraints of society. In this sense, these volumes together constitute a celebration of the process of maturation, the existential process of self-definition that involves both awesome responsibility and the potential joy of self-discovery. In integrity of craft and solemnity of theme, *Annie John* and *Lucy* constitute a major contribution to contemporary fiction, one that is certain to establish Jamaica Kincaid among the preeminent writers in modern American literature.

Notes

1. Jamaica Kincaid, *Annie John* (New York: Farrar Straus Giroux, 1985), p. 4. All quotations are from this edition.

2. I am indebted here to Susan Kenney, "Paradise with Snake," *New York Times Book Review*, 7 April 1985, p. 6.

3. Charlotte H. Bruner, "Antigua," *World Literature Today* 59 (1985): 644.

4. Diane Cole, in "The Pick of the Crop: Five First Novels," *Ms.*, April 1985, p. 14, comes to a similar conclusion.

5. See Bruner, "Antigua," p. 644.

6. See Nancy Chodorow, *The Reproduction of Mothering: Psychoanalysis and the Sociology of Gender* (Berkeley: University of California Press, 1978), pp. 79–80.

7. Annie's autobiographical essay is on pp. 41–45.

8. Nancy Chodorow has posited that in becoming independent, a young girl often becomes critical of her mother and seeks an emotional bond with a best friend, with whom she shares her innermost self (p. 137).

9. Even her father's most treasured memory is of playing an English game, cricket (p. 118).

10. Jamaica Kincaid gives full expression to the concept of racism and colonialism in Antigua in *A Small Place* (New York: Farrar, Straus and Giroux, 1988).

11. John Bemrose gives this chapter a similar interpretation. He states that "Annie suffers a nervous breakdown from the strain of being a good girl in public and a rebel in secret." See "Growing Pains of Girlhood," *MacLean's*, 20 May 1985, p. 61.

12. See Marianne Hirsch, "Spiritual *Bildung*: The Beautiful Soul as Paradigm," in *The Voyage In: Fictions of Female Development*, ed. Elizabeth Abel, Marianne Hirsch, and Elizabeth Langland (Hanover, NH: University Press of New England, 1983), p. 23.

13. See Chodorow, *Reproduction of Mothering*, p. 135.

14. Pamela Marsh even suggests that Annie's affection finally overcomes her resentment. See "Ambivalence in Antigua: Leaving Childhood Behind," *Christian Science Monitor*, 5 April 1985, p. B2.

15. All citations are to Jamaica Kincaid, *Lucy* (New York: Farrar Straus Giroux, 1990).

16. In one scene, in which she cares for the children at the summer home on the great lakes, Lucy herself assumes the role of mother toward Miriam: "She must have reminded me of myself when I was that age, for I treated her the way I remembered my mother treating me then" (p. 53).

17. Jane Mendelsohn sees the plot of *Lucy* as tracing "the process of one woman's dissolution and another's self-invention. A mournful book filled with betrayals and death, it follows the progress of longing, not of love." "Leaving Home: Jamaica Kincaid's Voyage Round Her Mother," *Village Voice Literary Supplement* 89 (October 1990): 21.

18. See Mendelsohn, "Leaving Home," p. 21.

Fundamentalist Views and Feminist Dilemmas: Elizabeth Dewberry Vaughn's *Many Things Have Happened Since He Died* and *Break the Heart of Me*

GLORIA L. CRONIN

There will be narratives of female lives only when women no longer live their lives isolated in the houses and stories of men.[1]

In order to avoid total annihilation, to escape man's habitual urge to colonize, she must conserve some space for herself, a sort of no-man's land which constitutes precisely what men fail to understand of her and often attribute to stupidity because she cannot express its substances in her totally alienated language.[2]

Introduction

THE question of what hinges for women on their entry into the symbolic order has been discussed extensively during the past thirty years of feminist theorizing. The general answer has been quite uniform—not less than everything to do with inventing, claiming, and making available their own stories. To live "isolated in the houses and stories of men" is to risk invisibility and "total annihilation." For nearly all feminist theorists the ultimate anonymity is to be storyless. What is remarkable in our age is the enormous outpouring in American literature of the last thirty years of female narratives of all kinds, including autobiography and autofictography (works of fiction purporting to be autobiographies). Elizabeth Dewberry Vaughn's *Many Things Have Happened Since He Died* is autofictography, which breaks new ground in that it tells that most obliterated of all female stories— the emotional geography of spouse abuse. Her *Break the Heart of Me*, however, is not autofictography but a conventional novel that does the same thing with the lost story of *childhood* sexual abuse. Vaughn attempts to chart this lost continent of women's and girls' experience and map the consequences. But her efforts face major technical challenges, as there are few precedents or patterns for her to follow. Neither can she avoid a thorough and harsh critique of one entire stratum of Southern American society: Christian fundamentalist patriarchy. This subject matter is timely, timeless, and transcultural.

When *Many Things Have Happened Since He Died*[3] appeared in 1992, reviewers were quick to note the appearance of a major new talent. But, clearly, most were ill-equipped to respond to her devastatingly accurate social critique and deeply emotional subject matter. The majority of reviewers preferred instead to discuss the arrival of a new heir to the Flannery O'Connor tradition and the remarkable, eccentric voice of the unnamed protagonist. Pat Conroy immediately called Vaughn "one of the most exciting new voices in American fiction." Others hailed Vaughn as "the new Flannery O'Connor of the South."[4] Most, however, noted the compelling quality of the narrator's voice. "Elizabeth Dewberry Vaughn has unleashed a narrative voice that is so original and captivating," said Joyce Sweeney, "it cannot be ignored."[5] Her monologues are "lively," "original," "offbeat," and "wickedly humorous,"[6] declared William Starr. Hers is a "stark, fearless vision,"[7] added Sweeney. To his credit, Madison Smart Bell recognized the connection between subject matter and style as "strangely fractured language . . . indiscriminately [smashing] together wish-fulfillment daydreams, lunatic-fringe fundamentalist dogmas and what seem to be shards of an incipient psychosis,"[8] but even he avoided her cultural critique. Katherine Dieckmann also noted the language—that is, how "the language buckles under its own weight" in much the way the "self splinters under abuse."[9] Dinty W. Moore called it a "tightly crafted first person stream of ramble approach,"[10] while John Carney identified her as "an astute reporter of both outward behavior and innermost feelings."[11] All in all her initial critics did recognize many of Vaughn's salient qualities as a writer, but they failed to deal adequately with her vision of violence and death as the substance of daily life for women and men in the American South's fundamentalist culture.

Several reviewers and scholars have attempted to locate Vaughn's literary genealogy in contemporary American fiction. Marian Carache perceptively noted that her narrative technique smacks of Samuel Beckett and Holden Caulfield.[12] Jacquie Brogan[13] quickly identified the feminist literary genealogy of the novel, though she noted forcefully Vaughn's obvious departures from prior feminist romances:

> In many ways *Many Things Have Happened Since He Died* is clearly related to *Their Eyes Were Watching God* [and *The Color Purple*]. All three expose the psychological and physical abuse a woman— or women—suffer at the hands of men in patriarchal society. All three are set in the South . . . the main characters of each . . . achieve self-revelation despite formidable obstacles to such growth. And, where Hurston uses the narrative device of having Janie speak the "truth"—the "other side" of her story to a friend, where Walker uses the device of having Celie write letters to God, Vaughn uses the device of having Elizabeth transcribe dictaphone tapes that she has been dictating to herself while suffering repeated and escalating abuse. The obvious twist is that Vaughn's character is white and, at least superficially, has from the beginning the advantage of education and employment.[14]

One might also include in this maternal genealogy several of Flannery O'Connor's female protagonists who mostly access a character's thoughts in a third-person voice and the wonderfully eccentric voice of Edna Earle in Eudora Welty's *The Ponder Heart*.

Elizabeth Dewberry Vaughn: A Profile

Vaughn's upbringing provides substantial clues to her cultural vision. Born Elizabeth Dewberry in 1962, she resided in Birmingham, Alabama, until 1983. She attended the Presbyterian-affiliated Christian-fundamentalist Briarwood Christian School from kindergarten to graduation from grade 12 in 1980. There she learned first-hand the fundamentalist culture from which she is now retreating. She notes with wry irony:

> I can't remember a time when I didn't know the importance of being prepared for death. Every Tuesday after school I went to a Bible study led by a former flight attendant, where my friends and I planned our weddings with fill-in-the-blank grooms, quoted the verses we'd memorized for the week, confessed our sins, and learned beauty tips from stewardess school. We wanted to be beautiful from the inside out.[15]

Her childhood summers were spent on Dauphin Island with her grandparents, a place where she courted and disposed of her first set of invisible friends and learned to overstock her suitcase with books.

At age seventeen Elizabeth Dewberry began her freshman year at Vanderbilt University, graduating with a B.S. in English in 1983. During the spring of 1983 she worked as an intern in the publicity department of CBS Records, an experience that becomes significant in her second novel, *Break the Heart of Me*. From the fall of 1983 until she moved to Atlanta in the fall of 1985, she attended The University of Alabama Graduate School of English as a non-degree-seeking student. In 1984 she married Robert Allen Vaughn, a third-year law student. Vaughn amusedly describes the wedding held in the sanctuary of her childhood church as the wedding all her Christian fundamentalist friends dreamed of—seven pink bridesmaids and a cake-and-strawberry-punch reception in the Fellowship Hall. It was also the wedding she had always planned. After Robert's graduation, the couple moved to Atlanta, Georgia, where she attended graduate school in English at Emory University. She graduated from Emory in 1989 with a Ph.D. in twentieth-century literature, with a dissertation on Ernest Hemingway entitled "Artifact and Inquest: Hemingway's Exploration of Realist and Metafictional Conventions in *In Our Time*." She wrote *Many Things* simultaneously with her dissertation, and it clearly combines the realistic and metafictional conventions she was examining in Hemingway's *In Our Time*.

The manuscript of *Many Things* was accepted in 1990 under the title "In the Dark" and subsequently renamed by editor Nan Talese. It was purchased within one month of acceptance and then published in hardback by Doubleday/Bantam in 1992. Vintage Books (Random House) published it in paperback in January 1992. *Break the Heart of Me* was published in February 1994 under the Nan Talese/Doubleday imprint. It, too, has a white Southern woman/first-person narrator experiencing the beginnings of self-revelation, in this instance about her sexual abuse as a child. Vaughn has two more novels in progress: one presently being reworked is entitled *The Last Southern Gentleman*, while the other is yet without title. She is planning at least one sequel to *Many Things Have Happened Since He Died*, probably to be set six years later. Vaughn is currently an assistant professor in the English department at Ohio State University, where she teaches Creative Writing and American Literature. She is active in Hemingway studies and writing.

The Unspeakable Story

In *Many Things* and *Break the Heart of Me* Elizabeth Dewberry Vaughn demonstrates two nearly invisible women's struggles: first, to stage their own "transgression" into autobiography from within the patriarchal mores of Bible Belt Alabama. Second, this battle to "report back" from within such an unconducive social space illustrates only too well the complex relationship between the very nature of culture and the nature of humanity itself. These two antiromantic feminist black comedies are really about the complex relationships of gender, culture, and narrative. But they are also about the importance of unearthing those very old/ new stories about the abuse of girls and women. Andrea Dworkin describes the usual fate of such narratives:

> The accounts of rape, wife-beating, forced childbearing, medical butchering, sex-motivated murder, forced prostitution, physical mutilation, sadistic psychological abuse, and other commonplaces of female experience that are excavated from the past or given by contemporary survivors should leave the heart seared, the mind in anguish, the conscience in upheaval. But they do not. No matter how often these stories are told, with whatever clarity or eloquence, bitterness, or sorrow, they might well have been whispered in the sand: they disappear, as if they were threatened back into silence or destroyed, and the experience of female suffering is buried in cultural invisibility and contempt. Because women's testimony is not and cannot be validated by the witness of men who have experienced the same events and given them the same value, the very old reality of abuse sustained by women, despite its overwhelming pervasiveness and constancy, is negated in the history books, left out, and is negated by those who claim to care about suffering but who are blind to this suffering. The problem simply stated is that one must believe in the existence of the person (the female as subject with dignity and agency) in order to recognize the authenticity of her suffering.[16]

Traditionally, women like O'Connor, Welty, and Vaughn, writing in their own private voices for public display, have been guilty of what writers and scholars like Bataille, Genet, and Sontag call transgressive writing. They refer to that writing which, like great art, makes magnificent forays into new frontiers of consciousness and reports back. However, in the case of women's narrative, the act of "voicing" the female self as a subject is still an unsanctioned activity. Within any discursive field of Western culture, the female subject exercises free speech or writing about self from an almost invisible and voiceless position. In *Many Things Have Happened Since He Died* (1992) and *Break the Heart of Me* (1994),[17] Vaughn insists we acknowledge both this invisibility and voicelessness as well as the subjectivity and dignity of such women. Her narratives break through this historic and cultural blindness by giving unquenchable voice to their experience. However, it is not merely the voice of the victim she gives us, but two genuine storytellers who write with power in the tradition of Faulkner, O'Connor, and Welty. Speaking of Elizabeth's quirky voice in *Many Things*, Vaughn comments: "Her mind is like a sponge. She can think in Biblical terms or like Helen Reddy or Donahue. Whatever she hears she then thinks . . . that's part of her problem."[18] Hélène Cixous's words describe best the immediacy of this voice:

> Feminine texts . . . are very close to the flesh of language . . . perhaps because there's something in them that's freely given, perhaps because they don't rush into meaning, but are straightway at the threshold of feeling. There's tactility in the feminine text.[19]

Vaughn confirms this impression of tactility or immediacy: "The heart of the writing process for me is hearing those voices. It's not that words conjure the person, it's that the character finds words. At the end of *Color Purple* Alice Walker says 'I want to thank my characters for coming.' When I'm writing I have a sense of gratitude to my characters being there and giving me the words. They talk to create an existence for themselves. I see them in dreams."[20] Vaughn describes the inception of her own novel:

> The speaker of *Many Things Have Happened Since He Died* came to me like an invisible friend in need of a voice, and the writing process was more like transcribing her thoughts than making them up. When I had finished writing the book, I dreamed that my home had many more rooms than I had realized and that hundreds of relatives I had never met were staying in them. I ran through the halls screaming, telling them to be quiet, and to leave, carrying their suitcases outside. When everyone else had gone, the speaker of *Many Things Have Happened Since He Died* sat down in my living room

and told me that she could not leave. She had nowhere else to go. I told her she could stay.[21]

Like Welty, Vaughn recognizes the power of the tradition of Southern tale-telling: "They make stories out of everything," she states; "they make stories out of just telling each other what happens on a regular basis."[22] This essay will discuss the cultural critique offered by both of her novels as they attempt to make visible the plight of sexually victimized women in Southern fundamentalist Christian patriarchy. It will also focus comparatively on their shared theme of emotional survival.

Patriarchal Christian Fundamentalism

In *Many Things Have Happened Since He Died*, Vaughn's protagonist, "Elizabeth" (she is not actually named), is part of a dysfunctional family within a dysfunctional, abusive Southern patriarchal culture. In addition, she is poor, female, and has completed only one year of college. The structure of abuse and oppression inherent in patriarchal Christian fundamentalism and families raised within it offers the biggest challenge to her ability to construct a viable self or self-narrative. Elizabeth's literal and symbolic relationship to her father, her husband, God the father, and patriarchy in general is problematic. The self-narrative is almost tragicomic in what it reveals: Uncle Dwight is an alcoholic. Her great grandfather and his son have killed each other with hunting rifles in a mutual suicide pact during the Great Alabama Depression. Her father, who has been dead just 101 days when her story begins, has probably also committed suicide over bankruptcy. For the most part, she views the violent and predatory nature of the men in her life through the images of taxidermy. All she has inherited from her own father is a stuffed duck that he had shot and hung over the mantelpiece. Mr. Brooks, her boss, she tells us, has a stuffed fox in a glass box in the office beside his sofa; it reflects its image in the glass covering the picture of his wife and two daughters that sits next to it (p. 4). Malone, her dental-student husband, gives her numerous black eyes, a broken finger, and a beating that leaves her senseless for many hours. In addition to this, he rapes her, leaving her psychologically maimed and pregnant. He, too, comes from a lineage of violent, dysfunctional men, and he, too, ends up stuffed and mounted—a gift to the medical chop-shop. After his accidental death, she donates his eyes, internal organs, and even his skin. She sums up in one poignant sentence the failure of masculine culture, human and godly, in her life: "I wanted a true relationship with my father, but I could not die for it" (p. 5). Her imaginative, childlike solution to the failure of men and God in particular is also poignant: "I used to have four invisible friends until I got tired of them and we went to the beach and I threw them in the ocean. None of them could swim. I wish I could do that to God" (p. 110).

Unfortunately, she has internalized most of Christian fundamentalism's destructive norms and formulas. "Marriage is sacred if you divorce it is a sin" (p. 15), she says after the first beating. "I believe forgiveness is like love it is not a feeling it is a commitment" (p. 27); "I have to forgive him so I do" (p. 26). Still suppressing her own feelings of betrayal and anger, she states optimistically: "Everything is fine now and God is taking so much care to build my character that I just know he is preparing me for something special whom the Lord loves he chastises" (p. 28). "We are starting over a new life in Christ and now our motto is love joy peace patience kindness gentleness self-control" (p. 29). Soon after this, when Malone breaks her finger in another violent argument over her father's money, she rationalizes that he is helping her develop character. To her mother, she explains: "I am becoming a better person a deeper person because I'm developing a patient long-suffering spirit. I'm learning to love unconditionally like Christ loves" (p. 35). The predictable results are deepening psychosis and an increasing number of suicide lists, not to mention even more demands from Malone. Her two terrible nightmares tell all. First she dreams that Malone has pulled out all her teeth, and next that there are predatory clacking teeth all over the apartment (p. 43).

Her intensifying psychological trauma further silences and isolates her, since there is no one to whom she can communicate her shame. When Malone rapes her and beats her senseless, we get a blank page with a few clues on the subsequent one. It is a textually arresting moment made more shocking when her patriarchally identified mother perpetuates the silencing process by lying to Elizabeth's bosses and failing to notify the authorities. Elizabeth responds to this near-erasure by begging for a piece of paper on which to write down her name before she forgets it or is killed. Trapped by the shame of her abusive treatment, she cannot confide in her mother, mother-in-law, workmates, church community, or the authorities. She can only deny her plight by rationalizing with more fundamentalist platitudes: "I don't care what non-Christians think of me. For example if they reject me then I am in good company because they have also rejected Christ and there is a special blessing in Heaven for those who have been persecuted for His name's sake" (p. 56).

Sylvia, in *Break the Heart of Me*, comes from an even more dysfunctional Southern family than does the unnamed "Elizabeth" of *Many Things*. She, too, confronts a series of patriarchal betrayals, and these cohere around the four violent deaths she "experiences" as a child. Ripped from her comatose, dying mother's womb following an almost suicidal car accident (her parents were unmarried teenage lovers), she is raised in her maternal grandparents' home. When at age twelve she experiences the trauma of finding her grandmother dead, she is taken to live with her father, euphemistically known to her as Uncle Mull, and his narcissistic twenty-five-year-old country-western-singing wife, Deedee. While attending Nashville Christian Academy, which specializes in its own exclusive brand of distorted fundamentalist Christianity, Sylvia lives in a hell of familial rejection. She also watches Mull and Deedee's marriage break down, joins the Rapture Club, and experiences two more bizarre deaths.

Sylvia connects the violence and betrayal enacted by the men in her life to what she observes as the irony of God's violence to his people, especially to his own son. She notes of the biblical record:

> God is killing everybody right and left when they don't do things His way, turning them into pillars of salt and changing their rivers to blood, setting locusts on them and killing their children and burning down their houses just to see if they'll love him after. You think too hard about that being God and somebody believing they're a prophet of God, and you start to feel scared. But you grow up listening to these stories every Sunday and reading books about them with color pictures and sometimes even pop-up illustrations, like Noah's Ark, all those little animals trotting into the ark and even snakes look cute like sideways S-es with an extra squiggle on the end they're smiling and the girl snake has eyelashes—somehow the destruction of the world becomes a pleasant thing to contemplate. The water turning into blood looks like pools of velvet, and the blood of Jesus is something you sing songs about, swaying to the music and saying halleluia, and I had comic books that showed Jesus on the cross with blood dripping down his legs and people swimming around in the lake of fire, only there was something about their arms and that made you think they were wearing roller skates under the fire. (pp. 298–99)

The Christian fundamentalist legacy of violence, guilt, horror, and distortion is as carefully delineated in this novel as it is in *Many Things*. Shocked into immobility by finding the dead body of her grandmother, Sylvia (like Elizabeth) tries to deal with her rising hysteria with adult formulas and fundamentalist platitudes. Remembering what she has learned of death from the local minister, she figures that if Memaw is in heaven already, then she needs nothing from Sylvia, and therefore neither misses her nor cares. Overcome by anger at such a betrayal of love, she says: "I was mad too, or maybe stunned is the word, like she'd slapped me in the face. And before I knew it I'd wished I could slap her back" (p. 3). The dead body seems "cold and eerie and sort of like sex" (p. 4), because there is something about it she is not supposed to know. All through these early hours, Reverend Tutwiler's voice unhelpfully intones in her head: "If you really love a brother or sister who's gone to be with the Lord, you'll be praising God with the angels" (p. 4). Then to be absolutely sure Memaw's death is just a death, she checks the afternoon sky: if it is cloudless, the Rapture cannot be coming. The Rapture, after all, will show Jesus' approach to earth trailing clouds of glory, not late-afternoon thunder clouds. It is the imminence of the apocalyptic violence of the Rapture that informs the emotional fabric of these early years. It necessitates her adoption of the persona and alter ego of Amazing Grace, her child faith-healer self, who tells her that if she really had faith she could just walk over to Memaw and raise her up from the dead. She acknowledges her betrayal by the entire adult world by concluding: "I didn't want to call Reverend Tutwiler because he'd already caused enough trouble with asleep in the Lord, and every single adult I could think of was like that—just not right, I mean" (p. 14). Death far exceeds fundamentalist platitudes for Sylvia. The Valley of the Shadow of Death feels as if "it comes and surrounds you and sits on your skin like Mist," she comments, and "then it seeps in like poison, like Agent Orange" (p. 16). There is for Sylvia no rejoicing with the souls in heaven.

Even the first flashback of sexual abuse by her grandfather reveals her violent betrayal by adults and their false religious formulas. While using her sexually, he had distracted her by placing a cloth over her eyes and counting with her to ten, after which he assures her God can no longer see anything. Sylvia remembers: "God watches us until when I got to the tens, and then the picture went blank and I could just hear my voice, my eight year old [voice]" (p. 21). The remembering, traumatized adult concludes: "My whole childhood smells like rot" (p. 30). The anguished pathos of Sylvia's Christian fundamentalist upbringing suggests distinct connections to the plight of Holden Caulfield; he had revealed a similar childlike vulnerability in imagining a "Catcher in the Rye," an alter ego who would save small children from the bad faith of the adult world. Sylvia's alter ego of "Amazing Grace, Child Faith-Healer," proceeds from a similar terror:

> Amazing Grace is from when I was eight. I was sitting in the Three Sisters' beauty parlor reading *Star* magazine while Memaw had her hair done, and I came across a page full of pictures of those little children who have some disease that makes them die of old age, and I looked at this little boy not any bigger than me, only he was bald and more shriveled up than Paw Paw, and chills went all the way through me and my hair stood up on my arms. It was as good as a burning bush. And I said Lord, that's my call, I got to heal those children. And before I knew it I had myself all fixed up in my head as Amazing Grace, child faith healer, and I was traveling around the world with the Amazing Grace choir, healing all the children who were dying of old age and going on TV telling everybody about the love of Jesus everywhere I went. So every night for a year I asked God for the gift of healing and I claimed every verse in the Bible I could think of about how God answers all prayer and if you ask God for it He'll give you the desires of your heart. So I don't know what went wrong. I guess I won't know until I get to heaven and my eyes are opened. Because I never did get the gift. (pp. 83–84)

Thinking about what she got instead of "a [spiritual] gift" leads to a painful summation of her childhood: "It's grotesque in the way a traffic accident involving bearded ladies and two-headed men would be" (p. 38). The other women in her life have fared no better. Of her grandmother's life Sylvia notes that "I think to this day she died of a broken heart" (p. 48). Then she recalls that her own mother died a desperate, pregnant, unmarried teenager at the precise moment she herself was born.

These deaths and rejections all underscore for Sylvia the failure of the patriarchy to care for anyone, women or men. Even as a teenager she realizes that her friend Bo's alienation has much to do with his rejection by his macho father. Bo is a skinny, part-Vietnamese, unathletic boy without the all-American-football-star potential of other men's sons. Coach Schifflett, his father, is known to be a violent wife-abuser and an ogler of cheerleaders. With considerable unconscious irony and pathos, Sylvia comments that Coach Schifflett's testimony is superior to that of others because he is a reformed drug addict and a heavy-metal-music listener. Plus he tells jokes. The compensatory psychopathology of Bo literally identifying with all the great figures of the Old and New Testaments before committing suicide provides Vaughn with her inevitable connections of apocalyptic fundamentalism, self-destructiveness, raw human violence, and the failure of the family.

Vaughn's delicately balanced black humor about the inanities of a fundamentalist Christianity gone mad is also evident in Sylvia's childhood amazement at the antics of another woman. Sylvia remembers that this woman had a fine testimony like Coach Schifflett's, but that she, unlike his completely silenced Vietnamese wife, had rebelled and run away from her Mafia husband after trying to shoot him on five different occasions. When she actually kills him on the fifth try and goes to jail, she gets saved and ends up witnessing to the judge and jury (p. 126). After all this, Sylvia notes admiringly, instead of serving time, the woman does public service by converting battered wives to Christ. Then there is the hilarious tale of the TV minister's wife who, like the Prov. 31 woman, had a log cabin moved into her yard called the "Gap House for God Answers Prayers" (p. 127). Funnier still is Vaughn's account of the scrapbook Sylvia and the members of the Rapture Club are preparing to leave behind after the Rapture "so the pagans could figure out what happened" (p. 129).

Self-Hatred, Suicide, and Silencing

However, there is little humor in the apocalyptic violence of Bo's graphic descriptions of the Second Coming. His accounts are replete with details about the Russian Bear of the North, helicopters instead of locusts, and an Armageddon reminiscent of a Civil War battleground. The only light touch is Sylvia's momentarily vengeful picture of the unrepentant Uncle Mull and Deedee "weeping and gnashing their teeth and dog-paddling around in the lake of fire" (p. 132). But Sylvia's pathetic sense of her developing female body causes her to prepare for the Rapture by dieting and bulimia: "I knew my body was a temple and I thought God deserved better than a fat temple, and I thought he was helping me because throwing up got easier and easier to the point where I hardly even had to try" (p. 134). Severely compromised in her development, Sylvia will later have great trouble developing a healthy attitude toward her body. Bo also turns inward to a pathological self-hatred and a spectacularly bizarre self-destruction. The apocalyptic violence climaxes in the graveyard when Bo dramatically slits his own throat in front of the horrified Sylvia as a reenactment of Abraham's sacrifice of Isaac. Both children have been violently orphaned in a so-called Christian community, and one is now dead.

For the protagonist in *Many Things Have Happened Since He Died*, contemplation of death and suicide is also a constant. So, too, is her warped sense of her own sexuality. Like Sylvia and Bo, she has no useful parents, siblings, mentors, fellow writers, or literary foremothers. Only Virginia Woolf appears as her suicidal death and bisexuality fascinate this bedeviled young woman. As she tries to understand her now-phobic response to sexual contact, she decides she must also be bisexual. The failure of her sense of gender identity is suggested when she finds Malone engaging in group masturbation under the influence of drugs—three men in her own marriage bed. Instead of labeling Malone as homosexual, she accuses herself of "monstrous" sins. She then intensifies her fundamentalist self-rhetoric about her obligations of forgiveness, loving, honoring, and obeying her husband. Hers is a perverted exercise in denial, self-hatred, and submission to the point of psychic disintegration. Her reaction leaves her wondering if her ashes will finally reside in an airtight vessel or in a Tupperware container that will leak her essential self out into the general mud. Denied the protective anger through which she might gain power and control, she is left only with a deepening depression and madness. These lead her to interpret the collapse of her own psyche and married life as Fate, God's will, or God's abandonment of her. Her only formulas for coping are pathetically inadequate fundamentalist platitudes: "Be a better wife." "Smile more often." "Think of happy things." "Experience the joy of the Lord all the time" (p. 88). These homilies go on for an entire hysterical page.

The marital-counseling classes the local minister encourages her and Malone to attend complete the pattern of abuse inflicted on women in such cultures. She is taught the classic formulas for being the submissive angel in the house, whereas Malone, the abusive husband, is empowered as the reigning patriarch and stand-in for Christ. He is valorized for simply attending the workshop despite his failure to cease his violent behavior, leaving Elizabeth to wonder how much more submissive she can be and still stay alive.

Speaking the Unspeakable

It is within this deadening cultural paradigm that Vaughn explores the failure of patriarchal fundamentalism to protect and empower women; the nonredemptive, nonpassionate nature of traumatized female sexuality; and the failure of heterosexual romance. She also explores the relationship between a woman's ability to write and the complex psychology of denial and disintegration occurring in such oppressive cultures. The only restorative processes she can suggest are those of self-revelation through self-talking as survival techniques. Her characters engage in cleansing anger and unconsciously motivated metaphorical or symbolic killings to rid themselves of abusive patriarchs. But, more importantly, they articulate their pain in narrative and song. For her protagonist this bloody mental process resembles a massive hemorrhage:

> When I started my pen wouldn't write I'm not saying writer's block I had plenty to say but no ink would come out so I started scribbling and scribbling so hard I tore the paper and right when I tore it ink started coming out in gobs the pen sort of quietly exploded and I couldn't help it if it looked like black blood it looked like either the pen or the paper was bleeding and I'm not saying I thought it was that it made me think of that [the rape] which made me feel like throwing up. (p. 173)

Clearly, Vaughn wishes to invert the redemptive formulas of some earlier twentieth-century feminist romances. For example, critic Jacquie Brogan has correctly pointed out a basic difference between *Many Things* and *The Color Purple* and *Their Eyes Were Watching God*. These latter two novels offer a green world in which both heroines come back to life and their respective communities also are redeemed. However, Vaughn, the white novelist, revises such versions of the feminist romance by "not establishing a redeeming patriarchy." Instead, she forestalls "altogether, any sense of communal redemption." Brogan puts it bluntly. "There is no redemptive Teacake or mellowed-out Mr. in this book," she declares, "nor any reconciliation with the general community."[23] Sylvia, in *Break the Heart of Me*, does not fall in love with a remarkably changed Buddy, nor does she leave him for a perfect relationship with Jake or rediscover her unmarred sexual self. She also fails to experience a great career success. Notably, there are no helpful religious leaders, therapists, friends, or family members for either woman. The unnamed protagonist of *Many Things* signs away her dead husband's body parts and gives up his baby for adoption in an act of revengeful exorcism. Her own and Sylvia's individual redemptions must come entirely from within, after they have rejected the guilt-promoting formulas and distortions of Christian fundamentalism. Vaughn's is a revisionist formula for grace that involves her protagonist in remembering, self-narration writing, and composing songs, but always alone. Sylvia, too, has no mentors or spiritual guides or patron saints. Her childhood friend, M'Lea, is gone, Memaw is dead, and Deedee runs away. Neither are there any women friends. Yet, as Sylvia eventually realizes, there are healing hiatuses in which "Life is sweet" (p. 349) and self-revelation is enough.

Many Things and *Break the Heart of Me*, for all their apparent simplicity, are novels of sophisticated artistry and complex structures of association and psychological progression. Both books offer self-conscious narration as self-revelation, but they do so in quite different ways. *Many Things* achieves its complex artistry through Vaughn's use of a self-conscious metafictionist woman narrator articulating some of the literary and gender problems of writing autobiography. The problems of silenced women in a fundamentalist culture are discussed as Vaughn foregrounds the special literary problems her unnamed narrator faces in constructing her *autos* (self), her *bios* (constructed self), and *graphia* (written version). This young woman has only a high school education, a minimal knowledge of literary techniques and conventions, and an idiom revealing confusion, self-abnegation, guilt, identity crises, suicidal thoughts, heartbreaking self-revelations, self-consolation, denial, platitudinous homilies, hilarious trivia, passive aggression, violent anger, blasphemy, and poignant silences. Her "style" is a vivid pastiche of run-on sentences, oblique dialogues, discontinuous forms, girlish diarist's lists, ironic masking, ellipses, blank sheets, fragmentary progressions, indecision, inferiority, and pages of asterisks reminiscent of *Tristram Shandy*.[24]

Vaughn's grasp of the linkage in gender, culture, genre, and voicing is conveyed by her unnamed protagonist's pained awareness that there are literary conventions she has not mastered or whose aesthetic will not work for her: "Authors find images like that to hide what they are saying. I don't know why they don't just come right out and say it I do but that's how its been done since time began and if you want to succeed at this game those are the rules you have to play by" (p. 120). Her mode of writing is to record events on a borrowed dictaphone and then transcribe the results; therefore, dense patterns of conventional allusion and metaphor as the "rules of the game" do not work in her spontaneous "speakerly" text. After all, everyday speech is the only language she has, and its success depends on the confidence of a sympathetic, probably female, implied reader. Hers is a specifically gender-based alienation from language. It is characterized by the special ambiguity of her simultaneous participation in and exclusion from the male literary hegemony. Although her speech becomes a rich, immediate, realistic, and droll idiom, it is one she has to invent for herself. Hence it lacks the assurance and legitimacy of an established convention. Besides, her own voice sounds strange to her as she plays the tapes back. She complains: "the tapes don't sound like me talking. That is not what happened. I am a liar on top of everything else I can't remember what I made up and what I didn't at least not where one stops and the other starts" (pp. 83–84). It is a discovery reminiscent of Roland Barthes's statement that an autobiography is really only a novel that does not speak its name. Despite all obstacles, she states her position courageously, if melodramatically:

I am going to use these notes to write an autobiography which will illustrate the strength of modern woman against tribulation and the loss of God in modern society and be a best seller and I will go on Oprah Winfrey and be rich and famous and everybody will know what he did to me and they will say that is one amazing woman do you know what he did to her. (p. 64)

However, Vaughn insists that the reader understand the harrowing power of self-revelatory narrative. To her heroine's surprise, the emerging book insists on its own writing: "I feel a certain strange power. Like I can rewrite the past and start over and certain things will never have happened and certain things will have" (p. 84). A self-conscious narrator in the contemporary metafictional sense, this young woman is also astutely aware that if anything is erased it leaves "a scar of silence which may be worse than what you erased" (p. 85). Besides, there are the demands of veracity. She contemplates leaving Malone out and then decides she might see him in the store or on the street. Similarly, she realizes she is the author of her own life story "and the life story of everyone I know and I tell a different one to every person I know" (pp. 200–201). In effect, she has learned that autobiography and fiction really are related, and that her actual life is not the same thing as a written life. "I am a character in my own book I have great power over part of me," she declares wonderingly, "and the other part of me is being constantly manipulated" (p. 201). But she knows that she, too, is a manipulator of truth: "I put it in there and it takes on a kind of truth" (p. 201). She is both amazed and pleased at this discovery.

Yet she is unprepared for the compulsion to speak that seizes her: "I have tried to stop writing this book . . . the whole book has gotten away from me it has its own life. . . . it's like going down hill on a bicycle I can't stop" (p. 213). Later she complains: "I have tried to gain some editorial control I have said start over rewrite leave certain things out let me have my dignity" (p. 213). As her emotional distress deepens, she slips into self-revelatory discourse: "I can be sound asleep and it's like somebody pulls me out of bed and makes me come in here and write and sometimes I can say I don't even want to think about that I'm not going to write about it but I still have to write about it sooner or later I never had insomnia before I started writing this book" (pp. 200–201). The climax comes when she remembers the details of the rape. She records with horror: "I remember I woke up in the middle of the night sweating and throbbing all over and I knew. But I will not write anything. I don't have to write anything I don't want to. I may never write again" (ch. 9, n.p.). But she knows she will and that when she does, it will be transgressive writing which will necessitate her hiding her tapes under the refrigerator. She also worries terribly over the newspaper account of a student whose dissertation went up in smoke when the local Kinko's burned down (p. 43).

Vaughn's real metafictional intent in this novel is to show how such a woman writer finds the appropriate narrative forms in which to couch her "unspeakable" transgressive act. Carolyn Heilbrun has stated that "If I had to emphasize the lack either of narrative or language to the formation of a new woman's life, I would unquestionably emphasize narrative."[25] Since Elizabeth has no traditional sense of history in which to couch her life, her narrative lacks any sense of public context. She can neither imagine nor write an apotheosis in the masculine sense, nor engage in carefree masculine self-exaggeration. For the same reasons, she cannot wax eloquent about the existential meaning of life, structure a symbolic journey around clearly recognizable rites of passage, or directly describe personal transformation. For instance, how should she discuss her sexual initiation? Elizabeth can offer only a list, a funny, perfunctory reporting of the exact number of sexual experiences she has had during this brief marriage. Likewise, the pivotal rape scene is never written. We must construct it ourselves from a searing, blank page masking horror, humiliation, and pain. In short, she is reluctantly deconstructing a heterosexual romance myth and writing the transgressive text that cannot be written. Hence she is not able to shape her narrative around a holistic female self whose holy, modern marriage and journey toward Christ can be structured within the masculine genre of an Augustinian or Bunyanesque spiritual journey. Vaughn's point is that the very gender problems connected with developing an *autos* have to do with genre problems inherent in constructing the *bios* and *graphia*. She also asks whether abused women can come to healing through the language of self-revelation, which may be their only hope for survival.

This cultural gender-genre difficulty is visually conveyed by Vaughn in the structural disaster Elizabeth enacts when trying to come up with chapter divisions. The jumbled numbering and nonnumbering devices that mark off the eighty episodes in the account suggest the latter has no ready-made narrative paradigm to give shape to her account. Initially there are three sets of chapters beginning Chapter One as she tries—and fails—to order the spiritual odyssey of her new marriage (ch. 1–6; ch. 1–10, 10 [16]; ch. 1–7). Apparently she had harbored some preconceived notion of an ideal heterosexual marriage; she would document its various stages of growth toward Christian harmony and fulfillment in redemptive progression—in a sort of spiritual *building*. However, each time she begins over again at Chapter One, the text signals the derailment of this living plot and she starts again with Chapter One, still obviously hoping to make the heterosexual-romance script work. She finally abandons the numbered progression as she abandons the myth. Thereafter, we see odd words for chapter titles, an occasional subtitle, and a few more random numbers as she goes back to the original numbering sequence. There then follow twenty-nine emotionally wrenching episodes titled only with an asterisk. The classic pilgrim's progress *bildung* of the Christian fundamentalist marriage with its romantic heterosexual and heavenward progression has

resoundingly failed as the organizing principle of a contemporary female *autos* or *bios*.

> ... I am not going to participate in the ridiculous fiction of naming
> this time of my life Chapter One it doesn't work. This is not the
> beginning. There is no such thing as a beginning beginning is a time
> before which is nothing and you always have something that comes
> before. . . . So I will start a new chapter but not a new beginning now
> every chapter. . . . Plus it doesn't matter because I will rewrite and
> renumber everything for the autobiography anyway. (p. 62)

Not only is she unable to appropriate masculine biographical
paradigms and aesthetics, and thereby create textual orderliness,
but she also has no famous public life or content to offer her
anticipated reading public. Although she bravely writes, "I am
woman hear me roar" (p. 167) from the Helen Reddy pop song,
she remembers with dismay the epic proportions of the burning
of Atlanta in *Gone with the Wind*; the scene represents her idea
of significant literary content. She realizes she has no comparable scene to offer, unless it be the unspeakable/unrepresentable
rape. But again she is confronted by the fact that language arts
are male and so, too, is the publishing world. The authorial irony
of juxtaposing her own rape with the burning or "raping" of
Atlanta is surely intentional. Vaughn seems to suggest that the
victim's final step toward validation of her subjectivity, truthful-
ness, and survival is her claiming a public voice. Self-narrative
or self-revelation does not finally connect one to the larger public
body where confirmation, acceptance, and companionship lie.
The route to a "Christian" or other "community" is public acknowledgment of violation and outrage. This is not an easy task.
She goes to the library to read *Writer's Market* but then reports
her frustration: "I read they don't want autobiographies unless
you're famous this is catch 22. I would be famous if they would
publish my autobiography. . . . Then, I can't afford to publish it
myself . . . I can't revolutionize the writing market but somebody
ought to" (pp. 204–5). As the manuscript nears completion, she
knows that an ordinary name like hers will not help the book to
sell. She thinks of calling herself Penelope Penn, but rejects that
as the name of a likely Harlequin romance writer. She knows
her chosen name must be long enough to sound important, and
that it should stick out and be close to the beginning of the
alphabet. All she can think of is a name that is already taken.
Renaming herself as important, as an author, is an act of masculine self-mythologizing or monumentalizing, but it is just too

hard for an inconsequential, yet-to-be-published woman. Yet ultimately only this kind of "male" assertion will heal the violation. It is Catch 22 again.

Memory and Survival

Vaughn's second novel, *Break the Heart of Me,* is no less invested in words and narrative connections as a woman's means of grace and survival. But this book does not focus on a self-conscious narrator probing the redemptive forces of fiction. Instead, it deals with the problems connected with the remembering and self-voicing of a character who has rarely confided in anyone. She is not trying to construct a public autobiography as is her counterpart. Rather she is trying to find the private language with which to access, organize, and heal her own painful and partially lost memories. She is not speaking to a potential reading public, and she has no desire to tell her story on the Oprah Winfrey show. Instead, Sylvia is trying to create a mature and integrated listening adult-self who can, like the self-conscious autobiographer of the previous novel, learn to connect and interpret all the voices of her own child-self and her alter ego, Amazing Grace. However, it is no accident that she is a would-be song writer and performer. Vaughn is suggesting perhaps that at heart all who try to uncover all the fragments of their own story are novelists, biographers, and song writers. Sylvia's self-appointed task is autobiography. But hers is a coherent, internal, self-narrative of remembering rather than a formal, public autobiography that has physical dimensions in print. This more complete consciousness must now weave all the forgotten or blocked narratives into one artistic or coherent whole, or it likely will collapse forever. In short, Sylvia must compose this new Whitmanesque song of the adult-self out of the traumatized child whose fragmented memories will destroy her if not fashioned into a consistent narrative.

It is hardly insignificant then that the title of the book comes from a Langston Hughes poem "Break the Heart of Me," which mourns the sexual mutilation and lynching of black men in the heart of Christian Dixie. Both Sylvia and the speaker of the Hughes poem express their pained reactions to the cultural violations of the individual by a violent Southern patriarchy. Sylvia is that white female victim (child and woman) whose greatest fear is sexual violation and death through the same patriarchal institution that has oppressed African Americans. Hence, Vaughn lays down the dark and powerful story of sexually violated Southern women (white and black) beside the dark and shameful story of sexually violated black men and women.

The structure of Sylvia's narrative of self-talking is even more artistically complex and mature than Elizabeth's in *Many Things*. The shambles of organization Elizabeth experiences because she wants her narrative to take a shape it ultimately cannot is missing here. Vaughn brilliantly fashions Sylvia's narrative into a mathematical chronology of a proceeding present and a receding past-come-to-consciousness. Considerable cumulative energy results from this near-classic modernist text with its suspenseful, associational swings. Her method enables Vaughn to juxtapose the theological, apocalyptic, and violent with those forces of self-hatred and sexual abuse that have seared the collective female psyche. Strategically, even comically, interwoven through this dark, death-dealing tale are numerous fundamentalist platitudes and references to death and heaven. These provide a referential catalog of abandonment, alienation, rotting corpses, cancer, blood, guilt, eating disorders, graveyards, and The Rapture—as well as of suicide, murder, sexual abuse, nightmares, sex-that-feels-like death, near-compulsive house-and-body-cleaning rituals, depression, and sexual violation. This deathly pattern emerges in the seventeen chapters from the death of Memaw to the planting of the spring garden. Vaughn's aesthetic and thematic achievement would do credit to a much more mature artist.

Sylvia's first step toward self-reclamation is typical Vaughn black humor. Distracted by Bo's disturbing phone call over his impulsive kiss, Sylvia, who is making milkshakes for herself and her grandfather, mistakes the Roachpruf-powder canister for the Slimfast one and feeds the dying man a fatal cocktail. It is a fitting feminist revenge: a rat's death for the sexual molester. Sylvia's next steps involve communicating the story of her abandonment and abuse to her hapless father, mentally excoriating Deedee for her selfishness, eliminating Jake, and insisting that Buddy help her remake her life. Only then can springtime planting, new songs harmonizing in her head, and a temporary sexual peace in her marriage signal the beginning process of forgiveness. Vaughn thereby redefines revelation, grace, and prayer through the revelatory powers of memory and narrative. Sylvia has abandoned the God of the Apocalypse, Christian fundamentalist formulas, and affiliation with organized religion.

But, miraculously, she still believes in a God, in love, and in the possibilities of her marriage. She is not crippled, blaming, embittered, unbelieving, or emotionally closed-off. Her residual anger is healthy and acceptable. For a time she hates but then forgives Mull and Deedee. She even confronts the fact that she loves but is not "in love" with Buddy. Yet she refuses to forgive her grandfather. He is now accountable to her for the "rot" he has brought to her childhood and into her grandmother's life. In the end, like Miss Celie in *The Color Purple*, she is engaged in quiet contemplation of nature. Like so many scarred heroines of contemporary American literature, she is consciously or unconsciously seeking an uncontaminated space outside an abusive patriarchal culture. For that culture has imposed on her four violent deaths, a lunatic, destructive religion, sexual abuse, repeated abandonments, and suicidal depression:

> I haven't prayed in a long time. I don't know if I believe in God anymore. I think about my grandmother planting flowers up the front walk. I think about how Memaw said God sees our lives—past, present, and future, beginning, middle, and end all at the same time. God exists outside of time where nothing begins, nothing ends, nothing happens, nothing is forgotten, everything just exists together like harmony. I hear the choir from Pell City Presbyterian Church singing it was beautiful. As it was in the beginning, is now and ever shall be, world without end, amen, amen. (p. 292)

Finally through the winter of her profound discontent, she plants spring flowers in her yard on a Sunday morning. "I feel the sun touch my back," she states. "I feel my soul unfolding. I say thank you to God. . . . I feel shy around God. I start getting a new song" (p. 292). But despite the significant personal peace and grace she is beginning to discover, she knows that she will spend the rest of her life reforgiving these people. She also will be imagining old Gilligan Island reruns and pretending that "they've all driven each other insane" (p. 294). The theme of memory then proves the key to revelation and a transformed future. It connects all the episodes and self-revelations in the novel. In *Break the Heart of Me*, more than in *Many Things*, Vaughn seems to be in agreement with Miguel de Unamuno: "We live in memory and by memory and our spiritual life is at bottom simply the effort of our memory to persist, to transform itself into hope . . . ."[26] After the picnic, the prayers, and the other rituals of forgiveness in the city graveyard, she lies in bed and tries to get Amazing Grace to sing to her. She then puts her hands

low on her stomach "and feels things there" (p. 294). It is both
a literal and spiritual beginning of new life.

In *Many Things* Vaughn employs a similar formula. Here also
are all the elements of black humor, tragicomedy, and feminist
revenge. When Malone accidentally dies of a drug overdose,
Elizabeth abandons Christian fundamentalist formulas and
allows a searing anger to guide her actions. In a posthumous
dismembering of his body, she donates his organs, eyes, and
skin, and gives up his baby for adoption. Erasure of Malone provides the turning point in Elizabeth's self-reclamation. Broken-
hearted, terrified, and driven alternately by remorse and outrage,
she goes back to her original plan to publish a best-selling autobiography. She is last seen putting it in the mail to the publisher,
praying that God will let him like it, and wishing the Protestant
community had a patron saint of manuscripts as the Catholics
surely do. Then she is off to buy a new notebook in which to
write the next stage of her life. She promises the reader that in
the new notebook she will give an account of whether or not the
baby grows up and tries to contact her.

Conclusion

Both the unnamed "autobiographer" (here referred to as Elizabeth) and Sylvia the "rememberer" have become autobiographers
and storytellers despite formidable cultural prohibitions. Like
all female tribal initiates, they have had to redraw the lines between self and nonself, purity and contamination, religion and
oppression, marriage and abuse, a girl's world and a woman's
world. In that marginal threshold or liminal space of self-
creation, such female initiates experience violent rites of passage
(rapes in more senses than one); in the process, they undergo
through violence the unceremonial transition from naïveté to
self-knowledge. But still no mentors appear. No one arrives to
tell the autobiographer that there is no patron saint of manuscripts in anybody's religion, or that few editors are subject to
divine influence. No one tells Sylvia that God will heal her by
sending Amazing Grace or a guardian angel. Neither female narrative takes the reader past the moment of self-revelation to support a bid for freedom beyond the assigned female script. Brogan
offers a blunt prediction for Vaughn's unnamed protagonist: "She

is utterly alone, in a contemporary culture which will in all probability continue to erase and abuse her."[27]

Notes

1. Carolyn G. Heilbrun, *Writing a Woman's Life* (New York: Ballantine, 1988), p. 47.

2. Claudine Herrman in Jane Miller, "Another Story" in *Women Writing About Men* (London: Virago Books, 1986), p. 163.

3. Elizabeth Dewberry Vaughn, *Many Things Have Happened Since He Died* (New York: Vintage-Random House, 1992). All quotations are from this paperback edition.

4. Pat Conroy, front cover blurb, Vintage paperback edition of *Many Things Have Happened Since He Died* (New York: Vintage-Random House, 1992).

5. Joyce Sweeney, "Highlights' Heroine Is Fool in All of Us," review of *Many Things Have Happened Since He Died*, *The Atlanta Journal/The Atlanta Constitution*, 18 March 1990, p. N8.

6. William W. Starr, "Heroine's Catharsis Tempered with Naïveté," review of *Many Things Have Happened Since He Died*, *The State*, 22 April 1990, p. 5–F.

7. Sweeney. "Highlights' Heroine Is Fool in All of Us," p. N8.

8. Madison Smart Bell, "Meanderings of a Twisted Mind: The Troubling Tale of a Woman in Fanaticism's Grip," review of *Many Things Have Happened Since He Died*, Book World Supplement, *The Washington Post*, 14 March 1990.

9. Katherine Dieckmann, "Paper Chase," review of *Many Things Have Happened Since He Died*, *Village Voice Literary Supplement*, April 1992, p. 22.

10. Dinty W. Moore, "*Many Things Have Happened Since He Died* and Here Are the Highlights." Louisiana State University. Review of *Many Things Have Happened Since He Died*. Spring/Summer 1990.

11. John Carney, "*Many Things* . . . Explores Christian Motives, Duty, Rules," review of *Many Things Have Happened Since He Died*, *The Tennessee Times Gazette*, 30 March 1990.

12. Marian Carache, "Novel Balances Humor and Horror." Review of *Many Things Have Happened Since He Died*. *Columbus Ledger-Enquirer*, 6 May 1990, p. 7.

13. Jacquie Vaught Brogan, "The Hurston/Walker/Vaughn Connection: Feminist Strategies in American Fiction." Unpublished paper. American Literature Association Convention, Cabo San Lucas, Mexico, November 1991, p. 6.

14. An early version of this paper was read at the Popular Culture Session of the MLA. It drew an enthusiastic response, and several members of the audience demanded to know who this new author was. Unable to offer particulars, I asked for responses from the audience. There was quite a stir when Nan Talese, esteemed fiction editor at Bantam-Doubleday, stood up and announced that she had edited the book and knew the author. After a moment or two of discussion, she grinned and said, "Let me introduce the author. Betsy Vaughn is here beside me." This was Vaughn's major introduction to the academic world beyond her own campus.

15. Elizabeth Dewberry Vaughn, "Elizabeth Dewberry Vaughn Author Bio." Unpublished document, author files, Doubleday Publishing House.

16. Andrea Dworkin, *Right Wing Women: The Politics of Domesticated Females* (London: The Women's Press, 1981), pp. 20–21.

17. Elizabeth Dewberry Vaughn, *Break the Heart of Me* (New York: Vintage-Random House, 1994). All quotations are from this paperback edition.

18. William Walsh, personal interview with Elizabeth Dewberry Vaughn. "In the Beginning Was the Word." In possession of Ms. Vaughn. 15 February 1994.

19. Hélène Cixous, "Castration and Decapitation." *Signs* (1981): 54.

20. Gloria L. Cronin, personal interview with Elizabeth Dewberry Vaughn. Tape One, Side A. 12 March 1993. Provo, Utah.

21. Elizabeth Dewberry Vaughn, unpublished author bio, Doubleday submission files.

22. Cronin, personal interview with Elizabeth Dewberry Vaughn. 12 March 1993.

23. Brogan, "The Hurston/Walker/Vaughn Connection," p. 6.

24. I am indebted to a variety of materials on the general subject of men and women's autobiographies. Of particular use were Judith Kegan Gardiner, "On Female Identity and Writing by Women," *Critical Inquiry* 8 (1981); Carolyn Heilbrun, *Writing a Woman's Life;* Estelle Jelinek, "Women's Autobiography and the Male Tradition," *Women's Autobiographies: Essays in Criticism* (Boston: Twayne Publishers, 1986); Susan S. Lanser, "Toward a Feminist Narratology," *Style* 20 (Fall 1986); Nancy K. Miller, "Arachnologies: The Woman, The Text, and The Critic" in *Subject to Change* (New York: Columbia University Press, 1988), pp. 77–101.

25. Heilbrun, *Writing a Woman's Life,* p. 43.

26. Miguel de Unamuno, *Tragic Sense of Life.* trans. J. E. Crawford Flitch (New York: Dover, 1954), p. 21.

27. Brogan, "The Hurston/Walker/Vaughn Connection," p. 15.

Dreams and Nightmares: "High-Tech Paranoia" and the Jamesonian Sublime— An Approach to Thomas Pynchon's Postmodernism

ELAINE SAFER

THOMAS Pynchon's fiction reveals the temper of our postmodern period. It represents what architect Charles Jencks has described as "the tension of our time." Jencks refers to the fact that "we have contradictory ideas and tastes which are equally valid and not resolvable [and which] reflect actual social and cultural tensions—even metaphysical realities."[1] America has many postmodern novelists. These include John Barth, John Hawkes, Robert Coover, Kurt Vonnegut, Donald Barthelme, Joseph Heller, William Burroughs, Don DeLillo, William Gass, and Thomas Pynchon. But Pynchon is considered by many critics to be the most influential of the group and his *Gravity's Rainbow* (1973) the truly monumental postmodern text.

Looking through what David Cowart terms a "postmodern lens,"[2] Pynchon exploits for comic-absurd purposes the history, resources, and aspirations of the twentieth-century world. He repeatedly finds fresh means of exhausting and replenishing our nation's history and culture.[3] He evokes myths: he grants some and deconstructs others. He uses and distorts history through parodic intertextuality. He develops premises and rejects them. He frustrates our desire for order by ironically disassembling the text and its characters. He presents situations that appear fantastic or bizarre and makes us aware that we share the comical dilemma of the characters. In sum, Pynchon disappoints our quest for correspondences by collapsing customary patterns. He creates a multifaceted "hybrid" fiction that shows what Linda Hutcheon describes as the "mixed, plural, and contradictory nature of the postmodern enterprise."[4] He also points to the work's artifice. In *Gravity's Rainbow*, for example, the narrator speaks directly to the reader who expects clarification of relationships: "You will want cause and effect. All right."[5]

In this essay, Thomas Pynchon's postmodernism will be discussed in terms of Fredric Jameson's sociopolitical critique of American society. It is a critique that focuses on "high-tech paranoia" and its relation to the sublime,[6] and it provides a particularly apt framework for an analysis of Pynchon's fiction.

The Postmodern Context

The postmodern facets of Pynchon's fiction have many links to postmodern architecture and art, psychology and sociology. Architect Robert Venturi, for example, explains that postmodern "architecture, which includes varying levels of meaning, breeds ambiguity and tension." In his *Complexity and Contradiction in Architecture*, Venturi draws heavily upon the literary criticism of Cleanth Brooks and William Empson to show that ambiguity and tension collect "precisely at the points of *greatest* poetic effectiveness." Venturi argues that "these ideas apply equally well to architecture."[7] Philip Johnson's prominent AT&T Building (completed in 1982) in midtown Manhattan provides an example. It has a Chippendale peak that looks like a highboy chest of drawers and suggests a mingling of architecture and furniture. Critic Paul Gapp, writing in 1978 in the *Chicago Tribune*, calls attention to this juxtaposition of different styles by titling his discussion of the building plan "Chippendale Architecture— Near Kitsch or Top Drawer?"[8] The eighteenth-century-style Chippendale pedimental crown also affords a striking juxtaposition of the historic and the modern: it is almost comically attached to a skyscraper composed of a modern masonry base and a steel skeleton shaft of pink granite veneer.

Still another example of postmodern architecture is Michael Graves's Portland Building (1982). Its square-box form of the modern International Style merges with decorative facades from classical architecture. Another outstanding combination of disparate styles is evident in the design that in November 1992 won the competition for Manhattan's Staten Island Ferry Terminal. Critic Herbert Muschamp declared that Robert Venturi and Denise Scott Brown aimed "to deflect nostalgia with humor" by superimposing a huge contemporary neon-illuminated clock on a building with a facade of Roman arches.[9] Similarly surprising postmodernist combinations and multiple points of view again were emphasized in the Sainsbury Wing of London's National Gallery (1991). Here Robert Venturi lined up elements of modernist realism and classical ornament: the rectangular wing with its large areas of glass and flat symmetrical surfaces connects to five facades whose moldings mesh with the nineteenth-century National Gallery and the buildings near it. The result is a building that connects "with its setting" but remains "a fragment." It becomes a structure that gives a "quintessential Post-Modern feeling of being at home" in both the twentieth and earlier centuries.[10] The total effect is a both/and condition rather than an either/or one.[11]

A postmodernist perspective emphasizes a departure from traditional theories. A famous example is architect Venturi's response to Mies van der Rohe's oft-quoted modernist tenet that "less is more." For Venturi, "less is a bore." He argues that "Blatant simplification means bland architecture."[12] This statement helped launch the postmodern movement in architecture as one in opposition to the "machine aesthetic" of the International Style, like that of Mies van der Rohe's Seagram Building in New York. This skyscraper is characterized by a plane of I-beams, right-angled geometric forms of glass-and-steel, and a clean, straightforward boxlike style that shows a concern with working out certain formal problems.[13] Venturi, in promoting postmodern architecture, explains: "I like elements which are hybrid rather than 'pure,' compromising rather than 'clean,' distorted rather than 'straightforward,' ambiguous rather than 'articulated' . . . inconsistent and equivocal rather than direct and clear. . . . I am for richness of meaning rather than clarity of meaning."[14]

Pop artist Andy Warhol conveys a similar sense of multiple orientations. He does so primarily by linking photography and pictorial art and by merging the grave and the trivial, the high fashion and the horrifying. He also dramatizes the postmodern consumer-oriented society's focus on multiple advertising images through his own representations of the Coca Cola bottle and Campbell's soup can.

A departure from traditional theory is evident also in postmodern psychology. Psychologist Steinar Kvale deviates from Freudian tenets by focusing on the language and cultural context of human behavior rather than on the unconscious and the past. Kvale emphasizes the change from focusing on the individual psyche to "studying the family as a linguistic system." Pathology is now believed to reside "in the structures of language" rather than in the psyche. Because therapists "work with language and

[are] masters of conversation," argues Kvale, the term "*psycho-therapist*" is inaccurate. Postmodern therapists, he asserts, do not try to heal the psyche, but to "heal with words."[15] This psychological focus on linguistic structure is strikingly similar to the postmodernist literary tenets of metafiction. William Gass, a major proponent of metafiction, explains that the language of fiction is not referential. It does not hold up the mirror to nature, but instead presents "the world within the word." Gass encourages the reader to respond to sound, rhythm, pace of language rather than to referential meaning, because this is the way to appreciate the creative process of fiction.[16] Here the emphasis, like that in the postmodern view of psychology, is on the power and complexity of language rather than on the way language connects to the world or the psyche.

Just as corresponding postmodern trends are observed in literature and in other cultural disciplines, so, too, such theoreticians as Michel Foucault, Jacques Derrida, Jean-François Lyotard, Jacques Lacan, and Fredric Jameson are studied in common by scholars in their respective fields.[17] Jameson's 1984 article, "Postmodernism, or the Cultural Logic of Late Capitalism,"[18] for example, provides an insightful view of postmodernism from a sociopolitical perspective. As such, it is a most helpful touchstone for the appreciation of Thomas Pynchon's critique of society; it will, therefore, be used here as a guide for discussion.

Jameson discusses the relationship between an "electronic and nuclear-powered" technology and a fast-moving, fragmented consumer society. He examines an information age that produces "machines of reproduction rather than of production" (p. 37). It is a process of "commodification" represented, he points out, in Andy Warhol's billboard images of the Campbell's soup can. It is also a process that signals the loss of the individual subject as it fragments into a proliferation of images and codes (pp. 16–17). Jameson points out that this age is one of information, an age in which people benefit from high-tech communication but are vulnerable to the abuse of sensitive personal information readily available to those in power. He contends that behind complex electronic technology is a "network of power and control even more difficult for our minds and imaginations to grasp" (p. 38). All this technology holds a "mesmerizing and fascinating" interest for us. Indeed, "the most energetic postmodernist texts" tap into this phenomenon and thereby afford us a "glimpse into a postmodern or technological sublime" (p. 37).[19]

The Jamesonian sublime is reflected in the "high-tech para-

noia" literature of science fiction. There "the circuits and networks of some putative global computer hookup are narratively
mobilized by labyrinthine conspiracies of . . . competing information agencies in a complexity often beyond the capacity of
the normal reading mind" (p. 38). When Pynchon's characters
whisper to one another "Watch the paranoia, please" (*Vineland*,
p. 160), we suspect that we are in the world Jameson describes.
It is a world where we are unable to map the "decentered com-
municational network in which we find ourselves caught as individual subjects" (p. 44).[20]

The Absurd and Entropy

The absurd, entropy, and "high-tech paranoia" are prevalent
themes in Thomas Pynchon's encyclopedic postmodern works.
In his fiction, characters search vainly for some form of order
(no matter how strange) as a means of self-preservation. What
they encounter is the absurd. Pynchon's novels thus exhibit what
Camus has defined as the absurd predicament: our perpetual
attempt to use reason to find significance in an illogical world.[21]
Pynchon portrays that postmodern world in which Joseph Heller's title *Catch-22* has been added to our dictionaries and in
which the scientific term *entropy* and the Second Law of Thermodynamics have become commonplace in literary discussions.
One obvious example is offered by Pynchon talking about his
early stories in the Introduction to *Slow Learner* (1984). There
he mentions his youthful enthusiasm for Norbert Wiener's discussion of the thermodynamic theory. Wiener argues that in a
closed system molecules move toward randomness—that is, toward loss of order and structure. This condition causes a sense
of "thermodynamical gloom."

Pynchon discusses this gloom and the "cosmic moral twist
[that entropy] continues to enjoy in current usage."[22] These concepts are reflected in Pynchon's well-known 1960 story "Entropy"[23] wherein all motion is reduced to zero. Callisto here uses
the third-person in a manner foreshadowing Stencil's narration
in V. He explains the ramifications of the Second Law of Thermodynamics. "As a young man at Princeton," he states, "Callisto
had learned a mnemonic device for remembering the Laws of
Thermodynamics: you can't win, things are going to get worse
. . . who says they're going to get better" ("Entropy," p. 72). In
later years, Callisto ruminates over entropy as a metaphor for

phenomena in his everyday life: "In American 'consumerism' [he] discovered a similar tendency from the least to the most probable, from differentiation to sameness, from ordered individuality to a kind of chaos" ("Entropy," p. 74). Callisto is afraid that all life will be like an endless party at Meatball Mulligan's apartment downstairs—where there is a breakdown of communication and a buildup of noise—or like the weather outside, which remains static, indicating that equilibrium has been reached.

The story's concluding paragraph dramatizes the inevitable progression of entropic decline. Callisto's girlfriend, Aubade, smashes the window of the hermetically sealed apartment, and disorder takes over:

> Suddenly then, as if seeing the single and unavoidable conclusion to all this she moved swiftly to the window before Callisto could speak; tore away the drapes and smashed out the glass with two exquisite hands which came away bleeding and glistening with splinters; and turned to face the man on the bed and wait with him until the moment of equilibrium was reached, when 37 degrees Fahrenheit should prevail both outside and inside, and forever, and the hovering, curious dominant of their separate lives should resolve into a tonic of darkness and the final absence of all motion. ("Entropy," pp. 85–86)

Sonorous rhythms combine with the richly assonantal effect of "i" sounds to move the passage relentlessly toward "the final absence of all motion."[24] The sound and horrific sense are linked (by the impact of the smashed glass on Aubade's "two exquisite hands") and evoke both despair and horror in the reader. This passage and the total story suggest the mesmerizing and fascinating effects of entropic decline and high-tech power to be found in Pynchon's fiction.

Pynchon's Novels

Thomas Pynchon's fiction has been the subject of over thirty-one books and more than four hundred articles. Early critics often commented on Pynchon's ability to catch and hold readers with the encyclopedic details of his fiction; these had been readers in quest of customary literary patterns depicting a metaphysical order. Having established this point, the critics then pursued more diverse organizing principles by which to comprehend and explain Pynchon's fiction.

Joseph Slade set the stage for discussions of entropy. Mark Richard Siegel did so for patterns of paranoia. David Cowart catalogued the references to painting, film, music, and literature. John Stark gleaned the texts for information from the science of cybernetics, information theory, and mathematics, as well as from psychology, history, religion, and film. Critics like Thomas Schaub and Molly Hite called attention to the fiction's "uncertainties" and to the need to focus on the stylistic medium itself— that is, on the literary nature of the text. Later critics like Thomas Moore, Kathryn Hume, and Dwight Eddins have returned to what Edward Mendelson has termed the encyclopedic quality of Pynchon's fiction. Deborah Madsen approaches Pynchon's fiction from the vantage point of postmodern allegory. For her, the "characteristics most frequently isolated by Pynchon criticism— ambiguity, uncertainty, semantic instability, the absence of a normative ethical base—define themselves as consequences of the way Pynchon's books function as allegory: specifically as postmodernist allegory."[25]

But the postmodern themes in Pynchon's fiction emphasized in the following discussion are linked, as already stated, to Fredric Jameson's "high-tech paranoia" and its relationship to the absurd and to entropy. According to Albert Camus, "to understand is, above all, to unify."[26] The desire for understanding and unity in a disordered universe leads to the absurd quests of Pynchon's central characters: Stencil (V.), Oedipa Maas (The Crying of Lot 49), Slothrop (Gravity's Rainbow), and Zoyd Wheeler (Vineland). Pynchon's shaping concept is that a "disintegrating world that has lost its unifying principle, its meaning, and its purpose" is an absurd one.[27] It is a world in which entropy prevails, for high entropy, disorder, and unpredictability are interrelated. "High-tech paranoia" then proves an understandable response of those individuals embarked on a futile quest in a complex world.

Herbert Stencil searches for signs of V. Even his personal identity is defined in relation to her: "He Who Looks For V" (V., p. 210). In talks with the dentist, Eigenvalue, and with the Whole Sick Crew, Stencil tries to find out how details fit into the "grand Gothic pile of inferences he was hard at work creating" (V., p. 209). The termination of the pursuit could result in a return to nothingness, a state of equilibrium or entropy, a life of "half-consciousness" (V., p. 44). He is ambivalent as to "which he was most afraid of, V. or [a life of] sleep" (*V.*, p. 324). As absurd hero, Stencil seems always on the verge of a spiritual experience. His adventures are so described as to develop a negative mirror-image of the spiritual model. At the beginning of his quest, he leafs through his father's Florentine journal "when the sentences on V. suddenly acquired a light of their own" (*V.*, p. 44). Stencil appears to undergo an epiphany like that experienced by Christian mystics. The epiphany is accompanied by the trappings of a spiritual "awakening" that involves an enigmatic light, a "shining vision of the transcendent spiritual world."[28] Yet this epiphany suggests a negation of any kind of spiritual revelation. The narrator sardonically explains: "Work, the chase—for it was V. he hunted—far from being a means to glorify God and one's own godliness (*as the Puritans believe*) was for Stencil grim, joyless; a conscious acceptance of the unpleasant for no other reason than that V. was there to track down" (*V.*, p. 44; italics added).

The Puritans had looked to the Bible for patterns on which to model their lives. Stencil, however, gets his patterns from the Parisian or Florentine journals written by his secret-agent father. Seeking transcendent signs, Stencil focuses on these peculiar spiritual notions as models for action. Instead, he gets involved in the profane machinations of governmental spy systems. He reads, for instance, that his father, Sidney, had interviewed someone who worked in the main sewer lines in France and that the person recalled having seen a woman "who might have been V." This provides Herbert Stencil reason enough to investigate the activities of the Alligator Patrol in Manhattan. Herbert thinks: "Having been lucky with sewers once . . . [there was] nothing wrong with trying again" (*V.*, p. 120). When someone in the Alligator Patrol misses his target and hits Stencil in the left buttock, his paranoid response appears comic: "How did they get on to you?" (*V.*, p. 119).

The paranoia continues as he tells this story to Eigenvalue while seated in the dentist/psychiatrist's consultation chair. His friend observes: "In a world such as you inhabit, Mr. Stencil, any cluster of phenomena can be a conspiracy" (*V.*, p. 140). Stencil is devoted to an "Ultimate Plot Which Has No Name" (*V.*, p. 210). He continually searches for V., who reappears under different identities throughout the novel; she is recognizable by her obsession with incorporating bits of inert matter into her body: namely her glass eye with the iris in the shape of a clock, a star sapphire in her navel, and her artificial feet (*V.*, pp. 321–22). At one point, Stencil observes that V. is part of a phenomenon "for which the . . . century had *as yet* no name" (*V.*, p. 386; italics added). Obsessed by his quest for V., Stencil refuses to end the chase even when others are certain of V.'s demise. The last one hears about Stencil is that he is in Malta aiming to track down the glass eye worn by the hypnotist, Mme. Viola. "It will do for the frayed end of another clue" (*V.*, p. 425), he tells Fausto, as he leaves for Stockholm.

The description of V.'s fascination for the inanimate—and Stencil's quest for her—suggests a twentieth-century nightmare: the entropic experience of annihilation. The historical details in the novel relate to many worldwide and national problems: the corporate alliances that have supported and manipulated wars, the rise of a mechanical energy that has resulted in rocket programs, the "nuclear weapons [that] multiply out of control," and the "racial sickness" in America and Europe that causes riots and violence.[29] In such a twentieth-century world, as Jameson has argued, "feelings . . . are now free-floating and impersonal and tend to be dominated by a peculiar kind of euphoria" (Jameson, p. 16). In such a society, there is a "derealization" of phenomena, a flattening that causes the earth to lose its depth and "to become a glossy skin, a stereoscopic illusion, a rush of filmic images without density." Jameson asks: "But is this now a terrifying or an exhilarating experience?" (Jameson, p. 34). We realize that it is both/and, and we glimpse the complexity of the postmodern sublime.

In *The Crying of Lot 49*, the quest of Oedipa Maas is, as it was for Stencil, a means of defining the self. For her, however, it is also a means of separating herself from a routine existence of Tupperware parties and TV watching. Her life had become a "fat deckful of days which seemed . . . more or less identical, or all pointing the same way subtly like a conjurer's deck, any odd one readily clear to a trained eye" (*Lot*, p. 2). Oedipa's search for the meaning of the mysterious Tristero is set into motion by the wealthy Pierce Inverarity, her former lover, who has made her executrix of his estate. The postmodern quest—linked to a "religious instant" (*Lot*, p. 13) and the unraveling of mystery—tempts Oedipa, and the reader as well. She drives to San Narciso to examine Pierce's books and records, and to meet with the lawyer Metzger. She looks downhill at the city and has a mystical experience, or at least a sense of "concealed meaning." Her reaction here is similar, the narrator says, to her reaction to high-tech phenomena when opening a transistor radio and seeing "her first printed circuit." The narrator explains:

a revelation . . . trembled just past the threshold of her understanding . . . she *and the Chevy* seemed parked at the centre of an odd, religious instant. As if, on some other frequency, or out of the eye of some whirlwind rotating too slow for her heated skin even to feel the centrifugal coolness of, words were being spoken. She suspected that much. (*Lot*, p. 13; italics added)

Later, she is in her motel room with the lawyer Metzger. There she watches a commercial for Fangoso Lagoons, a housing development that had interested Inverarity:

It was to be laced by canals with private landings for power boats, a floating social hall in the middle of an artificial lake, at the bottom of which lay restored galleons, imported from the Bahamas; Atlantean fragments of columns and friezes from the Canaries; real human skeletons from Italy; giant clamshells from Indonesia—all for the entertainment of Scuba enthusiasts. A map of the place flashed onto the screen, Oedipa drew a sharp breath, Metzger on the chance it might be for him looked over. But she'd only been reminded of her look downhill this noontime. Some immediacy was there again, some promise of hierophany: printed circuit, gently curving streets, private access to the water, Book of the Dead. (*Lot*, p. 18)

Both passages imply that Oedipa is having a spiritual experience. She has an uncanny feeling of apprehending what Evelyn Underhill terms "another order of reality."[30] Each passage seems to embody a strange, comic incongruity. On the one hand, Pynchon describes spiritual intimations of "a hieroglyphic sense of concealed meaning," the trembling presence of a "revelation," a sensation of being "on some other frequency," a suggestion of the awe of being in the "eye of some whirlwind" (*Lot*, p. 13). On the other hand, all implications seem deflated by the high-tech image of the material: the transistor radio and its printed circuit. Adding to the incongruity is the metallic image of the inanimate Chevy as being part of the religious center. What is particularly perplexing here, however, is that the concept of incongruity itself is questionable.

In our technologically driven society a mystical reaction to machines may not be incongruous with a religious experience in nature. In fact, as Jameson argues, the sense of astonishment at intimations of technological force often tends to supplant the traditional sense of the sublime. Similarly, the mysterious "promise of hierophany" in the second passage is offset somewhat by the crude setting: a room in a garish motel sporting a sign with a sexy nymph towering thirty feet into the air. The pervading crudity is intensified by the television commercial for the expensive new housing development (with its artificial lake and its leveling of the inanimate and animate—clamshells and "real human skeletons"). Also contributing to the general mood are the other commercials that flash on during the rerun of the movie *Cashiered*, and the banal comments of Metzger, who eventually engages Oedipa in a game of Strip Botticelli. "Go ahead," he tells her, ". . . ask questions. But for each answer, you'll have to take something off" (*Lot*, p. 22). However, this scene also eventually develops a feeling for the technically strange and uncanny, giving the reader a sense of Jameson's "high-tech sublime." The hair-spray can that Oedipa accidentally knocks over hits the floor, starts atomizing, and seems to charge ahead on its own pressured motion: "The can, hissing malignantly, bounced off the toilet and whizzed by Metzger's right ear . . . as [it] . . . continued its high-speed caroming. . . . The can knew where it was going, she sensed, or something fast enough, God or digital machine, might have computed in advance the complex web of its travel." But then, luckily, "the can did give up in midflight and fall to the floor, about a foot from Oedipa's nose" (*Lot*, pp. 22–23).[31]

This scene illustrates the way Pynchon moves the reader back and forth between what would be dichotomized traditionally as the sacred and the profane, but which in Pynchon's world partakes of both. Oedipa and the reader follow clues as they look for patterns in the maze of the Tristero. "Meaning what?" Oedipa often asks when confronted with puzzles. At the conclusion of *Lot 49*, there is no clarification as to whether Oedipa Maas is indeed Pierce Inverarity's heiress. The mystery of the Tristero still remains: "Another mode of meaning behind the obvious, or none. . . . For there either was some Tristero beyond the appearance of the legacy America, or there was just America" (*Lot*, p. 137).[32] At this point, the reader begins to appreciate that this situation is bigger than one of either/or. We are involved in the complexity and contradiction of a world of "both/and multiplicity."[33] It is a highly technological world in which there are many signifiers and an unclear signified. It is a world, the narrator explains, in which Oedipa would be "waiting for a symmetry of choices to break down, to go skew. She had heard all about excluded middles; they were bad shit, to be avoided" (*Lot*, p. 136).[34] What Inverarity had told her was "Keep it bouncing . . . that's all the secret, keep it bouncing" (*Lot*, p. 134). And Oedipa, like

Stencil in *V.,* continues her postmodern quest. It is a quest that mesmerizes the reader. For the latter senses that behind the computers and electronic circuits may be a multitude of decentered labyrinthine conspiracies whose complexity is too awesome to fathom. Fascinated by it all, Oedipa renews her pursuit: "The auctioneer cleared his throat. Oedipa settled back to await the crying of lot 49" (*Lot,* p. 138).

In *Gravity's Rainbow,* in an absurd World War II situation, Slothrop continually quests for answers about "Them," the controlling agents. The reader, too, follows clues as a means of comprehending how Dr. Jamf's conditioning of Slothrop in infancy could result in the strange connection between his sex acts and the V-2 rocket. Slothrop searches for answers about the rocket, about Imipolex G, about the Forbidden Wing in his past. He travels through London, Nice, Zurich, Berlin, and other parts of the Zone. At the end of his epic journey he not only fails to achieve fulfillment but also disintegrates, becoming "broken down . . . and scattered." Seaman Bodine observes him before the collapse is complete: "He's looking straight at Slothrop (being one of the few who can still see Slothrop as any sort of integral creature any more. Most of the others gave up long ago trying to hold him together, even as a concept—'It's just got too remote' [that is] . . . what they usually say)" (*GR,* pp. 738, 740). The reader likely will ponder this transformation and also the following:

> "There never was a Dr. Jamf," opines world-renowned analyst Mickey Wuxtry-Wuxtry—"Jamf was only a fiction, to help him explain what he felt so terribly, so immediately in his genitals for those rockets each time exploding in the sky . . . to help him deny what he could not possibly admit: that he might be in love, in sexual love, with his, and his race's, death." (*GR,* p. 738)

In *Vineland,* published seventeen years after *Gravity's Rainbow,* Pynchon is more specific about the government networks that control and mesmerize the members of a technologically oriented society. Zoyd Wheeler searches for meaning in Northern California's Vineland in 1984. The Orwellian vision of a society controlled by electronic surveillance has been metamorphosed into a Pynchonesque image of a society whose members are willingly seduced by television. Here power-hungry government officials control a variety of communications networks including the Tube. In such a world, Zoyd quests for a meeting with the ever-changing Frenesi, his former wife who progressed from student activist at Berkeley to government informer and lover of government-agent Brock Vond. Zoyd is obsessed with connecting to Frenesi even though she has rejected him. He, like Stencil in *V.*, seems to define himself in terms of another. Words seem inadequate as Zoyd tries to tell his daughter Prairie of his need for help in the quest for Frenesi: "Keep tryin' to find out. Try to read signs, locate landmarks, anything that'll give a clue, but— well the signs are there on street corners and store windows— but I can't read them. . . . [T]here's something between it and my brain that won't let it through" (*Vineland*, p. 40).

Zoyd engages in a series of fruitless maneuvers because of Frenesi. He rushes to Honolulu—"red-eyeing in" (*Vineland*, p. 56) to see Frenesi, who quickly departs from the hotel while he, in his room, indulges in sexual fantasies about her. In turn, he continually flees from Brock Vond and his secret agents who keep informed of Zoyd's whereabouts (because Prairie is with Zoyd and Brock hopes to use Prairie to make contact with her mother, Frenesi, once again). Zoyd also attends the yearly Traverse-Becker family reunions, even though he and Frenesi are divorced. Zoyd is always "at the periphery, in motion, out on one of the roads that had taken him away from his home, and that must [he hopes] lead back" (*Vineland*, p. 374).

Zoyd's inability to escape the surveillance of Brock Vond underlines the thematic assertion that "We're in th' Info Revolution here. Anytime you use a credit card you're tellin' the Man more than you meant to. Don't matter if it's big or small, he can use it all" (*Vineland*, p. 74). We are in a world where the rise of multinational corporations exerts a network of power and control over all aspects of living. It is a world where there are "labyrinthine conspiracies of . . . competing information agencies" (Jameson, p. 38) exerting fascistic control. Ditzah, trying to glimpse this force, tells Darryl Louise Chastain: "It's the whole Reagan program, isn't it—dismantle the New Deal, reverse the effects of World War II, restore fascism at home and around the world, flee into the past, can't you feel it, all the dangerous childish stupidity—'I don't like the way it came out, I want it to be my way.'" When Ditzah attempts to ward off such fears by explaining "We're probably just being paranoid" (*Vineland*, pp. 265, 264), we appreciate the hysteria and terror of Jameson's postmodern sublime.

Vineland displays a multitude of details that give an encyclopedic view of postmodern culture. But it is a flattened view.

For the novel operates on a diminished scale, as compared with Pynchon's highly allusive *Gravity's Rainbow* (with its evocative references to our country's Puritan past and the phantasmagorical suggestion of global communication networks in operation during World War II). The same holds true when it is compared with *V.* (wherein events take place in Manhattan, Malta, and in Florence, as well as in southwest Africa, ranging from 1904 to after World War II). In *Vineland*, the setting is reduced to American popular culture of the 1980s with flashbacks to the 1950s, 1960s, and 1970s. The popular-culture references, however, are overwhelming in their diversity and complexity: New Age music, designer clothes, talk shows, Mafia figures, zombie Thanatoids, TV characters—"Bigfoot" and "Jason"—a Tubaldetox institution, shopping mall therapists, self-help groups, pizza-parlor Buddhism at the Bodhi Dharma Pizza Temple, and feminist therapy at the Ninjette Sisterhood of the Kunoichi Attentives. There are also the technological machinations of bank machines, video cameras, surveillance equipment, satellite photos, and television; all of these assist in controlling the members of society.

Pynchon depicts the hypnotizing effects of television on Frenesi, Zoyd's former wife. We laugh at her dependence on TV, whose rays, she hopes, "would act as a broom to sweep the room clear of all spirits." We experience something close to Thomas Hobbes's feeling of "sudden glory" or "eminency"[35] as we contemplate this woman's foolish addiction to reruns of shows like "CHiPs," with its two motorcycle-cops, men in uniform who cause Frenesi to be so sexually stimulated that she has "a rising of blood, a premonitory dampness." We laugh at the narrator's ironic downgrading of Frenesi's desire for men in uniform: policemen, athletes, "actors in movies of war through the ages, or maître d's in restaurants" (*Vineland*, p. 83). But we get frightened when Frenesi, as an adult, moves from being a passive television viewer to being a double agent who unemotionally and mechanically uses a camera to film the overthrow of the People's Republic of Rock and Roll. The tone becomes progressively more painful as Frenesi, caught up in the intricacies of the machine ("it was herself and the [Canon] Scoopic" [p. 209]), puts a higher value on filmmaking than on her companionship with those who used to be her friends: activists of the sixties, college students who are upset at the double whammy of the Nixon presidency and of the Reagan governorship (of California). The tone gets darker as a student screams, "They're breaking people's heads" (*Vineland*, p. 207), and the narrator reports that "what [the police] lacked in coordination" was "made up for by their eagerness at a chance to handle, however briefly, some college-age flesh" (*Vineland*, p. 206).

Frenesi films Weed Atman as he is being shot, all the while thinking of herself as "attending a movie of it all" and watching Weed as "a character in a movie" (*Vineland*, p. 237). At the death scene, "Frenesi tried to find enough cable to get one of the floods on them . . . her camera, her shot . . . shapes may have moved somewhere in the frame, black on black, like ghosts trying to return to earthly form, but Sledge was right there on them, and the sound of the shot captured by Krishna's tape. . . . Weed was on his face with his blood all on the cement" (*Vineland*, p. 246).

The scene represents the evil forces that operate clandestinely in the information age. It is an age in which signifiers are machines and in which the signified seem to reside behind secret agents like Brock Vond who establishes the PREP (Political Re-Education Program) which turns sixties dissidents like Frenesi into informants for the government. PREP encourages people "to stay children forever . . . the sort of mild herd creatures who belonged, who'd feel," according to agent Vond, "much more comfortable behind fences" (*Vineland*, p. 269). The evil forces include the "faceless predators" who board the Kahuna Airlines plane while it is in the sky and turn it into a "gig of death." The dire consequence is that the "list of passengers who arrived was not always identical to the list of those who'd departed." Something, we are told, "was happening, in between, up here" (*Vineland*, pp. 383, 61).

A sense of hidden evil power is intimated throughout the novel.[36] By means of this evil, "Repression went on, growing wider, deeper, and less visible" (*Vineland*, p. 72). This obscure power is reminiscent of the strange influence behind the technological communication networks in *V.* There this elusive force is glimpsed when Kurt Mondaugen records and analyzes atmospheric radio disturbances (*V.*, p. 213), which take on implications of another world. Weissmann breaks the code and explains that the message states: "Kurt Mondaugen. . . . the world is all that the case is" (*V.*, pp. 258–59), but the mystery remains. The sense of the uncanny suggests the same frustrating puzzle that Oedipa Maas tries to unravel in *Lot 49*. It also seems to connect to the "Mystery Stimulus" in the descent of the V-2 rocket in *Gravity's Rainbow* (*GR*, p. 84), a mystery linking Slothrop to "Them"—the controlling agents during World War II. In *Vineland*, Frenesi, dwelling on the enigma, concludes that people may be "digits in God's computer," and all our actions may lie "beneath the notice of the hacker we call God" (*Vineland*, p. 91).

Not only are there no successful heroes in Pynchon's world, but also the concept of God has been transformed. Those who run the machines seem to run the world as well. Pynchon's novels illustrate Fredric Jameson's view that much contemporary literature focuses on our technologically oriented consumer society and its reproduction processes—including the use of video machines, movie cameras, tape recorders. In the best and most "energetic" works, Jameson explains, something else emerges that is able to show the processes and also the sinister power behind them; this something causes us to "glimpse" a "technological sublime" (Jameson, p. 37). This is what Pynchon's novels portray. In the process, they create an aesthetic experience that is both sublime and postmodern.

Notes

1. Charles Jencks, *Post-Modern Triumphs in London* (London: Architectural Design, 1991), p. 53.

2. David Cowart, "Attenuated Postmodernism: Pynchon's *Vineland*," *Critique* 32 (Winter 1990): 67.

3. John Barth discusses this method in "The Literature of Exhaustion," *Atlantic Monthly*, August 1967, pp. 29–34 and in "The Literature of Replenishment," *Atlantic Monthly*, January 1980, pp. 65–71.

4. Linda Hutcheon, *A Poetics of Postmodernism* (New York: Routledge, 1988), p. 20. Jean-François Lyotard explains: "The text [the postmodern artist] writes, the works he produces are not in principle governed by preestablished rules, and they cannot be judged according to a determining judgment, by applying familiar categories to the text or to the work. Those rules and categories are what the work of art itself is looking for." (See Jean-François Lyotard, *The Postmodern Condition*, trans. Geoff Bennington and Brian Massumi [Minneapolis: University of Minnesota Press, 1988], p. 81.) Postmodernism is an enterprise where fragmentation is emphasized and order systems are questioned. Even the notion of originality is questioned. Michel Foucault questions "the point of creation, the unity of a work, of a period, of a theme . . . the mark of originality." (See Michel Foucault, *The Archaeology of Knowledge*, trans. A. M. Sheridan Smith [New York: Random House, 1972], p. 230.) Ihab Hassan, after acknowledging that "no clear consensus about [postmodernism's] meaning exists among scholars," points out that "postmodernism veers toward open, playful, optative, provisional . . . disjunctive, or indeterminate forms, a discourse of ironies and fragments." (See Ihab Hassan, "Toward a Concept of Postmodernism," in *A Postmodern Reader*, ed. Joseph Natoli and Linda Hutcheon [New York: State University of New York Press, 1993], pp. 276, 283.) Todd Gitlin observes: "The 1960s exploded our belief in progress, which underlay the classical faith in linear order and moral clarity. Old verities crumbled, but new ones have not settled in. Self-regarding irony and blankness are a way of

staving off anxieties, rages, terrors and hungers that have been kicked up but cannot find resolution." (See Todd Gitlin, "Hip-Deep in Post-modernism," *New York Times Book Review*, 6 November 1988, p. 6.)

5. Thomas Pynchon, *Gravity's Rainbow* (New York: Viking, 1973), p. 663. Pynchon, of course, then disappoints reader expectation. George Levine and David Leverenz comment on Thomas Pynchon's success in frustrating the reader who looks for correspondences: "The temptation, clearly, has been irresistible to take his allusions, his dropped clues, his metaphors, and run, right into the ordering patterns that welcome us." (See Introduction to *Mindful Pleasures: Essays on Thomas Pynchon*, ed. George Levine and David Leverenz [Boston: Little, Brown, 1976], pp. 254–55). Page references from the following editions of Pynchon's novels will be placed parenthetically in the text. *V.* (1963; reprint, New York: Bantam, 1968); *The Crying of Lot 49* (1966; reprint, New York: Bantam, 1967); *Gravity's Rainbow* (New York: Viking, 1973); *Vineland* (Boston: Little, Brown and Co., 1990). I have discussed *V.* and *Gravity's Rainbow* in *The Contemporary American Comic Epic: The Novels of Barth, Pynchon, Gaddis, and Kesey* (Detroit: Wayne State University Press, 1988), pp. 79–110.

6. Fredric Jameson, *Postmodernism, or, The Cultural Logic of Late Capitalism* (Durham, NC: Duke University Press, 1991), pp. 1–54. References to Jameson will be to this edition and will be included parenthetically in the text.

7. Robert Venturi, *Complexity and Contradiction in Architecture* (New York: The Museum of Modern Art, 1977), pp. 22–23.

8. Gapp's essay, appearing on 23 April 1978, is cited in *The Critical Edge: Controversy in Recent American Architecture*, ed. Todd A. Marder (Cambridge, Mass: MIT Press, 1985), p. 49.

9. See Herbert Muschamp, "For Staten Island, A Ferry Terminal Rooted in the Past," *New York Times*, 22 November 1992, p. H32.

10. Robert Venturi, David Vaughan, and Charles Jencks, "National Gallery—Sainsbury Wing: An Interview," in Charles Jencks, *Post-Modern Triumphs in London* (London: Academy Group, 1991), pp. 50, 53.

11. See Venturi, *Complexity and Contradiction*, p. 23. Venturi stresses the need for such qualities so as to attain complexity and contradiction in architecture.

12. Venturi, *Complexity and Contradiction*, pp. 16–17.

13. See Charles Jencks, "The Death of Modern Architecture," *The Language of Post-Modern Architecture* (New York: Rizzoli, 1991), pp. 23–38.

14. Venturi, *Complexity and Contradiction*, p. 16.

15. Steinar Kvale, "Postmodern Psychology: A Contradiction in Terms?" in *Psychology and Postmodernism*, ed. Steinar Kvale (London: Sage, 1992), p. 49. See also Kenneth J. Gergen, *The Saturated Self: Dilemmas of Identity in Contemporary Life* (New York: Basic Books, 1991); Steven Seidman and David G. Wagner, ed. *Postmodernism & Social Theory* (Cambridge: Basil Blackwell, 1992).

16. William H. Gass, *The World Within the Word* (New York: Knopf, 1978); Gass, *Fiction and the Figures of Life* (Boston: Godine, 1971), p. 17. See also Gass, *In the Heart of the Heart of the Country* (Boston: Godine, 1989), pp. xiii–xlvi, 172–206.

17. See, for example, Steinar Kvale, ed. *Psychology and Postmodernism*, 1992; Steven Seidman and David Wagner, ed. *Postmodernism & Social Theory*, 1992; Joseph Natoli and Linda Hutcheon, ed. *A Postmodern Reader*; Linda Hutcheon, *A Poetics of Postmodernism* (1988); Hal Foster, ed. *The Anti-*

Aesthetic: Essays on Postmodern Culture (Seattle, Wash.: Bay Press, 1983); Ellen G. Friedman, "Where Are the Missing Contents? (Post) Modernism, Gender, and the Canon," *PMLA* 108 (1993): 240–52.

18. Fredric Jameson, *New Left Review* 146 (July–August 1984): 53–92; reprinted in *Postmodernism, or, The Cultural Logic of Late Capitalism*, pp. 1–54.

19. Jameson cites a contemporary phenomenon whose genealogy can be traced to Longinus's "heightened feeling" and also the Burkean and Kantian theories of sublime emotions evoked by the first temples and the building of Stonehenge, as well as by the Egyptian Pyramids and the dome of St. Peter's. For further elucidation of the postmodern sublime, see Anthony Vidler, "The Architecture of Allusion: Notes on the Postmodern Sublime," *Art Criticism* 2 (1985): 61–69. Vidler discusses the genealogy of the "sublime" (see esp. pp. 64–66). His essay is in response to Jean-François Lyotard's use of the term "sublime" in *The Postmodern Condition*.

20. Jameson does not refer to Pynchon, but I have not read a more fitting description of Pynchon's postmodern world. See Marc W. Redfield, "Pynchon's Postmodern Sublime," *PMLA* 104 (1989): 152–62. Redfield's focus is different from mine. He concentrates on the genealogy of Jameson's term "sublime" in Burkean and Kantian models as well as in the Romantic tradition, and he examines Pynchon's short fiction, not the novels. Several critics have indicated a connection between the mechanical and the transcendent (without specifically referring to Jameson or the sublime). See, for example, the discussion by David Porush, "'Purring into Transcendence': Pynchon's Puncutron Machine," *Critique* 32 (Winter 1990): 93–105; this is a keen analysis of how high-tech systems of information bear down on us in *Vineland*. See also Joseph W. Slade, "Communication, Group Theory, and Perception in *Vineland*," *Critique* 32 (Winter 1990): 126–44.

21. Albert Camus discusses our alienated experience in a world "divested of illusions and lights," our frustrating confrontation between the "nostalgia for unity [and] this fragmented universe." (See Albert Camus, *The Myth of Sisyphus*, trans. Justin O'Brien [New York: Vintage, 1955], pp. 5, 37.)

22. Thomas Pynchon, *Slow Learner* (New York: Bantam, 1985), pp. xxii–xxiv.

23. Thomas Pynchon, "Entropy," *Kenyon Review* 22 (1960): 277–92; rpt. in *Slow Learner* (New York: Bantam, 1985), pp. 65–86. References to this story will be placed parenthetically in the text.

24. See Redfield, "Pynchon's Postmodern Sublime," p. 155.

25. Joseph Slade, *Thomas Pynchon* (New York: Warner Paperbacks, 1974); Mark Richard Siegel, *Pynchon: Creative Paranoia in "Gravity's Rainbow"* (New York: Kennikat Press, 1978); David Cowart, *Thomas Pynchon: The Art of Allusion* (Carbondale: Southern Illinois University Press, 1980); John Stark, *Pynchon's Fictions: Thomas Pynchon and the Literature of Information* (Athens: Ohio University Press, 1980); Thomas Schaub, *Pynchon: The Voice of Ambiguity* (Urbana: University of Illinois Press, 1981); Molly Hite, *Ideas of Order in the Novels of Thomas Pynchon* (Columbus: Ohio State University Press, 1983); Thomas Moore, *The Style of Connectedness: "Gravity's Rainbow" and Thomas Pynchon* (Columbia: University of Missouri Press, 1987); Kathryn Hume, *Pynchon's Mythography: An Approach to "Gravity's Rainbow"* (Carbondale: Southern Illinois University Press, 1987); Dwight Eddins, *The Gnostic Pynchon* (Bloomington: Indiana University Press, 1990); Deborah L. Madsen, *The Postmodernist Allegories of Thomas Pynchon* (Leicester: Leicester University Press, 1991).

26. Camus, *The Myth of Sisyphus*, p. 13.

27. Martin Esslin, *The Theatre of the Absurd* (New York: Penguin, 1983), p. 411.

28. See Evelyn Underhill, *Mysticism: A Study in the Nature and Development of Man's Spiritual Consciousness* (New York: Dutton, 1930), pp. 196, 232–33.

29. These phrases are taken from Thomas Pynchon, "Is It O.K. to Be a Luddite?" *New York Times Book Review*, 28 October 1984, p. 40; Thomas Pynchon, "A Journey into the Mind of Watts," *New York Times Magazine*, 12 June 1966, p. 35. Although Pynchon is a writer who is intent on keeping his personal life out of the public eye (outdoing Salinger), he nevertheless keeps his own eyes sharply focused on current events and literary issues. This is evidenced by his *New York Times* discussions above, his piece on Gabriel García Márquez's *Love in the Time of Cholera* (*New York Times Book Review*, 10 April 1988, p. 1), and his contribution to the recent *New York Times* series on *The Deadly Sins*: "The Deadly Sins/Sloth: Nearer, My Couch, to Thee," *New York Times Book Review*, 6 June 1993, pp. 3, 57.

30. See Underhill, *Mysticism*, pp. 232–33.

31. See William Gleason, "The Postmodern Labyrinths of *Lot 49*," *Critique* 34 (Winter 1993): 93; see also Thomas Schaub, "'A Gentle Chill, An Ambiguity': *The Crying of Lot 49*," *Critical Essays on Thomas Pynchon*, ed. Richard Pearce (Boston: G. K. Hall, 1981). Schaub describes the scene as "an image of human life threatened, albeit comically, by the systems it has created" (p. 55).

32. Oedipa imagines herself as "walking among matrices of a great digital computer, the zeroes and ones twined above. . . . Behind the hieroglyphic streets there would either be a transcendent meaning, or only the earth" (*Lot*, p. 136).

33. Gleason, "Postmodern Labyrinths," p. 93.

34. See Joseph W. Slade, *Thomas Pynchon* (New York: Warner Paperbacks, 1974), p. 175. Slade points out: "Until the final revelation, excluded middles do not apply: They are bad shit indeed. . . . But it may also be a joke, a hoax. Oedipa fears what the revelation may bring. . . . Balancing her fear, however, is her courage. She goes to the auction, knowing that agents of Tristero will be there."

35. Thomas Hobbes, *The Elements of Law, Natural and Politic*, ed. Ferdinand Tonnies (Cambridge: Cambridge University Press, 1928), p. 32.

36. David Porush asserts that *Vineland* portrays "a world of dark revelation lurking just beyond our senses, of secret and inexplicable acts" (p. 99). Porush argues convincingly that there is a feeling that "'everything is connected' and that everything might refer both outside the text and to another part of the text [creating] a kind of 'infra-intertextuality' that lies at the heart of the Pynchon technique, hallmark of his singular genius" (p. 103). See also Elaine Safer, "Pynchon's World and Its Legendary Past: Humor and the Absurd in a Twentieth-Century *Vineland*," *Critique* 32 (Winter 1990): 107–25. This essay considers how the television-oriented culture of twentieth-century Vineland replaces the dreams of those who founded our nation, including the Vikings, in the eleventh century, who followed Leif the Lucky's exploration of Vinland.

Lingering Hopes, Faltering Dreams: Marilynne Robinson and the Politics of Contemporary American Fiction

THOMAS SCHAUB

THE term "political novel" was used to refer to novels of a particular kind or genre of fiction that was practiced more often by European than American writers. It was the kind of fiction "in which the *idea* of society, as distinct from the mere unquestioned workings of society, has penetrated the consciousness of the characters."[1] In the thirty-eight years since Irving Howe published *Politics and the Novel* (1957), readers and critics within the academy have become accustomed to think of narrative itself—any narrative—as political. At least they did so in the sense that in narrative the social and political are always present as an "unconscious" (Fredric Jameson), or in the sense that narrative is always "complicitous" (Linda Hutcheon) with its social and political temporality. By the use of such terms, contemporary practice converts the "context" of a work to an "in-text" that lurks within, shaping and guiding both the work's construction and reception. Vincent Leitch underscores this point: "Literary works are increasingly regarded as communal documents or as events with social, historical, and political dimensions rather than as autonomous artifacts within an aesthetic domain."[2] The idea that works of art exact experiences quite apart from the writer or reader's social and political history proved the dominant view of art during the postwar period when Irving Howe was writing political criticism. However, it is now taken to be an expression of both mystifying naiveté and patriarchal dominance.

Within the context of this current interpretive practice, Marilynne Robinson's views about her own and other American writers' work remind us that writers, not unreasonably, continue to think of themselves as authors fully in command of their own faculties. They believe that the writing of "political fiction" is something they may choose to do or not—that it is possible to avoid politics and stick to "art." In separate essays, both E. L. Doctorow and Robert Dunn, for example, lament the absence of fiction writers who take the panorama of contemporary social and political life as their dramatic object. Robert Dunn, in particular, criticized what he termed "private interest" fiction. Marilynne Robinson, on the other hand, responded to these plaintive exhortations by defending "private interest" fiction and attacking both political art and criticism.[3]

This exchange is another sign that the political role of art (theorized by Friedrich Schiller at the start of the modern era and given its current structure in the literary debates over mass culture and modernism in the middle of this century) remains a central issue in contemporary culture. However, it tends now to be argued through putatively more sophisticated Marxist and linguistic models. In her own assessment of contemporary criticism and fiction—titled "Writers and the Nostalgic Fallacy"—Robinson argues that political reading and art are "nostalgic," because they are based in modern European illusions of a former golden age. "Democratic impulses," she states, have been viewed by European intellectuals "as the trampling of culture under the feet of barbarians." European history, she adds, has created this contempt for the modern world: "European *history* is absolutely hair-raising, so European *culture* is mustered to serve as the political and moral defense of elites who could never hope to be justified by any other system of reckoning" (*WNF*, pp. 34–35).

Robinson rejects both the Left and the Right—for whom Marx and Burke stand as representative figures in her argument. Both positions have their roots in European history, and both participate in the "myth of the Fall in political dress." Their stance "permits and encourages scorn for one's fellows." From the contagion of this European modernism, she reasons, our writers and critics have caught "the habit of disparagement, persisted in with a kind of obsessiveness that seems like rigor." In another article she alludes to the influence in this country's intellectual life of European theories of language and literary theory, what she calls, in a pointed reference, a "Duke-and-the-Dauphin language of importations and neologisms."[4] She concludes her article "Writers and the Nostalgic Fallacy" with this declaration: "Somebody has stuffed Minerva's owl. It's time to clean house" (*WNF*, p. 35).

Perhaps most important for any consideration of her novel is Robinson's assertion that the "Great Ideas" of Europe's violent past are detrimental to both politics and art, for utopian (nostalgic) rationalism is hostile to the lived experience of the individual and the artist. Neither the left nor the right, for example, would "recognize a true emotion if it mugged them" (*WNF*, p. 35). This position also informs Robinson's literary criticism. In her preface to *The Awakening*, Robinson opposes applying ideological criticism to the representation of "human nature": "We are eager to coerce art into the service of politics and morality, both of which are concerned with controlling or changing human nature. We are not interested in according attention or doing justice to the gallant, sad, amazing, unregenerate form of it we have, which, for all we know is its true and final form."[5]

In these and other brief critical pieces, Robinson not only resurrects Emerson's charge to the American scholar, but also the nationalist rhetoric that is a recurrent feature of American culture in the wake of international conflict (in this case, the Vietnam War). In such rhetoric, Europe is represented as the place of origin of repression, ideological violence, and class conflict. Conversely, American culture is defined by its egalitarianism, democratic consciousness, private emotion and experience. Noam Chomsky characterizes this practice as "Visions of Righteousness."[6] In Robinson's formulation this cultural reflex merges with the literary aesthetics of the Cold War. For her version of American history and culture is virtually identical with the "end of ideology" thesis propounded by Louis Hartz, Reinhold Niebuhr, and Lionel Trilling in the aftermath of World War II: American culture is a liberal, centrist culture located in the dead center of life's contradictions. In this way, the idea of "America" was collapsed not only with reasonableness and "experience," but also with "reality" itself, just as, in the passage quoted above, "art" dissolves into "human nature." American culture, this point of view runs, is immune to ideological extremes—to ideas themselves. In Arthur Schlesinger's famous phrase, our culture occupies "the vital center."[7]

At the heart of her series of brief essays for the *New York Times Book Review* is Robinson's conviction that American culture and its citizens are getting a bad rap from Europeanized fiction and criticism. "For a long time it has been assumed by American writers that language reflects, or should reflect, the cultural level of its period and subject. . . . It has been assumed, furthermore, by many, that our cultural median is desolately low."[8] Because Robinson disagrees with both these assumptions, she argues that writers today must represent contemporary life by redeeming it with the power of their art. They should do so by revealing that a realm of experience worth valuing exists beneath the veneer of the public lingo, instead of using the degraded level of expression as a measure of the ordinary life. (In Robinson's censure there is an affinity with Saul Bellow. "We must get it out of our heads that this is a doomed time," Moses Herzog wrote to Professor Mermelstein three decades ago.) "Emerson and Whitman, among others," Robinson points out, "solved the problem of developing a democratic esthetic by finding the origins of poetry in the workings of consciousness, perception and language." By this solution, American culture was approached with "wonderful transparency and openness" (*WNF*, p. 34). Robinson, as F. O. Matthiessen once wrote of Emerson, is in "the optative mood."

This critical and cultural point of view played a central role in the language and style of Robinson's celebrated first novel, *Housekeeping* (1981):

> I made a world remote enough to allow me to choose and control the language out of which the story was to be made. It was a shift forced on me by the intractability of the *language* of contemporary experience—which must not be confused with contemporary experience itself. Merely speak the word "suburb," for example, and an entire world springs to mind, prepared for our understanding by sociologists and cultural commentators and novelists, good and bad. The language of present experience is so charged with judgment and allusion and intonation that it cannot be put to any new use or forced along any unaccustomed path. (*WNF*, p. 34)

These are striking remarks for two reasons. The first is that they are made in the midst of a literary critical culture convinced that experience and language are not separable in the way that Robinson's remarks seem to assume. The second is because contemporary language is generally thought to be the American writer's greatest resource.

In reviews of *Housekeeping*, the most remarked-upon quality of the story was the exceptional beauty and power of the language from which Robinson made the world of Ruth Foster.[9] Setting that language in the context of American fiction and its traditions further identifies the difference of this novel (in terms of its implicit cultural politics) from its contemporaries. In U.S. culture there is a tradition of respect for the colloquial. The American scholar, Emerson told his Harvard audience, learns from the "frank intercourse with many men and women" and the "rough, spontaneous conversation of men."[10] In the development of the

American novel particularly, as Richard Bridgman argued in *The Colloquial Style in America* (New York: Oxford University Press, 1966), the American idiom has been exactly the resource that helped produce a distinctly American prose fiction. What has made American literature "American" has been the steady incorporation by American writers of the variety of the culture's idiomatic voices until those voices infiltrated the narrative frame itself. This has been true from Huck Finn to Jake Barnes and Janie Starks to Invisible Man, Augie March and Holden Caulfield to Ellen Foster and Eugenio Castillo.

What is, perhaps, more to the point, the "plain style" of American social life was from the beginning of settlement set against the imported forms of European culture. In the twentieth century this simpler lifestyle supplied the language for the homegrown modernism of Robert Frost and Gertrude Stein, William Carlos Williams, Sherwood Anderson, Ernest Hemingway, Jean Toomer, Zora Neale Hurston, William Faulkner, and others. The local voice is counter-European. It is local and democratic in the best sense. Indeed, writers have counted on its idioms for all the complex social information coded within them to structure and enrich their writing. For Robinson to turn her back on what Williams called the "language of the day"[11] seems a rejection both of her best resource and of modernism's claim to the power of art to remake culture. Furthermore, if the definition of "the novel" held by such modernist critics as "the New York intellectuals" were applied, Robinson's book might not even qualify. In his seminal essay "Mass Society and Postmodern Fiction," Irving Howe argues that the kind of reflexive assumptions Robinson seeks to circumvent are the basis of the novel. He reasons that the erosion of those assumptions by the swelling "mass" society caused the death of the novel and the weakness of "postmodern" fiction. As a committed socialist, Howe defines the "novel" as an instrument of social critique uniquely suited to and produced by a class-stratified society.[12]

Many contemporary writers focus especially upon the "language of contemporary experience." They take it to be the most revealing dimension of social and historical reality available to them. Seemingly for them "experience" can only be that of a specific social and historical situation and constructed most efficiently from the languages at that intersection. The first sentence of Thomas Pynchon's *The Crying of Lot 49* offers an example. It makes a fictional world out of materials drawn from a particular cultural moment in U.S. history:

One summer afternoon Mrs. Oedipa Maas came home from a Tupperware party whose hostess had put perhaps too much kirsch in the fondue to find that she, Oedipa, had been named executor, or she supposed executrix, of the estate of one Pierce Inverarity, a California real estate mogul who had once lost two million dollars in his spare time but still had assets numerous and tangled enough to make the job of sorting it all out more than honorary.[13]

This sentence is patched together from a variety of cliché phrases ("had put perhaps too much," "real estate mogul," "once lost two million dollars in his spare time"), social (class-based) behaviors (Tupperware parties), legalisms, and camp references to Sophocles and Freud. These are but a few of the strands of discourse present within it. Indeed, this first sentence also begins to plot Oedipa's character development; it does so along a line defined by a gender-based activity of the leisure class on one end to the public (and equally gender-based) sphere of wills and contracts on the other. Pynchon may have meant his references to Tupperware parties, kirsch, and fondue to satirize his character (and through her a social practice), but likely he meant to initiate her development as well. Thus, when Oedipa distinguishes between "executor" and "executrix," her attention to gender inflection alerts the reader to a dawning awareness within the character that derives from two sources. The first is from the entry of larger numbers of women into public spheres of work during this period.[14] The second derives from the representation of this return in such books as The Feminine Mystique, women's magazines, nightly news programs, and movies. Having Oedipa distinguish between "executor" and "executrix" (making use of this resource from the "language of contemporary experience"), Pynchon positions her as a housewife poised between two decades. He attributes the distinction to her inner speech. Oedipa is perched on the cusp between the feminine mystique of the fifties and the assertion of disruptive power in the sixties—in which women, as well as men, may execute a public will.

For writers of fictions about social history and culture, the most valuable resource is likely to be contemporary language(s). For them, there is no useful distinction between language and experience, although most express a dismay comparable to Robinson's at the debasement of language. In this respect, one might suggest that Robinson and her colleagues are in full agreement. Yet Robinson chose in Housekeeping not to deploy techniques of satire and parody, which are central modes and characteristics of Pynchon, Don DeLillo, Raymond Carver, John Updike, Joan Didion, Bobbie Ann Mason, and others. All of these writers use idiom and artifact to delineate character. Thus Pynchon hones in precisely upon life in the suburbs:

> Through the rest of the afternoon, through her trip to the market in downtown Kinneret-Among-The-Pines to buy ricotta and listen to the Muzak ... then through the sunned gathering of her marjoram and sweet basil from the herb garden, reading of book reviews in the latest *Scientific American*, into the layering of a lasagna, garlicking of a bread, tearing up of romaine leaves, eventually, oven on, into the mixing of the twilight's whiskey sours against the arrival of her husband, Wendell ("Mucho") Maas from work, she wondered, wondered, shuffling back through a fat deckful of days which seemed (wouldn't she be the first to admit it?) more or less identical, or all pointing the same way subtly like a conjurer's deck, any odd one readily clear to the trained eye. It took her till the middle of Huntley and Brinkley to remember that last year at three or so one morning there had come this long-distance call (*TCL*, p. 11).

The assumptions and tone of this passage are radically different from any passage one might select from Ruth's narration in *Housekeeping*. Ruth's voice is the representation of a self that transcends history—or stands outside of—(or is meant to be such). However, all of Pynchon's novelistic powers are focused upon situating Oedipa within social and political realities of cultural history that Oedipa, a mock Rapunzel locked within the narcissism of her middle-class California life, had "forgotten." In Pynchon's satiric parable of American culture then, the heroine discovers what Michael Harrington identified so memorably as "the other America."[15]

In their common concern with the past, both novels represent the importance of memory. But Pynchon's novel is the representation of an action that results in social and political recognitions. Robinson's novel is the representation of a passion—and "emotion"—whose logic separates Ruth from society. Nothing in the language of Ruth's account would identify her as a child of our current cultural medium. Nor is there much besides Bernice's Ford and *Not as a Stranger* (1954), a novel that Ruthie reads, and "Good Night, Irene," a song by Leadbelly (1933) newly recorded after the war, to tell us the time is the mid-fifties. The place is Sandpoint, Idaho (Robinson's birthplace, beside Lake Pend Oreille, with the Bitterroot Range to the east). This social and historical background, even the geographic background, is purposely meager. However, for Pynchon, Howe's view of the artist's materials makes great sense.

It is precisely the social idiom of everyday language and locale that Pynchon, Didion, Toni Morrison, Updike, or Bobbie Ann Mason want to exploit, because the language itself is the bearer and representation of social meaning. Language constitutes the nightmare from which we cannot awake, as in Leslie Silko's *Ceremony*. In it the young Laguna man named Tayo hears a confusing medley of voices in his dreams. These voices are sometimes Spanish ("familiar love song, two words again and again, '*Y volvere*'"), sometimes Japanese ("angry and loud"—from his experience in the war), sometimes Laguna ("Uncle Josiah calling to him"):

> But before Josiah could come, the fever voices would drift and whirl and emerge again—Japanese soldiers shouting orders to him, suffocating damp voices that drifted out in the jungle steam, and he heard the women's voices then; they faded in and out until he was frantic because he thought the Laguna words were his mother's, but when he was about to make out the meaning of the words, the voice suddenly broke into a language he could not understand.[16]

Silko seems to imply that Tayo does not exist apart from the languages of his contemporary experience. They exist within him, and with them come the conflicting semantic and cultural content they communicate.

Contemporary writers as often as not seem to agree with Robinson that "contemporary language" is degraded, but they assume a close relationship between language and mental process. When Bobbie Ann Mason's character Cody tells his wife, "'A person has to follow his dream,'" Mason implies that what people think and the language they use to think aren't separable from who they are or the emotions they feel.[17] Like those of Robinson, Mason's stories argue that such language enters the lives of her characters from the beacons of radio and TV. (Cody's wife says to him, "'That sounds like some Elvis song.'") But the stories do not suggest that there is any rich emotional experience beneath Cody's words for thinking about his life.

As in the preceding sliver of dialogue taken from Mason's story "Hunktown," many contemporary writers take the state of the language—in popular music and MTV, in TV Evangelism, in movie advertisements, sitcoms and talk shows—to be a symptom of cultural illness that their own narrative voices seek to expose and purge through re-presentation (as Pierre Macherey theo-

rized) or in the use of art as negation—to recall Theodor
Adorno's approach to this subject. In their writing, the signs of
cultural decay are surrounded as it were by the vigilance of narrative "truth." Joan Didion states this possibility directly in her
essay "Slouching Toward Bethlehem":

> As it happens I am still committed to the idea that the ability to
> think for one's self depends upon one's mastery of the language, and
> I am not optimistic about children who will settle for saying, to
> indicate that their mother and father do not live together, that they
> come from a "broken home." They are sixteen, fifteen, fourteen years
> old, younger all the time, an army of children waiting to be given
> the words.[18]

Didion's account of her visit to San Francisco during the height
of Haight Ashbury describes the subculture there. It was then
populated by young people who didn't know what they were
talking about and who responded to the most serious events with
casual clichés supplied them by the public media. Their level of
response had been made superficial and trivial not only by the
dulling effects of drug habits but also by the pablum of paranoid
assumptions that served as their communal language. At the
same time, the precision of Didion's horrified observation surrounds this region of cultural failure with the reassuring example
of language competence existing outside, as it were, the world
it describes.

Don DeLillo, in his *White Noise*, depicts a world in which
experience and language coincide so completely they produce
the illusion of hierophany. Watching his children sleep, Jack
Gladney overhears his daughter utter the words "Toyota Celica,"
which are "familiar and elusive at the same time, words that
seemed to have a ritual meaning, part of a verbal spell or ecstatic
chant." Gladney asks himself how these "near-nonsense words"
could make him "sense a meaning, a presence"? Why do they
strike him "with the impact of a moment of splendid transcendence"?[19] In this novel, the encircling mechanism is not a contrary, insightful character or a journalistic narrator. Instead, it is
irony itself which creates both the comedy and critique of the
represented world. Readers are expected to understand this as a
critique of mass culture and the way it functions as totalizing
ideology. In such a culture brand names come to us as intimations of revelation.

It may well be an aspect of mass and postmodern culture that
the "language of the day" is no longer a source of either "local

color" or of authenticity. Thus the words people speak—like Gladney's daughter talking in her sleep—are increasingly those of someone else. This was the argument of Adorno and Hork-heimer, as well as of Dwight Macdonald and C. Wright Mills. Such is one implication of Irving Howe's argument in "Mass Society and Postmodern Fiction." Robinson's effort to circum-vent the "language of contemporary experience" should be placed within this continuing suspicion. But she refuses to col-lapse the public media and the private consciousness into the condition of overdetermination that drives this critique. It was this critique, as well as fictions like *White Noise* or Frederick Barthelme's *Moon Deluxe*, that Robinson had in mind when she wrote:

> Whole fictions are now made of stringing together brand names, me-dia phrases and minor expletives, the idea being, apparently, that these amount to a demonstration of how reduced people actually are, though they are in fact no more than the statement of a notably ungenerous faith. In any case, the model is wrong. There is no evi-dence that language contracts to conform itself to any current level of material or spiritual culture. (*LIS*, p. 8)

The "*language* of contemporary experience," which denies, de-grades, and prepackages our understanding, cannot, in Rob-inson's view, represent how "people actually are." For her, the satire and parody typical of so much American writing in the last fifty years are un-American. They result from an imported contempt for democratic life. They approach American life in the wrong spirit and with a misunderstanding of prerogatives and powers of literary language.

In these mini-essays, "Let's Not Talk Down" and "Language Is Smarter," Robinson insists upon two distinctions: one occurs between private experience and public language; the other lies between the language of the writer and the "level of material or spiritual culture." The writer, Robinson insists, has available to her (or him) a timeless, universal resource. "From all that lan-guage hoards we can take what is our own if we make good our claim. Freighted as it is, language remains possibility first of all" (*LIS*, p. 8). Failing to recognize the power of this resource, the writer not only underestimates the vitality of cultural experi-ence, but she also shortchanges the possibilities of art.

This distinction is especially clear in Robinson's view that language and experience are two different realms: one's experi-ence is not identical with the language one uses or in which one thinks. In this view the artist's language may not function as language at all, but as the verbal representation of an interior emotional life. Ruth's world, the novel implies, is radically *private* in a way that current critical thinking explicitly denies. It is made public to us only through the artist's invented or borrowed *language* and not through the idiom of contemporary language. The latter is too resonant with preconception and contempt to serve as the vehicle of (or provide access to) Ruth's story. In her literary art Robinson attempts to resurrect the experiential real by the centrifuge of the imagination; in the process she separates private experience from the public "language of contemporary experience." Robinson's novel is primarily a work of style. It implies that it is possible to fashion a style that differentiates between language and experience, and that experience, conversely, may be free of language. Her novel also suggests that the language of art, new or old, may provide access to that experience and set it free.

II

Housekeeping may be read as a representation of radically subjective consciousness and its narrative piecing by the logic and syntax of sorrow. But to say this only gives in, as it were, to the illusionist trick of representation. It does not answer the question of what the novel's style itself represents, or what we are to make of those words and habits that Robinson has taken as her own "from all that language hoards" (*LIS*, p. 8). In the context of Robinson's Americanist model, in which American literature represents and dignifies democratic "consciousness," we can say that Ruth's voice—Robinson's cobbled text—is the transparent medium of the very consciousness it constitutes. Yet it is important to see that by so doing *Housekeeping* also serves as a kind of domestic cultural policy. The reader may view the novel not from Ruth's sympathetic point of view, but from Robinson's as a kind of domestic czar of cultural affairs who is determined to "clean house." To see it this way is to understand the medium of her art as a form of cultural criticism.

To read *Housekeeping* in these terms also helps to underscore the paradoxes of the book's reception. Robinson explicitly distinguishes art from "politics and morality" (*Awakening*, p. viii), but her own cultural criticism invites readers to see the politics implicit in her novel. The critics of *Housekeeping*, on the other hand, have been quick to appropriate the novel's story for the work of social reform. They have done so without taking into account either the nationalism of Robinson's essays or of the novel itself. The novel has received the most attention from feminist scholars, but it also has drawn the attention of Marxist critics, as well as those who stress the "American" character of the book.

These reader-positions have effectively transformed the novel by converting the account of a young girl's grief into fables of liberation. This conversion has taken the form of several related arguments. In one, the novel depicts a return to the "great mother" and a "casting out [of] patterns that have been destructive" (Kirby, pp. 101, 107). In another, Ruth displays "heroic female resolve" and her choice of "the open road," though difficult, is "therapeutic" (Ravits, pp. 658–59, 666). In a Marxist reading, the novel's ending "implies . . . a form of historical agency with potentially radical results" (Foster, p. 86), and so on.[20] These examples suggest the interpretations of Housekeeping thus far are marked always by strategies of recruitment, by a determination to claim the novel for the "culture of redemption,"[21] however such restoration or freedom is imagined. The spirit of such readings has recently been canonized in The Columbia History of the American Novel. It informs readers that Housekeeping "reshapes American literary tradition by presenting a female protagonist . . . who lights out for the territory with the same autonomy and self-reliance usually reserved for male characters such as Cooper's Natty Bumppo, Twain's Huck Finn, and the eponymous hero of Jack Schaefer's Shane (1949)."[22]

It might be more appropriate to place Ruth's story in another tradition of American literature. That one would include Elizabeth Templeton fishing by firelight at night with Natty Bumppo and Chingachgook, or with Miles Coverdale recovering Zenobia's body from the river, and Marge, in Hemingway's In Our Time, leaving Nick to mope by himself and rowing herself home. In more contemporary work, Ruth's story may be set within the context of the more recent Diving into the Wreck, by Adrienne Rich, and Margaret Atwood's Surfacing. But perhaps the most resonant pairing is with Edna Pontellier, whose very name ("pons" or "bridge" and "tellier") implies a telling or teller—that is, a bridge. In addition, there is the French "tellière" meaning foolscap-paper; the result is a paper bridge or novel. Ruth's crossing of the bridge that removes her from the social dimensions of Fingerbone might also be contrasted with the leap Milkman Dead takes at the end of *Song of Solomon*. Another suggestive possibility is the headlong arc of the car that carries Thelma and Louise over the Grand Canyon.

Her novel's strong appeal to American critics is hardly surprising, despite those few reviewers who found the novel restricted by the "tortured argument" of Ruth's mourning. American feminists have long thought that death-of-the-self-and-author criticism does not have much to offer women and minorities who are just now acquiring both selves and authority. Still, to them, Ruth's rejection of Fingerbone's social structure and possibilities—benign as they are—seems a positive step.[23] But to argue in this way is to be persuaded by Ruth's example, as if her logic were ours rather than Robinson's representation of Ruth's perception.

Perhaps the more subliminal source of appeal—made explicit in the *Columbia History* entry—is the novel's Americanism. I refer to the way the novel invites comparison with Huck Finn or with Thoreau at Walden, Ishmael going to sea, and Holden Caulfield or Augie March, among others. The westernness of the book is striking; it suggests that feminist appreciation of Ruth's departure for "the open road" reinscribes dominant cultural stereotypes, as Ravits indicates by her title, "Extending the American Range." But fundamentally, as a fiction of words, *Housekeeping* is a brilliant, meditative resurrection of American romanticism. It is a resurrection that is thereby also nostalgic, evoking an emotion for "home" in the familiar language and belief of New England literary expression. "I am an Emersonian," Robinson has written ("Let's Not Talk Down"). "I must be influenced most deeply," she responded to a symposium, "by the 19th-century-Americans—Dickinson, Melville, Thoreau, Whitman, Emerson and Poe. Nothing in literature appeals to me more than the rigor with which they fasten on problems of language, of consciousness—bending form to their purposes, ransacking ordinary speech and common experience."[24] The transcendental inheritance of *Housekeeping* is evident throughout the novel. It can be seen in the logic of Ruth's mind, in the echo of Walden in Lake Fingerbone, in the Dickinson echo in the poem Ruth is asked to read ("I heard a fly buzz"), and so on. Indeed, the entire book is constructed somewhat like Emerson's journals—that is, from a compilation of Ruth's one-liners: these elaborate the homiletic phrasing of Puritan caution—as discovered and applied in the everyday life of domestic duty ("darkness is the only solvent").

From the "great repository of experience in memory" that is

language, Robinson borrows Emersonian transcendentalism. But what does this transcendentalism out of time mean to readers in 1981 or 1995? How does it function as style? What is being "dignified"? And in what sense does this choice of language and the remoteness of Ruthie's world concern itself with contemporary experience? Although the novel's story may be read as the powerful evocation of a young woman's mourning, of a certain "emotion" (to use Robinson's word), the medium of the story is explicitly nostalgic. If nostalgia is a form of mourning, we may say that the entire narrative is shaped and constituted by Ruth's nostalgia. But the nostalgia expressed by the novel's style—perhaps something like Jameson's "ideology of form"—is nostalgia for an idea of art that Robinson identifies with American democratic culture. Yet it is a culture which, 158 years since the publication of Emerson's "Nature," remains locked in struggle with Europe.

The central exhibit in this argument would be the novel's use of Emersonian correspondence as both the emotional logic of Ruth's consciousness and the stylistic device of Robinson's first-person narration. Evidence of this logic appears in every *Housekeeping* simile and analogy. The earth "brims," the pool in the backyard (like Walden itself) has "water clear as air," and "on it, slight as an image in an eye, sky, clouds, trees, our hovering faces and our cold hands."[25] From the very beginning, then, Ruth's world is the image of the transparent eyeball, and it is transformed by her into allegories of spiritual facts. The processes of nature and mind are deeply correspondent. When the lake begins to freeze, "fragments of transparent ice . . . knitted themselves up like bits of a reflection" (p. 7). Through Ruth's habit of analogy, Robinson reproduces the logic of Emerson's correspondence between natural and spiritual fact, a correspondence revealed by, or "in" the symbolic perception of, the poetic consciousness. In other words, these similes are "Emersonian" because they express a relationship between the natural world and the world of Ruth's consciousness or spirit. There is a "radical correspondence," Emerson wrote, "between visible things and human thoughts" (*Selections*, p. 33). For him, "every appearance in nature corresponds to some state of mind" (p. 32).

Ruth recalls that she first "noticed the correspondence between the space within the circle of my skull and the space around me" (p. 198) while learning to conquer her fear of the dark. Her emotional life is explained and made endurable by such correspondence: she fastens upon those "facts" of the natu-

ral world—the vortices of the moon-pulled lake, the elements of
night, water, and wind—and reads them as symbols of decay and
impermanence. This is Ruth's Gothic Emerson, as it were; all the
elements are translated into symbols of her spirit, tutored by the
repercussions of loss. Emerson's Hegelian idealism is reproduced
as *the way Ruth thinks*. The spiral of her emotional logic constitutes the novel's unfolding, as she propounds general truths from
the specificity of her own perceptions. She declares, for example,
that "darkness is the only solvent" (p. 116). The occasion of
"transients" drifting through Fingerbone stirs in her a melan-
choly observation: "The sorrow is that every soul is put out of
house" (p. 179). Later she notes that the stars are "pulled through
the dark along the whorls of an enormous vortex—for that is
what it is" (p. 211). In Ruth's perception, then, the natural and
social worlds repeatedly coincide and compose a metaphysical
brief in behalf of her totalizing desire. Translating perception
into "truth"—the great gift of Emerson's "poet"—Ruth is Emerson's American scholar, though one with a bad attitude.

Like Thoreau, Ruth reminds us that we are sojourners here
for only a short stay. But instead of a sunny call to a spiritual
awakening—and more in the spirit of Dickinson or Melville than
Thoreau—Ruth rejects the dream of ascension: "Dawn and its
excesses have always reminded me of heaven, a place where I
have always known I would not be comfortable." Set against the
image of salvation-as-ascension is the image of the lake's vortex.
Ruth imagines this vortex taking her and Sylvie "down into the
darker world." Here her language anticipates the crossing of the
bridge and its meaning—"where other sounds would pour into
our ears until we seemed to find songs in them" (pp. 149–50).
Of course the novel's genius and effectiveness derive from Ruth's
consciousness and its undeviating progress—what Brina Caplan
has called Ruth's "tortured argument."[26] This logic has not truly
been acknowledged in the criticism, yet it is this logic that reveals the novel as an inversion of the Western narrative of salvation. For Ruth's story begins with a Fall (the grandfather's tumble
in the train) and uses the Flood to introduce Sylvie. But it also
fails to light the Fire that ends the world, and it speculates that
Christ is a creation of memory rather than prophecy. There is no
more explicit sign of the book's engineering than Ruth's dream
that "Sylvie was teaching me to walk under water" (p. 175).[27]

Ruth's withdrawal is from society, not from injury. Ruth is not
a "victim" of society. Indeed, her withdrawal is into language
itself. This language ranges from the desire to "Let them come

unhouse me of this flesh" (p. 159) to her rebirth (crawling between Sylvie's legs [p. 17]) into the world of perished things. It includes also Ruth's (and the novel's) final metamorphosis into disembodied voice while crossing the bridge: "Did we really hear some sound too loud to be heard, some word so true we did not understand it, but merely felt it pour through our nerves like darkness or water?" (p. 215). Ruth's being asks this question from within language itself. For her being is now the being of words, those most absent of things, constituting a "presence" that is not there. This "word" pours through them in a reversal of the incarnation; it saturates them with darkness and water, the two elements most dear to Sylvie, and it reincarnates them in the Word. In effect, the argument of the novel rests on the correspondence between language and natural fact, which in turn is symbolic of spiritual truth. Thus the argument uses Emerson's discussion of "Language" (in *Nature*) to collapse the novel's central character (or "I") with its plot.

Ruth speaks of traveling with Aunt Sylvie to see friends here and there. But in imagining such journeys, Robinson works both sides of the fence: True, they are "drifters" and take jobs as waitresses or clerks, but Ruth's "silence" bothers those around her. It is "as if I put a chill on the coffee by serving it. What have I to do with ceremonies of sustenance, of nurturing?" she asks. The customers want to know why she does "not eat anything" herself (p. 214). Indeed, they visit Lucille as "ghosts" rather than substantial beings, traveling as air and water: "Sylvie and I have stood outside her window a thousand times, and we have thrown the side door open when she was upstairs changing beds, and we have brought in leaves, and flung the curtains and tipped the bud vase, and somehow left the house again before she could run downstairs, leaving behind us a strong smell of lake water" (p. 218).

Upon reflection, however, the reader decides that whether or not the ghostly pair have jumped, fallen, or crossed over the bridge, in either sense, is beside the point. The world in which these possibilities remain indeterminate is a world created of metaphor. It appears doubly so, in fact, since Ruth's narrative perception is one that translates the literal into symbol until the entire world has been converted from "fatuous light" (p. 172) to water. Even if we say she makes it to the other side, she remains immersed in the water since she no longer is on or desires "dry land." Ruth's insubstantiation haunts the world of light. (It was Henry Vaughan who wrote of those arriving in heaven, "they are all gone into the world of light.") Her intangibility lifts curtains and condenses upon Lucille's water glass in a Boston restaurant.

True to Emerson, the novel's language corresponds closely to the spiritual fact of Ruth's nonbeing: "Sylvie and I do not flounce in through the door. . . . We do not sit. . . . My mother, likewise, is not there. . . . We are nowhere in Boston" (pp. 218–19). These self-negated assertions enable Ruth to make her presence felt by her absence.[28] Indeed, in her adamant logic there is nowhere else for her to go or "be"—and still exist for the reader—than into language itself. First-person narration always has the special character of a voice speaking from another realm that haunts the reader's world. But Robinson's voice does not come to us as issuing from someone or somewhere else. Even more than is the case with Ralph Ellison's Invisible Man—who tells the reader it's time for him to end his hibernation—Ruth's disembodied voice is all there is of her.

III

To say this much is only to remain within the terms of the narrative's device for expressing Ruth's emotional being. But this withdrawal into language already takes us to considerations beyond the Emersonian workings of Ruth's consciousness. It leads the reader to a consideration of Robinson's transformation of Ruth's mourning into revelation—and then into the politics of her art. In performing this translation of Ruth's perception, Robinson completes the circuit of Emerson's idealism. Emerson had insisted that the poet's symbolic imagination is not merely subjective: "This relation between the mind and matter is not fancied by some poet, but stands in the will of God" (Selections, p. 35). In this way, the poet or scholar is able to speak for all men: "the deeper he dives into his privatest, secretest presentiment, to his wonder he finds this is the most acceptable, most public, and universally true" (p. 74). Thus Ruth's narrative rejects the idea of transcendence on the one hand, while elevating her experience of sorrow to transcendent scripture on the other.

This Hegelian romanticism is partly what leads the reader to interpret Ruth's development as a progress and an escape. In other words, this is so not only because Ruth and Sylvie say it is, but also because their story is given the form of truth. Ruth's decision is redeemed, so to speak, by the narrative form in which her author has created her: the language itself certifies the point of view articulated within it. This universalism affects the reader's reception of Ruth's experience; it substitutes for Ruth's particular experience the homiletic revelations that Robinson so powerfully elicits. George Toles puts it plainly: "I cannot talk myself out of believing that Robinson herself supports Ruth's calmly extravagant claims. . . . Nothing else that the narrative reveals to us requires us to draw back from the extremity of Ruth's declarations."[29]

Robinson's translation produces a paradox within the novel. Ruth's consciousness so lacks "perspective and horizon" that she finds herself "reduced to an intuition" (p. 70). Yet Robinson's approach converts Ruth's condition to the occasion of "absolute discovery" (p. 157). Robinson herself may think of what she has done as "dignifying" ordinary experience. Indeed, one of the most refreshing and winsome features of *Housekeeping* is the respect with which each character is treated—from the grandfather Edmund to the sister Lucille, to the kindly sheriff reluctant to do his duty. It seems quite likely that Robinson intended merely (and powerfully) to represent Ruth's sorrow, without attempting to wring from it anything but the reminder of mortality that afflicts us all. Her novel is arguably a marvelous evocation of a young woman's emotion. It shows that emotion respect and gives to it all the linguistic power and imagination Robinson can bring to bear upon a girl who cannot control her feet, who bites her knuckles and chews her hair, and speaks only to Sylvie for months at a time (pp. 183, 187).

Within the novel, Ruth's "sad, outcast state of revelation" results from shock waves generated by the grandfather's death. (Ruth's account begins and ends with the atomic image of "the shock wave" [pp. 15, 193].) "That event had troubled the very medium of their lives" (p. 15). But as a novel, Ruth's account models Robinson's idea of art and her inheritance from the nineteenth-century writers she admires. Having chosen to be a delineator of mind and consciousness, processes held in common by all, Robinson has paid due respect to the sturdy reality of experience, to "emotion." "I find no evidence," she notes in her response to Doctorow and Dunn, "that consciousness has ever been a comfortable experience" (*WNF*, p. 34). Thus her book of Ruth may be seen as a portrait of the American artist. It depicts a sensibility whose complex consciousness stands as a model of art against the simplifying (and violent) nostalgia of European modernism.

Language, in this way, is the medium both of thematized revelation (reminders of impermanence) and of a cultural faith. It penetrates the crust of public lingo to the still integral life of democratic experience and consciousness. Revelations have the liberating effect that accompanies any recognition, but it is hard to see them as pointing the way toward the "open road." They should be seen, perhaps, as the novel's Utopian element. This element is firmly contained in much American fiction by the stringencies of death and isolation, and it often is presented as truth itself: "This is the way it is." The social possibilities some critics have seen in the relationship between Ruth and Sylvie are present here. But these collective possibilities exist only within the story of a young woman unable to invest in another object of love.[30] For Sylvie, after all, is less another person than she is the medium of Ruth's memory and then of her self-image: Sylvie first becomes Helen to Ruth (p. 167), and finally the two become "almost a single person" (p. 209). Their "select society" (Emily Dickinson's presence throughout the novel is unmistakable) can exist only in a liminal world of art. This world is capable of affirming the ineluctable contradictions of life and giving to them, as Ruth does following Emerson, the metaphysical warrants of compensation, balance, and coherence.

Thus one may argue that Ruth's withdrawal into language is the action within the text of Robinson's withdrawal into art. It results not only, as Robinson claims, from "the intractability of contemporary language," but also from contemporary social history as well. Indeed, seen from this perspective, Ruth's voice comes to us from the world of style alone, or, as Robinson describes her novel, "a world remote enough." It is "a world elsewhere," notes Richard Poirier:

> American books are often written as if historical forces cannot possibly provide such an environment [of freedom], as if history can give no life to "freedom," and as if only language can create the liberated place. The classic American writers try through style temporarily to free the hero (and the reader) from systems, to free them from the pressures of time, biology, economics, and from the social forces which are ultimately the undoing of American heroes and quite often of their creators.[31]

Perhaps Poirier's "a world elsewhere" is always a world of nostalgia. It is as if American ideology here were a form of melancholia, unable to move through regret and mourning to an embrace of life's present and future possibility. Instead, this ideology may be seeking, against the current of social history, to recover a future that has been lost to time. Or, less nostalgically, it may be striving to re-member that which was never truly whole.

In this context, the image of the Other leaping into space (Milkman, Thelma and Louise, Ruth and Sylvie) is only willful rejection. It suggests an artistic embodiment of the "criminality implicit in the broadening of all freedom"[32] and explicitly removed from the social sphere in which freedom is a crime. These leaps of style, possible only in representation, are further instances then of what Poirier means by "a world elsewhere." In other words, Robinson's novel denies the very usefulness its critics wish to find in it. Madelon Sprengnether has referred to the novel's "radical alterity," but it is difficult to see anything radical in a (representation of a) consciousness that exists by virtue of its removal from society. Huck Finn's radical alterity, to take a point of contrast, exists precisely in his being radically "Other" in society. His narrative ends at just that point when he ceases to be radical, by heading west to "the territory."[33]

Robinson rejects an idea of art as political. Yet her own novel and criticism are complicit with a political view of art we now associate with the Cold War aesthetics of Arthur Schlesinger's "vital center" or Lionel Trilling's "liberal imagination." It is, in fact, a view that created the very canons that our profession is currently revising. This point of view is evident enough in her essays. But her novel *Housekeeping* also expresses those aesthetics: it reenacts the power of art to transform the popular and private into a universal experience that transcends history. "Every song recalls a thousand sorrows," Ruth says at one point. A repository of cultural memory, the novel's language proves a reservoir of universal experience. It functions much the way that Ellison said "the blues" do—by appropriating the particular (historical) experience of pain and transforming it into a transcendent, universal lyricism.

In Robinson's fiction the world of style originates in an esthetic similar to Ellison's. It is an idea of art as embodied contradiction, one that reemerged as a reaction to Stalinist communism and to embarrassments within the Old Left. Robinson's rejection of Doctorow and other contemporaries represents a persistent belief that art may or should be free of ideology. Hence it merges effortlessly with Cold War esthetics. Indeed, Robinson's idea of art is based on a similar interpretation of human nature. As in Lionel Trilling's Cold War formulation of "moral ambiguity," Robinson's view of art is rooted in a tragi-Christian idea of human nature. Her view is evident in her argument that the "religious version

of the . . . Fall is an idea that addresses the complexity of experi-
ence—how in one bosom divinity and depravity fight like broth-
ers" (*WNF*, pp. 34–35). Robinson's Americanist advocacy echoes
the narratives of American exceptionalism articulated during the
Cold War by Louis Hartz (*The Liberal Tradition in America* [New
York: Harcourt Brace, 1965]), Arthur Schlesinger, Jr. (*The Vital
Center* [Boston: Houghton Mifflin, 1949]), and Reinhold Niebuhr
(*The Irony of American History* [New York: Scribner's, 1952]).
Her stance results in traces of that particular history in her
novel's language. By evoking Emerson on behalf of an art and
democracy beyond ideology, Robinson exercises an Americanist
discourse of the most nationalist and centrist type. Little wonder
readers are moved by this representation of keeping house; it is
derived from the very text of New England idealism.

To sketch the nationalist dimension of Robinson's fiction and
criticism is not, I think, to deny those dimensions of her work
which critics with other viewpoints have identified. Her *Housekeeping* is a powerful and important novel. Still, its myriad and
subtle insights should not blind us to those complexities of a
text that may be more "residual" than "emergent." It gives one
pause to realize that Robinson's view of language, not so many
years ago, would be justly celebrated in a critical culture that
cherished art because (it was argued) art transcends history—by
1945 people had had enough history. Her language also has been
praised for exemplifying an esthetic view that celebrates that
part in each of us which we share with all others, past and present and future. In the last chapter of his *Anatomy of Criticism*
(1957), Northrop Frye wrote: "The ethical purpose of a liberal
education is to liberate, which can only mean to make one capable of conceiving society as free, classless, and urbane. No such
society exists, which is one reason why [*sic*] a liberal education
must be deeply concerned with works of imagination. The imaginative element in works of art, again, lifts them clear of the bondage of history."[34]

Turning again to the contrasting views of Doctorow and Robinson, we now may see them as the result of two different perceptions of art's relation to society and of society's dream of freedom.
Robinson, clearly, is of Frye's party. Today's prevailing critical
community has for over twenty years repudiated such universal-
izing idealism as a mystification of privilege. Hence Robinson's
esthetics have gone unnoticed because in her fiction the story
and its major figure resonate so sympathetically with the current
interests of contemporary intellectual culture. Granting this reso-

nance, we should recognize nonetheless the view of art and experience that Robinson enacts in the story of Ruth's loyal (and relentless) mourning. Admittedly, her story produces the effect of revelation, but it cannot be "true" in the sense that her story will set us free. Instead, as I have been suggesting, it may confirm us in our nostalgia.

Notes

1. Irving Howe, *Politics and the Novel* (New York: Horizon Press, 1957), p. 19.

2. Vincent Leitch, *Cultural Criticism, Literary Theory, Poststructuralism* (New York: Columbia University Press, 1992), p. ix.

3. See E. L. Doctorow, "The Passion of Our Calling," *New York Times Book Review*, 25 August 1985, pp. 1, 21–23; Robert Dunn, "Fiction That Shrinks from Life," *New York Times Book Review*, 30 June 1985, pp. 1, 24–25; and Marilynne Robinson, "Writers and the Nostalgic Fallacy," *New York Times Book Review*, 5 April 1985, pp. 1, 34–35. All textual references to this last essay are abbreviated *WNF*.

4. Marilynne Robinson, "Let's Not Talk Down to Ourselves," *New York Times Book Review*, 5 April 1987, p. 11.

5. Marilynne Robinson, "Introduction," *The Awakening* (New York: Bantam Books, 1988), p. viii.

6. Noam Chomsky, "Visions of Righteousness," *Cultural Critique* 3 (Spring 1986): 10–43.

7. See Thomas Schaub, *American Fiction in the Cold War* (Madison: University of Wisconsin Press, 1991), esp. pp. 3–24; Geraldine Murphy, "The Politics of Reading *Billy Budd*," *American Literary History* 1 (Summer 1989): 361–82; Donald Pease, "*Moby Dick* and the Cold War," *The American Renaissance Reconsidered*, ed. Walter Michaels and Donald Pease (Baltimore: Johns Hopkins University Press, 1985); Russell Reising, *The Unusable Past* (London: Methuen, 1986); and Mark Walhout, "The New Criticism and the Crisis of American Liberalism: The Poetics of the Cold War," *College English* 49 (December 1987): 861–71.

8. Marilynne Robinson, "Language Is Smarter Than We Are," *New York Times Book Review*, 1 January 1987, p. 8. All textual references to this essay are abbreviated *LIS*.

9. See, for example, Brina Caplan, "It Is Better to Have Nothing," *The Nation*, 7 February 1981, pp. 152, 154; Mark Granetz, "Brief Review," *The New Republic*, 21 February 1981, pp. 40–41; Rosemary Booth, "Three Insiders, One Outsider," *Commonweal*, 22 May 1981, pp. 306–07; Paul Gray, "Castaways," *Time*, 2 February 1981, p. 83; Alan Brownjohn, "Breaking the Rules," *Encounter*, 56 (May 1981): 87–88; and LeAnne Schreiber, "Pleasure and Loss," *New York Times Book Review*, 8 February 1981, pp. 14, 16.

10. *Selections from Ralph Waldo Emerson*, ed. Stephen E. Whicher (Boston: Houghton Mifflin, 1957), pp. 70–71.

11. William Carlos Williams, "Kora in Hell," *Imaginations*, ed. Webster Schott (New York: New Directions, 1971), p. 59.

12. Irving Howe, *A World More Attractive* (New York: Horizon Press, 1963), pp. 86–87.

13. Thomas Pynchon, *The Crying of Lot 49* (New York: Harper & Row Perennial, 1986), p. 1. All textual references to this novel are abbreviated *TCL*.

14. William H. Chafe, *The Unfinished Journey: America Since World War II* (New York: Oxford University Press, 1986), pp. 126–28, 329–30.

15. I had not seen this connection in print until Pierre-Yves Petillon's essay, "A Re-cognition of Her Errand into the Wilderness." See *New Essays on The Crying of Lot 49*, ed. Patrick O'Donnell (Cambridge: Cambridge University Press, 1991), p. 150. See also Michael Harrington, *The Other America* (New York: Macmillan, 1963), especially chapter one, "The Invisible Land."

16. Leslie Marmon Silko, *Ceremony* (New York: Penguin, 1977), p. 6.

17. Bobbie Ann Mason, *Love Life* (New York: Harper & Row, 1989), p. 49.

18. Joan Didion, *Slouching Toward Bethlehem* (New York: Dell, 1968), p. 123.

19. Don DeLillo, *White Noise* (New York: Penguin, 1985), p. 155.

20. Joan Kirby, "Is There Life After Art?" *Tulsa Studies in Women's Literature* 5 (Spring 1986): 101, 107; Martha Ravits, "Extending the American Range: Marilynne Robinson's *Housekeeping*," *American Literature* 61 (December 1989): 658–59, 666; and Tom Foster, "History, Critical Theory, and Women's Social Practices: 'Women's Time' and *Housekeeping*," *Signs* 14 (1988): 86. See also Ellen Friedman, "Where Are the Missing Contents?" *PMLA* 108 (March 1993): 240–52. Friedman, like Ravits, valorizes Ruth as a "nomad who seeks sanctuary in the interstices of culture" (p. 244). Like many feminist critics, Friedman sees the novel as a quest for the mother, and downplays or overlooks the fact that Ruth's family fell apart in the prior generation, when her mother (Helen) lost her father—and that Ruth repeatedly locates the origin of her homelessness in that first "shock."
For critics who aren't so certain about the novel's stance, see Paula Geyh, "Burning Down the House? Domestic Space and Feminine Subjectivity in Marilynne Robinson's *Housekeeping*," *Contemporary Literature* 34 (Spring 1993): 103–22; and Karen Kaivola, "The Pleasures and Perils of Merging: Female Subjectivity in Marilynne Robinson's *Housekeeping*," *Contemporary Literature* 34 (Winter 1993): 670–90.

21. See Leo Bersani, *The Culture of Redemption* (Cambridge: Harvard University Press, 1990).

22. *Columbia History of the American Novel*, ed. Emory Elliott and others (New York: Columbia University Press, 1991), p. 458.

23. In fact, the reviews provide interesting source material for reader-response studies. The more politically oriented of the critics showed the least patience with Ruth's character. They showed even less with the subtle ways in which the novel seems to advance Ruth's decision as a positive step. (See, for example, Caplan.)

24. "Inside the Skull—A Symposium," *New York Times Book Review*, 13 May 1984, p. 1.

25. Marilynne Robinson, *Housekeeping* (New York: Bantam Books, 1982), p. 5. Further references are cited in the text.

26. Caplan, "It Is Better to Have Nothing," p. 154.

27. The reading of this novel as the representation of a "female selfhood" is certainly the most characteristic kind of attention given to it. (See, for example, Roberta Rubenstein, *Boundaries of the Self* [Urbana: University of Illinois Press, 1987]). Several critics, including Ravits and Kirby, read the novel as an

intervention that "extends the range" of the male-dominated American literary tradition. My point of emphasis is that these elements of subversion, reinscription, and translation are part of an explicit structure of inversion.

28. In her *Crossing the Double-Cross* (Chapel Hill: University of North Carolina Press, 1986), Elizabeth Meese makes a related observation, while expressing a very different argument: "Ruth's narrative displaces loss or absence, as centered in her self-development and in her relationship with her mother" (p. 67). Madelon Sprengnether argues that "*Housekeeping,* as it deconstructs its title, deconstructs 'mother.' It is absence, the novel insists, that creates the dream of presence, a dream that must never be taken literally, since its fulfillment lies beyond the limits of human life." (See Madelon Sprengnether, "[M]other Eve: Some Revisions of the Fall in Fiction by Women Writers," *The Mother Tongue: Essays in Feminist Psychoanalytic Interpretation,* ed. Shirley Nelson Garner, Claire Kahane, and Madelon Sprengnether [Ithaca, N.Y.: Cornell University Press, 1985], p. 40.) This stipulation, it should be noted, is one that Ruth fails to observe and one that the book itself embodies as a "world elsewhere."

29. George Toles, "'Sighs Too Deep for Words': Mysteries of Need in Marilynne Robinson's *Housekeeping,*" *Arizona Quarterly* 47 (Winter 1991): 138.

30. See Sigmund Freud, "On Transience," *Collected Papers,* trans. Joan Riviere, V (London: Hogarth Press, 1956), pp. 79–82.

31. Richard Poirier, *A World Elsewhere* (New York: Oxford University Press, 1966), p. 5.

32. Ralph Ellison, *Shadow and Act* (New York: Vintage Books, 1964), p. 48.

33. Ralph Ellison suggests that the "Territory" reference in *Huckleberry Finn* is to the Oklahoma Territory. "Long before it became the State of Oklahoma," he notes, "the Territory had been a sanctuary for runaway slaves who sought there the protection of the Five Great Indian Nations." See Ralph Ellison, *Going to the Territory* (New York: Vintage Books, 1987), pp. 131–32.

34. Northrop Frye, *Anatomy of Criticism* (Princeton: Princeton University Press, 1957), p. 347.

Contributors

SUSAN BRIENZA was formerly on the English faculty at UCLA. The author of *Samuel Beckett's New Worlds: Style in Metafiction* and numerous articles on Beckett, she is active in the Samuel Beckett Society. Dr. Brienza has also written on James Joyce, Thomas Pynchon, and Sam Shepard. After receiving her J.D. from Stanford Law School, she published articles on Native American water rights and clerked for a federal judge in Denver, where she is now a practicing trial attorney. Between writing motions and briefs, she is planning articles on law and literature.

GLORIA L. CRONIN is Professor of English at Brigham Young University. Her specialties are critical theory, twentieth-century American literature, Jewish-American fiction, and women's literature. Her publications (alone or in collaboration) include *Saul Bellow: An Annotated Bibliography and Research Guide; Saul Bellow in the 1980s: A Collection of Critical Essays; Sixty Other Jewish Fiction Writers: An Annotated Bibliography; A Mosaic: Critical Essays on the Novels of Saul Bellow;* and *Tales of Molakai: The Voice of Harriet Ne.* The author of numerous essays on contemporary American fiction, she is currently writing a gender study of Saul Bellow's fiction. She is also coeditor of the *Saul Bellow Journal* and a board member of the Saul Bellow Society and the American Literature Association.

MELVIN J. FRIEDMAN is Professor of Comparative Literature and English at the University of Wisconsin–Milwaukee. His books (alone or in collaboration) include *The Added Dimension: The Art and Mind of Flannery O'Connor; William Styron; The Two Faces of Ionesco; Samuel Beckett Now; The Shaken Realist;* and *The Vision Obscured.* Formerly editor of *Wisconsin Studies in Contemporary Literature* and *Comparative Literature Studies,* he now serves on the editorial boards of *Contemporary Literature, Studies in American Fiction, Journal of Beckett Studies, Studies in the Novel,* and *International Fiction Review.* His awards include grants from Fulbright and ACLS, and he has served as

Visiting Senior Fellow at the University of East Anglia and as Canterbury Visiting Fellow at the University of Canterbury– New Zealand.

MICHAEL PATRICK GILLESPIE is Professor of English at Marquette University. He has published three studies on the works of James Joyce, coedited a volume of essays on Joyce, and written a monograph on Oscar Wilde. He has written more than two dozen essays on Modernist writers and their precursors. He is an advisory editor of the *James Joyce Quarterly* and is on the board of consultants of the Zurich James Joyce Foundation. He has received fellowships from the National Endowment for the Humanities, the American Philosophical Society, the American Council of Learned Societies, the Harry Ransom Humanities Research Center, and the William Andrews Clark Memorial Library.

SUZETTE HENKE is Thruston B. Morton, Sr. Professor of Literary Studies at the University of Louisville. She is the author of *Joyce's Moraculous Sindbook: A Study of "Ulysses"* and *James Joyce and the Politics of Desire* as well as coeditor of *Women in Joyce.* Her critical essays deal with such writers as Virginia Woolf, Dorothy Richardson, Anais Nin, Doris Lessing, Linda Brent, Janet Frame, Keri Hulme, Samuel Beckett, E. M. Forster, and W. B. Yeats. She is currently at work on a study of "women's life-writing" in the twentieth century.

JEROME KLINKOWITZ is Professor of English and University Distinguished Scholar at the University of Northern Iowa. His thirty published books range from the studies *Literary Disruptions* and *Structuring the Void* to *Their Finest Hours: Narratives of the RAF and Luftwaffe in World War II; Listen: Gerry Mulligan/An Aural Narrative in Jazz; Rosenberg/Barthes/Hassan: The Postmodern Habit of Thought; Short Season and Other Stories;* and *Writing Baseball.* He is presently completing two new story collections plus a study of Kurt Vonnegut's nonfiction (*Vonnegut in Fact*) and a memoir on working with America's innovative fictionists, *Ahead of the Game.*

CLAYTON KOELB is Guy B. Johnson Professor of German and Comparative Literature at the University of North Carolina, Chapel Hill. He is the author of *The Incredulous Reader: Literature and the Function of Disbelief; Inventions of Reading: Rhetoric and the Literary Imagination;* and *Kafka's Rhetoric: The Passion of*

Reading. He is editor or coeditor of *Thomas Mann's "Goethe and Tolstoy": Notes and Sources; The Current in Criticism: Essays on the Present and Future of Literary Theory; The Comparative Perspective on Literature: Approaches to Theory and Practice; Nietzsche as Postmodernist: Essays Pro and Contra;* and, most recently, a Norton critical edition of Thomas Mann's *Death in Venice.*

MARK KRUPNICK is Professor of Religion and Literature in the Divinity School of the University of Chicago. His books include *Displacement: Derrida and After* and *Lionel Trilling and the Fate of Cultural Criticism,* and he has recently edited a special issue of the *Journal of Religion* on the relations between contemporary literary theory and religious studies. A former associate editor of the quarterly journal *Modern Occasions,* he has published articles or review-essays on, among others, Daniel Bell, Clement Greenberg, Alfred Kazin, Irving Howe, Saul Bellow, Cynthia Ozick, Diana Trilling, Muriel Spark, and George Steiner. He is currently preparing a book on literary autobiography in the light of psychoanalytic self-psychology.

JAMES M. MELLARD is Professor of English at Northern Illinois University. He has been head of the Department of English, acting dean of the College of Liberal Arts and Sciences, and interim director of intercollegiate athletics. His specialties include twentieth-century American literature, literary criticism and theory, and the branch of psychoanalytic criticism associated with Jacques Lacan. His essays on contemporary fiction and modernist literature have appeared in such journals as *PMLA, JEGP, Modern Fiction Studies,* and the *Bucknell Review.* His books include *Four Modes: A Rhetoric of Modern Fiction; The Exploded Form: The Modernist Novel in America; Doing Tropology: Analysis of Narrative Discourse;* and *Using Lacan, Reading Fiction.*

JAMES NAGEL is the first J. O. Eidson Distinguished Professor of English at the University of Georgia. The founding editor of *Studies in American Fiction,* he is also the general editor of the G. K. Hall series "Critical Essays on American Literature." Executive coordinator of the American Literature Association, he has lectured in twelve countries and at numerous American universities. His publications include some fifty journal articles and more than a dozen books, the best known of which are *Stephen*

Crane and Literary Impressionism; Ernest Hemingway: The Writer in Context; and Hemingway in Love and War (a New York Times selection as one of 1989's best books). His current projects include a Viking edition of Steinbeck's The Pastures of Heaven and a study of the contemporary short-story cycle.

ELAINE B. SAFER is Professor of English at the University of Delaware. A specialist in the American comic novel and in the poetry and prose of John Milton, she has published essays on John Barth, Thomas Pynchon, William Gaddis, Ken Kesey, and Saul Bellow in Studies in the Novel, Critique, Studies in American Humor, Studies in American Fiction, Renascence, Critical Essays on Thomas Pynchon, and the Saul Bellow Journal. She is the current president of the Saul Bellow Society. The author of The American Comic Epic Novel, she has also published John Milton's "L'Allegro" and "Il Penseroso" and essays on Milton in the Milton Quarterly, Milton Studies, and A Milton Encyclopedia. She has been a Fulbright Scholar in France and has taught as a Visiting Distinguished Professor at Lyon III and at the Sorbonne (Paris III).

THOMAS SCHAUB is Professor of English and head of the department at the University of Wisconsin at Madison. He is also the editor of the journal Contemporary Literature and the author of Pynchon: The Voice of Ambiguity and American Fiction in the Cold War. His numerous articles deal with such writers as James Fenimore Cooper, William Carlos Williams, and Ralph Ellison.

BEN SIEGEL is Professor of English at California State Polytechnic University, Pomona. He has chaired the Department of English and directed the Annual Conferences in Modern American Writing held at the university's Kellogg West Center for Continuing Education. His books, alone or in collaboration, include The Puritan Heritage: America's Roots in the Bible; Biography Past and Present; Isaac Bashevis Singer; The Controversial Sholem Asch; The American Writer and the University; Critical Essays on Nathanael West; and Conversations with Saul Bellow. His critical essays deal with such writers as Saul Bellow, Daniel Fuchs, Bernard Malamud, Philip Roth, Isaac Bashevis Singer, and Israel Joshua Singer. He is on the editorial boards of Contemporary Literature, Studies in American Fiction, and the Saul Bellow Journal.

LINDA WAGNER-MARTIN is Hanes Professor of English and Comparative Literature at the University of North Carolina, Chapel Hill. She is the author or editor of numerous books, and her more recent ones include *The Modern American Novel, 1914–1945; Edith Wharton's The House of Mirth, a Novel of Admonition;* and *Telling Women's Lives, the New Biography.* Her biography of Gertrude Stein and her family will be published soon, and she is coediting *The Oxford Companion to Women's Writing in the U.S.,* with an accompanying anthology of women's writing.

JAMES L. W. WEST III is Distinguished Professor of English at The Pennsylvania State University, where he directs the Penn State Center for the History of the Book. His writings include *The Making of This Side of Paradise* (1983) and *American Authors and the Literary Marketplace Since 1900* (1988). He has edited scholarly editions of Theodore Dreiser's *Sister Carrie* and *Jennie Gerhardt* for the Pennsylvania Dreiser Edition. West has held fellowships from the Woodrow Wilson Foundation, the J. S. Guggenheim Foundation, the National Humanities Center, and, most recently, from the National Endowment for the Humanities. He has also held Fulbright appointments to England and Belgium. He is a founding coeditor of the journal *Review* and is now at work on the authorized biography of William Styron.

Index